The ABCs of TCP/IP

The ABCs of TCP/IP

GILBERT HELD

AUERBACH PUBLICATIONS

A CRC Press Company

Boca Raton London New York Washington, D.C.

Library of Congress Cataloging-in-Publication Data

Held, Gilbert, 1943-
The ABCs of TCP/IP / Gilbert Held.
p. cm.
Includes index.
ISBN 0-8493-1463-1
1. TCP/IP (Computer network protocol) I. Title.

TK5105.585 .H44695 2002
004.6′2—dc21 2002028013
CIP

This book contains information obtained from authentic and highly regarded sources. Reprinted material is quoted with permission, and sources are indicated. A wide variety of references are listed. Reasonable efforts have been made to publish reliable data and information, but the author and the publisher cannot assume responsibility for the validity of all materials or for the consequences of their use.

Direct all inquiries to CRC Press LLC, 2000 N.W. Corporate Blvd., Boca Raton, Florida 33431.

Trademark Notice: Product or corporate names may be trademarks or registered trademarks, and are used only for identification and explanation, without intent to infringe.

Visit the Auerbach Publications Web site at www.auerbach-publications.com

International Standard Book Number 0-8493-1463-1
Library of Congress Card Number 2002028013
Printed in the United States of America 1 2 3 4 5 6 7 8 9 0
Printed on acid-free paper

Contents

Preface

The TCP/IP protocol suite has evolved from an academic networking tool to the driving force behind the Internet, intranets, and extranets. Advances in networking and communications hardware based upon the TCP/IP protocol suite are opening a new range of technologies that provides the potential to considerably affect our lives. Such technologies as the new version of the Internet Protocol (IP), referred to as IPv6, the use of virtual private networks (VPNs), the convergence of voice and data through a technology referred to as Voice-over-IP (VoIP), and the expansion of data transmission over wireless communications (mobile IP) can be expected to govern the manner by which we perform many daily activities. Thus, the TCP/IP protocol suite is dynamically changing to reflect advances in technology, and, to paraphrase an often-used term, can be considered to represent "the protocol for the new millennium."

This book was written as a comprehensive guide to the TCP/IP protocol suite for both professionals and lay personnel who need to know a range of protocol-related information. Commencing with an overview of the protocol suite, this book examines the key components of the TCP/IP protocol suite. This examination includes the manner by which the various protocols operate, how applications operate, addressing issues, security methods, routing, and an overview of emerging technologies. Concerning security, it is important to understand both the threats we face as well as methods that can be used to overcome such threats. Thus, this book includes separate chapters focused on both areas.

The goal of this book is to explain both the "how" and the "why" of the TCP/IP protocol suite. The "how" refers to how various network protocols and applications operate, as this information can be important for selecting one application over another, as well as for attempting to resolve problems and network capacity issues. The "why" refers to this author's best guess as to the rationale for the structure of the TCP/IP protocol suite and the manner by which various components interact. Although no reader was probably present when various meetings occurred that defined the structure of the

TCP/IP protocol suite, a review of the manner by which different components of the suite operate allows one to note why it might have been designed. This in turn provides a considerable amount of information concerning both how and when to use certain members of the protocol suite.

As a professional author, I highly value reader feedback. Please feel free to contact me through the publisher of this book or e-mail me at gil_held@yahoo.com. Let me know if there are certain topics that you would like to see additional coverage on, if I omitted a topic of interest, or if I should expand coverage of an existing topic.

Gilbert Held
Macon, Georgia

Acknowledgments

The creation of a book is a team effort that requires the contribution of many people. Thus, I would be remiss if I did not acknowledge the efforts of the many people who were instrumental in converting the writings of this author into the book you are now reading.

It is always important to have the support of the acquisitions editor and publisher; however, it is even better to have a most enthusiastic backing for a writing project. Thus, I would like to thank Rich O'Hanley for his enthusiastic endorsement of this book.

As a frequent traveler to the four corners of the world, I often encounter electrical outlets that never quite mate with the various adapter kits that I have purchased. Due to this, my writing productivity is considerably enhanced by using pen and paper, especially at locations where it was only possible to shave with a razor, and a laptop battery had long ago reached an undesirable level of power. While I try to write legibly, this is not always the case. Thus, I am once more indebted to Mrs. Linda Hayes for turning my handwritten notes and sketches into a professional manuscript.

Last, but not least, the preparation of a book is a time-consuming task, requiring many hours of effort on weekends and evenings. Once again, I am indebted to my wife, Beverly, for her patience and understanding.

Dedication

This book is dedicated to the students of Georgia College & State University. Learning is a two-way experience and I appreciate the opportunity to educate and learn from my students.

Chapter 1

Overview

The TCP/IP protocol suite has evolved from primarily an academic and research communications protocol into a protocol that affects the lives of most individuals. Most, if not all, readers are familiar with the Internet, that mother of all networks which represents only one use of the TCP/IP protocol suite. Today, many organizations are creating private networks based on the use of the TCP/IP protocol suite that are referred to as intranets. In addition, the Internet is being used to interconnect geographically separated networks through a technology referred to as virtual private networks (VPNs).

To add to our knowledge of terms, when one business connects its network via the Internet to another corporate network, the resulting communications infrastructure is referred to as an extranet. Over the past few years, the use of intranets, extranets, and VPNs have significantly increased along with the use of the Internet.

Recognizing the versatility of the TCP/IP protocol suite, IP is now being used to transport voice, and the transmission of data over wireless communications is evolving to provide mobile users with the ability to access e-mail and surf the Web from their mobile phones. In offices and homes, the use of wireless LANs (local area networks) has literally exploded, permitting users to surf the Web, send and receive e-mail, participate in a videoconference, and perform other activities without requiring cabling. By alleviating the need for a wired infrastructure, office and home computer users obtain a high degree of computing flexibility and can rapidly satisfy their TCP/IP communications requirements. Thus, the TCP/IP protocol suite can be considered to represent the protocol for the new millennium.

This introductory chapter focuses on the role of the TCP/IP protocol suite. In doing so, the chapter concentrates on common and emerging applications supported by this technology, and takes the reader on a brief tour of the focus of succeeding chapters by previewing those chapters. This information, either by itself or in conjunction with the index, can be used to rapidly locate particular information of interest.

Applications

When the TCP/IP protocol suite was initially developed, it was used to support a relatively small handful of applications. Those applications included electronic mail, file transfer, and remote terminal operations. Since the initial development of the TCP/IP protocol suite, its modular architecture has enabled literally hundreds of applications to be developed that use the protocol suite as a transport for communications. This section briefly reviews a core set of current and emerging applications to obtain an appreciation for the role of the TCP/IP protocol suite.

TCP/IP applications can be subdivided into three general categories: obsolete or little used, current, and emerging. Although obsolete or little-used applications are interesting from a historical perspective, their value for the networking professional is minimal; thus, for the most part, this book focuses on current and evolving applications.

Current Applications

There is a core set of TCP/IP applications used by most people. Those applications include electronic mail, file transfer, remote terminal operations, and Web surfing. Although not directly used by most people, the domain name service (DNS) is crucial for the operation of TCP/IP-based networks as it provides the translation process between host names, such as www.gilheld.com, and IP addresses, such as 198.78.46.8. Because the vast majority of people who use TCP/IP-based networks enter host addresses while routing is based on the use of IP addresses, DNS provides the crucial link between the two. The remainder of this section briefly reviews the operation and utilization of the core set of current applications commonly used by people on TCP/IP-based networks. This information is presented to ensure that readers with different networking backgrounds obtain a common level of appreciation for the majority of current applications used on TCP/IP-based networks.

Electronic Mail

The TCP/IP protocol suite dates to the 1960s when government laboratories and research universities required a method to share ideas in an expedient manner. Among the first applications developed for the protocol suite was a text-based electronic mail system.

Over the past 30+ years, the use of electronic mail has evolved from a text-based messaging system into the development of sophisticated, integrated calendar, messaging, and documenting systems that perform electronic mail.

One example of a popular integrated e-mail system is Microsoft's Outlook, whose main screen is illustrated in Exhibit 1. Through the use of Outlook,

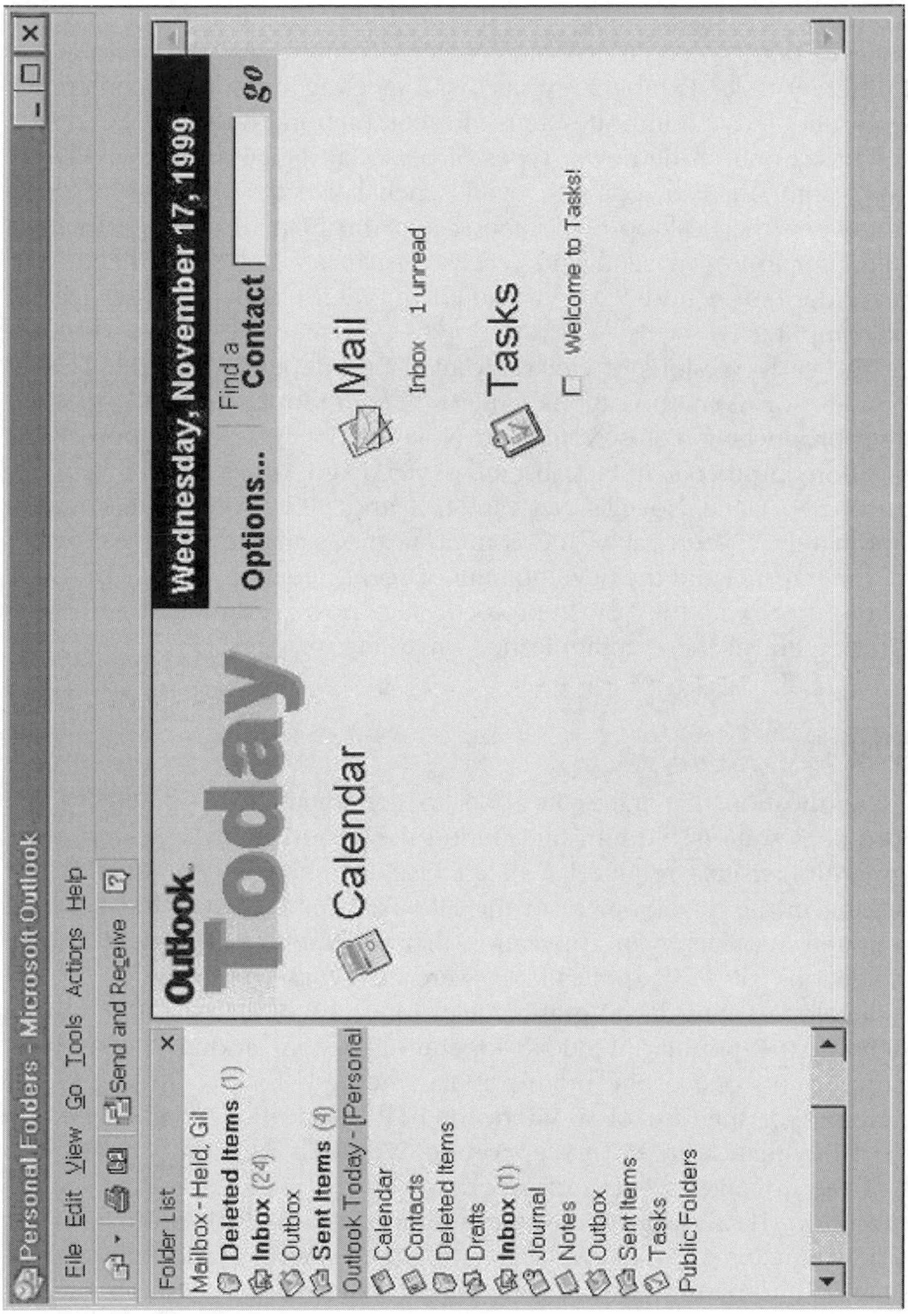

Exhibit 1. Viewing the Main Display of Microsoft's Outlook Program

one can send and receive conventional text-based messages, attach graphic images and word processing documents within that message, develop the equivalent of an electronic "Rolodex" via the use of a contact folder, and use its calendar facility as a reminder to perform different tasks.

Exhibit 2 illustrates a portion of the additional capability obtained through the use of Outlook. This example uses the program's calendar feature, which enables one to both schedule events as well as define tasks and indicate the status of different tasks. Exhibit 2 reveals that a meeting and a videoconference have been scheduled and indicates a task for completion on the indicated day. If one purchases one of the newer types of personal digital assistants (PDAs), such as the Compaq iPaq, one can even synchronize the contents of one's contacts between the desktop or notebook and the PDA. If equipped with a wireless adapter, one can send and receive e-mail as well as surf the Web using the under-one-pound PDA instead of a bulkier and certainly heavier notebook computer.

Unlike the early versions of electronic mail that depended on the TCP/IP protocol suite for communications, Microsoft's Outlook, as well as such competitive products as Lotus Notes and Novell's GroupWise, support many communications protocols. In fact, just a few years ago, IBM's System Network Architecture (SNA) and Novell's NetWare IPX and SPX protocols accounted for approximately 70 percent of the communications market. The growth in the use of the Internet and the development of corporate intranets has reversed protocol utilization, with the TCP/IP protocol stack now accounting for approximately 70 percent of the communications market.

File Transfers

A second application that traces its roots to the initial development of the TCP/IP protocol suite is file transfer. During the 1960s, many research laboratories and universities required a mechanism to share large quantities of data, resulting in the development of the File Transfer Protocol (FTP), which more accurately represents an application that facilitates file transfers.

Early versions of FTP applications were text based. Although several software developers introduced graphic user interface versions of FTP during the mid-1990s, the popular Windows operating system added a text-based FTP that represents one of the more popular methods for transferring files.

An example of the use of a Windows FTP application is illustrated in Exhibit 3. Note that, with the exception of Windows Version 3.1, all later versions of the ubiquitous Microsoft operating system include FTP as an MS-DOS application. Because it is free, the addition of a TCP/IP protocol stack with the introduction of Windows 95 to include several basic applications caused many third-party software developers that concentrated on TCP/IP applications to undergo a severe contraction in sales. In fact, although there are several graphic user interface versions of FTP available for use, most such products are now shareware instead of commercial products. Thus, the inclusion of the TCP/IP protocol suite in different versions of Windows had a significant impact on the market for stand-alone applications.

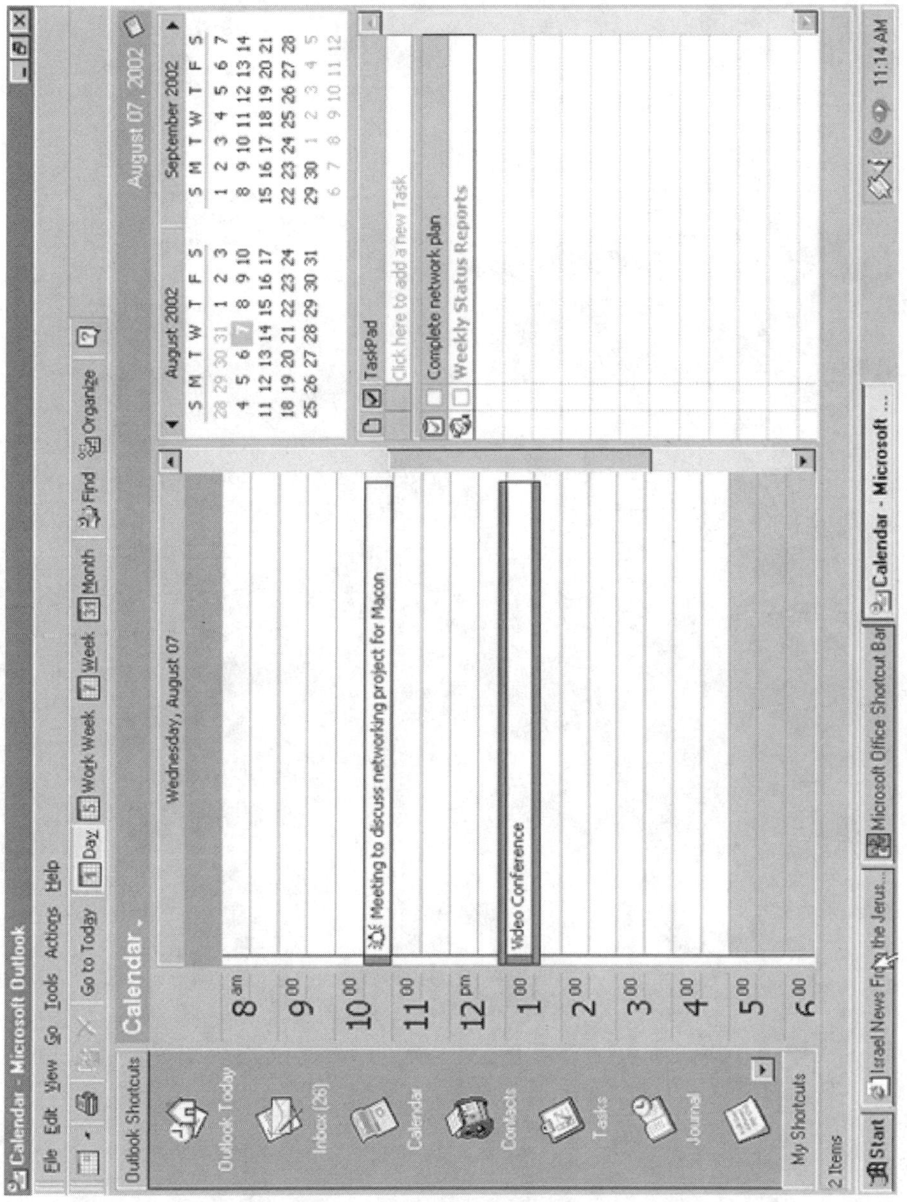

Exhibit 2. Using Microsoft's Outlook Calendar and Task Pad

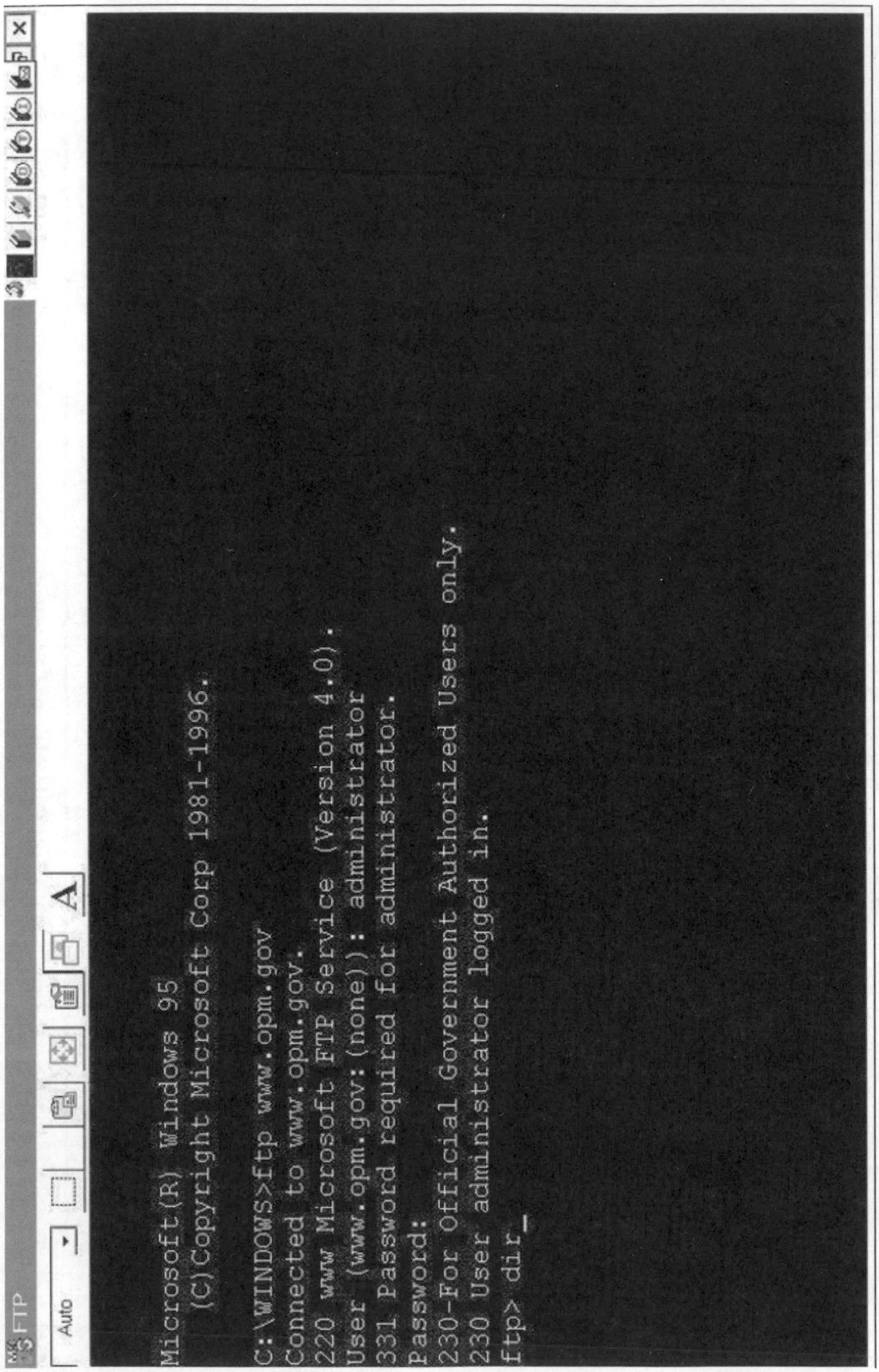

Exhibit 3. An Example of the Use of a Windows FTP Application

Remote Terminal Access

A third core application that dates to the 1960s is remote terminal access in the form of the Telnet application. During the 1960s, it was recognized that a mechanism to access distant computers as if a person's local computer was directly connected to the distant computer would be very desirable. This capability would allow people to configure remote devices as if they were directly connected to the remote device and resulted in the development of the Telnet application.

Exhibit 4 illustrates the use of a Telnet application program built into Microsoft's Windows. In this example, Telnet is being used to access a remote router and display information concerning the router's interfaces. Here, the ability to use Telnet saves a trip to the remote router and what would otherwise be a necessity to directly cable a terminal or PC into the router's console port.

Web Surfing

While it is true that most people correctly associate the use of the Internet with a Web browser, this is only one part of a complex story. The first commercial browser had limited capability and was primarily used for navigation to different Web sites and the display of Web pages. As Web sites proliferated, they began to add new applications that required browser developers and third-party software developers to add plug-ins to extend the capabilities of browser software. Examples of some common plug-ins include video- and audioconferencing, music playing, and authentication and encryption.

Exhibit 5 illustrates the display of the Netscape Communicator menu bar. On examining the entries in the drop-down menu, one notes that this browser more accurately represents an integrated application. Included in the software is a Web browser (Navigator), Web page creation (Composer), and calendar (Calendar) capability, as well as functions for performing conferencing. Looking at the background of the illustration shown in Exhibit 5, one notes the display of the home page for Amazon.com, a very popular electronic commerce site that expanded its initial focus from providing consumers with discounts for books to the online retailing of CDs, videos, toys, electronics, and other products. Within just a few years, electronic commerce on the Web grew from under $100 million to over $12 billion, with the TCP/IP protocol suite facilitating the growth in online sales due to the flexibility of the protocol suite to accommodate the new protocols and applications necessary to support electronic commerce.

One of the key factors that enabled electronic commerce on the Web to achieve exponential growth is the ability of consumers to transmit credit card information, view their security holdings, and perform similar functions in a secure manner. Exhibit 6 illustrates the use of the Microsoft Internet Explorer browser to establish a secure connection between this author's computer and the Salomon Smith Barney Web site. Note that the dialog box in the middle of the screen informs the Web surfer that he is about to view pages over a secure connection. This dialog box informs the user that he is attempting to

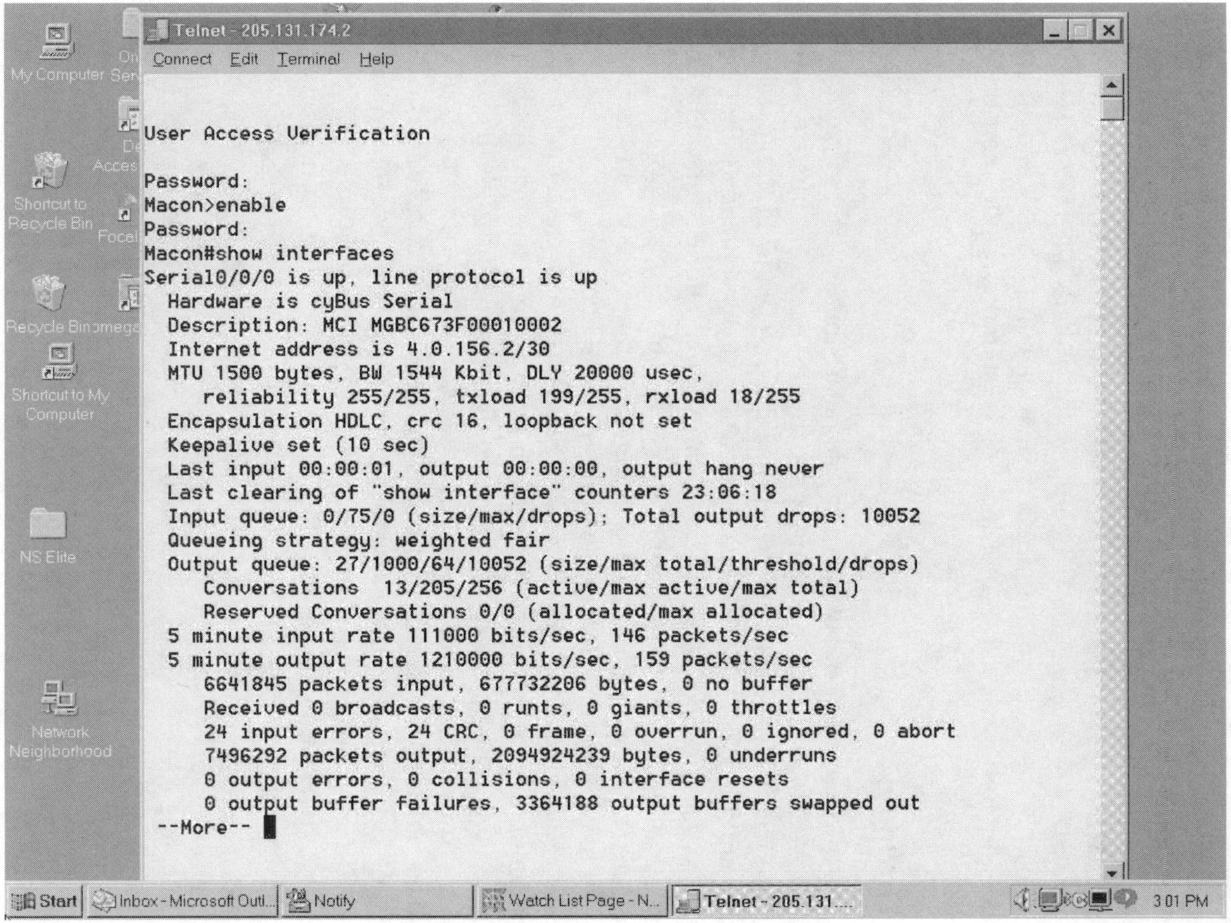

Exhibit 4. Using Telnet to Access a Remote Router and Determine the State of Its Interfaces

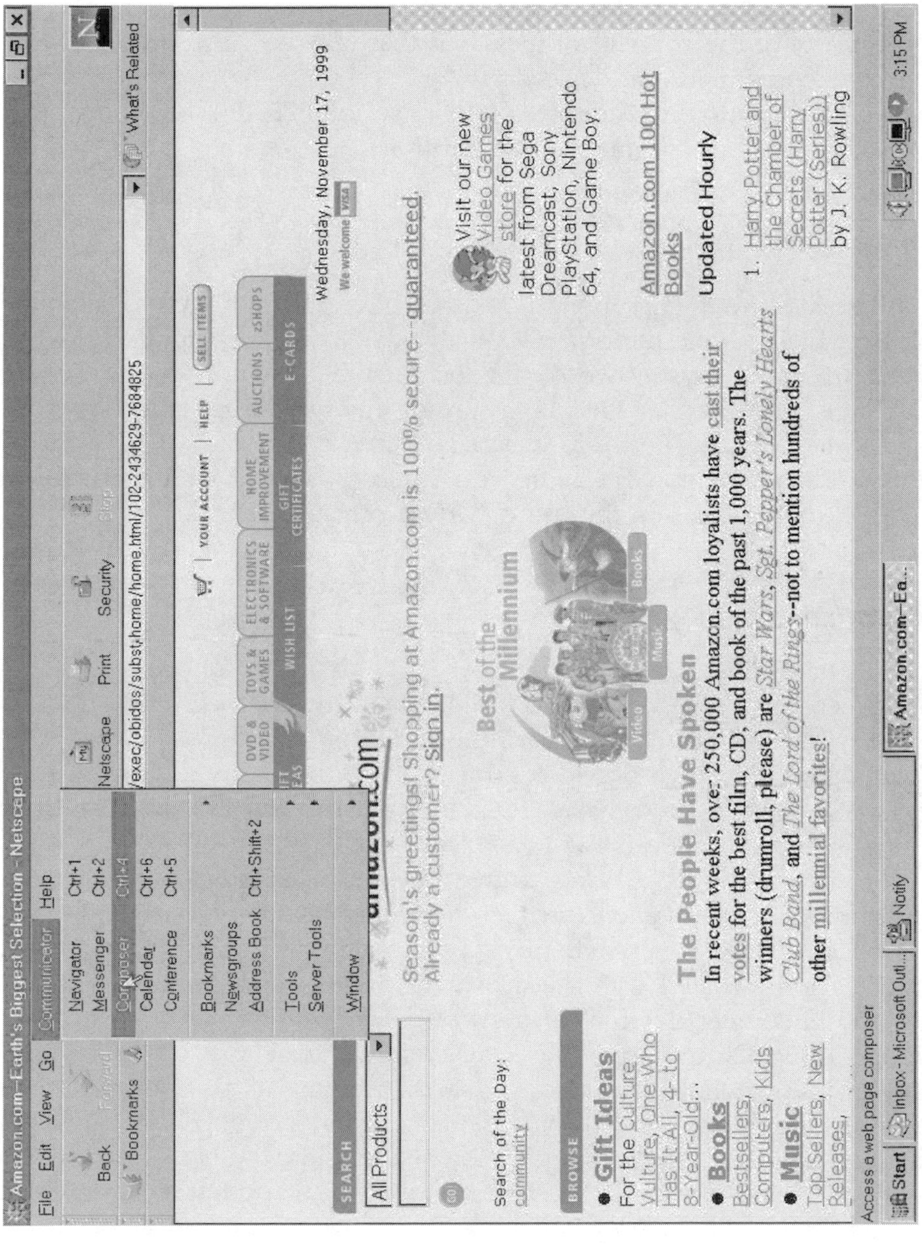

Exhibit 5. Examining the Major Components of the Netscape Communicator While Viewing a Popular Electronic Commerce Site

establish a secure connection to the Web site that has a valid certificate. The certificate, which is issued by a third party, contains information that authenticates the validity of a Web site. When a connection is established, the Microsoft browser transmits and receives data using a Secure Sockets Layer (SSL) connection. SSL uses a 128-bit key to encrypt and decrypt data, which secures communications between the browser and the Web site, enabling credit card information and similar data to flow over the Internet without fear of the discovery of the contents of messages that may be viewed on the path between two communicating devices.

With an appreciation for the role of a core set of TCP/IP applications, one can now focus on several emerging applications.

Emerging Applications

There are several emerging applications that have the potential to alter the manner by which people perform daily activities. While such applications are interesting from the perspective of a book on the evolution of the TCP/IP protocol suite, one also needs to be aware of emerging applications as they create new demands on network resources. Three emerging TCP/IP applications that deserve mention are audio and video players, the transmission of Voice-over-IP networks, and the use of virtual private networks.

Audio and Video Players

One of the major benefits of the Internet is its ability to function as a vast distribution center for information. While Web surfing has been very popular for several years, within recent years the distribution of music and the use of audio and video players to provide end users with the ability to convert their PCs into miniature televisions have gained in popularity. One popular example of an emerging application is the RealPlayer from RealNetworks.

The RealPlayer provides users with the ability to listen to music and conversations or to view events in near-real-time. The term "near-real-time" is used because the player buffers data to obtain the ability to eliminate random delays associated with the arrival of packets as they flow over the Internet and encounter different degrees of delay.

Exhibit 7 illustrates the use of the RealNetworks' RealPlayer on the author's desktop. In this example, the author is both listening and viewing a video clip from the Fox News Network. While audio and video players can turn the desktop into miniature televisions, they can also saturate the use of bandwidth on a network. In the example shown in Exhibit 7, the author was watching news about the crash of an airplane when network congestion occurred, forcing the player to freeze its audio and video presentation and buffer data at a lower rate until a sufficient amount of data was buffered to allow playback. Because it is very easy for 50 to 100 employees to click on different music and news items, the cumulative effects of such actions can result in the

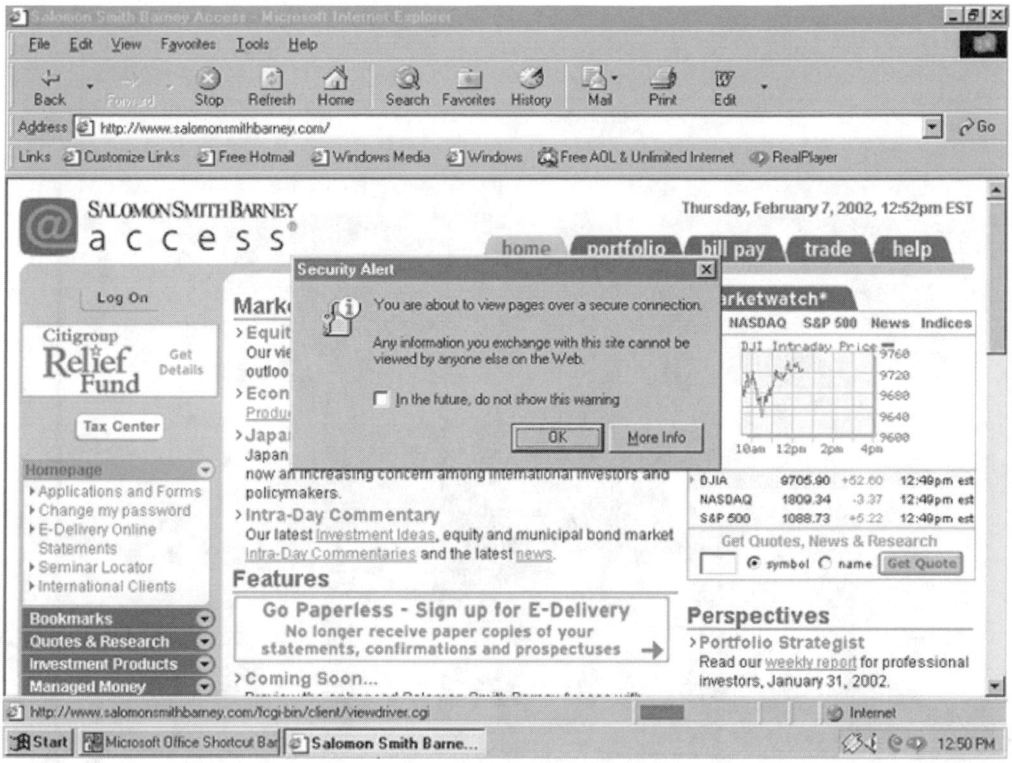

Exhibit 6. Establishing a Secure Connection to the Salomon Smith Barney Web Site

necessity to either upgrade a network or restrict the use of audio and video players.

Voice-over-IP

A second emerging application that can result in the restructuring of an existing network is the transmission of digitized voice over TCP/IP networks. Referred to as Voice-over-IP (VoIP), this technology is extremely delay sensitive and does not tolerate lengthy packets transporting data interspersed between packets transporting digitized voice. Thus, the ability to transmit voice over IP can require equipment or software that prioritizes packets transporting voice over those transporting data as well as fragmenting lengthy packets transporting data, so their transmission between voice-carrying packets has a minimal effect on the reconstruction of voice at the receiver.

Exhibit 8 illustrates the display of the Yahoo! Phone Card Web page. From this page one can access Yahoo Messenger to call any telephone in the world with rates as low as $0.02 per minute for U.S. calls. Yahoo is one of several Web portals that offers subscribers the ability to have their analog voice conversation digitized, compressed, and routed over an IP network to a server that decompresses the conversation, converts it back into an analog format, and out-dials the applicable telephone number of the called party. Because a compressed digitized voice call may require as little as 8 kbps of bandwidth,

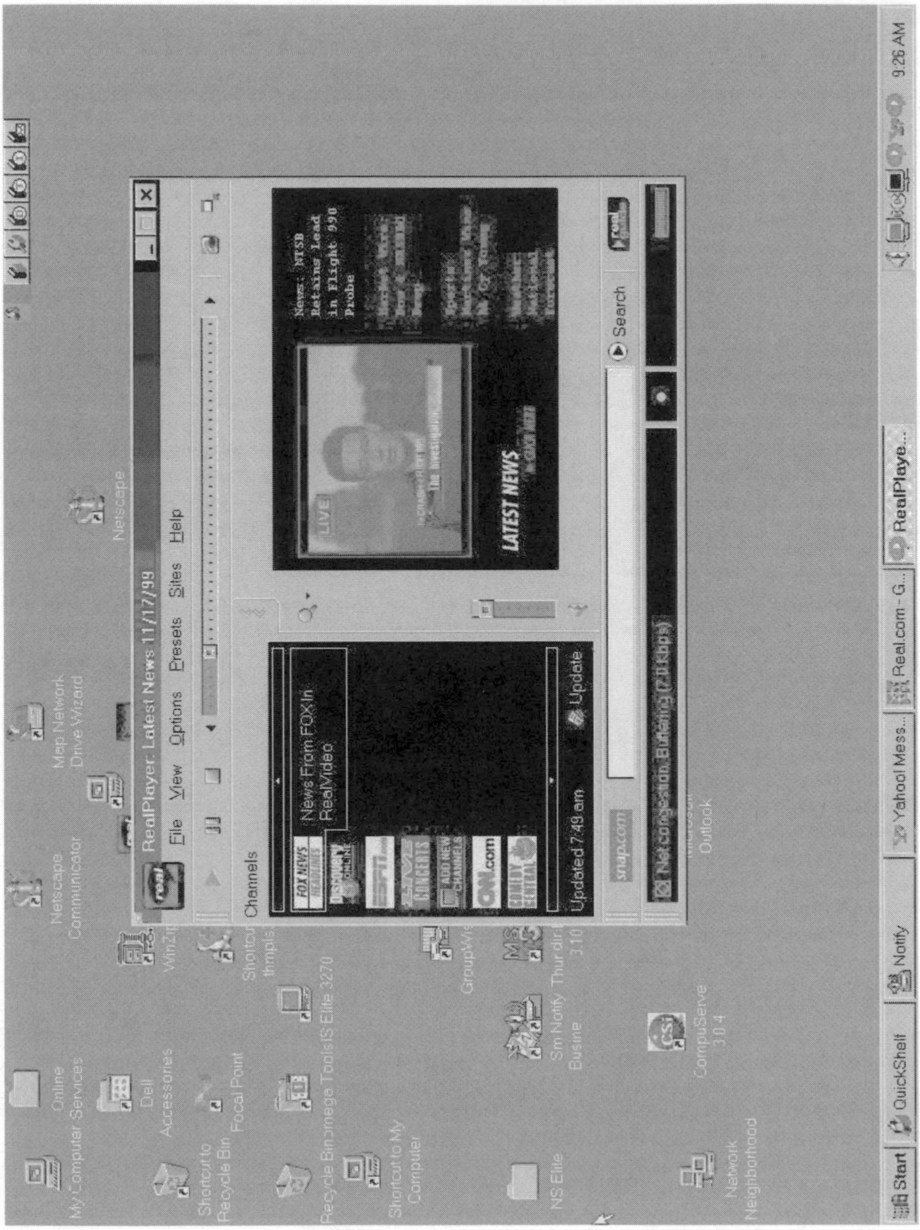

Exhibit 7. Using RealNetworks' RealPlayer to Obtain the Latest News from the Fox Network

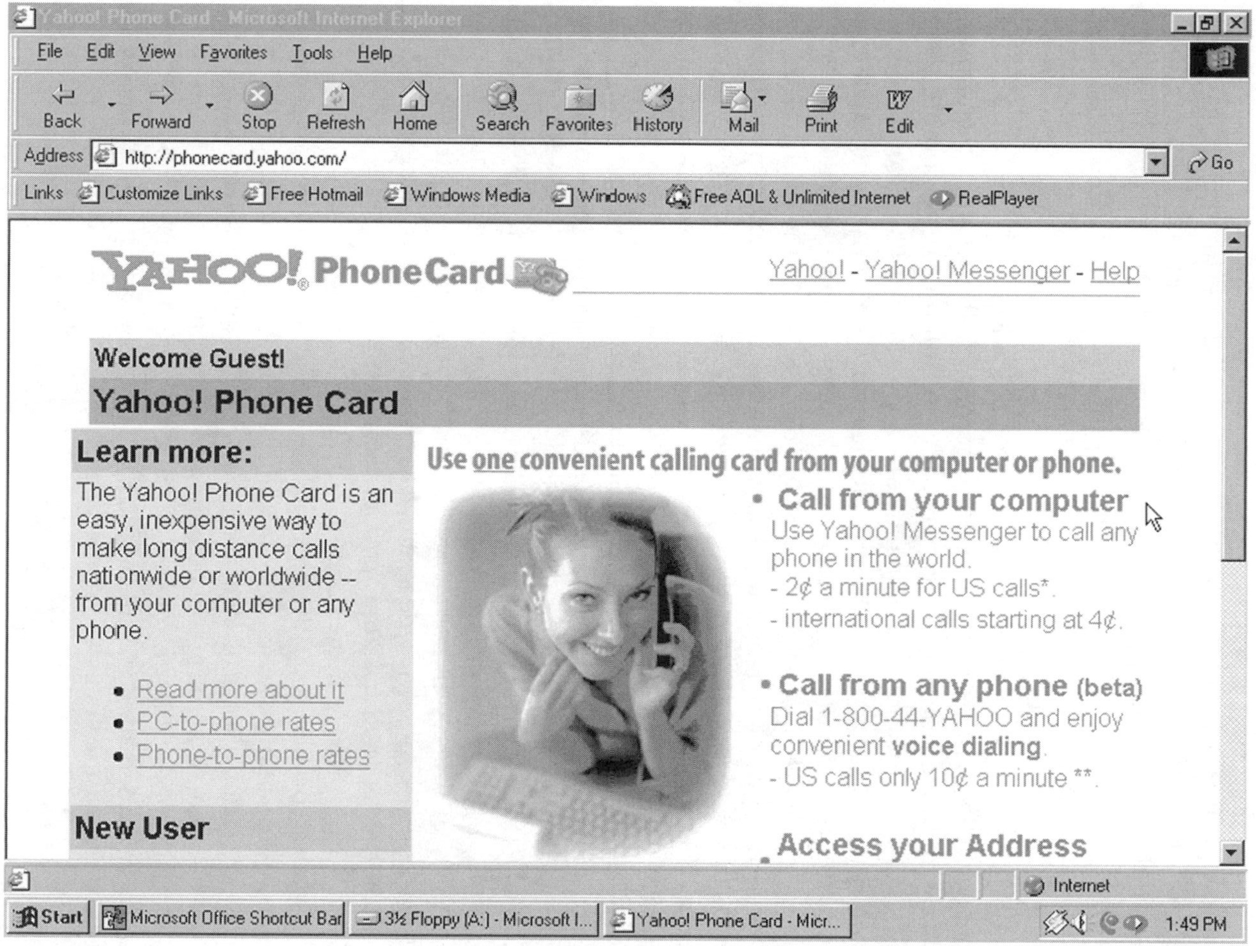

Exhibit 8. Yahoo Is Similar to Several Web Portals in that It Permits Subscribers to Use Their PCs to Initiate Discount Calls Carried over an IP Network

while a conventional switched telephone network requires 64 kbps, it is much more economical to route calls over an IP network.

Virtual Private Networking

A third emerging TCP/IP application is the use of the Internet as a virtual private network (VPN). The rationale for the use of the Internet as a VPN is economics. Leased lines are billed monthly based on distance between interconnected locations and operation rate. In comparison, the use of the Internet is distance insensitive, with corporations primarily billed on a monthly basis based on the operation rate of the access line that connects each corporate location to the Internet.

In addition to reducing the cost of communications, a VPN can save on equipment costs. This is because one connection to the Internet can support an almost unlimited number of virtual paths to different geographically separated corporate locations. In comparison, a private network would require routers at each location to have multiple ports to obtain the ability to interconnect one location with many other locations. Because router ports are relatively expensive, typically costing $1000 or more each, the internetworking of a large number of organizational locations via the use of an intranet can result in the expenditure of a considerable amount of money for additional router ports. Thus, VPNs can reduce the cost of both communications hardware and transmission facilities.

To illustrate an example of the potential economics associated with VPNs, consider Exhibit 9, which compares the use of a private network and the Internet to interconnect four geographically separated locations. In the top portion of Exhibit 9, six leased lines and 12 router ports are required to enable each location to directly connect with all other locations. In comparison, the VPN shown in the lower portion of Exhibit 9 only requires four local lines and four router ports to provide a similar capability because the mesh structure of the Internet is used as a transport facility.

While VPNs provide a mechanism to reduce networking costs, they open up networks connected to the Internet to potential attack from a virtually unlimited population of hackers. Thus, the use of VPNs introduces the need to consider various security measures to include firewalls, router access lists, and servers that perform authentication and encryption.

Given an appreciation for some of the emerging application being developed for use under the TCP/IP protocol suite, this chapter concludes with a brief preview of the focus of succeeding chapters in this book.

Book Preview

As indicated in the table of contents, this book is divided into ten chapters. Thus, this section reviews the focus of each chapter, commencing with Chapter 2, in the order in which they are incorporated into this book.

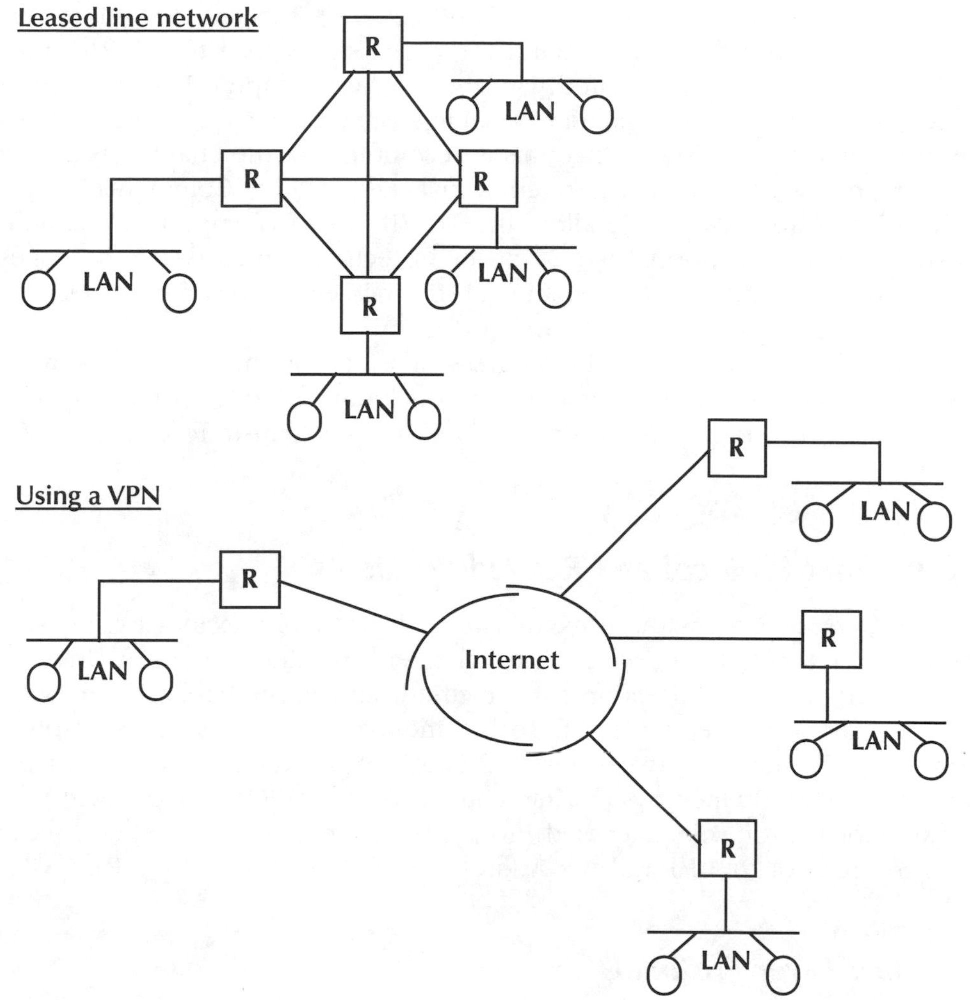

Exhibit 9. Comparing the Use of Leased Lines and a VPN to Interconnect Four Geographically Separated Locations

The Protocol Suite

Chapter 2 provides an introduction to the major components of the TCP/IP protocol suite. Information presented in this chapter will make us aware of the relationship of the various components of the protocol suite and their operations and functionality. By understanding the structure of the protocol suite, we will note its flexibility for adding new applications and protocols as well as how its use has evolved over the past four decades.

The Standards Process

A book covering the TCP/IP protocol suite would do disservice to its readers if it failed to provide information concerning the manner by which TCP/IP-related standards are developed. Thus, Chapter 3 focuses on this topic. Chapter 3 examines the TCP/IP standards process. Because the TCP/IP protocol suite is intimately associated with the Internet, Chapter 3 begins with a discussion of the various standards-making organizations and committees connected with the Internet. Once this is accomplished, the chapter examines how certain types of documents, referred to as Requests for Comments (RFCs), evolved into standards. These allow the TCP/IP protocol suite to be continuously updated to support both advances in technology as well as changes in the communications requirements of businesses, government agencies, academia, and individual end users.

Because RFCs are a work in progress, it is important to know how to access both old and new documents. In concluding Chapter 3 we will note several methods one can use to locate RFCs as a mechanism to examine their contents.

The Internet Protocol and Related Protocols

Chapter 4 commences with an examination of protocol specifics by focusing attention on the network layer. This chapter examines how the Internet Protocol (IP) operates, its addressing method, and several related protocols that are transported either by IP or at the data-link layer. This resolves addressing differences between layers 2 and 3 of the International Standards Organization (ISO) Open System Interconnection (OSI) Reference Model. The two additional protocols discussed in Chapter 4 include the Internet Control Message Protocol (ICMP) and the Address Resolution Protocol (ARP).

Transport Layer Protocols

Continuing the examination of the TCP/IP protocol suite, Chapter 5 focuses on the transport layer that represents layer 4 of the ISO OSI Reference Model.

Chapter 5 examines the operation of the two-layer protocols included in the TCP/IP protocol suite: the Transmission Control Protocol (TCP) and the User Datagram Protocol (UDP). In so doing, the chapter reveals how each one operates, the similarities and differences between the protocols, and how they are used by different applications.

Applications and Built-In Diagnostic Tools

The top layer of the TCP/IP protocol suite includes a variety of applications, some of which represent diagnostic tools one can utilize to check the operation of network components. Chapter 6 examines the operation and utilization of a core set of TCP/IP applications, including several applications whose use can be considered equivalent to the use of a diagnostic tool.

Routing

Chapter 7 focuses on the manner by which packets are transmitted through a TCP/IP network. Although there are over two dozen routing protocols, attention is focused on just a few that represent protocols that route a majority of network traffic. The protocols examined include a routing protocol commonly used by small- and medium-sized networks, and a routing protocol used to interconnect autonomous networks.

Security Threats

The ability to appropriately plan effective security measures requires an understanding of security threats, which is the focus of Chapter 8. This chapter examines the tools and techniques hackers use to break into systems, deny service to legitimate users, and create obstructions that can degrade network performance. In doing so, the chapter discusses the role of password crackers, port scanners, and other tools readily available to Internet users.

Enhancing Security

In Chapter 8 readers became familiar with a variety of security threats and tools hackers can use against individuals and corporations. Using that information as a base, Chapter 9 focuses on the methods one can use to enhance security. Chapter 9 examines the use of router access lists and firewalls as well as proxy services and network address translation.

Emerging Technologies

In concluding this book, the author examines the potential effect of four emerging technologies. First, we will describe and discuss how the new version of the Internet Protocol, IPv6, can be expected to literally open a window that will allow an extraordinary number of new devices to be connected to the Internet. Other topics to be covered in this chapter include the role of virtual private networks, the growing use of Voice-over-IP, and mobile IP.

Now that we have an appreciation for the orientation of this book, let us relax, grab a Coke© or a cup of coffee, and proceed to follow this author on a tour into the world of communications provided by the use of the TCP/IP protocol suite.

Chapter 2

The Protocol Suite

The primary purpose of this chapter is to obtain an appreciation for the general composition of the TCP/IP protocol suite. This can be accomplished by first examining the International Standards Organization (ISO) Open Systems Interconnection (OSI) Reference Model. Although the TCP/IP protocol suite predates the ISO's Reference Model, by examining the layering concept associated with communications defined by that model, one can obtain a better appreciation for the functioning of the TCP/IP protocol suite.

The ISO Reference Model

During the 1970s, approximately a dozen years after the development of several popular communications protocols to include TCP/IP, the International Standards Organization (ISO) established a framework for standardizing communications systems. This framework was called the Open System Interconnection (OSI) Reference Model and defines an architecture in which communications functions are divided into seven distinct layers, with specific functions becoming the responsibility of a particular layer.

Exhibit 1 illustrates the seven layers of the OSI Reference Model. Note that each layer, with the exception of the lowest, covers a lower layer, effectively isolating them from higher layer functions. Layer isolation is an important aspect of the OSI Reference Model as it allows the given characteristics of one layer to change without affecting the remainder of the model, provided that support services remain the same. This is possible because of well-known interface points in a layered model that enable one layer to communicate with another although one or both may change. In addition, the layering process permits end users to mix and match OSI or other layered protocol-conforming communications products to tailor their communications system to satisfy a particular networking requirement. Thus, the OSI Reference Model, as well

Layer 7	Application
Layer 6	Presentation
Layer 5	Session
Layer 4	Transport
Layer 3	Network
Layer 2	Data Link
Layer 1	Physical

Exhibit 1. The ISO Open System Interconnection Reference Model

as protocol suites that employ a layered architecture, provide the potential to directly interconnect networks based on the use of different vendor products. This architecture, which is referred to as an open architecture when its specifications are licensed or placed in the public domain, can be of substantial benefit to both users and vendors. For users, an open architecture removes them from dependence on a particular vendor, and can also prove economically advantageous as it fosters competition.

For vendors, the ability to easily interconnect their products with the products produced by other vendors opens up a wider market. Consider now the functions of the seven layers of the OSI Reference Model.

OSI Reference Model Layers

As previously noted, the OSI Reference Model consists of seven layers, with specific functions occurring at each layer. This section provides an understanding of the functions performed at each layer in the OSI Reference Model. This information can then be used in the next section of this chapter to better understand the components of the TCP/IP protocol suite.

Layer 1: The Physical Layer

The physical layer represents the lowest layer in the ISO Reference Model. Because the physical layer involves the connection of a communications system to communications media, the physical layer is responsible for specifying the electrical and physical connection between communications devices that connect to different types of media. At this layer, cable connections and the electrical rules necessary to transfer data between devices are specified. Examples of physical layer standards include RS-232, V.24, and the V.35 interface.

The RS-232 interface specifies the voltage level of the transmit and receive signals as well as the operation of a large number of control circuits. Altogether, RS-232 specifies the operation of 25 control circuits, of which a lesser amount is normally used by most applications. For example, the connection of a terminal to a modem typically occurs using a 25-pin connector on each end of a cable; however, only nine or ten conductors may actually be used within the cable. The V.24 standard is the international version of the RS-232 standard and for most applications can be considered equivalent. The V.35 standard represents a high-speed 35-pin data interface that is commonly used to connect routers to channel service units (CSUs). A CSU can be considered to represent a digital modem that is commonly connected to a T1 transmission line operating at 1.544 Mbps. For all three standards, the specification of operation voltages and the manner by which different conductors operate represent physical layer functions.

Layer 2: The Data-Link Layer

The second layer in the ISO Reference Model is the data-link layer. This layer is responsible for defining the manner by which a device gains access to the medium specified in the physical layer. In addition, the data-link layer is also responsible for defining data formats to include the entity by which information is transported, error control procedures, and other link control procedures.

Most trade literature and other publications reference the entity by which information is transported at the data-link layer as a frame. Depending on the protocol used, the frame will have a certain header composition with fields that normally indicate the destination address and the originator of the frame through the use of a source address. In addition, frames will have a trailer with a Cyclic Redundancy Check (CRC) field that indicates the value of an error checking mechanism algorithm performed by the originator on the contents of the frame. The receiver will apply the same algorithm to an inbound frame and compare the locally generated CRC to the CRC in the trailer. If the two match, the frame is considered to be received without error, while a mismatch indicates that a transmission error occurred and the receiver will then request the originator to retransmit the frame. Examples of common layer 2 protocols include such LAN protocols as Ethernet and Token Ring, as well as such WAN protocols as High Level Data Link Control (HDLC) and Frame Relay.

The original development of the OSI Reference Model targeted wide area networking. This resulted in its applicability to LANs requiring a degree of modification. The Institute of Electrical and Electronic Engineers (IEEE), which is responsible for developing LAN standards, subdivided the data-link layer into two sub-layers: logical link control (LLC) and media access control (MAC). The LLC layer is responsible for generating and interpreting commands that control the flow of data and performing recovery operations in the event errors are detected. In comparison, the MAC layer is responsible for providing access to the local area network, which enables a station on the network to transmit information. The subdivision of the data-link layer allows a common LLC layer to be used regardless of differences in the method of network access. Thus, a common LLC is used for both Ethernet and Token Ring, although their access methods are dissimilar.

Layer 3: The Network Layer

Moving up the ISO Reference Model, the third layer is the network layer. This layer is responsible for arranging a logical connection between a source and destination on the network to include the selection and management of a route for the flow of information between source and destination based on the available paths within a network.

Services or functions provided at the network layer are associated with the movement of data through a network to include addressing, routing, switching, sequencing, and flow control procedures. At the network layer, units of information are placed into packets that have a header and trailer, similar to frames at the data-link layer. Thus, the network layer packet will contain addressing information as well as a field that facilitates error detection and correction.

In a complex network, the source and destination may not be directly connected by a single path. Instead, a path may be required to be established through the network that consists of several sub-paths. Thus, the routing of packets through the network, as well as the mechanism in the form of routing protocols that provide information about available paths, are important features of this layer.

Several protocols are standardized for layer 3, to include the International Telecommunications Union Telecommunications body (ITU-T) X.25 packet switching protocol and the ITU-T X.75 gateway protocol. X.25 governs the flow of information through a packet network, whereas X.75 governs the flow of information between packet networks. In examining the TCP/IP protocol suite in the next section of this chapter, one sees that the Internet Protocol (IP) represents the network layer protocol used in the TCP/IP protocol suite. One also notes that addressing at the network layer and the data-link layer differ from one another, and a discovery process is used for packets to be correctly delivered via frames to their intended destination.

Layer 4: The Transport Layer

Continuing the tour of the ISO Reference Model, the transport layer is responsible for governing the transfer of information after a route has been established through the network by the network layer protocol. There are two general types of transport layer protocols: connection oriented and connectionless. A connection-oriented protocol first requires the establishment of a connection prior to data transfer occurring. This type of transport layer protocol performs error control, sequence checking, and other end-to-end data reliability functions. A second type or category of transport layer protocol operates as a connectionless, best-effort protocol. This type of protocol depends on higher layers in the protocol suite for error detection and correction. TCP in the TCP/IP protocol suite represents a layer 4 connection-oriented protocol, while UDP represents a connectionless layer 4 protocol.

The support of connection-oriented and connectionless transport layer protocols permits two basically opposite types of activities to be supported.

A connection-oriented protocol's handshaking activity used to establish a connection prior to the actual transfer of data is well suited for file transfers, Web browsing, and similar activities where one would not want to transfer data until sure the receiver is available. Because handshaking requires an exchange of information, it results in the delay of the actual data transfer operation. In comparison, a best-effort connectionless transport protocol transmits data without knowing if the intended recipient is available. While this may at first sound peculiar, this type of protocol avoids handshaking delay and overhead. Thus, a connectionless protocol is well-suited for transmitting small quantities of data, such as network management queries and responses. To ensure that the transmitter does not wait forever for a response from a destination that is not reachable or active, the transmitting station will set a timer. If the timer expires prior to the receipt of a response, the transmitter assumes that the recipient is not available.

Layer 5: The Session Layer

The fifth layer in the OSI Reference Model is the session layer. This layer is responsible for providing a set of rules that govern the establishment and termination of data streams flowing between nodes in a network. The services that the session layer can provide include establishing and terminating node connections, message flow control, dialogue control, and end-to-end data control. In the TCP/IP protocol suite, layers 5 through 7 are grouped together as an application layer.

Layer 6: The Presentation Layer

The sixth layer of the OSI Reference Model is the presentation layer. This layer is concerned with the conversion of transmitted data into a display format appropriate for a receiving device. This conversion can include data codes as well as display placement. Other functions performed at the presentation layer can include data compression and decompression and data encryption and decryption.

Layer 7: The Application Layer

The top layer of the OSI Reference Model is the application layer. This layer functions as a window through which the application gains access to all of the services provided by the model. Examples of functions performed at the application layer include electronic mail, file transfers, resource sharing, and database access. Although the first four layers of the OSI Reference Model are fairly well defined, the top three layers can vary considerably between networks. As previously mentioned, the TCP/IP protocol suite, which is a layered protocol that predates the ISO Reference Model, combines layers 5 through 7 into one application layer.

Data Flow

The design of an ISO Reference Model compatible network is such that a series of headers are opened to each data unit as packets are transmitted and delivered by frames. At the receiver, the headers are removed as a data unit flows up the protocol suite, until the "headerless" data unit is identical to the transmitted data unit. The next chapter section examines the flow of data in a TCP/IP network that follows the previously described ISO Reference Model data flow.

The ISO Reference Model never lived up to its intended goal, with ISO protocols achieving a less-than-anticipated level of utilization. The concept of the model made people aware of the benefits that could be obtained by a layered open architecture as well as the functions that would be performed by different layers of the model. Thus, the ISO succeeded in making networking personnel aware of the benefits that could be derived from a layered open architecture and more than likely contributed to the success of the acceptance of the TCP/IP protocol suite.

The TCP/IP Protocol Suite

The Transmission Control Protocol/Internet Protocol (TCP/IP) actually represents two distinct protocols within the TCP/IP protocol suite. Due to the popularity of those protocols, and the fact that a majority of traffic is transferred using those protocols, the members of the protocol suite include TCP and IP and are collectively referred to as TCP/IP. However, when discussing the TCP/IP protocol suite we are actually referencing a large number of protocols that operate at different layers in the ISO Reference Model. Some protocols, such as TCP and IP, are used by tens of millions of people on a daily basis. In comparison, other protocols, such as CBT and Chaos, are primarily known by historians. The primary focus of this book is on protocols within the TCP/IP protocol suite that are being actively used.

Exhibit 2 provides a general comparison of the structure of the TCP/IP protocol suite to the OSI Reference Model. The term "general comparison" is used because the protocol suite consists of hundreds of applications, of which only a handful are shown. Another reason that Exhibit 2 is a general comparison results from the fact that the TCP/IP protocol suite actually begins above the data-link layer. Although the physical and data-link layers are not part of the TCP/IP protocol suite, they are shown in Exhibit 2 to provide a frame of reference to the OSI Reference Model as well as to facilitate an explanation of the role of two special protocols within the TCP/IP protocol suite.

The Network Layer

The network layer of the TCP/IP protocol stack primarily consists of the Internet Protocol (IP). The IP includes an addressing scheme that identifies the source and destination address of the packet being transported. In TCP/IP terminology, the unit of data being transmitted at the network layer is referred to as a datagram. Also included in what can be considered to represent the

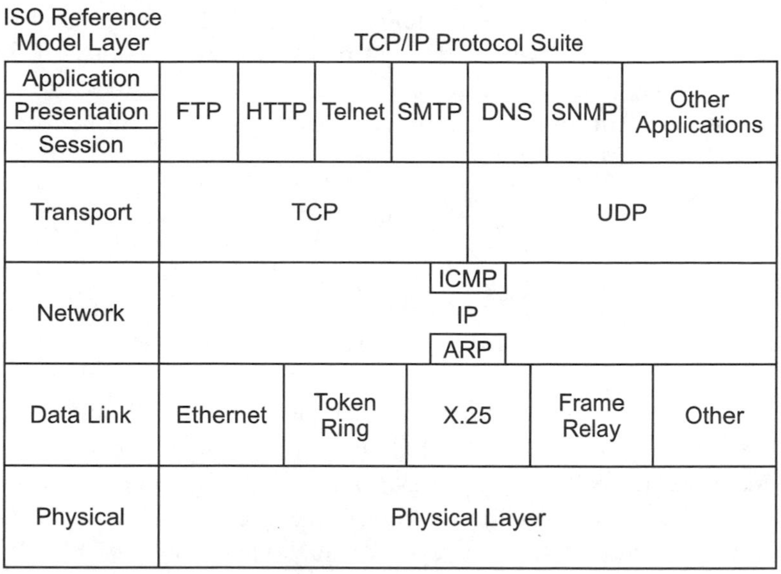

Exhibit 2. Comparing the TCP/IP Protocol Suite to the ISO Reference Model

network layer are two additional protocols that perform very critical operations. Those protocols are the Address Resolution Protocol (ARP) and the Internet Control Message Protocol (ICMP).

IP

The Internet Protocol (IP) provides the addressing capability that allows datagrams to be routed between networks. By itself, IP represents a connectionless protocol that makes a best effort to deliver datagrams. To add reliability to the delivery of datagrams requires IP to transport TCP, because the latter represents a connection-oriented error detection and correction protocol.

The current version of IP is IPv4, under which IP addresses consist of 32 bits. There are currently five classes of IP addresses, referred to as Class A through Class E, with Classes A, B, and C having their 32 bits subdivided into a network portion and a host portion. The network portion of the address defines the network where a particular host resides, while the host portion of the address identifies a unique host on the network. Chapter 4 examines the Internet Protocol in detail to include its current method of 32-bit addressing. Chapter 10 focuses on emerging technologies and on the next-generation Internet Protocol referred to as IPv6.

ARP

One of the more significant differences between the data-link layer and the network layer is the method of addressing used at each layer. At the data-link layer, such LANs as Ethernet and Token Ring networks use 48-bit MAC addresses. In comparison, TCP/IP currently uses 32-bit addresses under the current version of IP and the next generation of IP, IPv6, uses a 128-bit address. Thus, the delivery of a packet or datagram flowing at the network layer to a station on a LAN requires an address conversion. That address conversion is performed by the Address Resolution Protocol (ARP) whose operation is discussed in detail in Chapter 4.

ICMP

The Internet Control Message Protocol (ICMP), as its name implies, represents a protocol used to convey control messages. Such messages range in scope from routers responding to a request that cannot be honored with a "destination unreachable" message to the requestor, to messages that convey diagnostic tests and responses. An example of the latter is the echo-request/echo-response pair of ICMP datagrams that is more popularly referred to collectively as Ping.

ICMP messages are conveyed with the prefix of an IP header to the message. Thus, one can consider ICMP to represent a layer 3 protocol in the TCP/IP protocol suite. The structure of ICMP messages as well as the use of certain messages are examined in Chapter 4 where the network layer of the TCP/IP protocol suite is examined in detail.

The Transport Layer

As indicated in Exhibit 2, there are two transport layer protocols supported by the TCP/IP protocol suite: the Transmission Control Protocol (TCP) and the User Datagram Protocol (UDP).

TCP

TCP is an error-free, connection-oriented protocol. This means that prior to data being transmitted by TCP, the protocol requires the establishment of a path between source and destination as well as an acknowledgment that the receiver is ready to receive information. Once the flow of data commences, each unit, which is referred to as a TCP segment, is checked for errors at the receiver. If an error is detected through a checksum process, the receiver will request the originator to retransmit the segment. Thus, TCP represents an error-free, connection-oriented protocol.

The advantages associated with the use of TCP as a transport protocol relate to its error-free, connection-oriented functionality. For the transmission of relatively large quantities of data or important information, it makes sense to use this transport layer protocol. The connection-oriented feature of the protocol means that it will require a period of time for the source and destination to exchange handshake information. In addition, the error-free capability of the protocol may be redundant if the higher layer in the protocol suite also performs error-checking. Recognizing the previously mentioned problems, the developers of the TCP/IP protocol suite added a second transport layer protocol referred to as UDP.

UDP

The User Datagram Protocol (UDP) is a connectionless, best effort, non-error-checking transport protocol. UDP was developed in recognition of the fact that some applications may require small pieces of information to be transferred, and the use of a connection-oriented protocol would result in a significant overhead to the transfer of data. Because a higher layer in the protocol suite could perform error-checking, error detection and correction could also be eliminated from UDP. Because UDP transmits a piece of information referred to as a UDP datagram without first establishing a connection to the receiver, the protocol is also referred to as a best-effort protocol. To ensure that a series of UDP datagrams is not transmitted into a black hole if a receiver is not available, the higher layer in the protocol suite using UDP as a transport protocol will wait for an acknowledgment. If one is not received within a predefined period of time, the application can decide whether to retransmit or cancel the session.

In examining Exhibit 2, note that certain applications use TCP as their transport protocol while other applications use UDP. In general, applications that require data integrity, such as remote terminal transmission (Telnet), file transfer (FTP), and electronic mail, use TCP as their transport protocol. In comparison, applications that transmit relatively short packets, such as the Domain Name Service (DNS) and the Simple Network Management Protocol (SNMP) that is used to perform network management operations, use UDP.

One relatively new TCP/IP application takes advantage of both the TCP and UDP transport protocols. That application is Voice-over-IP (VoIP). VoIP commonly uses TCP to set up a call and convey signaling information to the distant party. Because real-time voice cannot be delayed by retransmission if an error in a packet is detected, there is no need to perform error detection. Thus, digitized voice samples are commonly transmitted using UDP once a session is established using TCP.

The Application Layer

As previously noted, the development of the TCP/IP protocol suite predated the development of the ISO's OSI Reference Model. At the time the TCP/IP protocol suite was developed, functions above the transport layer were combined into one entity that represented an application. Thus, the TCP/IP protocol suite does not include separate session and presentation layers. Now having an appreciation for the manner by which the TCP/IP protocol stack can be compared and contrasted to the OSI Reference Model, this chapter concludes by examining the flow of data and the use of headers within a TCP/IP network.

Data Flow and Header Utilization

Data flow within a TCP/IP network commences at the application layer where data is provided to an applicable transport layer protocol — TCP or UDP. At layer 4, the transport layer appends either a TCP or UDP header to the application data, depending on the transport protocol used by the application layer. The purpose of the transport layer header is to provide information about the type of application being transported, as well as data necessary for the transport protocol to perform its intended operation. Concerning the latter, the TCP header, as will be noted later in this book, includes a field for sequence information that enables datagrams received out of order to be placed back into their correct order. Other fields within the TCP header are used to verify the receipt of data as well as perform other connection-oriented functions.

The transport layer protocol uses a port number to distinguish the type of application data being transported. Through the use of port numbers, it becomes possible to distinguish one application from another flowing between a common source and destination.

For lay personnel not familiar with TCP or IP, this explains how a common hardware platform, such as a Windows NT server, can support both Web and FTP services. That is, although the server has a common IP address contained in an IP header, the port number in the TCP or UDP header indicates the application.

Application data flowing onto a network is first formed into a TCP segment or UDP datagram. The resulting UDP datagram or TCP segment is then passed to the network layer where an IP header is opened. The IP header contains network addressing information that is used by routers to route datagrams through a network. Similar to TCP, UDP results in the appending of a header to application data. However, because UDP represents a best-effort connectionless transport protocol, as one might expect, its header is not as extensive as the TCP header. For example, because data sequencing is not required, the UDP header does not have a Sequence field. Similarly, because data is transmitted on a best-effort basis, there is no need for an Acknowledgment field. Chapter 5 examines TCP and UDP headers in detail.

In comparison to the TCP and UDP headers that identify the application being transported, the purpose of IP is to provide a mechanism for the routing of data from source to destination. The IP header that is appended to either a TCP or UDP header includes a Destination Address field, which facilitates the routing of the datagram. Chapter 4 focuses attention on IP, to include the fields within the IP header.

When an IP datagram reaches a LAN, the difference between the network layer and LAN address is first resolved through ARP. Once this is accomplished, the IP datagram is placed into a LAN frame using an appropriate MAC address in the LAN header. Exhibit 3 illustrates the data flow within a TCP/IP network for delivery to a station on a LAN.

The TCP/IP protocol suite represents a methodically considered and developed collection of protocols and applications. As noted in subsequent chapters of this book, it is a very flexible open architecture that allows new applications and protocols to be developed. Concerning that development, it is the standards process that ensures the orderly development of additions to the protocol suite. Thus, Chapter 3 focuses on this important topic.

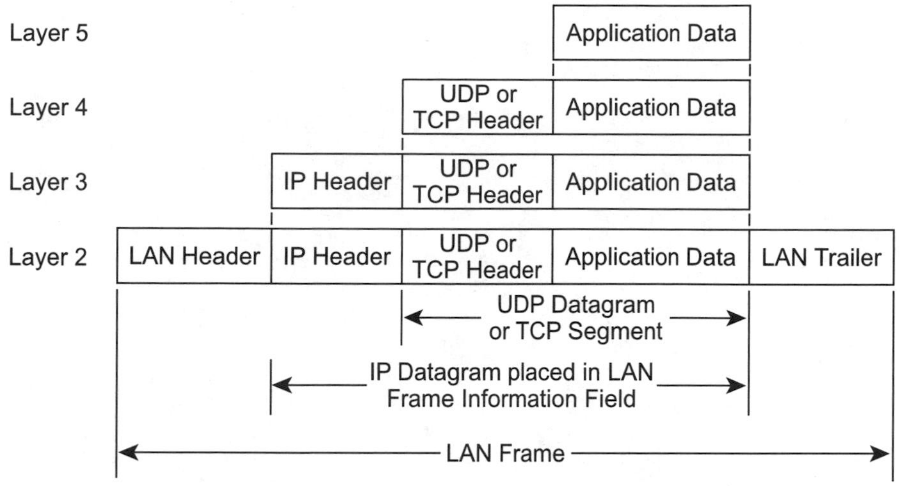

Exhibit 3. Data Flow within a TCP/IP Network for Delivery to a Station on a LAN

Chapter 3

Internet Governing Bodies and the Standards Process

Standards are the glue that enables hardware and software products to interoperate. Without standards it would be difficult, if not impossible, for different vendors to create products that could operate with products made by other organizations. For the TCP/IP protocol suite, standards are developed by several organizations that can be considered the governing bodies of the Internet. Thus, the first section of this chapter concentrates on this topic. Once this is accomplished, attention turns to the standardization process and the relationship of different governing bodies to the publication of documents that affect the use of the TCP/IP protocol suite. Because Internet standards are available online, this chapter also examines how one can access needed documents. In doing so, we discuss and examine several document searching techniques that can be used to satisfy information requirements in a timely manner.

Internet Governing Bodies

Any discussion of the role of various bodies in governing the manner by which networks that form the Internet connect to one another and how they control the evolution of the TCP/IP protocol suite is facilitated by examining the evolution of the mother of all networks. Thus, let us digress a bit and focus attention on the manner by which funding by the U.S. Department of Defense was used to develop communications between research centers that evolved into the Internet.

Internet Evolution

The evolution of the TCP/IP protocol suite can be traced to the efforts of the U.S. Department of Defense Advanced Research Projects Agency (DARPA). During the latter portion of the 1960s, DARPA funded a project to facilitate communications between computers that resulted in the development of a protocol referred to as the Network Control Program (NCP). For a period of approximately seven years, NCP was used to support process-to-process communications between host computers via a packet switching network operated by the Advanced Research Project Agency (ARPA) and referred to as ARPAnet.

Although NCP allowed peer-to-peer communications, it lacked a degree of flexibility that resulted in DARPA providing research grants to the University of California at Los Angeles (UCLA), Stanford Research Institute (SRI), and several additional universities. This resulted in a recommendation to replace NCP with a protocol referred to as the Transmission Control Program (TCP). Between 1975 and 1979, DARPA funding resulted in the development of TCP and the protocol responsible for the routing of packets that was given the name Internet Protocol (IP). Within a short period of time, the protocol suite was referred to as TCP/IP. In 1983, ARPA required all organizations that wished to connect their computers to ARPAnet to use the TCP/IP protocol suite.

In 1983, ARPAnet was subdivided into two networks. One network, known as Military Network (MILNET), was developed for use by the Department of Defense. The second network that now represents nonmilitary sites was called the DARPA Internet.

During the mid-1980s, a large number of networks were created using the TCP/IP protocol suite. Some networks, such as the Southeastern Universities Research Association Network (SURANet), represented associations of universities within a geographical area, while other networks were developed by commercial organizations. Each of these networks was interconnected using ARPAnet as a backbone and resulted in the beginning of what is now known as the Internet.

At the same time that ARPAnet was being used as a backbone by geographically separated regional networks, a new network was formed. The initial goal of this new network was to link five supercomputer sites. This network, operated by the National Science Foundation (NSF) and referred to as NSFnet, was established in 1986. As a relatively new network, the NSF built a backbone with 56-kbps circuits that were upgraded to 1.544-Mbps T1 circuits by July 1988.

Within a short period of time, several regional networks began to link their facilities to the NSFnet. Although the NSFnet was a noncommercial enterprise, several commercial networks were developed during the late 1980s that were interconnected to the NSFnet via points or locations referred to as commercial Internet exchanges (CIXs). Later, the CIXs evolved to become peering points that represent locations where modern-day Internet service providers interconnect their networks.

By 1989, the original ARPAnet had become expensive to operate, while NSFnet provided a faster backbone infrastructure while providing a mirror image of the ARPAnet. This resulted in DARPA deciding to take ARPAnet out of service. In turn, the use of the NSFnet further increased. As LANs became prevalent and were connected to the NSFnet, the term "Internet" was commonly used to reference the network of interconnected networks. As the use of the Internet expanded, the NSF did not have the staff required for various administrative duties associated with running the network, and issued contracts to facilitate the orderly growth in connectivity. Some companies were given the responsibility to operate network access points (NAPs) through which companies could connect commercial networks to the Internet, while other companies received contracts to register domain names, such as xyz.com and myuniversity.edu. Eventually, the NSF contracted out all of the functions associated with operation of the Internet. By 1995, the NSF shut down its backbone as the number of NAPs, which later became known as peering points, proved sufficient for network interconnection purposes and made the NSFnet obsolete. Today, there are literally thousands of Internet service providers (ISPs) whose networks are interconnected to one another through peering points. To ensure interoperability, several organizations have been formed over the past 30 years to govern various aspects of the TCP/IP protocol suite. Some of the more prominent organizations include the Internet Activities Board (IAB), which was renamed the Internet Engineering Task Force (IETF); the Internet Assigned Numbers Authority (IANA); and the Internet Society (ISOC).

The IAB and IETF

In 1983, the Internet Activities Board (IAB) was formed as an umbrella organization to coordinate the activities of independent task forces that were previously formed to focus attention on a particular area of technology, such as routing protocols, addressing, and standards. One of the working groups that gained a significant degree of prominence and a literal explosion in attendance was the Internet Engineering Task Force (IETF).

In 1992, the Internet Activities Board was both reorganized and renamed with the new name Internet Architecture Board that allowed the same initials to be used. Today, the IAB represents a technical advisory group of the Internet Society, with the latter formed in 1991 as an umbrella organization for the IAB, IETF, and Internet Research Task Force (IRTF). The new IAB is responsible for providing oversight of the architecture for the protocols and procedures used by the Internet as well as for editorial management and publication of Request for Comments (RFC) documents and for administration of Internet assigned numbers. As noted in the second section of this chapter, RFCs are documents that define the TCP/IP protocol suite.

The IANA

The Internet Assigned Numbers Authority (IANA) until recently was supported by the U.S. Government, but is now a not-for-profit organization with an international board of directors. The IANA is responsible for IP addresses, domain names, and protocol parameters and serves as the central coordinating location for the Internet.

The IANA uniform resource locator (URL) is www.iana.org. At that location, one can examine online a comprehensive listing of port number assignment services, obtain links and information concerning domain names, view IP address allocation data, and note contact information. From the IANA Web site one can also use a link to the Internet Corporation for Assigned Names and Numbers (ICANN), and organization we will shortly discuss.

The IANA dates to the creation of the Internet and was originally funded by the NSF. Due to international growth, it was felt that it would be more appropriate for the IANA's activities to be supported by organizations that rely upon it. Thus, many of the IANA functions converted into a new, not-for-profit organization. That new organization is the Internet Corporation for Assigned Names and Numbers (ICANN). ICANN represents a nonprofit corporation that was established to assume the responsibility for IP address space allocation, protocol parameter assignment, domain name system management, and other functions previously performed by the IANA and other organizations under U.S. Government contract. While ICANN took over many IANA functions, the former's role with respect to RFCs remains the same. Although the IAB is responsible for RFCs, the IANA retains responsibility for any new numbering required to identify protocols, ports, or other components of the TCP/IP protocol suite. To accomplish this, the IANA carefully coordinates its activities with the IAB and ICANN to ensure that RFCs do not adversely impact the TCP/IP protocol suite. Given an appreciation for the governing bodies of the Internet related to the development of RFCs, one can now focus on the manner by which the TCP/IP protocol suite is standardized by examining a Request for Comments.

Request for Comments

As noted earlier in this chapter, Requests for Comments (RFCs) are documents that define the TCP/IP protocol suite. RFCs date to 1969 and examine a variety of topics covering many aspects of computer communications, such as networking protocols, procedures, and metrics. For the most part, RFCs are technical documents. However, they can cover a variety of topics, to include an instruction for authors that defines the procedures for writing an RFC. There are currently approximately 4000 RFCs, and it was not until RFC 1543 that instructions for the author were standardized.

The RFC Editor is the publisher of the RFCs and is responsible for the final editorial review of the document. The URL of the RFC Editor is www.rfc-editor.org. At that Web address one can obtain information about the RFC series and the RFC process, search for and retrieve RFCs from the RFC Editor's repository, and obtain other RFC-related information. Such information includes obtaining a list of RFCs that were submitted to the RFC Editor but have yet to be published, news about the RFC process, and the ability to search and retrieve Internet Drafts. As will be shortly noted, all RFCs at one time were Internet Drafts; however, not all Internet Drafts will become RFCs.

Originally, when the Internet was a fraction of its current size, the RFC Editor was a single person. Today, the RFC Editor is actually a group of people and the editorship effort is now performed by the Networking Division of the USC Information Sciences Institute (ISI) in Marina del Rey, California.

The Standards Process

Anyone can submit an RFC. However, the primary source of such documents is the IETF. The actual submission of an RFC begins as a memorandum that is reviewed by the Internet Engineering Steering Group (IESG) that operates under the IAB. If the memorandum is approved, the IESG sends it to the RFC Editor. At this point in time, the document becomes a draft RFC.

Draft RFC

A draft RFC is considered a public document, and a peer review process occurs during which comments are received and reviewed concerning whether or not the RFC removes its draft status and is distributed as an RFC standard.

Although most of the literature, to include this book, uses the term "draft RFC," this is technically incorrect. The correct term is "Internet Draft" (ID) because a document that never leaves the draft stage cannot become an RFC. Thus, all RFCs at one time in their life were Internet Drafts; however, not all Internet Drafts will become RFCs.

Proposed Standard and Draft Standard

An RFC is normally issued as a preliminary draft. After a period of time allowed for comments, the RFC will normally be published as a proposed standard. However, if circumstances warrant, the RFC draft can also be dropped from consideration. Assuming that favorable — or a lack of nonfavorable — comments occur concerning the proposed standard, it can be promoted to a draft standard after a minimum period of six months.

RFC Standard

After a review period of at least four months, the Internet Engineering Steering Group (IESG) can recommend a draft standard for adoption as a standard. Although the IESG must recommend the adoption of an RFC as a standard, the IAB is responsible for the final decision concerning its adoption. Exhibit 1

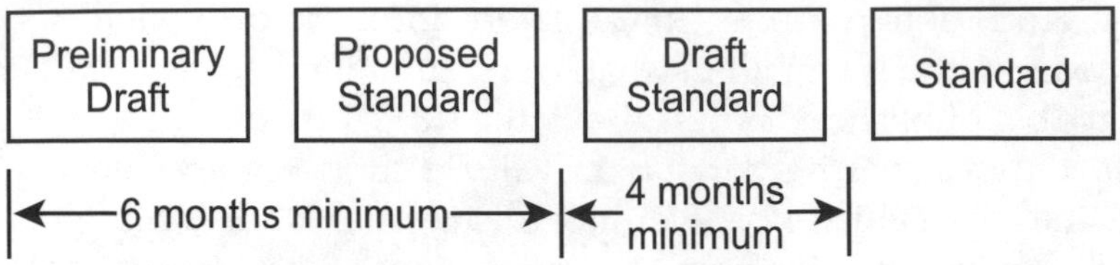

Exhibit 1. Internet Standards Track Time

illustrates the previously mentioned time track for the development of an RFC that represents both an Internet and TCP/IP protocol suite standard. As indicated in Exhibit 1, a minimum of ten months is required for an RFC to be standardized, and many times the process can require several years.

RFC Details

Once issued, an RFC is never revised. Instead, an RFC is updated by new RFCs. When this situation occurs, the new RFC will indicate that it obsoletes or updates a previously published one. This means that if an error occurs in a published RFC, it cannot be changed. Instead, a revised RFC can be written that obsoletes the one in error.

RFC Categories

There are currently three categories of RFCs: Track, Informational, and Experimental. A Standards Track RFC specifies an Internet Standards Track protocol for the Internet community and requests discussion and suggestions for improvement. An Informational RFC provides information for the Internet community and does not specify an Internet Standard of any kind. The third category for RFCs is Experimental, which defines an experimental protocol for the Internet community that may or may not be adapted by the community.

Accessing RFCs

There are several locations on the Internet that maintain a repository of RFCs. Two such organizations are the RFC-Editor (a public organization) and Ohio State University. In addition, one can also join several mailing groups to obtain RFC announcements. If one enters the keyword "RFC index" in a Web search engine, one can usually retrieve several locations where one can point the browser to access a list of RFCs. The RFC-Editor and Ohio State University operate very useful Web sites for accessing and retrieving RFCs, and probably should be considered prior to using other sites.

Exhibit 2 illustrates the RFC search and retrieval page of the RFC-Editor. Its Web address is http://www.rfc-editor.org/rfc.html. In examining Exhibit 2, note that one can search for an RFC by number, author, title, date, or keyword.

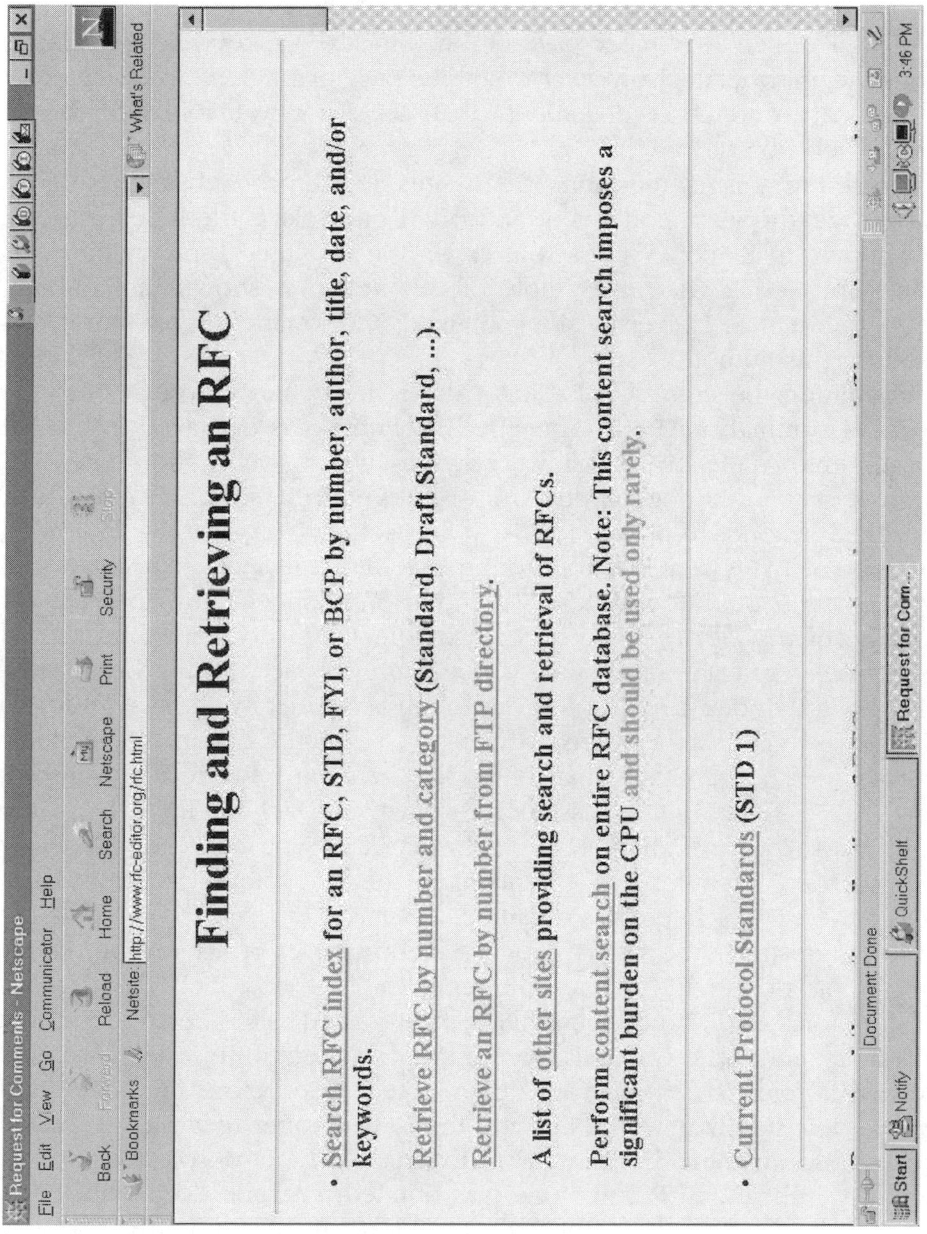

Exhibit 2. The Public RFC-Editor Provides Several Methods for Finding and Retrieving RFCs

In addition, one can retrieve RFCs by number and category or use the screen shown in Exhibit 2 to access the ability to search for and retrieve the RFC.

The Computer and Information Science Department of Ohio State University operates a second Web site that warrants consideration in a search for RFCs. The uniform resource locator (URL) of this site is http://www.cis.ohio-state.edu/hypertext/information/rfc.html.

Exhibit 3 illustrates RFC-Editor and Ohio State University's support and retrieval of RFCs in a number of ways that include a keyword search. In addition, the Ohio State University Web site provides access to an Internet Users' Glossary and other documents that can be a valuable addition to anyone's "Web library."

In concluding this examination of RFC sites, it will probably be of interest to many readers to view portions of an RFC. If one selects the Index retrieval method shown in Exhibit 3 and scrolls down the resulting display, one notes recently published RFCs. An example of this action is shown in Exhibit 4, where the Ohio State University site contained 2719 online RFCs when it was accessed by this author.

In examining the entries in Exhibit 4, note the common format used for displaying a summary of RFCs. After the RFC number is displayed in the left margin, the title of the RFC is followed by the author's publication date, RFC format, and status. Although all RFCs must be written in seven-bit ASCII text, an approved secondary publication is in postscript. Note that by indicating the number of bytes required for storing the RFC, the index allows one to consider if one should download it via an existing connection that might not provide the bandwidth required for an expedient delivery, or if one should request its delivery via e-mail if time is not of the essence. As another option, if accessing the Index from home, one might consider waiting a return to work to access via a higher speed connection a lengthy document needed.

To illustrate the general format of an RFC, examine the relatively recent document RFC 2710 Multicast Listener Discovery (MLD) for IPv6. From the Index listing shown in Exhibit 4, one sees that it is a proposed standard. By clicking on the RFC number 2710 shown in the left column in Exhibit 4, a display of the RFC of interest is obtained.

Exhibit 5 illustrates the view through a Web browser of the top portion of the beginning of the RFC. In examining Exhibit 5, note that the persons responsible for the RFC and their affiliations are listed at the beginning of the document, as is the date of publication of the document. If this RFC obsoleted or updated a prior RFC, one would then note a line before the "Category" line on the left side that would indicate the RFC number that was obsoleted or updated. Because the RFC viewed in Exhibit 5 did not obsolete or update a previously published RFC, that line was omitted from the document.

Continuing the examination of the structure of an RFC, note that the title appears on a line below the submission date. Under the title is a status section that contains a paragraph that describes the RFC. Each RFC must include on its first page a "Status of this Memo" section, which functions as a brief introduction to the RFC. Here, the term "Memo" is used, in actuality, as a memo following a format and structure that evolves into an RFC.

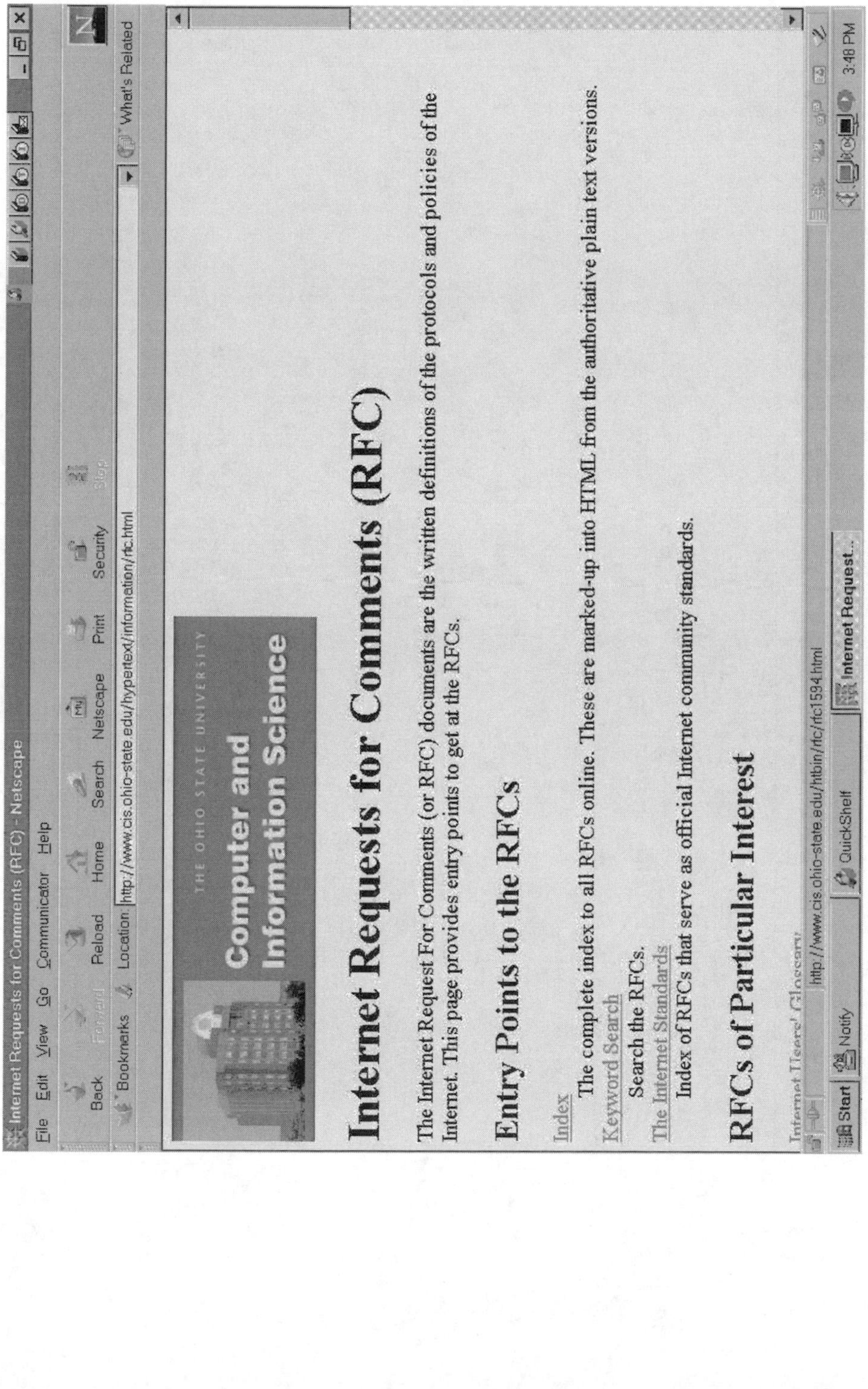

Exhibit 3. Viewing Access to RFCs via the Computer and Information Science Department of Ohio State University

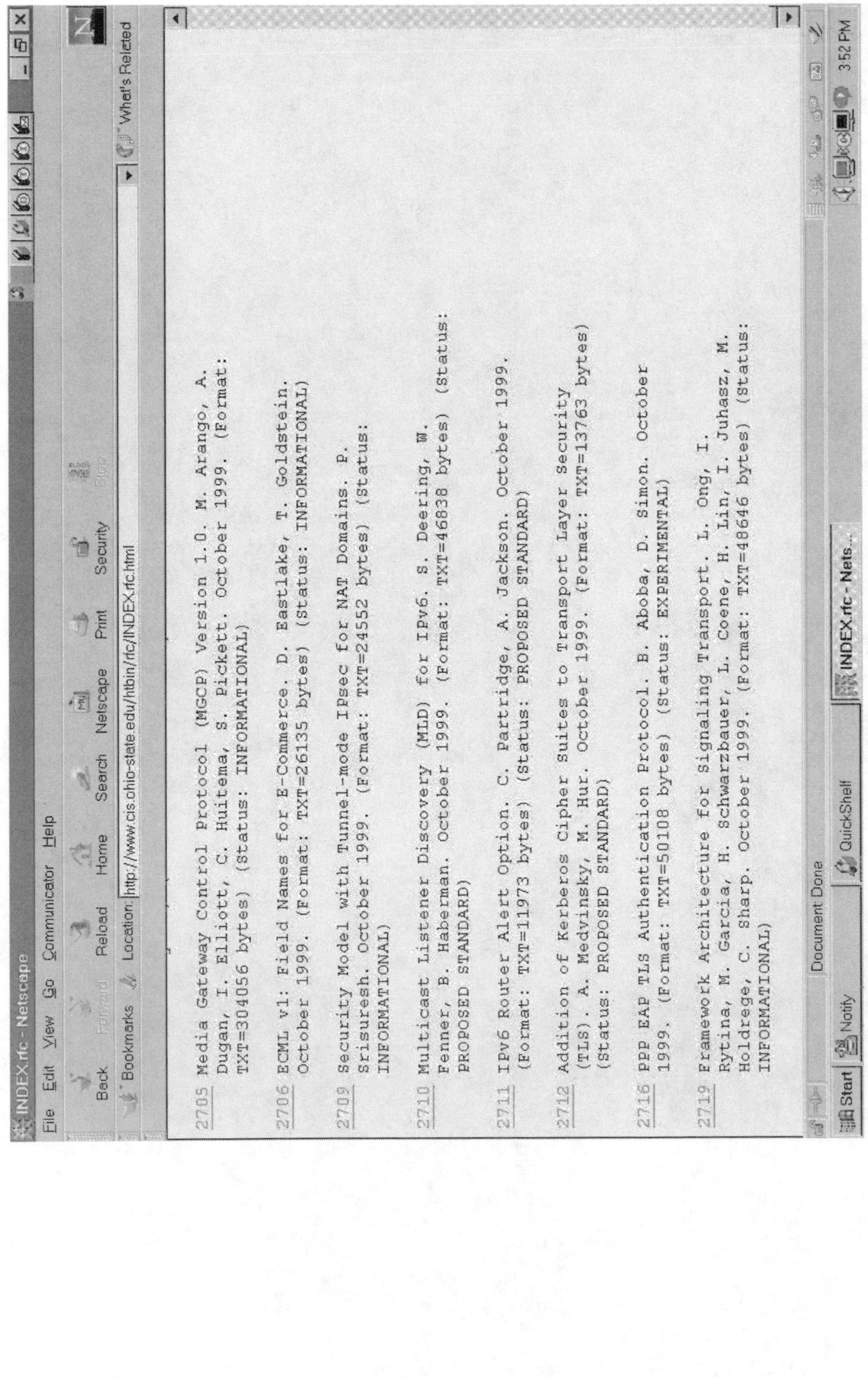

Exhibit 4. Viewing a Portion of the Ohio State University RFC Index List

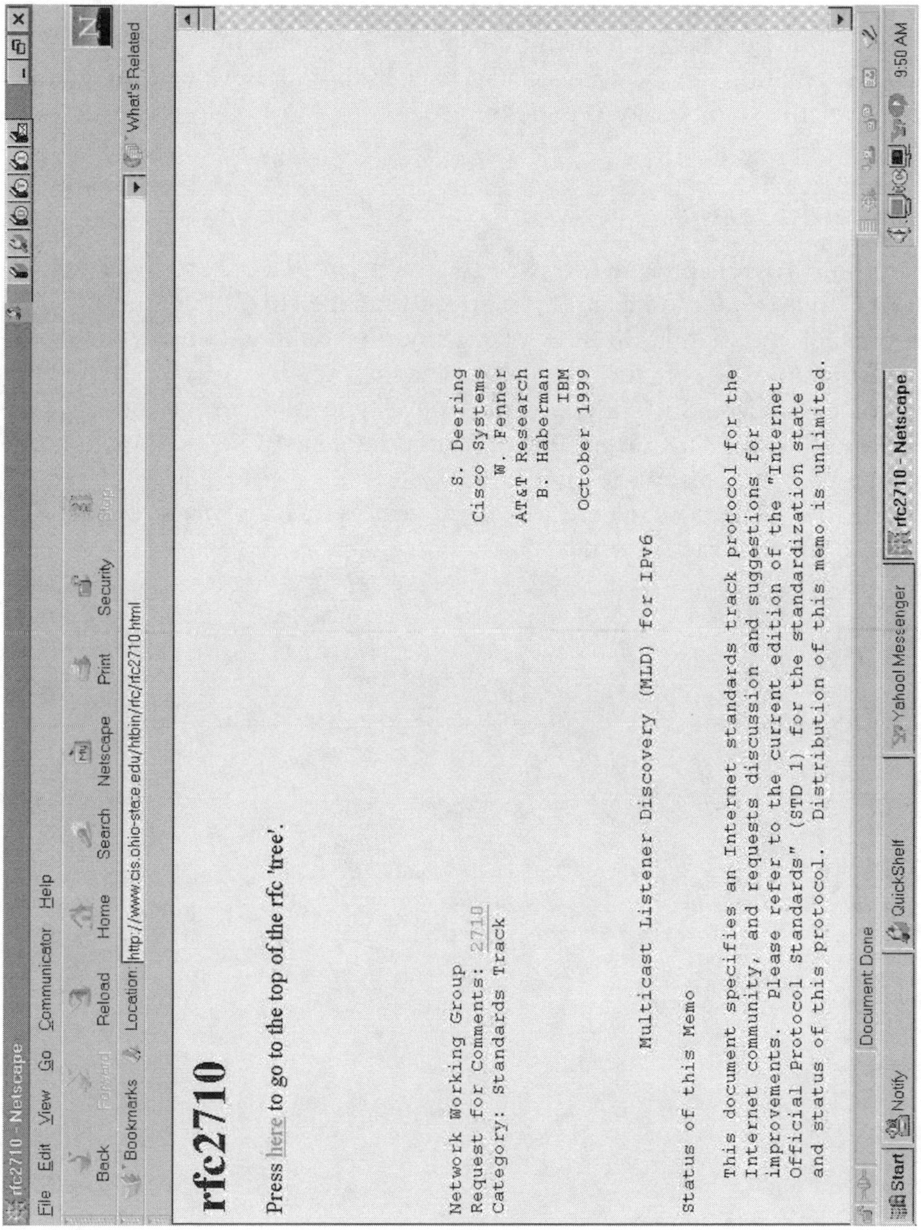

Exhibit 5. Viewing the Initial Portion of RFC 2710

In continuing to view the contents of an RFC, one will encounter a copyright notice, followed by an abstract of the document. Some documents will also include a table of contents, followed by the body of the document. Most modern RFCs now terminate with three sections. The second from last section contains a section entitled Authors' Addresses, which lists the authors, their organization, mailing address, telephone number, and e-mail address. The next to last section in the RFC contains a complete copyright notice. The last section in an RFC contains an acknowledgment section. Thus, the basic RFC provides information on how to contact the authors as well as a detailed description of the technology it is defining.

Best Current Practice

In concluding this chapter, a few words are in order concerning a special type of RFC that is adopted as a Best Current Practice (BCP) document. Some RFCs represent the standardization of community deliberations about statements of principle or conclusions about what is the best way to perform a function or operation. Such RFCs form a new type of Internet specification that is adopted as a Best Current Practice document. A BCP document retains its RFC number and its place in the RFC series; however, it is given the additional label "BCPxxx," where the "xxx" represents the place of the RFC in the Best Current Practice series.

Chapter 4

The Internet Protocol and Related Protocols

The focus of this chapter is on the first layer of the TCP/IP protocol suite. While the Internet Protocol (IP) is the primary protocol most people associate with the network layer, there are two related protocols that must be considered when discussing the TCP/IP protocol suite. Those protocols are the Address Resolution Protocol (ARP) and the Internet Control Message Protocol (ICMP).

This chapter focuses attention on what this author commonly refers to as the Network Layer Troika of the TCP/IP protocol suite: IP, ARP, and ICMP. In examining the Internet Protocol, pay particular attention to the structure of the IP header and its fields, which are examined by routers as a mechanism for making forwarding decisions. Another specific IP area of focus is addressing, as the composition of IP addresses determines the manner by which datagrams are routed from source to destination, as well as the number of hosts that can be connected to a specific type of network. In addition, in examining IP addressing, this chapter also discusses several little-known areas of IP that having knowledge about can provide the user with network design and operation flexibility. Two examples of such topics are the assignment of multiple network addresses to an interface and the use of a zero subnet. Because the filtering of IP datagrams by routers and firewalls can occur based on IP addresses, as well as ICMP message types and control field values, the information presented in this chapter will also provide a firm foundation for discussion of security in later chapters in this book.

The initial focus in this chapter is on IP, to include its use for routing datagrams across a network and between interconnected networks. The composition of the IP header and the use of different fields in the header are examined in detail. Once this is accomplished, attention turns to the role and operation of the Address Resolution Protocol (ARP) and includes examining the rationale for a little-known ARP technique that can considerably facilitate the operation of delay-sensitive transmissions, such as Voice-over-IP. A discussion of Internet Control Message Protocol (ICMP) concludes this chapter. Because some ICMP types of messages are commonly used by hackers as a mechanism to begin an attack upon a network, information about ICMP presented in this chapter will also be used when examining security as a separate entity later in this book.

The Internet Protocol

The Internet Protocol (IP) represents the network layer of the TCP/IP protocol suite. IP was developed as a mechanism to interconnect packet-switched TCP/IP-based networks to form an internet. Here, the term "internet" with a lowercase "i" is used to represent the connection of two or more TCP/IP-based networks.

Datagrams and Segments

The Internet Protocol transmits blocks of data referred to as datagrams. As indicated in Chapter 2, IP receives upper layer protocol data containing either a TCP or UDP header, referred to as a TCP segment or UDP datagram. The prefix of an IP header to the TCP segment or UDP datagram results in the formation of an IP datagram. This datagram contains a destination IP address that is used for routing purposes.

Datagrams and Datagram Transmission

To alleviate potential confusion between datagrams and an obsolete transmission method referred to as datagram transmission, a few words are in order. When the ARPAnet evolved, two methods of packet transmission were experimented with. One method was referred to as datagram transmission and avoided the use of routers to perform table lookups. Under datagram transmission, each node in a network transmits a received datagram onto all ports other than the port on which the datagram was received. While this technique avoids the need for routing table lookup operations, it can result in duplicate datagrams being received at certain points within a network. This results in the necessity to develop software to discard duplicate datagrams, adding an additional level of complexity to networking. Thus, datagram transmission was soon discarded in favor of the creation of virtual circuits that represent a temporary path established between source and destination. When referring to datagram transmission in the remainder of this book, one is actually referencing the transmission of datagrams via a virtual circuit created between source and destination.

Routing

The actual routing of an IP datagram occurs on a best-effort or connectionless delivery mechanism. This is because IP by itself does not establish a session between the source and destination before it transports datagrams. When IP transports a TCP segment, the TCP header results in a connection-oriented session between two layer 4 nodes transported by IP as a layer 3 network protocol.

The importance of IP can be noted by the fact that routing between networks is based on IP-addresses. As noted later in this chapter, the device that routes data between different IP-addressed networks is known as a router. Because it would be extremely difficult, if not impossible, to statically configure every router in a large network to know the route to other routers and networks connected to different routers, routing protocols are indispensable to the operation of a dynamic series of interconnected IP networks. Thus, information presented in this chapter will also form a foundation for understanding the use of routing protocols, which is covered as a separate entity in a later chapter of this book. The best way to obtain an appreciation for the operation of the Internet Protocol is through an examination of the fields in its header.

The IP Header

The current version of the Internet Protocol is version 4, resulting in IP commonly referred to as IPv4. The next generation of the Internet Protocol is IPv6. This section focuses attention on IPv4; IPv6 is discussed in the chapter that examines evolving technologies (Chapter 10).

Exhibit 1 illustrates the fields contained in the IPv4 header. In examining the IPv4 header in Exhibit 1, note that the header consists of a minimum of 20 bytes of data, with the width of each field shown with respect to a 32-bit (four-byte) word.

Bytes versus Octets

In this book, the term "byte" is used to reference a sequence of eight bits used in a common manner. During the development of the TCP/IP protocol suite and continuing today, most standards documents use the term "octet"

<table>
<tr><td>0</td><td>4</td><td>8</td><td>16</td><td>31</td></tr>
<tr><td>Vers</td><td>Hlen</td><td>Service Type</td><td colspan="2">Total Length</td></tr>
<tr><td colspan="3">Identification</td><td>Flags</td><td>Fragment Offset</td></tr>
<tr><td colspan="3">Time to Live Protocol</td><td>Header</td><td>Checksum</td></tr>
<tr><td colspan="5">Source IP Address</td></tr>
<tr><td colspan="5">Destination IP Address</td></tr>
<tr><td colspan="5">Options + Padding</td></tr>
</table>

Exhibit 1. The IPv4 Header

to reference a collection of eight bits. The use of the term "octet" is due to differences in the composition of a byte during the 1960s.

During the early development of computer systems, differences in computer architecture resulted in the use of groupings of five to ten bits to represent a computer byte. Thus, the term "byte" at that time was ambiguous, and standards-making bodies decided to use the term "octet" to reference a grouping of eight bits. Because all modern computers use eight-bit bytes, the term "byte" is no longer ambiguous. Thus, the term "byte" is used throughout this book.

To obtain an appreciation for the operation of IP, examine the functions of the fields in the header. When appropriate, there is discussion of the relation of certain fields to routing and security, topics that will be discussed in detail in later chapters.

Vers Field

The Vers field is four bits in length and is used to identify the version of IP used to create an IP datagram. The current version of IP is v4, with the next generation of IP assigned version number 6.

The four bits in the Vers field support 16 version numbers. Under RFC 1700, a listing of Internet version numbers can be obtained and a summary of that listing is included in Exhibit 2. In examining Exhibit 2, note that the reason the next-generation Internet Protocol is IPv6 instead of IPv5 relates to the fact that version 5 was previously assigned to an experimental protocol referred to as the Streams 2 Protocol.

Hlen Field

The length of the IP header can vary due to its ability to support options. To allow a receiving device to correctly interpret the contents of the header from

Exhibit 2. Assigned Internet Version Numbers

Numbers	*Assignment*
0	Reserved
1–3	Unassigned
4	IP
5	Streams
6	IPv6
7	TP/IX
8	P Internet Protocol (PIP)
9	TUBA
10–14	Unassigned
15	Reserved

the rest of an IP datagram requires the receiving device to know where the header ends. This function is performed by the Hlen field, the value of which indicates the length of the header.

The Hlen field is four bits in length. In Exhibit 1, note that the IP header consists of 20 bytes of fixed information followed by options. Because it is not possible to use a four-bit field to directly indicate the length of a header equal to or exceeding 320 bytes, the value in this field represents the number of 32-bit words in the header. For example, the shortest IP header is 20 bytes, which represents 160 bits. When divided by 32 bits, this results in a value of 160/32 or 5, which is the value set into the Hlen field when the IP header contains 20 bytes and no options.

Service Type Field

The Service Type field is an eight-bit field that is commonly referred to as a Type of Service (ToS) field. The initial development of IP assumed that applications would use this field to indicate the type of routing path they would like. Routers along the path of a datagram would examine the contents of the Service Type byte and attempt to comply with the setting in this field.

Exhibit 3 illustrates the format of the Service Type field. This field consists of two sub-fields: Type of Service (ToS) and Precedence. The Type of Service sub-field consists of bit positions that, when set, indicate how a datagram should be handled. The three bits in the Precedence sub-field allow the transmitting station to indicate to the IP layer the priority for sending a datagram. A value of 000 indicates a normal precedence, while a value of 111 indicates the highest level of precedence and is normally used for network control.

The value in the Precedence sub-field is combined with a setting in the Type of Service sub-field to indicate how a datagram should be processed.

7	6	5	4	3	2	1	0
R	Type of Service				Precedence		

where:

R represents reserved

Precedence provides eight levels, 0 to 7, with 0 normal and 7 the highest.

Type of Service (ToS) indicates how the datagram is handled.

0000 Default
0001 Minimize monetary cost
0010 Maximize reliability
0100 Maximize throughput
1000 Minimize delay
1111 Maximize security

Exhibit 3. The Service Type Field

As indicated in the lower portion of Exhibit 3, there are six settings defined for the Type of Service sub-field. To understand how this sub-field is used, assume an application is transmitting digitized voice that requires minimal routing delays due to the effect of latency on the reconstruction of digitized voice. By setting the Type of Service sub-field to a value of 1000, this would indicate to each router in the path between source and destination network that the datagram is delay sensitive and its processing by the router should minimize delay.

In comparison, because routers are designed to discard packets under periods of congestion, an application in which the ability of packets to reach their destination is of primary importance would set the ToS sub-field to a value of 0010. This setting would denote to routers in the transmission path that the datagram requires maximum reliability. Thus, routers would select other packets for discard prior to discarding a packet with its ToS sub-field set to a value of 0010.

Although the concept behind including a Service Type field was a good idea, from a practical standpoint it is rarely used. The reason for its lack of use is the need for routers supporting this field to construct and maintain multiple routing tables. While this is not a problem for small networks, the creation and support of multiple routing tables can significantly affect the level of performance of routers in a complex network such as the Internet.

Although routers in most networks ignore the contents of the Service Type field, this field is now being used to map IP datagrams being transmitted over an ATM backbone. Because ATM includes a built-in Quality of Service (QoS) that, at the present time, cannot be obtained on an IP network, many organizations are transmitting a variety of data to include Voice-over-IP over an ATM backbone, using the Service Type field as a mechanism to map different IP service requirements into applicable types of ATM service. A second emerging application for the Service Type field is to differentiate the requirements of different applications as they flow into an IP network. In this situation, the Service Type byte is renamed as the DiffServe (Differentiated Service) byte. The Internet Engineering Task Force is currently examining the potential use of the DiffServe byte as a mechanism to define an end-to-end QoS capability through an IP network.

Total Length Field

The Total Length field indicates the total length of an IP datagram in bytes. This length indicates the length of the IP header to include options, followed by a TCP or UDP header or another type of header, as well as the data that follows that header. The Total Length field is 16 bits in length, resulting in an IP datagam having a maximum defined length of 2^{16} or 65,535 bytes.

Identification and Fragment Offset Fields

Unlike some types of clothing where one size fits all, an IP datagram can range up to 65,535 bytes in length. Because some networks only support a transport frame that can carry a small portion of the theoretical maximum-length IP datagram, it can become necessary to fragment the datagram for transmission between networks. One example of this would be the routing of a datagram from a Token Ring network to another Token Ring network via an Ethernet network. Token Ring networks that operate at 16 Mbps can transport approximately 18 kbytes in their Information field. In comparison, an Ethernet frame has a maximum-length Information field of 1500 bytes. This means that datagrams routed between Token Ring networks via an Ethernet network must be subdivided, or fragmented, into a maximum length of 1500 bytes for Ethernet to be able to transport the data.

The default IP datagram length is referred to as the path MTU (or maximum transmission unit). The MTU is defined as the size of the largest packet that can be transmitted or received through a logical interface. For the previous example of two Token Ring networks connected via an Ethernet network, the MTU would be 1500 bytes. Because it is important to commence transmission with the lowest common denominator packet size that can flow through different networks and, if possible, adjust the packet size after the initial packet reaches its destination, IP datagrams use a default of 576 bytes when datagrams are transmitted remotely (off the current network).

Fragmentation is a most interesting function as it allows networks capable of transmitting larger packets to do so more efficiently. The reason efficiency increases is due to the fact that larger packets have proportionally less overhead. Unfortunately, the gain in packet efficiency is not without cost. First, although routers can fragment datagrams, they do not reassemble them, leaving it to the host to perform reassembly. This is because router CPU and memory requirements would considerably expand if they had to reassemble datagrams flowing to networks containing hundreds or thousands of hosts. Second, although fragmentation is a good idea for boosting transmission efficiency, a setting in the Flag field (see below) can be used to indicate that a datagram should not be fragmented. Because many routers do not support fragmentation, many applications by default set the do not fragment flag bit and use a datagram length that, while perhaps not most efficient, ensures that a datagram can flow end-to-end as its length represents the lowest common denominator of the networks it will traverse. A third problem associated with long packets results from the fact that their processing can impose undue queuing delays. For example, a packet containing time-dependent digitized voice that reaches a queue just after a packet containing a relatively delay-insensitive file transfer packet can be delayed to the point where the reconstruction of voice at the recipient sounds awkward. Because of this, most organizations will use multiple queues to subdivide traffic into different classes and normally do not fragment datagrams.

However when an IP datagram is fragmented, this situation results in the use of three fields in the IP header. Those fields are Identification, Flags, and Fragment Offset.

The Identification field is 16 bytes in length and is used to indicate which datagram fragments belong together. A receiving device operation at the IP network layer uses the Identification field as well as the source IP address to determine which fragments belong together. To ensure fragments are put back together in their appropriate order requires a mechanism to distinguish one fragment from another. That mechanism is provided by the Fragment Offset field, which indicates the location where each fragment belongs in a complete message. The actual value in the Fragment Offset field is an integer that corresponds to a unit of eight bytes that indicates the offset from the previous datagram. For example, if the first fragment were 512 bytes in length, the second fragment would have an offset value that indicates that this IP datagram commences at byte 513. By using the Total Length and Fragment Offset fields, a receiver can easily reconstruct a fragmented datagram.

Flags Field

The third field in the IP header directly associated with fragmentation is the Flags field. This field is three bytes in length, with two bits used to denote fragmentation information. The setting of one of those bits is used as a direct fragment control mechanism, because a value of "0" indicates the datagram can be fragmented, while a value of "1" indicates do not fragment the datagram. The second fragment bit is used to indicate fragmentation progress. When the second bit is set to a value of "0," it indicates that the current fragment in a datagram is the last fragment. In comparison, a value of "1" in this bit position indicates that more fragments follow.

The following diagram illustrates the composition of the three-bit Flags field. Note that the first bit position, which is reserved for future use, is set to a value of 0. The next bit position is referred to as the "don't fragment" (DF) bit, which indicates whether or not a datagram should be fragmented. If this bit position is not set, fragmentation is not allowed. The third bit is the "more fragments" (MF) bit. When set, this bit position indicates more fragments follow. Thus, a setting of 0 in the MF bit position indicates the last fragment.

0	1	2
0	DF	MF

To illustrate the use of the Flags field, assume a datagram needs to be subdivided into three fragments. The following illustration indicates the change in the value of the Flags field with respect to the initial datagram and its three fragments:

Datagram	*Flags*	*Field*
Initial	DF	MF
Fragment 1	0	1
Fragment 2	0	1
Fragment 3	0	0

Time to Live Field

The Time to Live (TTL) field is eight bits in length. The setting in this field is used to specify the maximum amount of time that a datagram can exist. It is used to prevent a mis-addressed datagram from endlessly wandering the Internet or a private IP network, similar to the manner by which a famous American folk hero was noted in a song to wander the streets of Boston.

Because an exact time is difficult to measure, the value placed into the TTL field is actually a router hop count. That is, routers decrement the value of the TTL field by 1 as a datagram flows between networks. If the value of this field reaches zero, the router will discard the datagram and, depending on the configuration of the router, generate an ICMP message that informs the originator of the datagram that the TTL field expired and the datagram, in effect, was sent to the great bit bucket in the sky.

Many applications set the TTL field default value to 32, which should be more than sufficient to reach most destinations in a very complex network, to include the Internet. In fact, one popular application referred to as traceroute will issue a sequence of datagrams commencing with a value of 1 in the TTL field to obtain a sequence of router-generated ICMP messages that enables the path from source to destination to be noted. The operation of the traceroute application and how it can be used as a diagnostic tool are examined in detail in Chapter 6.

Protocol Field

It was noted in Chapter 2 that an IP header prefixes the transport layer header to form an IP datagram. While TCP and UDP represent a large majority of layer 4 protocols carried in an IP datagram, they are not the only protocols transported. In addition, even if they were, one would need a mechanism to distinguish one upper layer protocol from another that is carried in a datagram.

The method used to distinguish the upper layer protocol carried in an IP datagram is obtained through the use of a value in the Protocol field. For example, a value of decimal 6 is used to indicate that a TCP header follows the IP header, while a value of decimal 17 indicates that a UDP header follows the IP header in a datagram. Other popular protocols include ICMP, which results in an IP Protocol field value of 1; Exterior Gateway Protocol, which results in an IP Protocol field value of 8; and ICMP for IPv6, which results in the use of 58 for the assigned Internet protocol number.

The Protocol field is eight bits in length, permitting up to 256 protocols to be defined under IPv4. Exhibit 4 lists the current assignments of Internet protocol numbers. Note that although TCP and UDP by far represent the vast majority of TCP/IP traffic on the Internet and corporate intranets, other protocols can be transported and a large block of protocol numbers are currently unassigned. Also note that under IPv6, the Protocol field is named the Next Header field. Chapter 10 examines IPv6 in detail.

Exhibit 4. Assigned Internet Protocol Numbers

Decimal	*Keyword*	*Protocol*
0	HOPOPT	IPv6 Hop-by-Hop Option
1	ICMP	Internet Control Message Protocol
2	IGMP	Internet Group Management Protocol
3	GGP	Gateway-to-Gateway Protocol
4	IP	IP in IP (encapsulation)
5	ST	Stream
6	TCP	Transmission Control Protocol
7	CBT	CBT
8	EGP	Exterior Gateway Protocol
9	IGP	Any private interior gateway (used by Cisco for their IGRP)
10	BBN-RCC-MON	BBN RCC Monitoring
11	NVP-II	Network Voice Protocol, Version 2
12	PUP	PUP
13	ARGUS	ARGUS
14	EMCON	EMCON
15	XNET	Cross Net Debugger
16	CHAOS	Chaos
17	UDP	User Datagram Protocol
18	MUX	Multiplexing
19	DCN-MEAS	DCN Measurement Subsystems
20	HMP	Host Monitoring Protocol
21	PRM	Packet Radio Measurement
22	XNS-IDP	XEROX NS IDP
23	TRUNK-1	Trunk-1
24	TRUNK-2	Trunk-2
25	LEAF-1	Leaf-1
26	LEAF-2	Leaf-2
27	RDP	Reliable Data Protocol
28	IRTP	Internet Reliable Transaction Protocol
29	ISO-TP4	ISO Transport Protocol Class 4
30	NETBLT	Bulk Data Transfer Protocol
31	MFE-NSP	MFE Network Services Protocol
32	MERIT-INP	MERIT Internodal Protocol
33	SEP	Sequential Exchange Protocol
34	3PC	Third Party Connect Protocol
35	IDPR	Inter-Domain Policy Routing Protocol
36	XTP	XTP
37	DDP	Datagram Delivery Protocol
38	IDPR-CMTP	IDPR Control Message Transport Protocol
39	TP++	TP++ Transport Protocol
40	IL	IL Transport Protocol
41	IPv6	IPv6

Exhibit 4. Assigned Internet Protocol Numbers (continued)

Decimal	*Keyword*	*Protocol*
42	SDRP	Source Demand Routing Protocol
43	IPv6-Route	Routing Header for IPv6
44	IPv6-Frag	Fragment Header for IPv6
45	IDRP	Inter-Domain Routing Protocol
46	RSVP	Reservation Protocol
47	GRE	General Routing Encapsulation
48	MHRP	Mobile Host Routing Protocol
49	BNA	BNA
50	ESP	Encapsulation Security Payload for IPv6 and IPv4
51	AH	Authentication Header for IPv6 and IPv4
52	I-NLSP	Integrated Net Layer Security
53	SWIPE	IP with Encryption
54	NARP	NBMA Address Resolution Protocol
55	MOBILE	IP Mobility
56	TLSP	Transport Layer Security Protocol (using Kryptonet key management)
57	SKIP	SKIP
58	IPv6-ICMP	ICMP for IPv6
59	IPv6-NoNxt	No Next Header for IPv6
60	IPv6-Opts	Destination Options for IPv6
61		Any host internal protocol
62	CFTP	CFTP
63		Any local network
64	SAT-EXPAK	SATNET and Backroom EXPAK
65	KRYPTOLAN	Kryptolan
66	RVD	MIT Remote Virtual Disk Protocol
67	IPPC	Internet Pluribus Packet Core
68		Any distributed file system
69	SAT-MON	SATNET Monitoring
70	VISA	VISA Protocol
71	IPCV	Internet Packet Core Utility
72	CPNX	Computer Protocol Network Executive
73	CPHB	Computer Protocol Heart Beat
74	WSN	Wang Span Network
75	PVP	Packet Video Protocol
76	BR-SAT-MON	Backroom SATNET Monitoring
77	SUN-ND	SUN ND PROTOCOL-Temporary
78	WB-MON	WIDEBAND Monitoring
79	WB-EXPAK	WIDEBAND EXPAK
80	ISO-IP	ISO Internet Protocol
81	VMTP	VMTP
82	SECURE-VMTP	SECURE-VMPT
83	VINES	VINES

Exhibit 4. Assigned Internet Protocol Numbers (continued)

Decimal	Keyword	Protocol
84	TTP	TTP
85	NSFNET-IGP	NSFNET-IGP
86	DGP	Dissimilar Gateway Protocol
87	TCF	TCF
88	EIGRP	EIGRP
89	OSPFIGP	OSPFIGP
90	Sprite-RPC	Sprite RPC Protocol
91	LARP	Locus Address Resolution Protocol
92	MTP	Multicast Transport Protocol
93	AX.25	AX.25 Frames
94	IPIP	IP-within-IP Encapsulation Protocol
95	MICP	Mobile Internetworking Control Protocol
96	SCC-SP	Semaphore Communications Sec. Protocol
97	ETHERIP	Ethernet-within-IP Encapsulation
98	ENCAP	Encapsulation Header
99		Any private encryption scheme
100	GMTP	GMTP
101	IFMP	Ipsilon Flow Management Protocol
102	PNNI	PNNI over IP
103	PIM	Protocol Independent Multicast
104	ARIS	ARIS
105	SCPS	SCPS
106	QNX	QNX
107	A/N	Active Networks
108	IPPCP	IP Payload Compression Protocol
109	SNP	Sitara Networks Protocol
110	Compaq-Peer	Compaq Peer Protocol
111	IPX-in-IP	IPX in IP
112	VRRP	Virtual Router Redundancy Protocol
113	PGM	PGM Reliable Transport Protocol
114		Any 0-hop protocol
115	L2TP	Layer-Two Tunneling Protocol
116	DDX	D-II Data Exchange (DDX)
134–254		Unassigned
255	Reserved	

Header Checksum Field

It was previously noted that IP represents a connectionless protocol. As such, it does not include any type of error correction mechanism, such as a sequencing field in its header. As a best-effort protocol, IP simply transmits datagrams and leaves it up to higher layers in the protocol suite to determine if data correctly arrived at its destination. Because IP represents a connectionless, best-effort protocol, it may appear strange that the header includes a 16-bit Checksum field. However, the checksum is included to verify the integrity of the header and data being transported. Because one or more fields in the IP header change in value as a datagram flows from one router to another, such as the Time-to-Live field that is decremented by each router, every intermediate device must recalculate the Header Checksum field. As each router or gateway receives a datagram, it first computes the checksum and compares its compute value to the value in the Checksum field in the IP header. If the two do not match, the datagram is sent to the great bit bucket in the sky; however, no message to this effect is sent to the originator. Instead, IP relies upon upper layer protocols, such as TCP, to determine that a datagram was lost and to recover from this condition by requesting a retransmission.

Source and Destination Address Fields

Both the Source and Destination Address fields are 32 bits in length under IPv4. The Source Address represents the originator of the datagram, while the Destination Address represents the recipient.

Under IPv4, there are five classes of IP addresses, referred to as Class A through Class E. Classes A, B, and C are subdivided into a network portion and a host portion and represent addresses used on the Internet and private IP-based networks. Classes D and E represent two special types of IPv4 network addresses. Because it is extremely important to understand the composition and formation of IP addresses to correctly configure devices connected to an IP network, as well as to design and modify such networks, the next section in this chapter focuses on this topic. Given an appreciation of IP addressing, one can then examine the use of the Address Resolution Protocol (ARP), noting how ARP is used to enable layer 3 IP datagrams that use 32-bit IP addresses to be correctly delivered by LANs using 48-bit layer 2 MAC addresses.

Options

The IP Options field is optional and, for the most part, rarely used under IPv4. The intention of the Options field was to permit the IP header to convey additional information on an as required basis, such as requesting a particular route for certain datagrams.

The Options field is variable in length and can include several parameters that are concatenated to one another. Each parameter will be identified by a "type" byte that contains three fields — a copied flag, class field, and number field — as indicated below.

C	Class	Number

The purpose of the copied flag (C) is to indicate if an option must be copied in all fragments in the event a datagram is fragmented. If the copied flag is not set, then the option is only copied in the first fragment. Options are grouped by class. Under RFC 791, two option classes were defined: 0 for Control and 2 for Debugging and Measurements. Eight examples of IP header options defined in RFC 791 are summarized in the following table.

Class	*Number*	*Length*	*Destination*
0	0	N/A	End of Option List
0	1	N/A	No Operation
0	2	11	Security
0	3	Variable	Loose Source Routing
0	7	Variable	Record Route
0	8	4	Stream ID
0	9	Variable	Strict Source Routing
2	4	Variable	Internet Timestamp

To obtain an appreciation of the capability of IP Options, focus attention on some of the options listed in the above table.

End of Option List

This option indicates the end of the option list. Thus, it is only one byte and does not have a length beyond its basic format.

No Operation

An option with a Class value of 0 and Number value of 1 is a No Operation option. Similar to the End of Option List option, the No Operation option is one byte in length and has no length component. The No Operation option is commonly used to insert padding between separate options so that they begin on 32-bit word boundaries.

Security

A Class value of 0 and Number value of 2 indicates a Security option. This option is used to carry security, compartmentalization, user group, and handling restriction codes compatible with Department of Defense (DoD) requirements.

Loose Source Routing

The Loose Source Routing option is used to route a datagram based upon information supplied by the source. This option is identified by a Class value of 0 and Number value of 3.

Record Route

A Record Route option permits the route a datagram takes to be recorded. This option is variable in length and defined through a Class value of 0 and Number value of 7.

Stream ID

The Stream ID option is used to transport the stream identifier that occurred in an application known as the Satnet experiment identifier. This option is defined through a Class value of 0 and Number value of 8.

Strict Source Routing

The Strict Source Routing option is defined by a Class value of 0 and Number value of 9. This option is used to route a datagram based upon information provided by the source.

Of the previously mentioned options, only two are in moderate use today: Loose and Strict Source Routing. Both source routing options have a common format, which is shown below.

Type	Length	Pointer	Route Data

The Pointer field contains an index or byte count commencing at the beginning of the option. Thus, its minimum length is 4. If the Pointer field is greater than the Options Length, this indicates that the datagram has reached its final destination. If not, the header's destination address will be replaced by the four bytes (32 bits) following the pointer. When the source routing is strict (type 137), this must be the address of an adjacent router. In comparison, when routing is loose (Type 131), there is no such restriction.

IP Addressing

This section focuses on the mechanism that enables IP datagrams to be delivered to unique or predefined groups of hosts. That mechanism is the addressing method used by the Internet Protocol, commonly referred to as IP addressing.

Under the current version of the Internet Protocol, IPv4, 32-bit binary numbers are used to identify the source and destination address in each datagram. It was not until RFC 760 that the Internet Protocol as we know it was defined and the next IP-related RFC, RFC 791 that obsoleted RFC 760, included the concept of IP address classes. Another key IP-related addressing RFC is RFC 950, which introduced the concept of subnetting. Subnetting represents a method of conserving IP network addresses and is described and discussed in detail later in this section.

Overview

Although a host is normally associated with a distinct IP address, in actuality IP addresses are used by the Internet Protocol to identify distinct device interfaces. That is, each interface on a device has a unique IP address. This explains how a router with multiple interfaces can receive communications addressed to the device on different router ports connected to LANs and WANs. Devices such as hosts, routers, and gateways can have either single or multiple interfaces. When the latter situation occurs, the device will be assigned multiple IP addresses — one for each interface.

Because most hosts are connected to a LAN via a single interface, most readers familiar with IP addressing associate a single IP address with a host. Although not as common as host workstations that use a single network connection, some servers and all firewalls and routers have multiple network connections. Exhibit 5 illustrates a network structure used to connect a corporate private network to the Internet. In this example, a demilitarized (DMZ) LAN is used to interconnect the router and firewall. A DMZ LAN is a LAN without servers or workstations, in effect forcing all communications to and from the Internet to pass through a firewall. Note that both the router and firewall have multiple ports. Thus, in an IP networking environment, each communications device would be assigned two IP addresses: one for each device interface.

In examining Exhibit 5, the DMZ LAN can be placed into effect by simply cabling the firewall to the router through the use of a crossover cable. However,

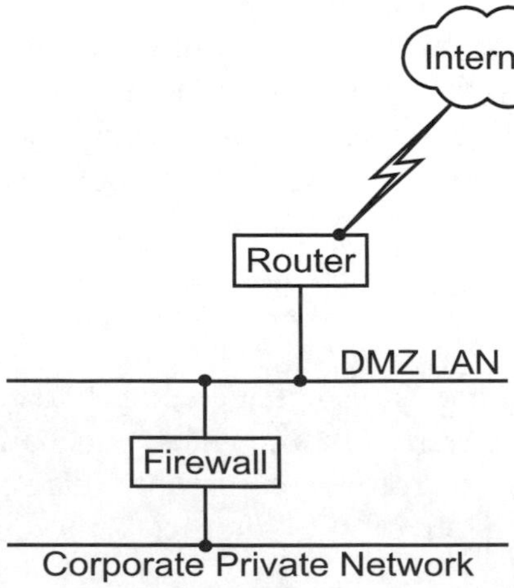

Exhibit 5. Several Types of Communications Devices with Multiple Interfaces, with an IP Address Assigned to Each Interface

most organizations should consider the use of a hub, permitting the firewall and router to interconnect with one another through the hub. The rationale for using the hub is the fact that it allows one to easily insert a monitor, probe, or another device into a spare hub port if the need should arise. In comparison, directly cabling the firewall to the router via the use of a crossover cable would not provide this level of flexibility.

The IP Addressing Scheme

As previously mentioned, IPv4 uses 32-bit binary numbers to identify the source and destination address in each datagram. The use of 32-bit numbers provides an address space that supports 2^{32} or 4,294,967,295 distinct addressable interfaces. While this number probably exceeded the world's population when the Internet was initially developed as a mechanism to interconnect research laboratories and universities, the proliferation of personal computers and the development of the Web significantly expanded the role of the "mother of all networks." Recognizing that many individuals would eventually use personal digital assistants (PDAs), and even all phones, to access the Web, as well as the fact that hundreds of millions or possibly billions of persons in the Third World would eventually be connected to the Internet, it became obvious that IP address space would eventually be depleted. In 1992, the Internet Architecture Board (IAB) began work on a replacement for the current version of IP. Although its efforts were primarily concerned with the addressing limitations of IPv4, the IAB also examined the structure of IP and the inability of the current version of the protocol to easily indicate different options within the header. The result of the IAB effort was a new version of IP that is referred to as IPv6. IPv6 was finalized during 1995 and is currently being evaluated on an experimental portion of the Internet. Under IPv6, source and destination addresses were expanded to 128 bits, and the IP header was considerably altered, with only the Ver field retaining its position in the IPv6 header. Although the use of IPv6 will considerably enhance the support of an expanded Internet as well as facilitate various routing operations, it will be many years before the new protocol moves from an experimental status into production. Due to this, the focus on addressing in this section is on IPv4, and coverage of IPv6 is deferred to Chapter 10.

Address Changes

During the development of the Internet Protocol, it was recognized that hosts would be connected to different networks and that those networks could be interconnected to one another to form a network of interconnected networks, now commonly referred to as the Internet. Thus, in developing an IP addressing scheme, it was also recognized that a mechanism would be required to identify a network as well as a host connected to a network. This recognition

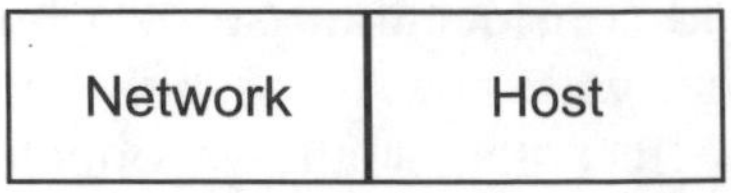

Under the two-level IP addressing hierarchy, the 32-bit IP address is subdivided into network and host portions. The composition of the first four bits of the 32-bit word specifies whether the network portion is 1, 2, or 3 bytes in length, resulting in the host portion being either 3, 2, or 1 bytes in length.

Exhibit 6. The Two-Level IP Addressing Hierarchy used for Class A, B, and C Addresses

resulted in the development of an addressing scheme in which certain classes of IP addresses are subdivided into a two-level addressing hierarchy.

Exhibit 6 illustrates the two-level addressing hierarchy used by Class A, B, and C addresses whose composition and utilization are reviewed below. In examining the two-level IP addressing scheme shown in Exhibit 6, it should be noted that all hosts on the same network are usually assigned the same network prefix, but must have a unique host address to differentiate one host from another. As noted later in this chapter, it is possible (although little noted) that multiple network addresses could reside on a common network. This is the exception rather than the rule. Similarly, two hosts on different networks should be assigned different network prefixes; however, the hosts can have the same host address. In thinking about this addressing technique, one can consider it in many ways to be similar to the structure of a telephone number. That is, no two people in the same area code can have the same phone number. It is both possible and likely that somewhere the same phone number exists in a different area code.

One can also view Class A, B, and C addresses as having the following general format:

< Network Number, Host Number >

where the combined network number and host number have the form xxxx.xxxx.xxxx.xxxx, with each x representing a decimal value. Probing deeper into IP addressing, one sees that the above format uses dotted decimal notation to reference IP addresses. By the end of this section, the reader will be conversant in the use of this method of IP address notation.

Rationale

During the IP standardization process, it was recognized that a single method of subdivision of the 32-bit address space into network and host portions would be wasteful with respect to the assignment of addresses. For example, assume all addresses are evenly split. This would result in the use of 16 bits for a network number and a similar number of bits for a host number. Without considering host and network addressing restrictions (discussed later in the section), the use of 16 bits results in a maximum of 65,536 (2^{16}) networks with up to 65,536 hosts per network. Not only would the assignment of a network address to an organization that has only 100 computers result in a waste of 65,436 host addresses that could not be assigned to other organizations, but in addition, there could only be 65,536 networks. This limited number of networks would be clearly insufficient in an era where over 50,000 colleges, universities, high schools, and grade schools are now connected to the Internet via LANs, with each LAN having a distinct network address. Recognizing that the use of IP addresses could literally mushroom beyond their expectations, the designers of IP came up with a methodology whereby the 32-bit IP address space was subdivided into different address classes. The result of the efforts of IP designers was the definition of five address classes, referred to as Class A through Class E.

Overview

Class A addresses were developed for use by organizations with extremely large networks or for assignments to countries. Class B addresses were developed for use by organizations with large networks, while Class C addresses are used by organizations with small networks. Two additional address classes are Class D and Class E. Class D addresses are used for IP multicasting, a technique where a single message is distributed to a group of hosts dispersed across a network. Class E addresses are reserved for experimental use. Unlike Classes A through C that incorporate a two-level IP addressing structure, Classes D and E use a single addressing structure.

Exhibit 7 illustrates the structure or format of the five defined IP address classes. In examining the entries in Exhibit 7, note that an address identifier of variable length is the prefix to each address class. The address identifier prefix is a single "0" bit for a Class A address, the bits "10" for a Class B address, "110" for a Class C address, "1110" for a Class D address, and "1111" for a Class E address. Note that the address class bit(s) are structured to enable a simple test to determine the address class of a 32-bit IP address. That is, if the first bit in the address is a "0," the address is a Class A address. If not, the next bit is examined. If the second bit is "0," then the address represents a Class B IP address. If the second bit is a "1," then the third bit position must be examined. If the third bit position is "0," then the address represents a Class C address. If not, the fourth bit position is then examined to determine if the address is a Class D or Class E address. Once an address class is identified, the subdivision of the remainder of the address into the network and host address portions can easily be obtained from a table lookup or from predefined data within a program. For example, if a 32-bit address is a Class A address due to the first bit being binary 0, then the next seven bits represent the actual network address, while the remaining 24 bits represent the host address. Similarly, if the first two bits of the 32-bit address have the value "10," then the next 14 bits represent the actual network address, while the

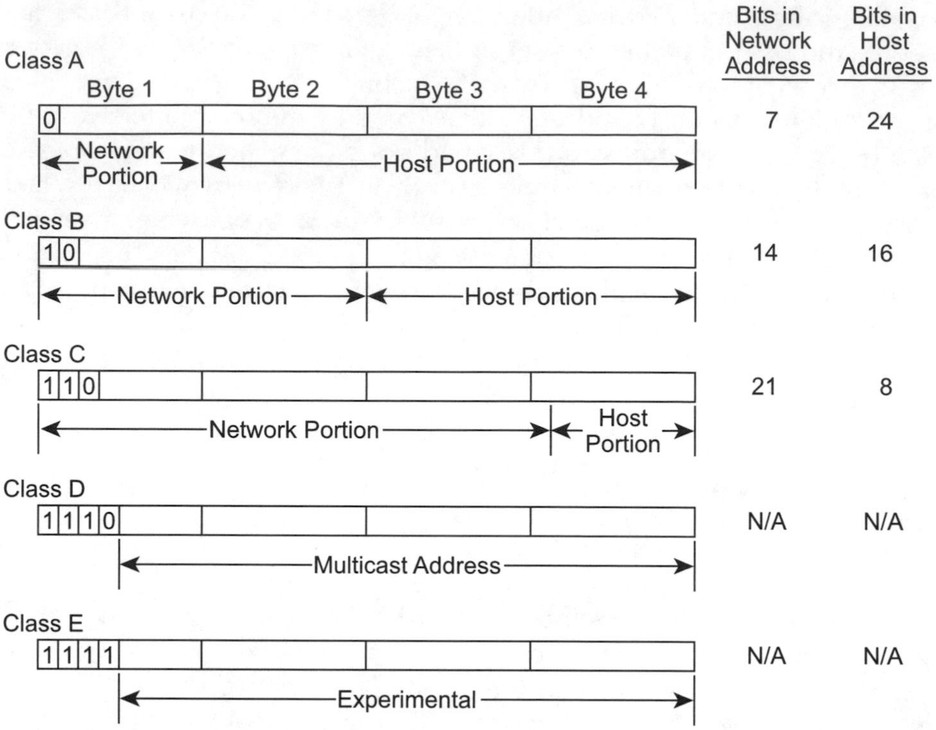

Exhibit 7. IP Address Formats

trailing 16 bits represent the host address. To obtain an appreciation of the use of each IP address class, a detailed examination of each address class follows, with particular attention to the composition of the network and host portion of each address for Classes A through C, as well as the manner by which all five classes are used.

Class A Addresses

As indicated in Exhibit 7, a Class A address has the four-byte form of <network-number.host.host.host>, with seven bits used for the actual network address because the first bit position must be set to a value of binary 0 to indicate the address is a Class A address. Because seven bits are available for the network address, one would logically assume that 2^7 or 128 Class A networks can be defined. In actuality, networks 0 and 127 are reserved and cannot be used, resulting in Class A addressing supporting 126 networks. Because there are 24 bits used for a host identifier, this means that each network is capable of supporting up to $2^{24} - 2$ (or 16,277,214) hosts. The reason 2 is subtracted from the possible number of hosts results from the fact that no host can be assigned a value of all 0s nor a value of all 1s. As noted later in this chapter, a host value of all 1s indicates a broadcast address.

Because only a small number of Class A networks can be defined, they were used up many years ago. Due to the large number of hosts that can be assigned to a Class A network, Class A addresses were primarily assigned to large organizations and countries that have national networks.

Loopback

One Class A network address that warrants attention results from the setting of all seven bits in the network address to 1, representing 127 in decimal. A network address of 127.x.x.x is reserved as an internal loopback address and cannot be assigned as a unique IP address to a host. Thus, a question one may have is, "why reserve a network address of 127 if it is not usable?" The answer to this question is the fact that one can use a network address of 127.x.x.x as a mechanism to determine if one's computer that loaded TCP/IP protocol stack has an operational stack. An example of the use of a 127-network address is illustrated in the top of Exhibit 8, which shows the use of the Ping command to query the device at address 127.1.1.1. Because this is a loopback address, this action tests the protocol stack on the author's computer. Note that in this example, Microsoft's version of Ping uses the IP address 127.1.1.1 as a loopback. If one enters the address 127.0.0.0 as shown in the lower portion of Exhibit 8, Microsoft's implementation of the TCP/IP protocol stack treats the IP address as an invalid address.

All TCP/IP protocol stacks should, as a minimum, recognize the IP address 127.0.0.1 as an internal loopback address. Most protocol stacks will also consider a prefix of 127 for a network address with any non-zero host address as a loopback. Thus, one can normally use 127.1.2.3, 127.4.5.6, and any other combination other than 127.0.0.0 as a loopback.

Class B Addresses

Continuing this exploration of IPv4 address classes, a Class B address has the form <network-number.network-number.host.host> for the four bytes in the address. A Class B network address is defined by setting the two high-ordered bits of an IP address to the binary value "10." Because two bits are used to identify the address, this means that the actual Class B network address is 14 bits in width, while the host portion of the address is two bytes or 16 bits in width. Thus, a Class B address is capable of supporting 2^{14} (or 16,384) networks, with each network capable of supporting up to $2^{16} - 2$ (or 65,534) hosts. Due to the manner by which Class B addresses are subdivided into network and host portions, such addresses are normally assigned to relatively large organizations. In addition, through the process of subnetting, which is described later in this section, one Class B address can be provided to multiple organizations, with each organization informed as to the correct subnet mask to use to identify the portion of a Class B address provided for their use.

If familiar with binary, one can easily convert permissible binary values in the first byte of a Class B address into a range of decimal values. For example, because a Class B address commences with binary values 10, the first byte

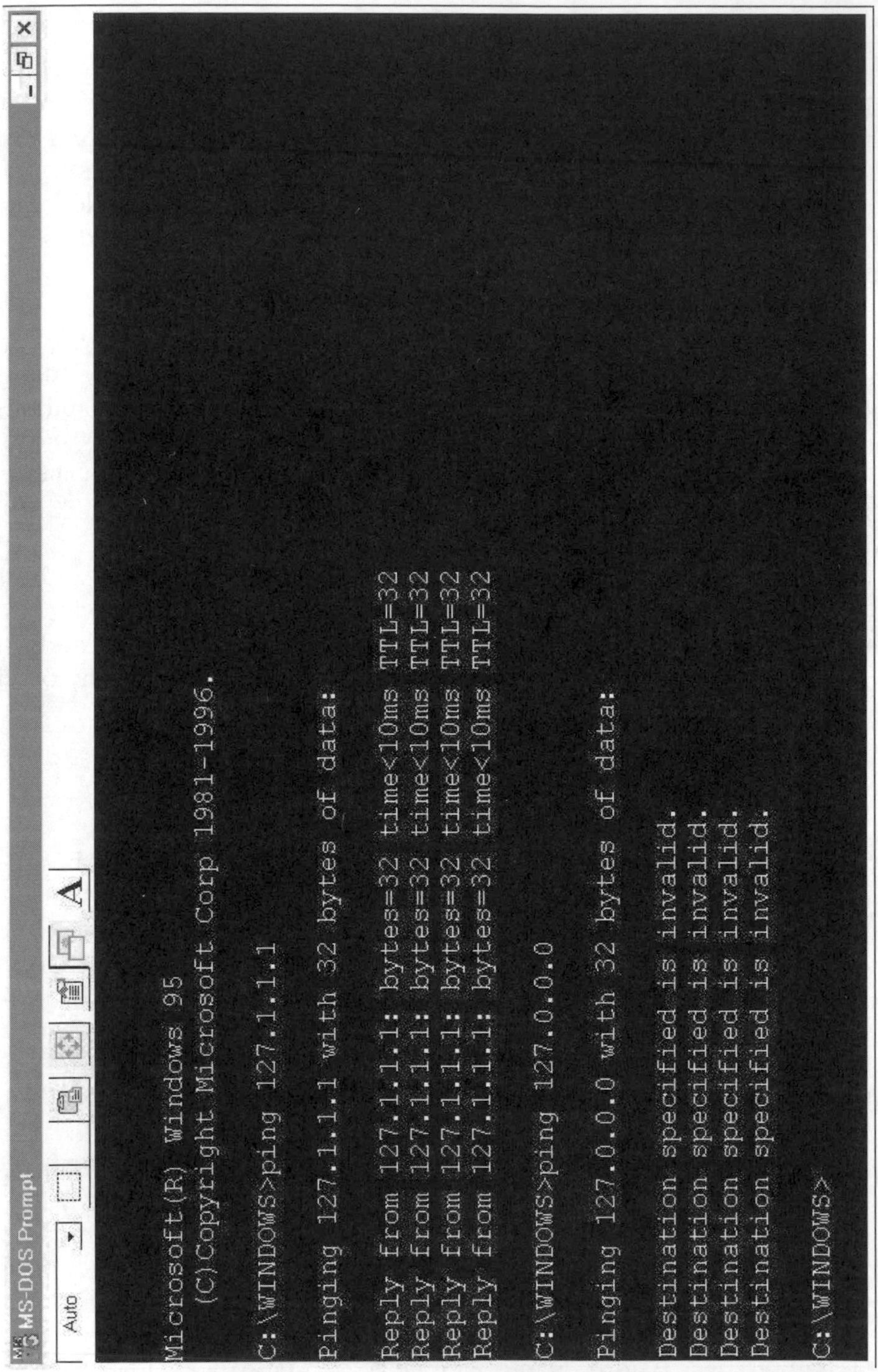

Exhibit 8. Using an IP Loopback Address with a Ping Application to Verify the Status of the TCP/IP Protocol Stack

must range between 1000000 and 10111111. One can convert to decimal by noting that the value of each position in a byte is as follows:

128 64 32 16 8 4 2 1

Thus, binary 10000000 is equivalent to decimal 128, while binary 10111111 is equivalent to decimal 191. Thus, the first byte of a Class B address is restricted to the range 128 to 191, with 0 to 255 permitted in the second byte of the network address.

Class C Addresses

A Class C address is identified by the first three bits in the IP address being set to the binary value of 110. This value denotes the fact that the first three bytes in the 32-bit address identify the network, while the last byte identifies the host on the network. Because the first three bits in a Class C address are set to a value of 110, this means there are 21 bits available for the network address. Thus, a Class C address permits 2^{21} (or 2,097,152) distinct network addresses. Since the host portion of a Class C address is 1 byte in length, the number of hosts per network is limited to $2^8 - 2$ (or 254).

Due to the subdivision of network and host portions of Class C addresses, they are primarily assigned for use by organizations with relatively small networks, such as a single LAN that requires a connection to the Internet. Because it is common for organizations to have multiple LANs, it is also quite common for multiple Class C addresses to be assigned to organizations that require more than 254 host addresses, but are not large enough to justify a Class B address. It is also common for an organization with multiple LANs located within close proximity to one another to share one Class C address through subnetting, a topic covered later in this chapter.

Similar to the manner in the decimal range of Class B addresses was computed, one can compute the range of permitted Class C addresses. That is, because the first three bits in the first byte are set to a value of 110, the binary range of values are 11000000 to 11011111, representing decimal 192 through 223. The second and third bytes in a Class C address range in value from 0 to 255, while the last byte, which represents the host address, ranges in value from 1 to 254, because host values of 0 and 255 are not permitted.

Class D Addresses

Class D IP addresses represent a special type of address referred to as a multicast address. A muticast address is assigned to a group of network devices and allows a single copy of a datagram to be transmitted to a specific group. The members of the group are then able to receive a common sequence of datagrams instead of having individual series of datagrams transmitted to each member on an individual basis, in effect conserving network bandwidth.

A Class D address is identified by the assignment of the binary value 1110 to the first four bits of the address. The remaining 28 bits are then used to define a unique multicast address. Because a Class D address always has the prefix 1110, its first byte varies from 11100000 to 11101111, resulting in the address range 224 through 239. Thus, the multicast address range becomes 224.0.0.0 through 239.255.255.255, with the use of a Class D address enabling approximately 268 million multicast sessions to simultaneously occur throughout the world.

To obtain an appreciation for the manner by which Class D addressing conserves bandwidth, consider a digitized audio or video presentation routed from the Internet onto a private network for which users working at 15 hosts on the private network wish to receive the presentation. Without a multicast transmission capability, 15 separate data streams, each containing a repetition of the audio or video presentation, would be transmitted through the Internet onto the private network, with only the destination address in each datagram in one stream differing from the datagram in a different stream. Here, 14 data streams are unnecessary and only function to clog the Internet as well as the private network. In comparison, through the use of multicasting, the 15 users requiring the presentation would join the multicast group, permitting one data stream to be routed through the Internet onto the private network.

Common examples of the use of multicast include access to many news organization video feeds that result in a 2 × 2-inch television on a computer monitor. With frame refresh rates of 15 or more frames per second, a server of unicast transmissions would consume a relatively large amount of bandwidth. Thus, the ability to eliminate multiple data streams via multicast transmission can prevent networks from being saturated. In addition, this capability reduces the number of datagrams that routers must route. This minimizes the necessity of routers that discard packets when they become saturated.

Unicast, Broadcast, and Multicast Comparison

To facilitate a comparison of the three basic types of addressing, consider Exhibit 9, which shows five stations connected to the Class C network whose address is 205.131.175.0. For simplicity of illustration, this author has only indicated the host address or fourth dotted decimal number for each station on the network in Exhibit 9 varying from 2 to 6. A router connected to the 205.131.175.0 network, which provides connectivity to the Internet, is shown as having the host address of 1. If a datagram is received from the Internet destined to a single station, such as 205.131.175.3, this source address represents a unicast address. If a datagram is to be delivered to all hosts on the network, its destination address will be set to 205.131.175.255, which represents a broadcast address, resulting in all stations on the network receiving the datagram. Thus, two types of IP addressing are unicast and broadcast. To indicate the third type of IP address, assume stations 205.131.175.2 and 205.131.175.3 wish to participate in receiving the annual Victoria Secrets fashion show. Instead of having both stations receive datagrams transporting real-time video at 30 frames per second, which are duplicates of one another

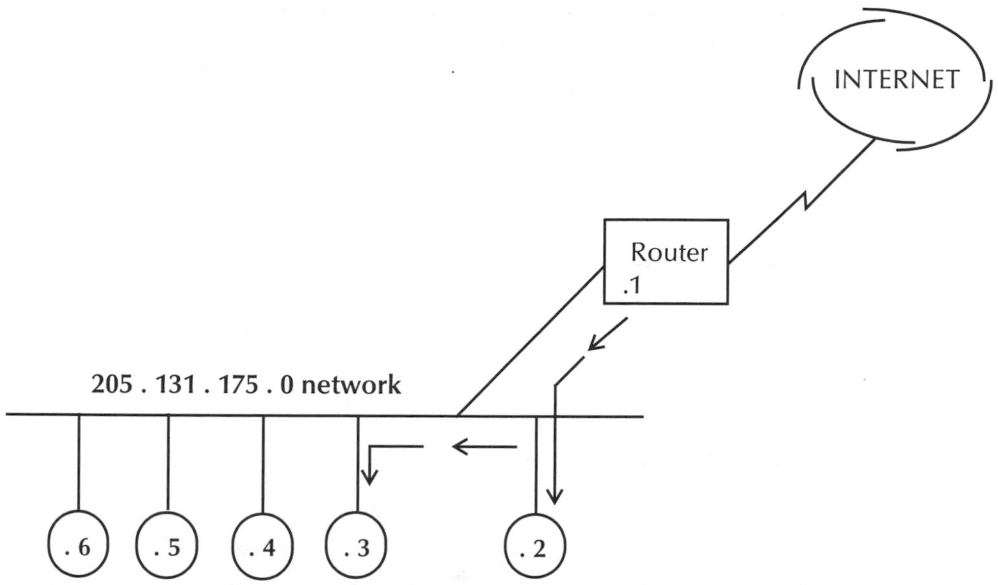

Exhibit 9. Multicast Addressing Enables a Common Data Stream to Be Received by Multiple Stations on a Network or on Different Networks

with the exception of the destination address in the IP header, we can reduce the data flow onto the network via multicast operations. Each of the IP addresses on the local network would join the multicast group address, which is to be used by the fashion show. To do so, each station sends a request to the router. When the router receives the multicast transmission, it transmits it onto the 205.131.175.0 network as a single stream of datagrams that are read by both members of the multicast group. This halves the amount of datagrams transporting real-time video onto the network. If more employees joined the multicast group, the traffic savings would proportionally increase. Thus, a multicast group represents two or more stations that receive a common stream of datagrams as a mechanism to reduce network traffic.

Class E Addresses

The fifth address class defined for IPv4 is Class E. A Class E address is defined by the setting of the first four bits in the 32-bit IP address to the binary value of 1111. Thus, a Class E address has a first byte value between 11110000 and 11111111, or between 240 and 255 decimal.

Class E addresses are currently reserved for experimental usage. Because there are 28 bits in a Class E address that can be used to define unique addresses, this means there are approximately 268.4 million available Class E addresses.

One common method used to denote Class A through E addresses is by examining the decimal value of the fist byte of the 32-bit IPv4 address. To

Exhibit 10. IPv4 Address Class First Byte Values

Address Class	*First Byte Address Range*
Class A	1 to 126
Class B	128 to 191
Class C	192 to 223
Class D	224 to 239
Class E	240 to 255

facilitate this examination, Exhibit 10 summarizes the range of decimal values for the first byte of each address class.

Dotted Decimal Notation

Only a brief examination of how to convert the binary value of a byte into decimal has been given, with no discussion of the rationale for the use of decimal numbers in IP addresses. Thus, the rationale is presented here.

Because humans do not like to work with strings of 32-bit binary addresses, the developers of IP looked for a technique that would make it easier to specify IPv4 addresses. The resulting technique is referred to as "dotted decimal notation," in recognition of the fact that a 32-bit IP number can be subdivided into four eight-bit bytes. Because of this, it is possible to specify a 32-bit IPv4 address via the use of four decimal numbers in the range 0 through 255, with each number separated from another number by a decimal point.

To review the formation of a dotted decimal number, first focus on the decimal relationship of the bit positions in a byte. Exhibit 11 indicates the decimal values of the bit positions within an eight-bit byte. Note that the decimal value of each bit position corresponds to 2^n, where "n" is the bit position in the byte. Thus, the first or rightmost bit position in a byte has the decimal value of 2^0 or 1 when set. Similarly, the second bit position from the right has the decimal value of 2^1 or 2, and so on. Using the decimal values of the bit positions shown in Exhibit 11, assume one wants to convert the following 32-bit binary address into dotted decimal notation:

01010100110011101111000100111101

The first eight bits that correspond to the first byte in an IP address have the binary value 01010100. Then, the value of that byte expressed as a decimal number becomes 64 + 16 + 4, or 84. Next, the second bit in the binary string has the binary value of 11001110. From Exhibit 11, the decimal value of the second byte is 128 + 64 + 8 + 4 + 2, or 206. Similarly, the third byte, whose binary value is 11110001, has the decimal value 128 + 64 + 32 + 16 + 1, or 241. The last byte, whose bit value is 00111101, would have the decimal value 32 + 16 + 8 + 4 + 1, or 61. Based on the preceding, one would enter the 32-

128	64	32	16	8	4	2	1

The decimal value of the bit positions in a byte correspond to 2^n where n is the bit position that ranges from 0 to 7.

Exhibit 11. Decimal Values of Bit Positions in a Byte

bit address in dotted decimal notation as 84.206.241.61, which is certainly easier to work with than a 32-bit string.

Basic Workstation Configuration

The use of dotted decimal notation can be appreciated when examining the configuration of a workstation. If using Microsoft Windows 95, Windows 98, Windows ME, Windows 2000 or the recently introduced Windows XP, one would go to Start> Control Panel> Network and double-click on the TCP/IP entry in the configuration tab to assign an applicable series of dotted decimal values to configure a host on an IP network.

To correctly configure a host on a TCP/IP network requires the entry of three dotted decimal addresses and a subnet mask, the latter also specified as a dotted decimal number. The three addresses one must specify include the IP address of the host being configured, the IP address of a gateway, and the IP address of a domain name server.

The term "gateway" dates from the early days of ARPAnet when a device that routed datagrams between networks was referred to by that name. Today, this device is referred to as a router; however, in the wonderful world of TCP/IP configuration, the term "gateway" is still used. The second new device is the DNS that resolves (a fancy name for translates) host names into IP addresses, and its operation will be described in more detail later in this book (Chapter 6). At the present time, simply note that the DNS allows one to enter addresses into Web browsers, such as www.whitehouse.gov, and allows the TCP/IP protocol stack to perform the translation into an applicable IP address. All routing in an IP network occurs via an examination of IP addresses.

Exhibit 12 illustrates the setting of the IP address tab in the TCP/IP Properties dialog box on the author's personal computer. Note that the button labeled "Specify an IP address" is shown selected, which indicates to the Windows operating system that a fixed IP address will be assigned to the computer. In Exhibit 12, that address is 198.78.46.8, which, if one converts 198 into binary rather than glancing at Exhibit 10, one will note a value of 11000000. Because the first three bits are set to binary 110, this denotes a Class C address. If one does not like working with binary, one could then use Exhibit 10 to determine that the setting of the first byte to 198 is indeed a Class C address.

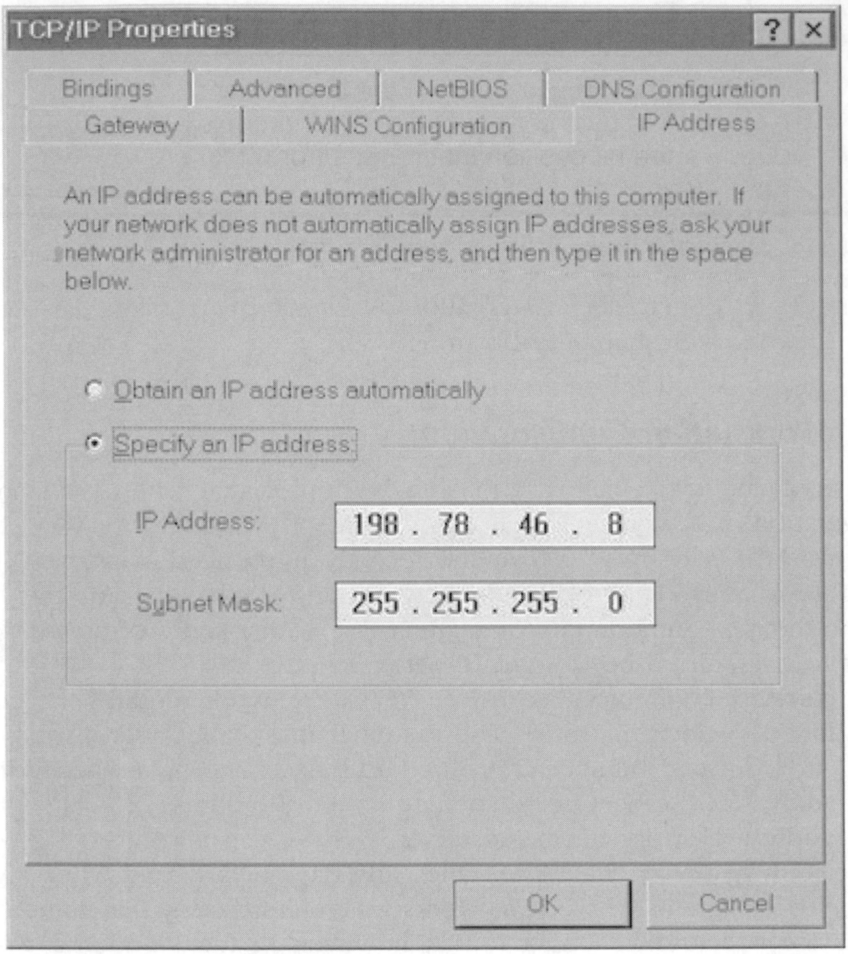

Exhibit 12. Setting the IP Address and Subnet Mask

If one focuses the two radio buttons shown in Exhibit 12, one will note that the lower one is shown selected and corresponds to the entry "Specify an IP address." This selection provides the ability to enter a specific IP address and subnet mask into the dialog box. If one selects the upper radio button associated with the label "Obtain an IP address automatically," the rectangular areas that previously allowed one to enter an IP address and subnet mask will become shaded and one will not be able to enter those dotted decimal numbers. Instead, the Dynamic Host Configuration Protocol (DHCP) will be invoked to obtain the required IP address and subnet mask as well as the gateway and DNS addresses automatically from a DHCP server. In a Windows NT or Windows 2000 environment, DHCP represents a service one can enable on the server. Once enabled, the server becomes responsible for distributing IP addresses to workstations configured to obtain IP addresses automatically. For now, assume we selected the radio button associated with the label "Specify an IP address" and continue the examination of different configuration settings.

Although the subnet mask will be discussed shortly, at the present time one can note here that its setting "extends" the network portion of an address internally within an organization. That is, the set bits in a subnet mask indicate the new length of the network portion of the address. Examining the subnet mask shown in Exhibit 12 and remembering that a value of 255 represents the setting of all bits in a byte to 1, this indicates that the network portion of the address is 24 bits long. Because a Class C address uses three bytes for the network address and one byte for the host address, this also means that a subnet mask of 255.255.255.0 for a Class C address indicates that the network is NOT subnetted.

By selecting the tab labeled "Gateway," one can view the manner by which one can add and remove the IP addresses of routers. Exhibit 13 illustrates the TCP/IP Properties dialog box with its Gateway tab selected. In this example, the IP address 198.78.46.1 was entered to denote the address of the router that will route datagrams with an IP network address other than 198.78.46.0 off the network.

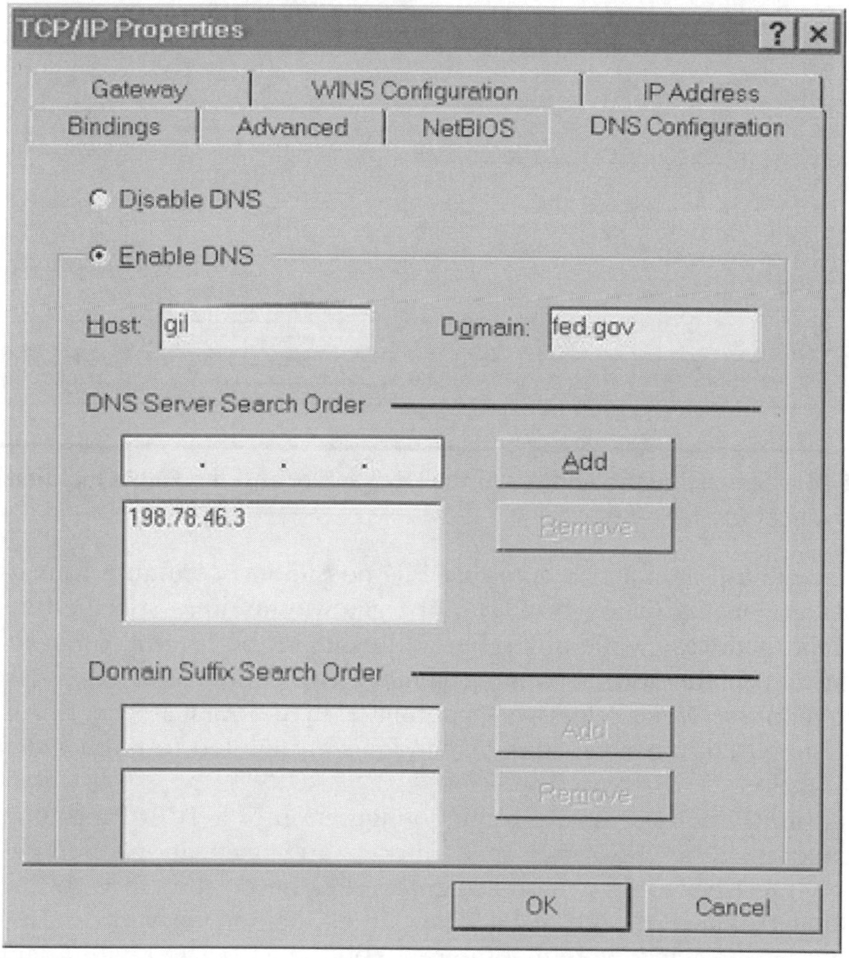

Exhibit 13. Configuring the Gateway Address under Windows 95/98

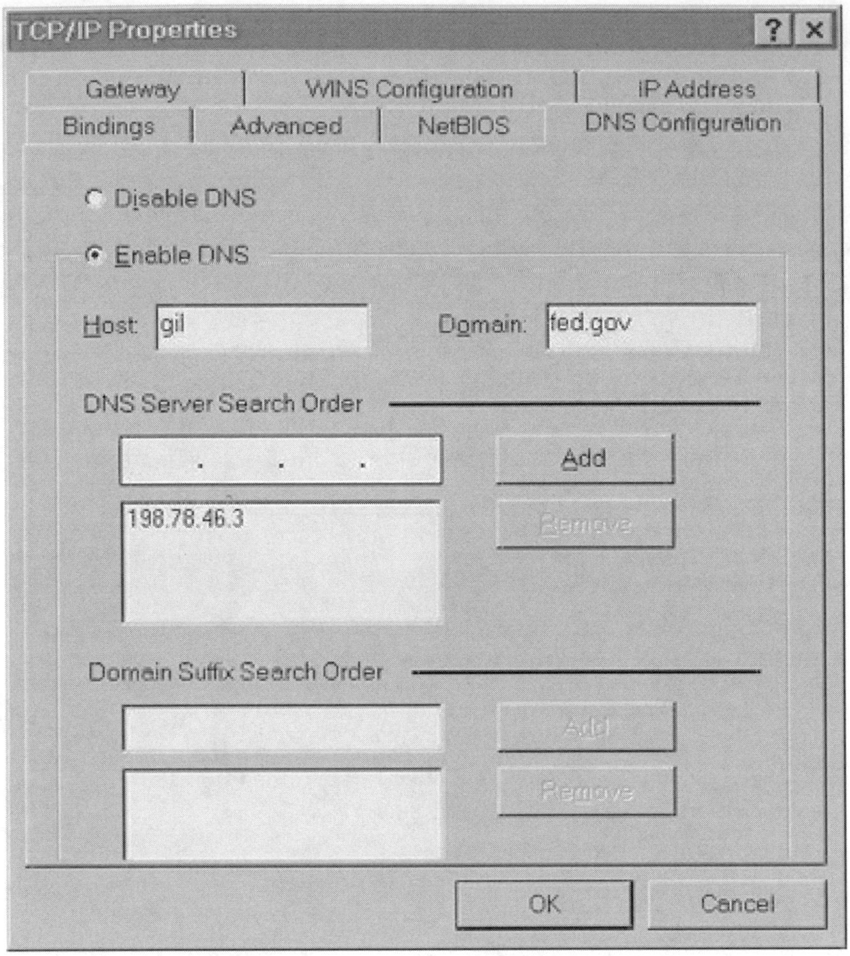

Exhibit 14. Specifying the Address of the DNS Server and the Fully Qualified Name of the Host at the DNS Tab

In examining Exhibit 13, note that it is possible to configure four gateway IP addresses in the dialog box. The first gateway address specified becomes the default gateway, while any other addresses in the list will be used in the order in which the addresses are entered if the default is not responsive to routing requests. While Windows 95 permitted up to four Gateway IP addresses to be configured, other versions of Windows are limited to three Gateway IP addresses.

The third IP address used for the configuration of a TCP/IP protocol stack is the address of a DNS server that supports an organization's network. One can view the DNS configuration screen by clicking on the tab with that label.

Exhibit 14 illustrates the TCP/IP Properties dialog box with its DNS Configuration tab selected. Note that the radio button associated with Enable DNS is shown selected, and a host name of "gil" was entered for this computer which is part of the domain fed.gov. Thus, the complete host name of this computer is gil.fed.gov. Note that one does not have to specify either host or domain. Doing so results in the IP address previously assigned to this computer, along with the host name entered in a record in the DNS server. This would then allow someone to access this computer by entering gil.fed.gov instead of the IP address of 198.78.46.8. If no one accesses the computer, one could safely omit the host and domain entries. If the computer is a popularly used server, one would want to include the host name because it would be easier to remember than a sequence of dotted decimal numbers.

The combination of host and domain is commonly referred to as a fully qualified domain name (FQDN). An FQDN means that the name is unique. In comparison, the host portion of the name (gil) could exist on many domains. Similarly, many computers could have a common domain name (fed.gov).

Returning to Exhibit 14, note that one can specify up to four DNS server addresses. In addition, one can specify one or more domain suffix search orders where common domain suffixes include gov (government), com (commercial), edu (educational), mil (military), and org (nonprofit organization).

Reserved Addresses

It was previously noted that the address block 127.0.0.0 through 127.255.255.255 is used for loopback purposes and can thus be considered to represent a block of reserved addresses. When considering IPv4 addressing, there are three additional blocks of reserved addresses that warrant attention. Those address blocks are defined in RFC 1918, entitled *Address Allocation for Private Internet,* and are summarized in Exhibit 15.

The original intention of RFC 1918 addresses was to define blocks of IP addresses organizations could use on private networks that would be recognized as such. As the use of the Internet grew, the ability to obtain IP addresses became more difficult because existing network addresses were assigned to different organizations. This resulted in a second role for RFC 1918 addresses under a process referred to as network address translation (NAT). Under NAT, internal RFC 1918 addresses can be dynamically translated to public IP addresses while reducing the number of public addresses that need to be used. For example, consider an organization with 500 stations that only has one Class C address. One possibility is to use RFC 1918 addresses behind a router connected to the Internet, with the router translating RFC 1918 addresses dynamically into available Class C addresses. Although no more than 254 RFC

Exhibit 15. Reserved IP Addresses for Private Internet Use (RFC 1918)

Address Blocks
10.0.0.0–10.255.255.255
172.16.0.0–172.31.255.255
192.168.0.0–192.168.255.255

1918 addresses could be translated into valid distinct Class C addresses at any point in time, it is also possible to use TCP and UDP port numbers to extend the translation process so each RFC 1918 address can be simultaneously used and translated. To do so, a router would translate each RFC 1918 address into a Class C address using a different port number, permitting thousands of translations for each Class C address.

Another device that can provide address translation is a proxy firewall. In addition to translating addresses, a proxy firewall also hides internal addresses from the Internet community. This address hiding provides a degree of security because any hacker that attempts to attack a host on a network where a proxy firewall operates must first attack the firewall.

Two additional items to note about RFC 1918 addresses are that they cannot be used directly on the Internet, and they are a favorite source address used by hackers. The reason RFC 1918 addresses cannot be directly used on the Internet results from the fact that if one company does so, a second could also do so, resulting in addressing conflicts and the unreliable delivery of information. Thus, as discussed, RFC 1918 addresses are translated into Class A, B, or C addresses when a private network using such addresses is connected to the Internet. Concerning hacker use, because source IP addresses are not checked by routers, it is quite common for an RFC 1918 address to be used as the source address by a hacker, making it difficult — if not impossible — to locate the hacker.

Because it is quite common for hackers to use an RFC 1918 address as their address in configuring a TCP/IP protocol stack, it is also quite common to create a router access list that filters datagrams that have an RFC 1918 address. When network security is discussed in Chapter 9, also included will be applicable access list statements to send datagrams with RFC 1918 source addresses to the great bit bucket in the sky.

The WINIPCFG Utility

One of the most common applications that uses RFC 1918 addresses is wireless LANs. When one sets up a wireless LAN, stations communicate via an access point to the wired infrastructure. To facilitate IP addressing, the access point will support DHCP and lease RFC 1918 addresses to its client stations.

If one is using a modern version of Windows, one can use the WINIPCFG utility program to determine a variety of fixed and variable addresses assigned to one's workstation. Exhibit 16 illustrates the use of the WINIPCFG utility program on a notebook computer used by this author in his home to connect to the Internet via a combined access point/router that in turn was connected to a cable modem. In examining the entries in Exhibit 16, the host name and DNS Server address represent metrics assigned by Cox Cable, which is this author's Internet service provider. The Ethernet Adapter Information section in the lower portion of Exhibit 16 provides one with the ability to view address assignments and other metrics for each adapter installed. In the example shown in the lower portion of Exhibit 16, the SMC Networks EZ Connect

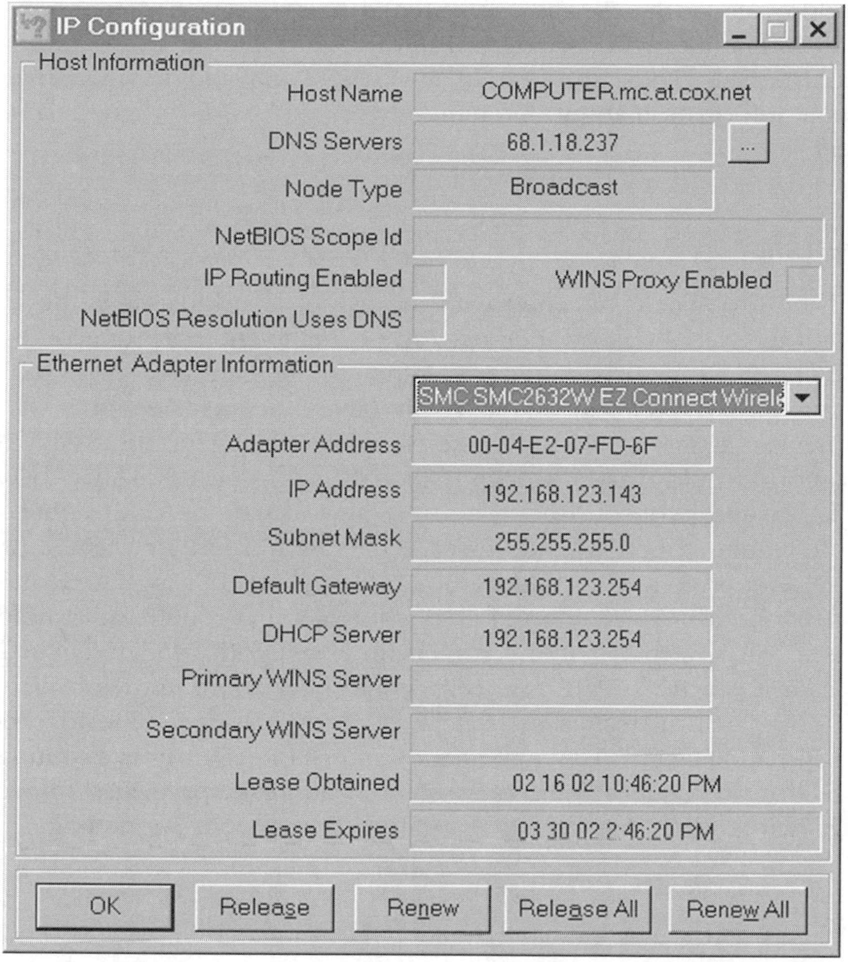

Exhibit 16. Using the WINIPCFG Utility Program, One Can Determine a Significant Amount of Information Concerning Hardware and IP Addresses Assigned to Network Adapters

wireless adapter is shown selected. Below the adapter selection, the 48-bit Media Access Control (MAC) hardware address is shown as 12 hex characters. Under WINIPCFG, the MAC address is referred to as the Adapter Address. Below the adapter address, the IP address assigned to the adapter is shown. If one compares this address (192.168.123.143) to the entries in Exhibit 15, one will note that it represents an RFC 1918 Class C IP address. Similarly, the default gateway and DHCP server IP addresses are also RFC 1918 Class C addresses.

In the wireless network established by this author, each client and the access point use RFC 1918 addresses to communicate with one another, with the access point functioning as both the default gateway and DNS server. As a DHCP server, the access point leases IP addresses to wireless clients and lease information is shown at the bottom of Exhibit 16. Because the access point includes a network address translation (NAT) capability, it converts RFC

1918 addresses to the IP address assigned by this author's Internet service provider to his Internet connection. Later in this book we will note how NAT is accomplished. Thus, the use of WINIPCFG can be a valuable tool to determine information about different network addresses assigned to network adapters.

Subnetting

One of the problems associated with the use of IP addresses is the fact that even with the use of classes, their use can be inefficient. For example, consider the use of a Class A network address. Although one can have up to 16,277,214 hosts per Class A network, one can only have 127 such networks. Thus, the assignment of a Class A network address to a large organization with 100,000 workstations would waste over 16 million IP addresses. Similarly, because a single LAN is incapable of supporting 100,000 workstations, one might consider asking for multiple network addresses, which would further waste a precious resource referred to as IPv4 addresses. Another problem associated with using more network addresses than required is the fact that routers must note those addresses. This means that the routers in a network, which could be the Internet or a private TCP/IP network, would have more entries in its routing tables. This, in turn, results in routers requiring a longer time to check the destination address in a datagram against entries in each router's routing table. The solution to the problems of wasted IP address space and unnecessary routing table entries is provided through the process of subnetting.

Overview

Subnetting was standardized in RFC 950 in 1985. This RFC defines a procedure to subnet or divide a single Class A, B, or C network into two or more subnets. Through the process of subnetting, the two-level hierarchy of Class A, B, and C networks previously illustrated in Exhibit 6 is converted into a three-level hierarchy. Exhibit 17 provides a comparison between the two-level hierarchies initially defined for Class A, B, and C networks and the three-level subnet hierarchy. In examining the lower portion of Exhibit 17, note that to convert the two-level hierarchy into a three-level hierarchy, the extension of the network address occurs by taking away a portion of the host address portion of an IPv4 address.

Subnetting Example

As previously noted, any of the IPv4 A through C address classes can be subnetted. To illustrate the subnet process, as well as obtain an appreciation for how subnetting facilitates the use of IPv4 address space, one can examine the process by understanding the concept of masking and the use of the subnet mask, both of which are essential to the extension of the network portion of an IP address beyond its predefined location.

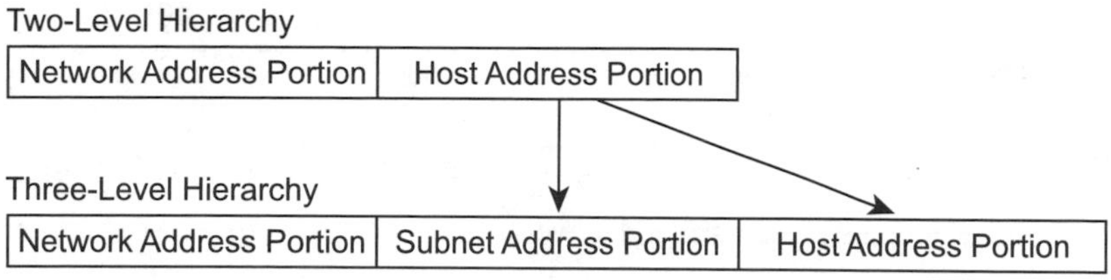

Exhibit 17. Comparing the Three-Level Subnet Hierarchy to the Two-Level Network Class Hierarchy

To illustrate the concept of subnetting, assume an organization has the need to install five LANs within a building, with each network supporting between 10 and 15 workstations and servers. Further assume that the organization was previously assigned the IP Class C network address 198.78.46.0. Although the organization could apply for four additional Class C addresses, doing so would waste precious IPv4 address space because each Class C address supports a maximum of 254 interfaces. In addition, if one anticipates connecting the organization's private networks to the Internet, the use of four additional Class C network addresses would be required in a number of routers in the Internet as well as the organization's internal routers.

Instead of asking for four additional Class C addresses, one can use subnetting by dividing the host portion of the 198.78.46.0 IPv4 address into a subnet number and a host number. Because one needs to support five networks, one must use a minimum of three bits from the host portion of the IP address as the subnet number. The reason a minimum of three bits from the host portion of the address must be used is due to the fact that the number of subnets one can obtain is 2^n, where n is the number of bits. When n = 2, this yields four subnets, which is too few. When n = 3, one obtains eight subnets, which provides enough subnets for this example.

Because a Class C address uses 24 bits for the network portion and eight bits for the host portion, the use of a three-bit subnet extends the network address such that it becomes 27 bits in length. This also means that a maximum of five bits (8 – 3) can be used for the host portion of the address.

Exhibit 18 illustrates the creation of the three-level addressing scheme just described. Note that the three-bit subnet permits eight subnets (000 through 111).

To the outside world, the network portion of the address remains the same. This means that the route from the Internet to any subnet of a given IP network address remains the same. This also means that routers within an organization must be able to differentiate between different subnets; however, routers outside the organization do not consider subnets.

To illustrate the creation of five subnets, assume one wants to commence subnet numbering at 0 and continue in sequence through subnet 4. Exhibit 19, illustrates the creation of five subnets from the 198.78.46.0 network address. Note that the top entry in Exhibit 19, which is labeled "Base Network," represents the Class C network address with a host address byte field set to all zeroes.

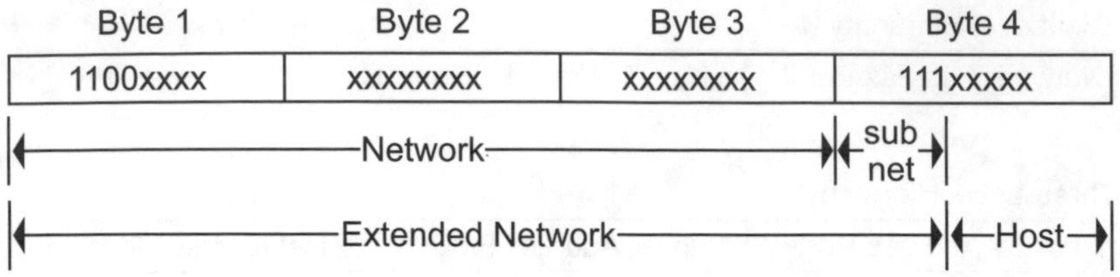

Exhibit 18. Creating a Class C Three-Level Addressing Scheme

Because it was previously determined that three bits from the host address portion of the network would be required to function as a subnet identifier, the network address is shown extended into the host byte by three portions.

Host Restrictions

In examining the subnets formed in Exhibit 19, it would appear that the hosts on the first subnet can range from 0 through 31, while the hosts on the second subnet can range in value from 33 through 63, etc. In actuality, this is not correct because there are several restrictions concerning host addresses on subnets. First, one cannot use a base subnet address of all zeroes nor all ones. Thus, for subnet 0 in Exhibit 19, valid addresses would range from 1 to 30. Similarly for subnet 1, valid addresses would range from 33 to 62. Thus, subnetted host address restrictions are the same as for a regular IP non-subnetted network.

Another host address restriction that requires consideration is the fact that for all classes, one must have the ability to place some hosts on each subnet. Thus, as a minimum, the last two bit positions into the fourth byte of Class A, B, and C addresses cannot be used in a subnet. Exhibit 20 illustrates the number of bits that are available for subnetting for Class A, B, and C network addresses.

The Zero Subnet

Another item concerning subnetting that warrants attention is the fact that at one time, the zero subnet was considered anathema by the Internet community, and its use was and to a degree still is discouraged. While this viewpoint has

Exhibit 19. Creating Extended Network Prefixes via Subnetting

Base Network:1100110.01010000.00101110.00000000 = 198.78.46.0
Subnet #0:1100110.01010000.00101110.00000000 = 198.78.46.0
Subnet #1:1100110.01010000.00101110.00100000 = 198.78.46.32
Subnet #2:1100110.01010000.00101110.01000000 = 198.78.46.64
Subnet #3:1100110.01010000.00101110.01100000 = 198.78.46.96
Subnet #4:1100110.01010000.00101110.10000000 = 198.78.46.128

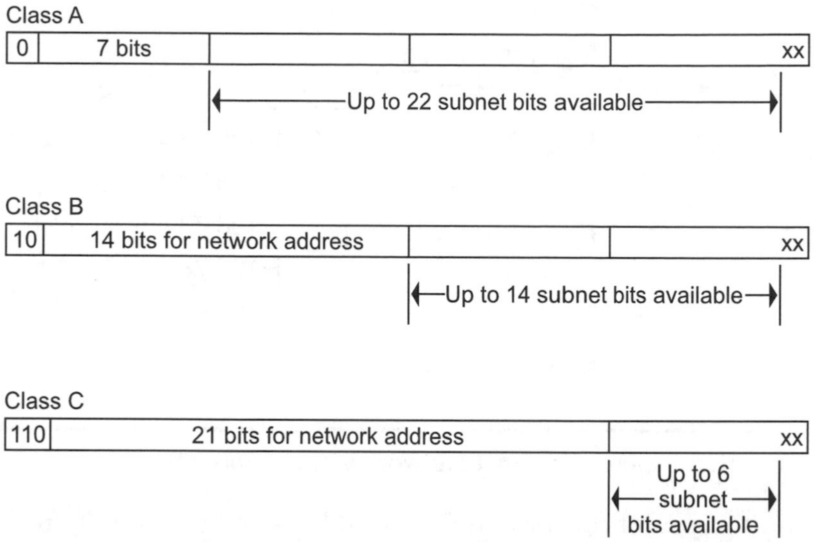

Exhibit 20. Available Bit Positions for Subnet Formation

somewhat fallen from favor, it is important to note that some devices will not support the use of subnet zero and will not allow one to configure their interface address as being on a zero subnet. The reason for this restriction results because confusion can arise between a network and a subnet that have the same address. For example, assume network address 129.110.0.0 is subnetted as 255.255.255.9. This would result in subnet zero being written as 129.110.0.0, which is the same as the network address.

When configuring TCP/IP devices, it is important to note that some devices that support a zero subnet must be explicitly configured to do so. For example, the most popular manufacturer of routers is Cisco Systems. Although all Cisco routers support the use of subnet zero, one must use the router command ip subnet-zero to configure a Cisco router to do so. If one attempts to configure a subnet zero, one will receive an "inconsistant network mask" error message.

Internal versus External Subnet Viewing

Returning to the subnetting example in which five subnets were created from one Class C network address, one can easily understand why subnetting saves router table entries. This is illustrated in Exhibit 21, which depicts an internal intranet view of the use of subnets versus a view from the Internet for the prior example. In examining Exhibit 21, note that all five subnets appear as the IP network address 198.78.46.0 to routers on the Internet. This means that each router must have knowledge of one IP network address. At the router connected to the Internet, that device becomes responsible for examining each inbound datagram and determining the appropriate subnet where the datagram should be routed. To do so, this router uses a subnet mask whose composition and use are discussed below. Prior to doing so, a few points

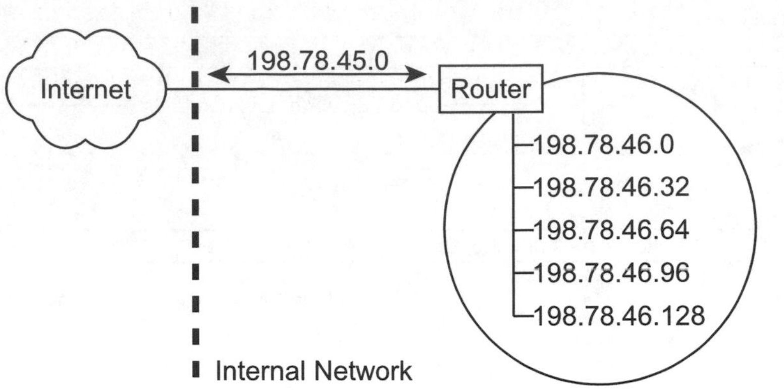

Exhibit 21. Internet versus Internal Network View of Subnets

concerning the use of the base network address of 198.78.46.0 are in order. First, to each router the destination address in each datagram appears as a 32-bit sequence. Thus, there is no knowledge of dotted decimal numbers except for the configuration of devices because routing occurs by the examination of the network portion of the address in each datagram. Second, each router begins its address examination by first focusing attention on the first bit in the destination address to determine if it is a Class A address. If the first bit position is set to a binary 0, the router knows it is a Class A address, as well as knows that the first byte in the 32-bit destination address represents the network address. Similarly, if the first bit in the destination address is not a binary 0, the router examines the second bit to determine if the address is a Class B address, etc. Thus, a router can easily determine the address class of the destination address in a datagram that then indicates the length of the network portion of the address. The router can then use this information to search its routing table entries to determine the appropriate port to output the datagram, all without having to consider whether or not the address represents a subnetted address.

Thus far, this chapter has discussed how to create a subnet and extend the network portion of an IPv4 address, but has not addressed the manner by which a router at the edge of the Internet knows how to route datagrams to their appropriate subnet. In addition, there is the question of how a station on an internal network can recognize subnet addressing. For example, if an IP datagram arrives at an organizational router with the destination address 198.78.46.38, how does the router know to place the datagram on subnet 1? The answer to these questions is the use of a subnet mask.

Using the Subnet Mask

The subnet mask provides a mechanism that enables devices to determine the separation of an IPv4 address into its three-level hierarchy of network, subnet, and host addresses. To accomplish this task, the subnet mask consists of a sequence of set to "1" bits that denotes the length of the network and subnet portions of the IPv4 network address associated with a network. That is, the subnet mask indicates the internal extended network address.

To illustrate the use of the subnet mask, again assume the network address to be 198.78.46.0. Further assume that one wants to create a subnet mask that can be used by a router or workstation to note that the range of permissible subnets is 0 to 7. Because this requires the use of three bits, the subnet mask becomes:

11111111.11111111.11111111.11100000

Similar to the manner by which IP addresses can be expressed more efficiently through the use of dotted decimal notation, one can also express subnet masks using that notation. Because each byte of all set bits has a decimal value of 255, the dotted decimal notation for the first three bytes of the subnet mask is 255.255.255. Because the first three bits of the fourth byte are set, its decimal value is 128 + 64 + 32, or 224. Thus, the dotted decimal specification for the subnet mask becomes:

255.255.255.224

Because a device can easily determine the address class of the destination address in a datagram, the subnet mask then informs the device of which bits in the address represent the subnet and indirectly which bits represent the host address on the subnet. To illustrate how this is accomplished, assume a datagram has arrived at a router with the destination IP address 198.78.46.97, and that the subnet mask was previously set to 255.255.255.224. The relationship between the IP address and the subnet mask would then appear as indicated in Exhibit 22.

Because the first two bits in the destination address are set to 11, this indicates the address is a Class C address. The TCP/IP protocol stack knows that a Class C address consists of three bytes used for the network address, and one byte used for the host address. Thus, this means that the subnet must be 27 – 24, or three bits in length. This fact tells the router or workstation that bits 25 through 27, which are set to a value of 011 in the IP address, identify the subnet as subnet 3. Because the last five bits in the subnet mask are set to zero, this indicates that those bit positions in the IP address identify the host on subnet 3. Because the setting of those five bits have the value

IP Address:	198.78.46.97	11000110.01010000.00101110.01100001
Subnet Mask:	255.255.255.244	11111111.11111111.11111111.11100000
		Extended Network Address

Exhibit 22. Examining the Relationship between an IP Address and a Subnet Mask

00001, this means that the IP address of 198.78.46.97 references host 1 on subnet 3 on the IPv4 network 198.78.46.0.

To assist readers who need to work with subnets, Exhibit 23 provides a reference to the number of subnets that can be created for Class B and Class C networks, their subnet mask, the number of hosts per network, and the total number of hosts supported by a particular subnet mask. In examining the entries in Exhibit 23, one notes that the total number of hosts can vary considerably, based on the use of different length subnet extensions. Thus, one should carefully consider the effect of a potential subnetting process prior to actually performing the process.

Multiple Interface Addresses

One of the lesser-known aspects of IP addressing is the fact that it is possible to assign multiple logical network addresses to one physical network. Prior

Exhibit 23. Class B and Class C Subnet Mask Reference

Number of Subnet Bits	*Subnet Mask*	*Number of Subnetworks*	*Hosts/ Subnet*	*Total Number of Hosts*
Class B				
1	—	—	—	—
2	255.255.192.0	2	16382	32764
3	255.255.224.0	6	8190	49140
4	255.255.240.0	14	4094	57316
5	255.255.248.0	30	2046	61380
6	255.255.252.0	62	1022	63364
7	255.255.254.0	126	510	64260
8	255.255.255.0	254	254	64516
9	255.255.255.128	510	126	64260
10	255.255.255.192	1022	62	63364
11	255.255.255.224	2046	30	61380
12	255.255.255.240	4094	14	57316
13	255.255.255.248	8190	6	49140
14	255.255.255.252	16382	2	32764
15	—	—	—	—
16	—	—	—	—
Class C				
1	—	—	—	—
2	255.255.255.192	2	62	124
3	255.255.255.224	6	30	180
4	255.255.255.240	14	14	196
5	255.255.255.248	30	6	170
6	255.255.255.252	62	2	124
7	—	—	—	—
8	—	—	—	—

to examining how this occurs, one will probably want to understand the rationale for doing this. Thus, let us assume an organization originally operated a 10BASE-5 network with 100 users and wants to construct a distributed network within a building that will consist of 350 workstations and server. Further assume that the organization's previously installed 10BASE-5 coaxial-based backbone will be used by adding 10BASE-T hubs to the backbone, with a single router providing a connection to the Internet.

If the organization previously obtained a Class C address when it operated a 10BASE-5 network, adding 250 stations means that a second router interface and two networks would be required because each Class C address supports a maximum of 254 hosts.

TCP/IP supports the ability to assign multiple network addresses to a common interface. In fact, TCP/IP also supports the assignment of multiple subnet numbers to a common interface. This can only be accomplished through the use of a router. Exhibit 24 illustrates an example in which three network addresses were assigned to one interface. For low volumes of network traffic, this represents an interesting technique to reduce the number of costly router interfaces required.

As indicated in Exhibit 24, the router connection to the coaxial cable would result in the assignment of two IP addresses to its interface — one for each network. In this example, the addresses 205.131.175.1 and 205.131.176.1 were assigned to the router interface. Conversations between devices on the 205.131.175.0 network and the 205.131.176.0 network would require datagrams to be forwarded to the router. Thus, each station of each network would be configured with the "gateway" IP address that represents an applicable assigned router IP interface address.

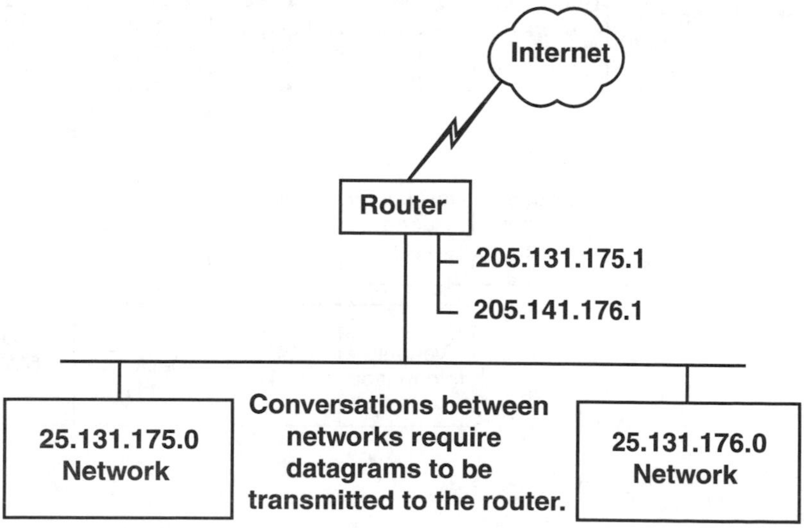

Exhibit 24. Assigning Multiple Network Addresses to a Common Router Interface

Address Resolution

The TCP/IP protocol suite begins at the network layer, with an addressing scheme that identifies a network address and a host address for Class A, B, and C addresses. This addressing scheme actually evolved from an ARPAnet scheme that only required hosts to be identified, because that network began as a mechanism to interconnect hosts via serial communications lines. At the same time ARPAnet was being developed, work progressed separately at the Xerox Palo Alto Research Center (PARC) on Ethernet, a technology in which multiple stations were originally connected to a coaxial cable.

Ethernet used a 48-bit address to identify each station on the network. As ARPAnet evolved as a mechanism to interconnect multiple hosts on geographically separated networks, IPv4 addressing evolved into a mechanism to distinguish the network and the host. Unfortunately, the addressing used by the TCP/IP protocol suite bore no relationship to the MAC address used first by Ethernet and later by Token Ring.

Ethernet and Token Ring Frame Formats

Exhibit 25 illustrates the frame formats for Ethernet and Token Ring. Note that the IEEE standardized both types of LANs and uses six-byte (48-bit) source and destination addresses. The IEEE assigns blocks of addresses six hex characters in length to vendors. Those six hex characters represent the first 24 bits of the 48-bit field used to uniquely identify a network adapter card. The vendor then encodes the remaining 24 bits or six hex character positions

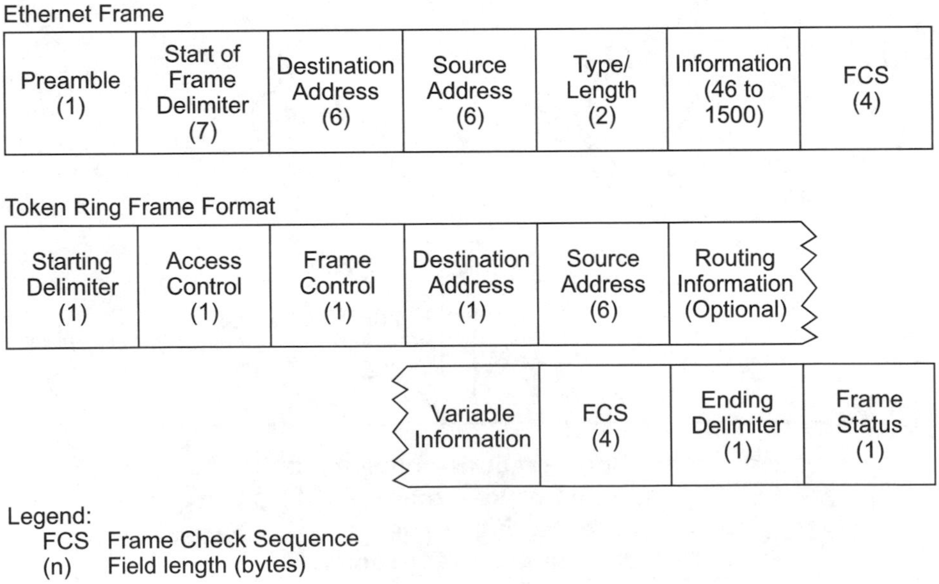

Exhibit 25. Ethernet and Token Ring Frame Formats

to identify the adapter card manufactured by the vendor. Thus, each Ethernet and Token Ring adapter has a unique hardware burnt-in identifier that denotes both the manufacturer and the adapter number produced by the manufacturer.

LAN Delivery

When an IP datagram arrives at a LAN, it contains a 32-bit destination address. To deliver the datagram to its destination, the router must create a LAN frame with an appropriate MAC destination address. Thus, the router needs a mechanism to resolve or convert the IP address into the MAC address of the workstation configured with the destination IP address. In the opposite direction, a workstation may need to transmit an IP datagram to another workstation. In this situation, the workstation must be able to convert a MAC address into an IP address. Both of these address translation requirements are handled by protocols specifically developed to provide an address resolution capability. One protocol, referred to as the Address Resolution Protocol (ARP), translates an IP address into a hardware address. A second protocol, referred to as the Reverse Address Resolution Protocol (RARP), performs a reverse translation process, converting a hardware layer address into an IP address.

The Address Resolution Protocol dates to November 1982 when it was defined in RFC 826. In comparison, the Reverse Address Resolution Protocol is defined in RFC 902, which was published in June 1984.

Address Resolution Operation

The address resolution operation begins when a device needs to transmit a datagram. First, the device checks its memory to determine if it previously learned the MAC address associated with a particular destination IP address. This memory location is referred to as an ARP cache. Because the first occurrence of an IP address means its associated MAC address will not be in the ARP cache, it must learn the MAC address. To do so, the device will broadcast an ARP packet to all devices on the LAN. Exhibit 26 illustrates the format of an ARP packet. Note that the numbers shown in some fields in the ARP packet indicate the byte numbers in a field when a field spans a four-byte boundary.

ARP Packet Fields

To illustrate the operation of ARP, one can examine the fields in the ARP packet. The 16-bit Hardware Type field indicates the type of network adapter, such as 10 Mbps Ethernet (value = 1), IEEE 802 network (value = 6), etc. The 16-bit Protocol Type field indicates the protocol for which an address resolution process is being performed. For IP, the Protocol Type field has a value of hex 0800.

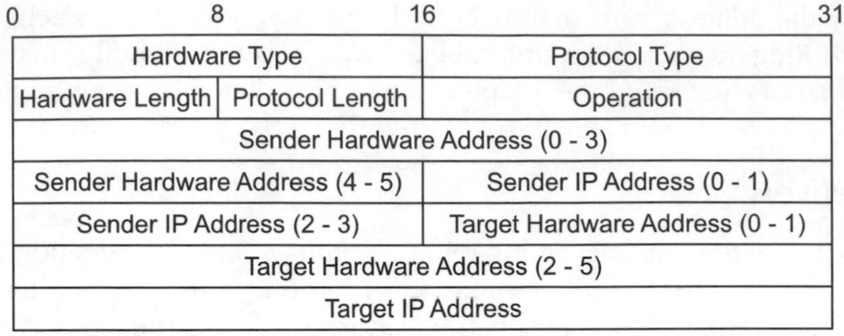

Exhibit 26. The ARP Packet Format

The Hardware Length field defines the number of bytes in the hardware address. Thus, the ARP packet format can be varied to accommodate different types of address resolutions beyond IP and MAC addresses. Because Ethernet and Token Ring have the same MAC length, the value of this field is 6 for both.

The Protocol Length field indicates the length of the address for the protocol to be resolved. For IPv4, the value of this field is set to 4. The Operation field indicates the operation to be performed. This field has a value of 1 for an ARP Request. When a target station responds, the value of this field is changed to 2 to denote an ARP Reply.

The Sender Hardware Address field indicates the hardware addresses of the station generating the ARP Request or ARP Reply. This field is six bytes in length and is followed by a four-byte Sender IP Address field. The latter indicates the IP address of the originator of the datagram.

The next to last field is the Target Hardware Address field. Because the ARP process must discover its value, this field is originally set to all zeros in an ARP request. Once a station receives the request and notes it has the same IP address as that in the Target IP Address field, it places its MAC address in the Target Hardware Address field. Thus, the last field, Target IP Address, is set to the IP address the originator needs for a hardware address.

Locating the Required Address

To put the pieces together, assume a router receives a datagram from the Internet with the destination address of 205.131.175.5. Further assume that the router has a connection to an Ethernet network, and one station on that network has that IP address. The router needs to determine the MAC address associated with the IP address so it can construct a frame to deliver the datagram. Assuming there is no entry in its ARP cache, the router creates an ARP frame and transmits the frame using a MAC broadcast address of FFFFFFFFFFFF. Because the frame was broadcast to all stations on the network, each device reads the frame. The station that has its protocol stack configured to the same IP address as that of the Target IP Address field in the ARP frame would respond to the ARP Request. When it does, it will transmit an ARP

Reply in which its physical MAC address is inserted into the ARP Target Hardware Address field that was previously set to zero.

The ARP standard includes provisions for devices on a network to update their ARP table with the MAC and IP address pair of the sender of the ARP Request. Thus, as ARP Requests flow on a LAN, they contribute to the building of tables that reduce the necessity of additional broadcasts.

Gratuitous ARP

There is a special type of ARP referred to as a "gratuitous ARP" that deserves mention. When a TCP/IP stack is initialized, it issues a gratuitous ARP, which represents an ARP Request for its own IP address. If the station receives a reply containing a MAC address that differs from its address, this indicates that another device on the network is using its assigned IP address. If this situation occurs, an error message warning of an address conflict will be displayed.

Proxy ARP

A proxy is a device that works on behalf of another device. Thus, a proxy ARP represents a mechanism that enables a device to answer an ARP Request on behalf of another device.

The rationale for the development of proxy ARP, which is also referred to as ARP Hack, dates to the early use of subnetting when a LAN could be subdivided into two or more segments. If a station on one segment required the MAC address of a station on another subnet, the router would block the ARP Request because it is a layer 2 broadcast, and routers operate at layer 3. Because the router is aware of both subnets, it could answer an ARP Request on one subnet on behalf of other devices on the second subnet by supplying its own MAC address. The originating device will then enter the router's MAC address in its ARP cache and will correctly transmit packets destined for the end host to the router.

RARP

The Reverse Address Resolution Protocol (RARP) was at one time quite popular when diskless workstations were commonly used in corporations. In such situations, the workstation would know its MAC address, but be forced to learn its IP address from a server on the network. Thus, the RARP would be used by the client to access a server on the local network and would provide the client's IP address. Similar to ARP, RARP is a layer 2 protocol that cannot normally cross router boundaries. Some router manufacturers implemented RARP, which allows requests and responses to flow between networks.

To obtain the assignment of an IP address, a diskless workstation will first transmit a local RARP broadcast. The workstation will indicate its hardware address and request the assignment of an IP address from an RARP server that receives the request. Upon receipt of the RARP request, the server checks its database for an entry that associates the hardware address received in the request to an IP address previously configured for the hardware address. If the server locates an applicable entry, it will transmit a frame to the hardware address of the workstation requesting an IP address with the station's assigned address. If the IP address does not exist in the server's database, by design it will not respond to the RARP Request and the workstation will terminate its effort to participate on the network.

The RARP frame format is the same as for ARP. The key difference between the two is the setting of field values. RARP fills in the sender's hardware address and sets the IP address field to zeroes. Upon receipt of the RARP frame, the RARP server fills in the IP Address field and transmits the frame back to the client, reversing the ARP process.

ICMP

This chapter concludes by focusing on the Internet Control Message Protocol (ICMP). If one thinks about IP for a while, one realizes that there is no provision to inform a source of the fact that a datagram encountered some type of problem. This is because one of the functions of ICMP is to provide a messaging capability that reports different types of errors that can occur during the processing of datagrams. In addition to providing an error reporting mechanism, ICMP includes certain types of messages that provide a testing capability.

ICMP dates to RFC 792 where it was originally described. Although ICMP provides a mechanism for transmitting messages containing information about network problems and errors, it can also have an adverse effect on network security. The reason for the latter results from the fact that ICMP can be used to scan a network, providing a third party with information that can be extremely useful in determining what stations are present on a network and the services they support. Such information can then be used to attack a network. Due to this, many security experts recommend using a firewall or a router access list to block all ICMP messages. This author is of a different opinion and believes that when a firewall or router access list is properly constructed, several ICMP messages should be allowed because they facilitate the ability of a user to obtain information on the status of computers as well as the path to a particular computer. Due to the value of such information for many users, appropriate firewall or router access list filtering can be used to allow useful ICMP messages, while blocking other types of ICMP messages. Such techniques are described later in this book.

Overview

ICMP messages are transmitted within an IP datagram as illustrated in Exhibit 27. Note that although each ICMP message has its own format, they

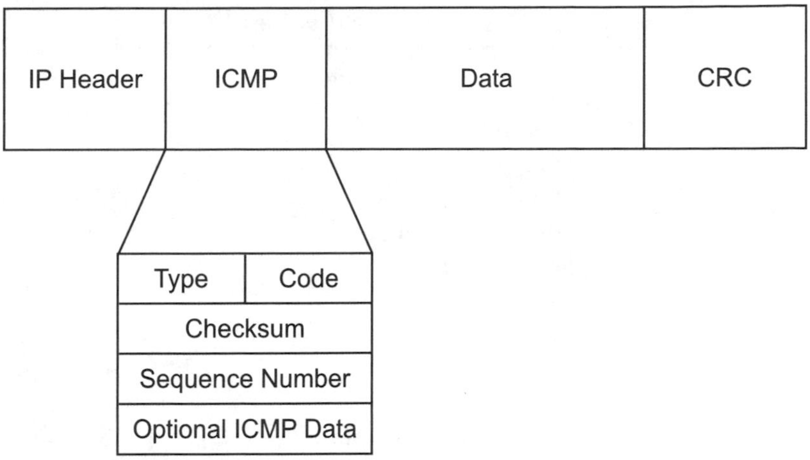

Exhibit 27. ICMP Messages Are Transported via Encapsulation within an IP Datagram

all begin with the same three fields. Those fields are an eight-bit Type field, an eight-bit Code field, and a 16-bit Checksum field.

One can obtain familiarity with the capability of ICMP by examining the use of some of the fields within an ICMP message. The Type and Code fields within an ICMP message are discussed first.

The ICMP Type Field

The purpose of the ICMP Type field is to define the meaning of the message as well as its format. Two of the most popularly used ICMP messages use type values of 0 and 8. A Type field value of 8 represents an Echo Request, while a Type field value of 0 denotes an ICMP Echo Reply. Although their official names are Echo Request and Echo Reply, most people are more familiar with the term Ping, which is used to reference both the request and the reply. Exhibit 28 lists ICMP Type field values that currently identify specific types of ICMP messages.

The ICMP Code Field

The ICMP Code field provides additional information about a message defined in the Type field. The Code field may not be meaningful for certain ICMP messages. For example, both Type field values of 0 (Echo Reply) and 8 (echo request) always have a Code field value of 0. In comparison, a Type field value of 3 (Destination Unreachable) can have one of 16 possible Code field values, which further defines the problem. Exhibit 29 lists the Code field values presently assigned to ICMP messages based upon their Type field values.

Exhibit 28. ICMP Type Field Values

Type	*Name*
0	Echo Reply
1	Unassigned
2	Unassigned
3	Destination Unreachable
4	Source Quench
5	Redirect
6	Alternate Host Address
7	Unassigned
8	Echo Request
9	Router Advertisement
10	Router Selection
11	Time Exceeded
12	Parameter Problem
13	Timestamp
14	Timestamp Reply
15	Information Request
16	Information Reply
17	Address Mask Request
18	Address Mask Reply
19	Reserved (for Security)
20–29	Reserved (for Robustness Experiment)
30	Traceroute
31	Datagram Conversion Error
32	Mobile Host Redirect
33	IPv6 Where-Are-You
34	IPv6 I-Am-Here
35	Mobile Registration Request
36	Mobile Registration Reply
37	Domain Name Request
38	Domain Name Reply
39	SKIP
40	Photuris
41–255	Reserved

Examining Message Types and Code Field Values

As indicated in Exhibit 26, there are 40 defined ICMP message type field values, with message types 41 through 255 reserved for future use. This section examines the use of some of the more popular ICMP message types as a mechanism for understanding why allowing the Internet Control Message Protocol to flow through firewalls and routers without restriction can be harmful to the health of the network.

Exhibit 29. ICMP Code Field Values Based on Message Type

Message Type	*Code Field Values*
3	Destination Unreachable **Codes** 0 Net Unreachable 1 Host Unreachable 2 Protocol Unreachable 3 Port Unreachable 4 Fragmentation Needed and Don't Fragment was Set 5 Source Route Failed 6 Destination Network Unknown 7 Destination Host Unknown 8 Source Host Isolated 9 Communication with Destination Network Is Administratively Prohibited 10 Communication with Destination Host Is Administratively Prohibited 11 Destination Network Unreachable for Type of Service 12 Destination Host Unreachable for Type of Service 13 Communication Administratively Prohibited 14 Host Precedence Violation 15 Precedence Cutoff in Effect
5	Redirect **Codes** 0 Redirect Datagram for the Network (or subnet) 1 Redirect Datagram for the Host 2 Redirect Datagram for the Type of Service and Network 3 Redirect Datagram for the Type of Service and Host
6	Alternate Host Address **Codes** 0 Alternate Address for Host
11	Time Exceeded **Codes** 0 Time to Live Exceeded in Transit 1 Fragment Reassembly Time Exceeded
12	Parameter Problem **Codes** 0 Bad IP Header 1 Missing a Required Option 2 Bad Length

Exhibit 29. ICMP Code Field Values Based on Message Type *(continued)*

Message Type	*Code Field Values*
40	Photuris
	Codes
	0 Reserved
	1 Unknown Security Parameters Index
	2 Valid Security Parameters, but Authentication Failed
	3 Valid Security Parameters, but Decryption Failed

Echo Reply

A Type field value of 0 represents an Echo Reply message. The Echo Reply message is generated in response to a Type 8 ICMP message or Echo Request. In comparing Exhibits 28 and 29, note that an Echo Reply represents one of several ICMP message types that are not further quantified by a code value. Thus, this explains why Exhibit 29 does not indicate Code field values for a Type 0 ICMP message.

Destination Unreachable

A Type field value of 3 represents an ICMP Destination Unreachable message. This message is generated by a router that cannot forward a packet toward its destination. To further clarify the reason why a packet cannot be forwarded, one of 16 Code types is included in the ICMP Type 3 message. As indicated in Exhibit 29, a Code value of 0 would indicate that the network was unreachable, a Code value of 1 would indicate that the host was unreachable, etc.

Network Unreachable

A Code value of 0 (Network Unreachable) indicates that a router or gateway cannot locate the route to the destination network. This can result from the fact that the destination network does not exist or the router does not know how to route traffic to the requested network. Thus, the receipt of an ICMP Type 3, Code value 0 message informs the client that a path to the destination network is not available.

Host Unreachable

A Code value of 1 indicates that the destination host on the destination network cannot be located. For example, if a host is powered down or does not exist, the router attached to the destination network will respond with a Type 3, Code 1 ICMP message to the source address in the datagram.

Protocol Unreachable

If IP is carrying a higher layer protocol, such as TCP, it is possible that the destination host is not configured to support that transport layer protocol. In this situation, either the distant router or the destination host will return a Type 3, Code 2 Protocol Unreachable ICMP message.

Port Unreachable

If one transmits an application, it uses a defined port number. If the destination device is not configured to support the application, it does not service the port conveyed in the transport header. Instead, the destination host or router connected to the distant network will respond with a Type 3, Code 3 Port Unreachable ICMP message.

Fragmentation Needed and Don't Fragment Was Set

If the DF (Don't Fragment) bit position in the Flags field is set but a router receives a datagram that requires fragmentation, it responds with a Type 3, Code 4 ICMP message. Because the originator is responsible for fragmentation, it can use this ICMP message as an indicator to adjust its datagram size.

Source Route Failed

Suppose a router encounters a next hop in the source route that does not reside on the network to which it is connected. To inform the originator of this problem, the router generates an ICMP Type 3, Code 5 message.

Destination Network Unknown

If a router cannot deliver a datagram or forward it due to not knowing where the destination network resides, it will generate an ICMP Type 3, Code 6 Destination Network Unknown message.

Source Host Isolated

At one time, a Type 3, Code 8 value was used to indicate that a host was known but not reachable. Today, this message code is considered obsolete.

Destination Network Is Administratively Prohibited

If a router is not allowed to forward datagrams onto another network, it will generate a Type 3, Code 9 Communications with Destination Network Is Administratively Prohibited message.

Destination Host Is Administratively Prohibited

A Type 3, Code 10 ICMP message indicates that a router is not permitted to transmit or forward datagrams to a particular host.

Destination Network Unreachable for Type of Service

A router will generate a Type 3, Code 11 ICMP message that it cannot deliver due to the Type of Service requested not being supported. Because the use of ToS is rare, so is a Type 3, Code 11 ICMP message.

Destination Host Unreachable for Type of Service

When an IP datagram cannot be delivered to a host due to the requested Type of Service being unavailable, the router generates a Type 3, Code 12 Destination Host Unreachable for Type of Service ICMP message. Similar to a Type 3, Code 11 message, this message is rarely encountered.

Communications Administratively Prohibited

A Type 3, Code 13 Communications Administratively Prohibited ICMP message is generated by a router when it receives a datagram it cannot deliver to a host because it is not allowed. This message indicates that an administrator configured a filter to block certain types of traffic from flowing to the host.

Host Precedence Violation

When a router receives a datagram for delivery to a particular host with a precedence value, it can only deliver the data if the destination has the same precedence level. If not, the router returns a Type 3, Code 14 Host Precedence Violation ICMP message.

Precedence Cutoff in Effect

If a packet is dropped due to cutoff, the router will return a Type 3, Code 15 Precedence Cutoff in Effect ICMP message. This message rarely occurs today.

Source Quench

A Source Quench ICMP message represents a Type 4 message. This message is transmitted by a receiver to an originator to show the rate at which data is transmitted and functions as a flow control mechanism.

Redirect

A Redirect message is an ICMP Type 5 message. This message supports four code values that further clarify the redirection. The use of a Redirect results in an adjustment to a routing table that redirects traffic.

As indicated in Exhibit 29, there are four Redirect codes supported by a Type 5 ICMP message. Those codes indicate Redirect for a Network or Subnet (Code 0), Redirect for a Host (Code 1), Redirect for the Type of Service and Network (Code 2), and Redirect for the Type of Service and Host (Code 3).

Echo

A Type 8 message represents the most popular type of ICMP message. An Echo message forms the first part of the Echo-Echo Reply pair of messages referred to as a Ping. The address of the source in an Echo message represents the destination of the Echo Reply. To form the Echo Reply, the destination swaps source and destination addresses in the Echo message and changes the Type value from 8 to 0.

Time Exceeded

An ICMP Type 11 message, referred to as Time Exceeded, indicates that the Time to Live (TTL) field in an IP header was decremented to zero and the datagram was discarded. When this situation occurs, a gateway or router notifies the source of the datagram via an ICMP Type 11 Time Exceeded message.

In addition to informing a host that a message was discarded, a Type 11 ICMP message is used by the Traceroute command to discover a path from source to destination. To do so, the Traceroute command initially sets the TTL field value to 1 and increments its value in subsequent datagrams that are transmitted to map a route from source to destination. Later in this book when examining diagnostic testing methods, we will examine the use of the Traceroute program in detail.

Router Advertisement and Solicitation

Types 9 and 10 ICMP messages are for router Advertisement and Solicitation, respectively. Instead of initializing a routing table with static routes specified in a router configuration file, it is possible to use router ICMP Advertisement and Solicitation messages for a router to learn available routes dynamically and update its routing table.

Parameter Problem

A Type 12 message is used to indicate that a gateway or router has encountered a problem processing a datagram and sent it to the great bit bucket in the sky. One example of a Parameter Problem is an incorrect parameter in an option or a datagram that does not end on a correct byte boundary. There are two code values used to clarify the reason for a Parameter Problem. A Code 0 indicates a bad IP header, while a Code 1 indicates a required option is missing.

Timestamp and Timestamp Reply

An ICMP Type 13 message represents a Timestamp. The Timestamp encodes in 32 bits the time in milliseconds since midnight. An ICMP Type 14 message represents a Timestamp Reply. The Timestamp Reply includes the original data in the Timestamp message as well as an additional timestamp.

The use of Timestamp and Timestamp Reply messages were included in ICMP as a mechanism to facilitate the synchronization of clocks over an IP network. To accomplish this, the following three-step process is performed.

1. The requestor stamps the originate time and transmits a Timestamp message.
2. The destination stamps the receive time when it received the query.
3. The destination stamps the transmit time when it responds to the query with a Timestamp Reply.

Each station uses the three timestamps to adjust, if necessary, their transmit and receive clocks. Although transmit and receive clocks can be set to different values, by convention most systems use the same setting for both clocks and use a common clock to transmit and receive.

Information Request and Information Reply

ICMP Type 15 and Type 16 messages represent Information Request and Information Reply messages, respectively. The use of an Information Request message permits a device to determine the number of the network to which it is connected. To do so, the host sends an ICMP Type 15 message with an IP header whose Source Network and Destination Address field values are set to zero. This is used as a mechanism to mean "this network" and the station on "this network" replies with an Information Reply that indicates the number of the network it is on.

Address Mask Request and Reply

Similar to Timestamp Request and Reply, Address Mask Request and Reply work as a linked pair of ICMP messages. Hosts can use the Address Mask Request (Type 17) to acquire a subnet mask from a remote device that generates an Address Mask Reply (Type 18) ICMP message.

Traceback

Unlike previously described ICMP messages that are standardized, the Traceback message represents a work in progress in the form of an Internet Draft. The purpose of the Traceback message is to learn the path that packets take through the Internet. Although many hackers spoof IP addresses to hide their identity, the implementation of support by routers on the Internet for a Traceback message could break the shield of IP address spoofing. That is, a Traceback message would allow packets to be traced back to their origin, which would provide knowledge of the originator of certain activities. Given an appreciation for some current and a pending ICMP message, one can examine why ICMP messages can be risky to the health of a network.

ICMP Vulnerabilities

The initial goal behind the use of Ping (Echo Request Type 8 followed by an Echo Reply Type 0 response) was to enable users to determine if a remote system was operational and reachable. That is, an Echo Reply would indicate that the remote system was both operational and reachable. However, Ping can also be used for scanning a network. For example, if the network address is 205.131.175.0, which represents a Class C address, a hacker could easily write a script or use one of many readily available scanning programs to Ping each possible host address from 205.131.175.1 through 205.131.175.254 to determine which IP addresses within a network have computers operating a TCP/IP protocol stack.

In addition to ICMP Echo Requests, other types of ICMP messages can be used for scanning. For example, ICMP Timestamp (Type 13) will elicit a Timestamp Reply (Type 14) from UNIX hosts. Because Microsoft did not include a Timestamp function into its protocol stack, it becomes possible to use Echo Request and Timestamp to determine if a system is both operational and running a Microsoft operating system.

Another ICMP message type that conveys information that gives hackers an edge is the Address Mask Request (Type 17). The resulting Address Mask Reply (Type 18) can identify routers as well as provide subnet information that can be of valuable assistance in mapping a target network.

A Redirect (Type 5) message can be dangerous because it is used to adjust routing tables. Another dangerous ICMP message is Source Quench (Type 4), which informs the recipient to slow down the rate at which it transmits messages. When improperly used, the Source Quench message can result in a denial-of-service attack by slowing data transmission to a crawl.

Although it might appear that a Time Exceeded message is relatively harmless, it can also be used to map a network. For example, a hacker can transmit only the first portion of a fragment and wait for a Time Exceeded Code 1 message that indicates Fragment Reassembly Time Exceeded. In addition to mapping the IP addresses on a network, this technique can also be used to map ports. In fact, some popular scanning software makes use of fragmentation to determine both active stations on a network and the services they support. Because some ICMP messages can be quite helpful, this author believes their utility needs to be weighed against their vulnerability to determine if such messages should be allowed to flow through firewalls and routers rather than simply blocking all ICMP messages.

Later in this book when examining router access lists in detail, we will note that it is possible to allow only Echo Reply messages from the Internet to our hosts. Thus, certain types of access lists can be used to block Pinging from the Internet while allowing employees to determine if certain hosts on the Internet are reachable.

Chapter 5

The Transport Layer

The purpose of this chapter is to acquaint the reader with the two transport layer protocols supported by the TCP/IP suite. These protocols are the Transmission Control Protocol (TCP) and the User Datagram Protocol (UDP).

As indicated in Chapter 3, either TCP or UDP can be identified by setting an applicable value in the IP header. Although the use of either protocol results in the placement of the appropriate transport layer header behind the IP header, there are significant differences between the functionality of each transport protocol. Those differences make one protocol more suitable for certain applications than the other protocol, and vice versa.

TCP

The Transmission Control Protocol (TCP) is a connection-oriented protocol. This means that the protocol will not forward data until a session is established in which the destination acknowledges it is ready to receive data. This also means that the TCP setup process requires more time than when UDP is used as the transport layer protocol. However, because one would not want to commence certain operations, such as remote log-on or a file transfer, unless one knows the destination is ready to support the appropriate application, the use of TCP is more suitable than UDP for certain applications. Conversely, in examining UDP, one will realize that this transport layer protocol similarly supports certain applications better than other applications. Although there are many advantages associated with a connection-oriented protocol, as noted later in this chapter, it requires a handshaking process to be completed prior to establishing a connection. This means that it is possible to initiate a connection request and then fail to respond to the subsequent reply, in effect tying up some of the resources of the recipient for a period of time. If this action is repeated, it forms the basis for a denial-of-service (DoS) attack. The manner by which TCP connections occur, referred to as a three-way handshake, is examined later in this chapter. Because the best way to become familiar with TCP is by first examining the fields in its header, let us do so.

The TCP Header

The TCP header consists of 12 fields as illustrated in Exhibit 1. In comparing TCP and UDP, one realizes that the TCP header is far more complex. The reason for this additional complexity results from the fact that TCP is not only a connection-oriented protocol, but, in addition, supports error detection and correction as well as packet sequencing, with the latter used to note the ordering of packets and includes determining if one or more packets are lost.

Source and Destination Port Fields

The Source and Destination Port fields are each 16 bits in length. Each field denotes a particular process or application. In actuality, most applications use the Destination Port number to denote a particular process or application, and either set the Source Port field value to a random number greater than 1024 or to zero. The reason the Destination Port number defines the process or application results from the fact that an application operating at the receiver normally operates acquiescently, waiting for requests, looking for a specific destination port number to determine the request.

The reason the originator sets the Source Port to zero or a value above 1023 is due to the fact that the first 1023 out of 65,536 available port numbers are standardized with respect to the type of traffic transported via the use of

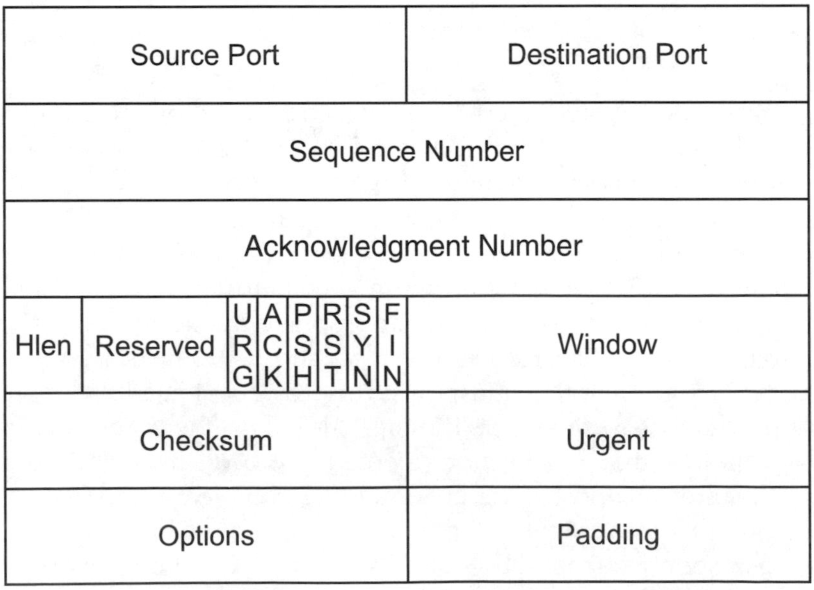

Exhibit 1. The TCP Header

specific numeric values. To illustrate the use of port numbers, assume one station wishes to open a Telnet connection with a distant server. Because Telnet is defined as port 23, the application will set the Destination Port value to that numeric. The Source Port will normally be set to a random value above 1023 and an IP header will then add the destination and source IP addresses for routing the datagram from the client to the server. In some literature, one may encounter the term "socket," sometimes incorrectly used as a synonym for port. In actuality, the destination port in the TCP or UDP header plus the destination IP address cumulatively identify a unique process or application on a host. The combination of port number and IP address is correctly referenced as a socket. At the server, the Destination Port value of 23 identifies the application as Telnet. When the server forms a response, it first reverses source and destination IP addresses. Similarly, the server places the Source Port number in the Destination Port field, which enables the Telnet originator's application to correctly identify the response to its initial datagram.

Multiplexing and Demultiplexing

Port numbers play an important role in TCP/IP as they enable multiple applications to flow between the same pair of stations or from multiple nonrelated stations to a common station. This flow of multiple applications to a common address is referred to as multiplexing. Upon receipt of a datagram, the removal of the IP and TCP headers requires the remaining portion of the packet to be routed to its correct process or application, based on the Destination Port number in the TCP header. This process is referred to as demultiplexing.

Both TCP and UDP use port numbers to support the multiplexing of different processes or applications to a common IP address. An example of this multiplexing and demultiplexing of packets is illustrated in Exhibit 2. The top left portion of Exhibit 2 illustrates how both Telnet and FTP, representing two TCP applications, can be multiplexed into a stream of IP datagrams that

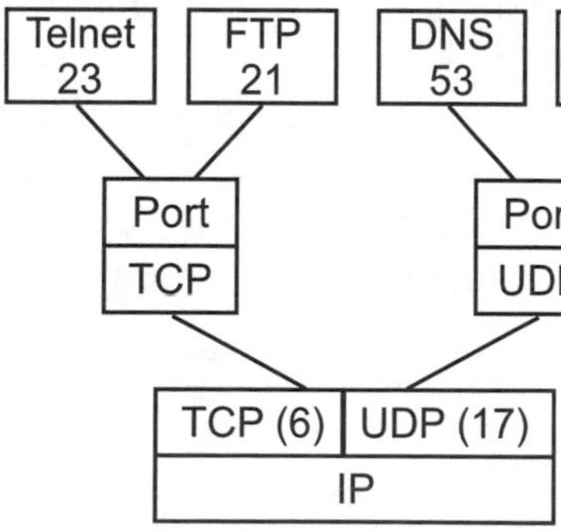

Exhibit 2. Port Numbers with Multiple Applications Multiplexed via Serial Communications to a Common IP Address

flow to a common IP address. In comparison, the top right portion of Exhibit 2 illustrates how, through port numbering, UDP ports permit a similar method of multiplexing of applications.

Many servers connected to the Internet are commonly configured to support two or more applications on a single hardware platform. One common example of multiple applications involves operating a Web server and an FTP server on a common hardware platform. To illustrate an example of this situation let us first point a browser to http:www.opm.gov/ as illustrated in Exhibit 3. In examining Exhibit 3, note that the Web page viewed through the browser is the home page of the United States Office of Personnel Management. To determine if this federal agency operates an FTP site, this author changed the uniform resource locator (URL) from http://www.opm.gov/ to ftp://ftp.opm.gov/.

Exhibit 4 illustrates the result obtained when the URL was changed to ftp://ftp.opm.gov/. Note that this FTP site does not support anonymous log-ins and requires a user accessing the account to enter his user name and password. While Exhibits 3 and 4 indicate that the United States Office of Personnel Management operates both Web and FTP servers, how can one determine that they both reside on the same hardware platform? The answer to this question can be obtained in one of several ways. First, one could use the Ping utility program that is described later in this book to obtain the IP address of each application. However, the United States Office of Personnel Management is similar to many other organizations in that it blocks Pings via the use of router access lists. Thus, another method must be employed to determine if the IP addresses for each application are the same. One method to consider is the use of the NSLOOKUP command.

NSLOOKUP represents an application that can use the default name server or another domain name server to obtain the IP address associated with a host name. Exhibit 5 illustrates the use of NSLOOKUP, which in a Windows environment operates in the command Prompt. In this example, after invoking the command, we entered the host address of ftp.opm.gov and determined that the IP address was 205.131.177.3. Next, we entered the host address www.opm.gov and determined that the IP address of the Web server operated by the United States Office of Personnel Management is the same as its FTP server IP address. Thus, both the Web server and the FTP server represent applications operating on a common host. Later in this book the use of Ping, NSLOOKUP, and other utility programs is examined in more detail.

The key to the ability to operate multiple applications on a common hardware platform is through the use of port numbers. Thus, let us turn our attention to this important topic.

Port Numbers

The "universe" of both TCP and UDP port numbers can vary from a value of 0 to 65535, resulting in a total of 65,535 ports capable of being used by each transport protocol. This so-called port universe is divided into three

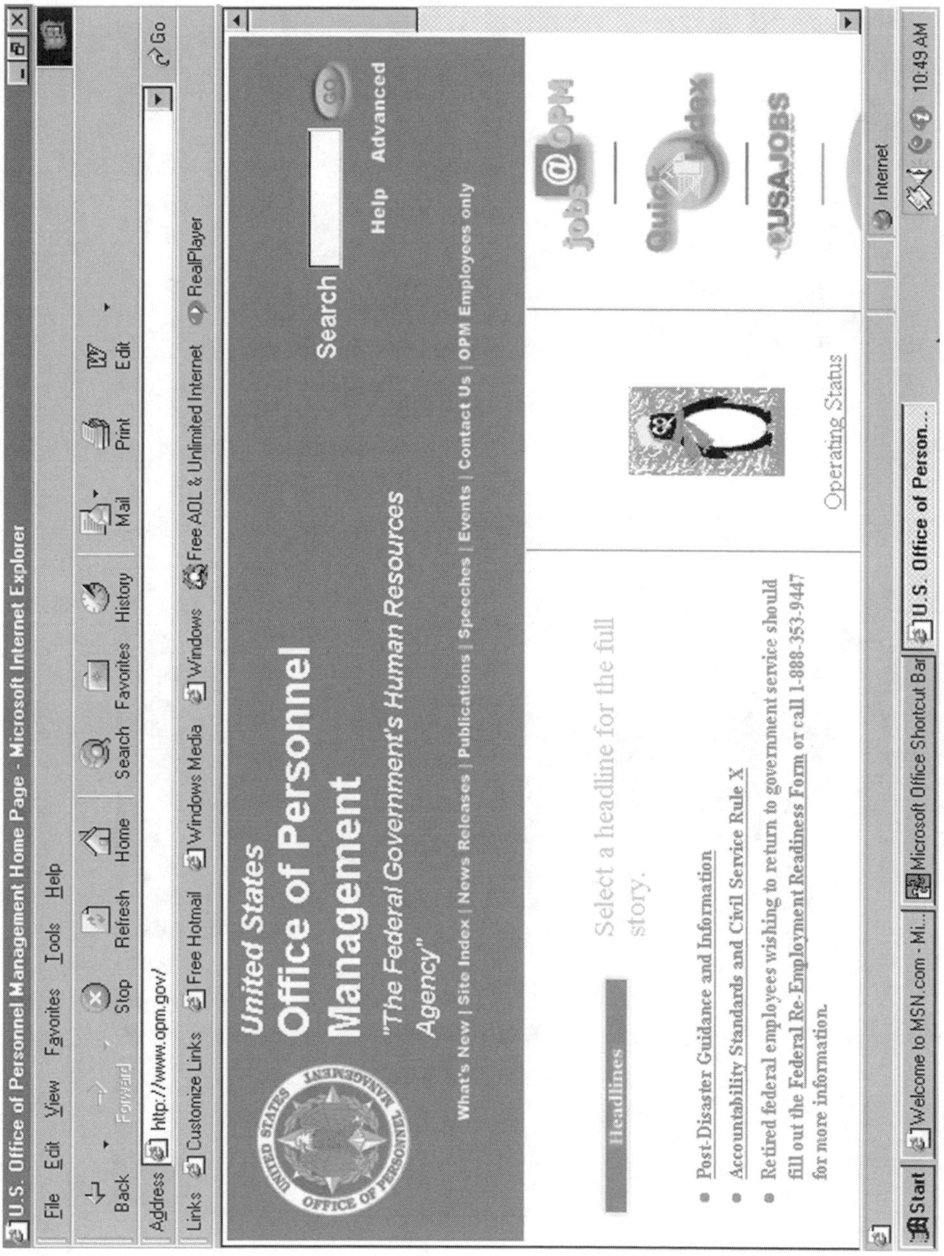

Exhibit 3. Viewing the Home Page of the United States Office of Personnel Management

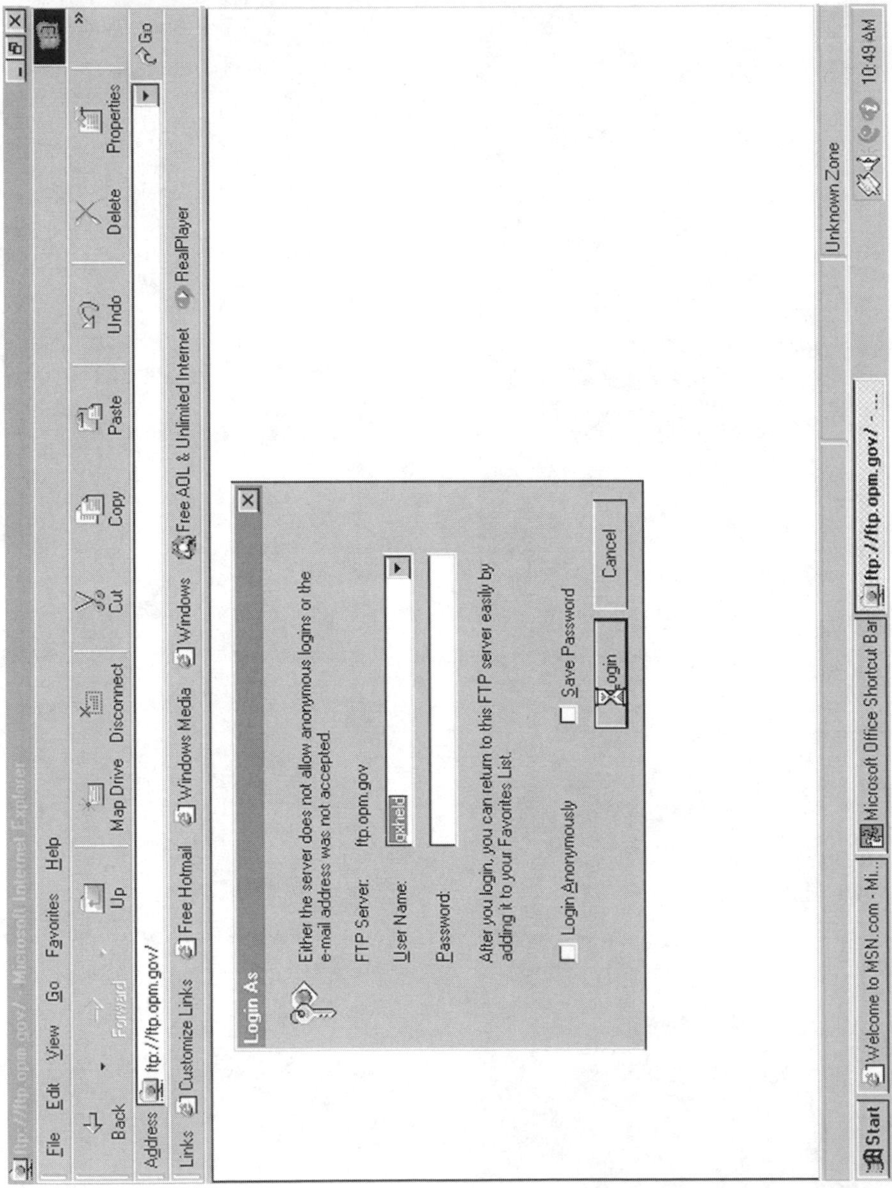

Exhibit 4. Attempting to Log On to the FTP Site Operated by the United States Office of Personnel Management

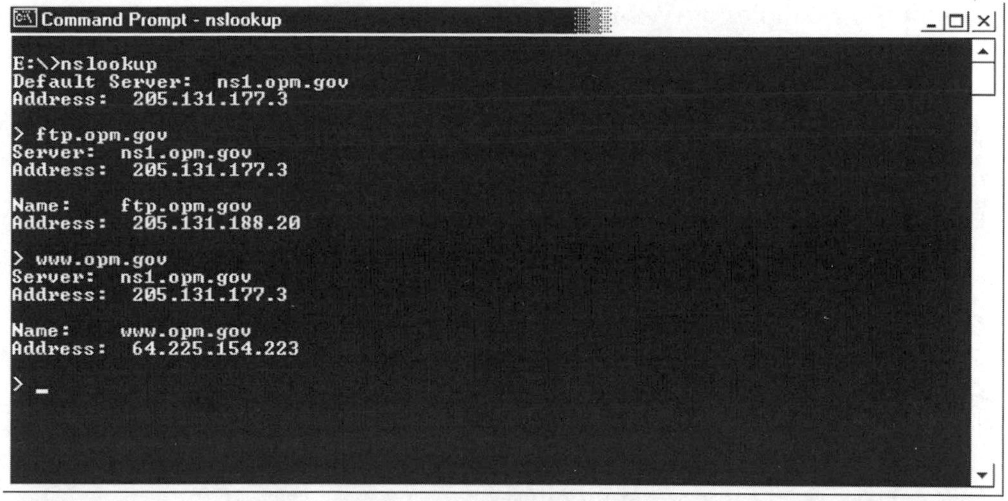

Exhibit 5. Using the NSLOOKUP Utility Program to Obtain the IP Address Associated with Different Hosts

ranges referred to as Well-Known Ports, Registered Ports, and Dynamic or Private Ports.

Well-Known Ports

Well-Known Ports are the most commonly used port values as they represent assigned numerics that identify specific processes or applications. Ports 0 through 1023 represent the range of Well-Known Ports. These port numbers are assigned by the Internet Assigned Numbers Authority (IANA) and are used to indicate the transportation of standardized processes. Where possible, the same Well-Known Port number assignments are used with TCP and UDP. Ports used with TCP are normally used to provide connections that transport long-term conversations. In some literature, one may encounter Well-Known Port numbers being specified as in the range of values from 0 to 255. While this range was correct many years ago, the modern range for assigned ports managed by the IANA was expanded to cover the first 1024 port values from 0 to 1023. Exhibit 6 provides a summary of the port value assignments from 0 through 255 for Well-Known Ports, to include the service supported by a particular port and the type of port — TCP or UDP — for which the port number is primarily used. A good source for the full list of assigned port numbers is RFC 1700.

Registered Ports

Registered ports are those whose values range from 1024 through 49151. Although all ports above 1023 can be used freely, the IANA requests vendors to register their application port numbers with them.

Exhibit 6. Examples of Well-Known TCP and UDP Services and Port Use

Keyword	*Service*	*Port Type*	*Port Number*
TCPMUX	TCP Port Service Multiplexer	TCP	1
RJE	Remote Job Entry	TCP	5
ECHO	Echo	TCP and UDP	7
DAYTIME	Daytime	TCP and UDP	13
QOTD	Quote of the Day	TCP	17
CHARGEN	Character Generator	TCP	19
FTP-DATA	File Transfer (Default Data)	TCP	20
FTP	File Transfer (Control)	TCP	21
TELNET	Telnet	TCP	23
SMTP	Simple Mail Transfer Protocol	TCP	25
MSG-AUTH	Message Authentication	TCP	31
TIME	Time	TCP	37
NAMESERVER	Host Name Server	TCP and UDP	42
NICNAME	Who Is	TCP	43
DOMAIN	Domain Name Server	TCP and UDP	53
BOOTPS	Bootstrap Protocol Server	TCP	67
BOOTPC	Bootstrap Protocol Client	TCP	68
TFTP	Trivial File Transfer Protocol	UDP	69
FINGER	Finger	TCP	79
HTTP	World Wide Web	TCP	80
KERBEROS	Kerberos	TCP	88
RTELNET	Remote Telnet Service	TCP	107
POP2	Post Office Protocol Version 2	TCP	109
POP3	Post Office Protocol Version 3	TCP	110
NNTP	Network News Transfer Protocol	TCP	119
NTP	Network Time Protocol	TCP and UDP	123
NETBIOS-NS	NetBIOS Name Server	UDP	137
NETBIOS-DGM	NetBIOS Datagram Service	UDP	138
NETBIOS-SSN	NetBIOS Session Service	UDP	139
NEWS	News	TCP	144
SNMP	Simple Network Management Protocol	UDP	161
SNMPTRAP	Simple Network Management Protocol Traps	UDP	162
BGP	Border Gateway Protocol	TCP	179
HTTPS	Secure HTTP	TCP	443
RLOGIN	Remote Login	TCP	513
TALK	Talk	TCP and UDP	517

Dynamic or Private Ports

The third range of port numbers is from 49152 through 65535. This port number range is associated with dynamic or private ports. This port range is usually used by new applications that remain to be standardized, such as Internet telephony.

Sequence and Acknowledgment Number Fields

TCP is a byte-oriented sequencing protocol. Thus, a Sequence Number field is necessary to ensure that missing or misordered packets are noted or identified. That field is 32 bits in length and provides the mechanism for ensuring that missing or misordered packets are noted or identified.

The actual entry in the Sequence Number field is based on the number of bytes in the TCP Data field. That is, because TCP was developed as a byte-oriented protocol, each byte in each packet is assigned a sequence number. Because it would be most inefficient for TCP to transmit one byte at a time, groups of bytes, typically 512 or 536, are placed in a segment and one sequence number is assigned to the segment and placed in the Sequence Number field. That number is based on the number of bytes in the current segment as well as previous segments, as the Sequence Number field value increments its count until all 16-bit positions are used and then continues via a rollover through zero. For example, assume the first TCP segment contains 512 bytes. Then, a second segment will have the sequence number 1024.

When the SYN flag bit (discussed later in this section) is set, the Sequence Number field indicates that the sequence number is an Initial Sequence Number (ISN). An algorithm is used to compute the ISN, which is included in the Sequence Number field during session setup. This number represents the identifier of the first byte in the first datagram, with subsequent sequence number identifying the first byte within subsequent datagrams.

The Acknowledgment Number field, which is also 32 bits in length, is used to verify the receipt of data. The number in this field also reflects bytes. For example, returning to the example sequence of two 512-byte segments, when the first segment is received, the receiver expects the next sequence number to be 513. Therefore, if the receiver were acknowledging each segment, it would first return an acknowledgment with a value of 513 in the Acknowledgment Number field. When it acknowledges the next segment, the receiver would set the value in the Acknowledgment Number field to 1025, etc. From the preceding, it is obvious that the Acknowledgment Number should equal the other side's previously transmitted sequence number and length value.

Because it would be inefficient to have to acknowledge each datagram, a variable or "sliding" window is supported by TCP. That is, returning an Acknowledgment Number field value of n + 1 would indicate the receipt of all bytes through byte n. If the receiver has the ability to process a series of multiple segments and each is received without error, it would be less efficient to acknowledge each datagram. Thus, a TCP receiver can process a variable number of segments prior to returning an acknowledgment that informs the transmitter that n bytes were received correctly. To ensure that lost datagrams or lost acknowledgments do not place TCP in an infinite waiting period, the originator sets a timer and will retransmit data if it does not receive a response within a predefined period of time.

The previously described use of the Acknowledgment Number field is referred to as Positive Acknowledgment Retransmission (PAR). Under PAR, each unit of data must be either implicit (sending a value of n + 1 to acknowledge receipt of n bytes) or explicit. If a unit of data is not acknowledged by the time the originator's timeout period is reached, the previous transmission is retransmitted. When the Acknowledgment Number field is in use, a flag bit, referred to as the ACK flag in the Code field, will be set. The six bit positions in the Code Bits field are discussed below.

Hlen Field

The Header Length (Hlen) field is four bits in length. This field, which is also referred to as the Offset field, contains a value that indicates where the TCP header ends and the Data field begins. This value is specified as a number of 32-bit words. It is required due to the fact that the inclusion of options can result in a variable-length header. Because the minimum length of the TCP header is 20 bytes, the minimum value of the Hlen field would be 5, denoting five 32-bit words, which equals 20 bytes.

Code Bits Field

As previously indicated in Exhibit 1, there are six individual one-bit fields within the Code Bits field. Each bit position functions as a flag to indicate whether or not a function is enabled or disabled. Thus, to obtain an appreciation for the use of the Code Bits field, one should examine each bit position in that field.

URG Bit

The Urgent (URG) bit or flag is used to denote an urgent or priority activity. When such a situation occurs, an application will set the URG bit position, which acts as a flag and results in TCP immediately transmitting everything it has for the connection instead of waiting for additional characters. An example of an action that could result in an application setting the Urgent flag would be a user pressing the CTRL-BREAK key combination.

A second meaning resulting from the setting of the Urgent bit or flag is that it also indicates that the Urgent Pointer field is in use. Here, the Urgent

Pointer field indicates the offset in bytes from the current sequence number where the Urgent data is located.

ACK Bit

Setting the ACK bit indicates that the segment contains an acknowledgment to a previously transmitted datagram or series of datagrams. Then the value in the Acknowledgment Number field indicates the correct receipt of all bytes through byte n by having the byte number n + 1 in the field.

PSH Bit

The third bit position in the Code Bit field is the Push (PSH) bit. This one-bit field is set to request the receiver to immediately deliver data to the application and flags any buffering. Normally, the delivery of urgent information would result in setting both the URG and PSH bits in the Code Bits field.

RST Bit

The fourth bit position in the Code Bits field is the Reset (RST) bit. This bit position is set to reset a connection. By responding to a connection request with the RST bit set, this bit position can also be used as a mechanism to decline a connection request.

SYN Bit

The fifth bit in the Code Bits field is the Synchronization (SYN) bit. This bit position is set at start-up during what is referred to as a three-way handshake.

FIN Bit

The sixth and last bit position in the Code Bits field is the Finish (FIN) bit. This bit position is set by the sender to indicate that it has no additional data, and the connection should be released.

Window Field

The Window field is 16 bits in length and provides TCP with the ability to regulate the flow of data between source and destination. Thus, this field indirectly performs flow control.

The Window field indicates the maximum number of bytes that the receiving device can accept. Thus, it indirectly indicates the available buffer memory of the receiver. Here, a large value can significantly improve TCP performance as it permits the originator to transmit a number of segments without having to wait for an acknowledgment while permitting the receiver to acknowledge the receipt of multiple segments with one acknowledgment.

Because TCP is a full-duplex transmission protocol, both the originator and recipient can insert values in the Window field to control the flow of data in each direction. By reducing the value in the Window field, one end of a session in effect informs the other end to transmit less data. Thus, the use of the Window field provides a bi-directional flow control capability.

Checksum Field

The Checksum field is 16 bits (or two bytes) in length. The function of this field is to provide an error detection capability for TCP. To do so, this field is primarily concerned with ensuring that key fields are validated instead of protecting the entire header. Thus, the checksum calculation occurs over what is referred to as a 12-byte pseudo-header. This pseudo-header includes the 32-bit Source and Destination Address fields in the IP header, the eight-bit Protocol field, and a Length field that indicates the length of the TCP header and data transported within the TCP segment. The TCP pseudo-header is illustrated in Exhibit 7. Because the TCP pseudo-header is computed based on 32-bit words, the Zero field represents a field in which all bits are set to zero. The primary purpose of the Checksum field is to ensure that data has arrived at its correct destination, and the receiver has no doubt about the address of the originator nor the length of the header and the type of application data transported.

Urgent Pointer Field

The Urgent Pointer field is one byte in length and functions as a mechanism to identify the position of urgent data within a TCP segment. To do so, it relies on an inverse relationship. That is, the value in this field acts as a pointer to the sequence number of the byte following the urgent data. Thus, the Urgent Pointer actually indicates the beginning of routine or non-urgent data, resulting in urgent data by default occurring before the pointer location. As previously noted, the URG bit position in the Code field must be set for the data in the Urgent Pointer field to be interpreted.

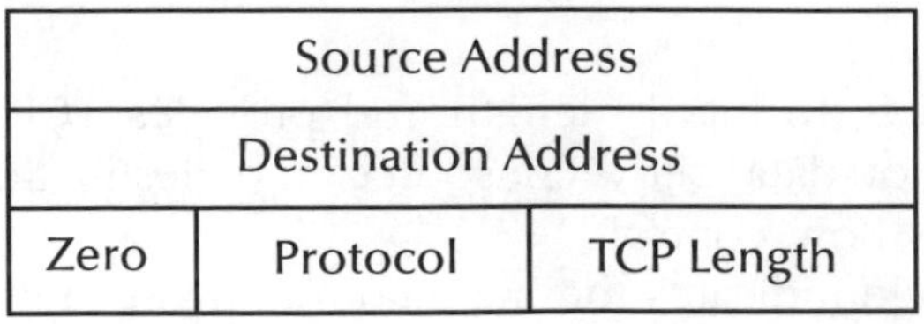

Exhibit 7. The TCP Pseudo-Header

Options

The Options field, if present, can be variable in length. The purpose of this field is to enable TCP to support various options, with Maximum Segment Size (MSS) representing a popular TCP option. Because the header must end on a 32-bit boundary, any option that does not do so is extended via pad characters that in some literature are referred to as a Padding field.

TCP options are identified by an option Kind field. Exhibit 8 lists some of the Kind field values associated with different TCP options. Options 1 and 2 are exactly one byte in length. All other options have a one-byte Kind field, followed by a one-byte Length field. The Length field indicates the length of the option, to include both the Kind and Length fields. Thus, the length of the option data is the value of the Length field – 2.

One of the most popular TCP options is the Maximum Segment Size (MSS). When a TCP connection is being established, each station will transmit its desired MSS to the remote endpoint in a SYN packet. The desired MSS is the Maximum Transmission Unit (MTU) of the interface being used, minus the IP and TCP frame overhead, which is normally 40 bytes. The MTU is usually set when a device driver initializes an interface and its value represents the payload portion of the frame. Most protocol stacks support MTUs up to 65,535 bytes; however, the interface MTU needs to be compared to the route MTU. The route MTU represents the MTU that can be used without causing fragmentation. For example, if a datagram flows from a Token Ring network to an Ethernet network, the maximum frame length supported by Ethernet is 1500 bytes, which is significantly less than that supported by a Token Ring network. Thus, the per-route MTU would be Ethernet's 1500 bytes. A per-route MTU is usually maintained as a field value in a host's routing table and learned via an MTU discover process or manually configured. When a large packet must be transferred via an interface with a smaller MTU, the routing entity will either fragment the datagram or drop it.

Exhibit 8. TCP Options

Kind	*Length*	*Description*
0	—	End of Option List
1	—	No-operation
2	4	Maximum Segment Size
3	3	Window Scale
4	2	SACK Permitted
5	2	SACK
6	6	Echo (obsoleted by Option 8)
7	6	Echo Reply (obsoleted by Option 8)
8	10	Timestamp Option
9	2	Partial Order Connection Permitted
10	3	Partial Order Service Profile

Returning to our discussion of the MSS, when two networks with differing MTUs are to be connected, TCP stations can exchange their MSS(s). The smaller of the two can then be selected, which enables communications to occur without IP fragmentation.

Padding Field

The Padding field is optional and is included only when the Options field does not end on a 32-bit boundary. Thus, the purpose of the Padding field is to ensure that the TCP header, when extended, falls on a 32-bit boundary.

Given an appreciation for the composition of the TCP header, one can now focus on the manner by which this protocol operates. In doing so, the reader will examine how TCP establishes a connection with a distant device and its initial handshaking process, its use of sequence and acknowledgment numbers, how flow control is supported by the protocol, and how the protocol terminates a session.

Connection Establishment

As mentioned earlier in this section, TCP is a connection-oriented protocol that requires a connection between two stations to be established prior to the actual transfer of data occurring. The actual manner by which an application communicates with TCP is through a series of function calls. To obtain an appreciation for the manner by which TCP establishes a session, one must first examine connection function calls used by applications, for example, Telnet and FTP.

Connection Function Calls

Exhibit 9 illustrates the use of the OPEN connection function calls during the TCP connection establishment process. This process commences when an application requires a connection to a remote station. At that time, the application will request TCP to place an OPEN function call. There are two types of OPEN function calls: passive and active. A passive OPEN function call represents a call to allow connections to be accepted from a remote station. This type of call is normally issued upon application start-up, informing TCP that, for example, FTP or Telnet is active and ready to accept connections originating from other stations. TCP will then note that the application is active, note its port assignment, and then allow connections on that port number.

Port Hiding

One of the little-known aspects of TCP is the fact that some organizations attempt to hide their applications by configuring applications for ports other than well-known ports. For example, assigning Telnet to port 2023 instead of

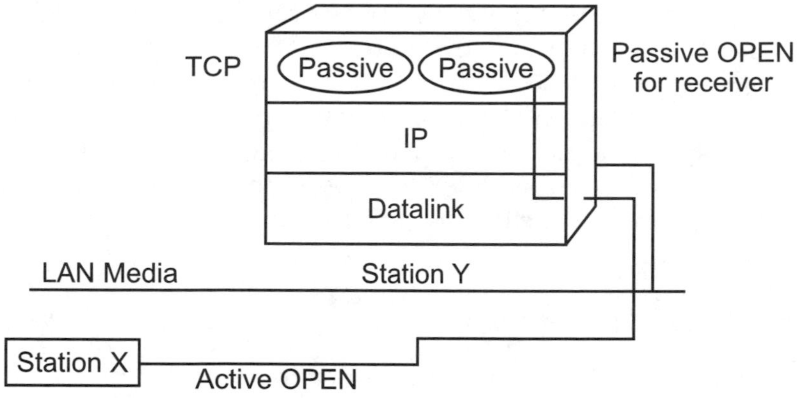

Exhibit 9. Using Function Calls to Establish a TCP Connection

port 23 is an example of port hiding. Although a person with port scanning software would be able to easily discover that port 2023 is being used, the theory behind port hiding is that it reduces the ability of lay personnel to easily discover applications at different network addresses and then attempt to use those applications.

Passive OPEN

Returning to the use of a passive OPEN function call, its use governs the number of connections allowed. That is, while a client would usually issue one passive OPEN, a server would issue multiple OPENs because it is designed to service multiple sessions. Another term used for the passive end of the TCP action is responder or TCP responder. Thus, a TCP responder can be thought of as an opening up of connection slots to accept any inbound connection request without waiting for any particular station request.

Active OPEN

A station that needs to initiate a connection to a remote station issues the second type of OPEN call. This type of function call is referred to as an active OPEN. In the example illustrated in Exhibit 9, station X would issue an active OPEN call to station Y. For the connection to be serviced by station Y, that station must have previously issued a passive OPEN request which, as previously explained, allows incoming connections to be established. To successfully connect, station X's active OPEN must use the same port number that the passive OPEN used on station Y. In addition to active and passive OPEN calls, other calls include CLOSE (to close a connection), SEND and RECEIVE (to transfer information), and STATUS (to receive information for a previously established connection).

Given an appreciation for the use of active and passive OPEN calls to establish a TCP connection, one can now explore the manner by which TCP segments are exchanged. The exchange of segments enables a session to occur. The initial exchange of datagrams that transport TCP segments is referred to as a three-way handshake. It is important to note how and why this process occurs. It has been used in modified form as a mechanism to create a denial-of-service (DoS) attack, which is discussed in Chapter 5 and 10.

The Three-Way Handshake

To ensure that the sender and receiver are ready to commence the exchange of data requires that both parties to the exchange be synchronized. Thus, during the TCP initialization process, the sender and receiver exchange a few control packets for synchronization purposes. This exchange is referred to as a three-way handshake. This functions as a mechanism to synchronize each endpoint at the beginning of a TCP connection with a sequence number and an acknowledgment number.

Overview

A three-way handshake begins with the originator sending a segment with its SYN bit in the Code Bit field set. The receiving station will respond with a similar segment with its ACK bit in the Code Bit field set. Thus, an alternate name for the three-way handshake is an "initial SYN-SYN-ACK" sequence.

Operation

To illustrate the three-way handshake, one can continue from the prior example shown in Exhibit 9, in which station X placed an active OPEN call to TCP to request a connection to a remote station and an application on that station. Once the TCP/IP protocol stack receives an active OPEN call, it will construct a TCP header with the SYN bit in the Code Bit field set. The stack will also assign an initial sequence number and place that number in the Sequence Number field in the TCP header. Other fields in the header, such as the destination port number, are also set and the segment is then transferred to IP for the formation of a datagram for transmission onto the network.

To illustrate the operation of the three-way handshake, consider Exhibit 10, which illustrates the process between stations X and Y. Because the initial sequence number does not have to start at zero, assume it commenced at 1000 and then further assume that the value was placed in the Sequence Number field. Thus, the TCP header flowing from station X to station Y is shown with SYN = 1 and SEQ = 1000.

Because the IP header results in the routing of a datagram to station Y, that station strips the IP header and notes that the setting of the SYN bit in the TCP header represents a connection request. Assuming station Y can accept a new connection, it will acknowledge the connection request by building a

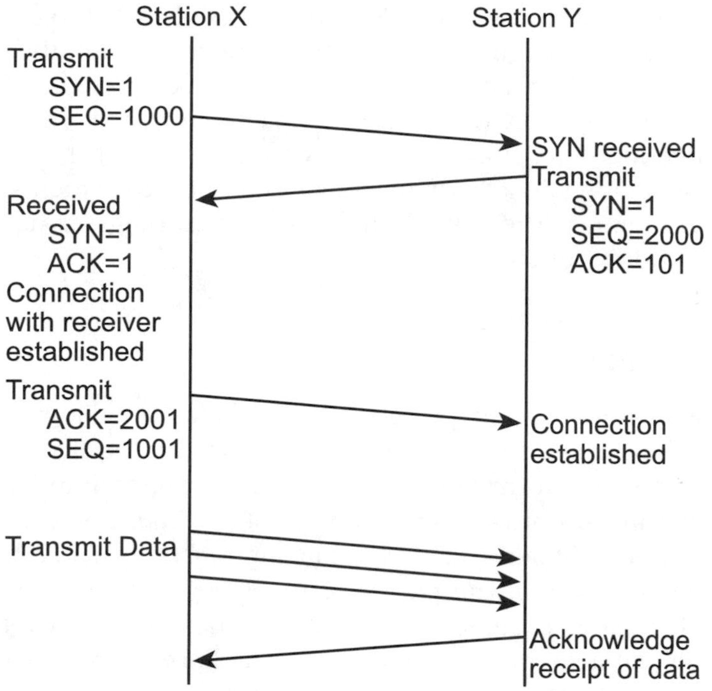

Exhibit 10. The Three-Way Handshake

TCP segment. That segment will have its SYN and ACK bits in its Code Bit field set. In addition, station Y will place its own initial sequence number in the Sequence Number field of the TCP header it is forming. Because the connection request had a sequence number of 1000, station Y will acknowledge receipt by setting its Acknowledgment field value to 1001 (station X sequence number plus 1), which indicates the next expected sequence number.

Once station Y forms its TCP segment, the segment has an IP header added to form a datagram. The datagram flows to station X. Station X receives the datagram, removes the IP header, and notes via the setting of the SYN and ACK bits and Sequence Number field value that it is a response to its previously issued connection request. To complete the connection request, station X must, in effect, acknowledge the acknowledgment. To do so, station X will construct a new TCP segment in which the ACK bit will be set and the sequence number will be incremented by 1 to 1001. Station X will also set the Acknowledgment Number to 2001 and form a datagram that is transmitted to station Y. Once station Y examines the TCP header and confirms the correct values for the Acknowledgment and Sequence Number fields, the connection becomes active. At this point in time, both data and commands can flow between the two endpoints. As this occurs, each side of the connection maintains its own set of tables for transmitted and received sequence numbers. Those numbers are always in ascending order. When the applicable 16-bit field reaches its maximum value, the settings wrap to 0.

In examining the three-way handshake illustrated in Exhibit 10, note that after the originating station establishes a connection with the receiver, it transmits a second TCP initialization segment to the receivers and follows that segment with one or more IP datagrams that transport the actual data. In Exhibit 10, a sequence of three datagrams is shown being transmitted prior to station Y, generating an acknowledgment to the three segments transported in the three datagrams. The actual number of outstanding segments depends on the TCP window, discussed next.

The TCP Window

TCP is a connection-oriented protocol that includes a built-in capability to regulate the flow of information, a function referred to as flow control. TCP manages the flow of information by increasing or decreasing the number of segments that can be outstanding at any point in time. For example, under periods of congestion when a station is running out of available buffer space, the receiver may indicate it can only accept one segment at a time and delay its acknowledgment to ensure it can service the next segment without losing data. Conversely, if a receiver has free and available buffer space, it may allow multiple segments to be transmitted to it and quickly acknowledge the segments.

TCP forms segments sequentially in memory. Each segment of memory waits for an IP header to be added to form a datagram for transmission. A "window" is placed over this series of datagrams that structures three types of data: data transmitted and acknowledged; data transmitted, but not yet acknowledged; and data waiting to be transmitted. Because this "window" slides over the three types of data, the window is referred to as a "sliding window."

Exhibit 11 illustrates the use of the TCP sliding window for flow control purposes. Although the actual TCP segment's size is normally 512 bytes, for simplicity of illustration, a condensed sequence of segments with sequence numbers varying by unity are shown. In this example, assume that sequence numbers 10 through 15 have been transmitted to the destination station. The remote station acknowledges receipt of those segments. Datagrams containing segment sequence numbers 16 through 20 were transmitted by the source station, but at this particular point in time have not received an acknowledgment.

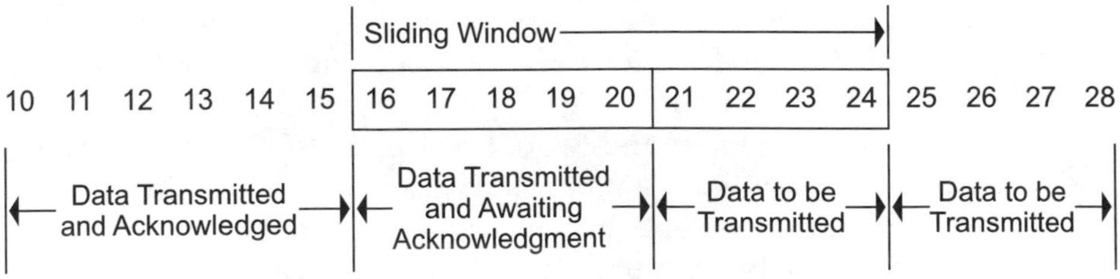

Exhibit 11. Flow Control and the TCP Sliding Window

Thus, that data represents the second type of data covered by a sliding window. Note that this window will slide up the segments as each datagram is transmitted. The third type of data covered by the sliding window is segments. In Exhibit 11, segments 21 through 24 are in the source station awaiting transmission, while segments 25 through 28 are awaiting coverage by the sliding window.

Returning to Exhibit 1, which illustrated the TCP header, note the field labeled "Window." That field value indirectly governs the length of the sliding window. In addition, the setting of that field provides a flow control mechanism. For example, the Window field transmitted by a receiver to a sender indicates the range of sequence numbers, which equates to bytes, that the receiver is willing to accept. If a remote station cannot accept additional data, it would then set the Window field value to 0. The receiving station continues to transmit TCP segments with the Window field set to 0 until its buffer is emptied a bit, no pun intended, in effect allowing the resumption of transmission conveying data by the originator. That is, when the transmitting station receives a response with a Window field value of 0, it replies to the response with an ACK (Code field ACK bit set to 1) and its Window field set to a value of 0. This inhibits the flow of data. When sufficient buffer space becomes available at the receiver, it will form a segment with its Window field set to a non-zero value, an indication that it can again receive data. At this point, the transmitting of data goes to the receiver.

Avoiding Congestion

One of the initial problems associated with TCP is the fact that a connection could commence with the originator transmitting multiple segments, up to the Window field value returned by the receiver during the previously described three-way handshake. If there are slow-speed WAN connections between originator and recipient, it is possible that routers could become saturated when a series of transmissions originated at the same time. In such a situation, the router would discard datagrams, causing retransmissions that continued the abnormal situation. The solution developed to avoid this situation is referred to as a TCP slow start process.

TCP Slow Start

Slow start represents an algorithm procedure added to TCP that implicitly uses a new window, referred to as the congestion window. This window is not contained as a field in the TCP header. Instead, it becomes active through the algorithm that defined the slow start process. That is, when a new connection is established, the congestion window is initialized to a size of one segment, typically 512 or 536 bytes. Each time an ACK is received, the congestion window's length is increased by one segment. The originator can transmit any number of segments up to the minimum value of the congestion window or the Window field value (Advertised Window). Note that flow control is imposed by the transmitter in one direction through the congestion window, while it is imposed in the other direction by the receiver's advertised Window field value.

Although slow start commences with a congestion window of one segment, it builds up exponentially until it reaches the Advertised Window size. That is, it is incremented by subsequent ACKs from 1 to 2, then it is increased to 4, 8, 16, etc. until it reaches the Advertised Window size. Once this occurs, segments are transferred using the Advertised Window size for congestion control and the slow start process is terminated.

The Slow Start Threshold

In addition to working at initiation, slow start will return upon the occurrence of one of two conditions: duplicate ACKs or a timeout condition where a response is not received within a predefined period of time. When either situation occurs, the originator commences another algorithm referred to as the congestion control algorithm.

When congestion occurs, a comparison is initiated between the congestion window size and the current advertised window size. The smaller number is halved and saved in a variable referred to as a slow start threshold. The minimum value of the slow start threshold is 2 segments unless congestion occurred via a timeout, with the congestion window then set to a value of 1, the same as a slow start process. The TCP originator has the option of using the slow start start-up or congestion avoidance. To determine which method to use, the originator compares the congestion value to the value of the slow start threshold. If the congestion value matches the value of the slow start threshold, the congestion avoidance algorithm will be used. Otherwise, the originator will use the slow start method. Having previously described the slow start method, the focus shifts to the congestion avoidance method and to the algorithm it uses.

Upon the receipt of ACKs, the congestion window will be increased until its value matches the value saved in the slow start threshold. When this occurs, the slow start algorithm terminates and the congestion avoidance algorithm starts. This algorithm multiplies the segment size by two, divides that value by the congestion window size, and then continually increases its value based on the previously described algorithm each time an ACK is received. The result of this algorithm is a more linear growth in the number of segments that can be transmitted in comparison to the exponential growth of the slow start algorithm.

TCP Retransmissions

While it is obvious that the negative acknowledgment of a segment by the receiver returning the same segment number expected indicates a retransmission request, what happens if a datagram is delayed? Because delays across a TCP/IP network depend on the activity of other routers in the network, the number of hops in the path between source and destination, and other factors, it is relatively impossible to have an exact expected delay prior to a station assuming data is lost and retransmitting. Recognizing this situation, the developers of TCP included an adaptive retransmission algorithm in the protocol. Under this algorithm, when TCP submits a segment for transmission, the protocol records the segment sequence number and time. When an acknowledgment is received to that segment, TCP also records the time, obtaining a round-trip delay. TCP uses such timing information to construct an average round-trip delay that is used by a timer to denote, when the timer expires, that a retransmission should occur. When a new transmit-response sequence occurs, another round-trip delay is computed, which slightly changes the average. Thus, this technique slowly changes the timer value that governs the acceptable delay for waiting for an ACK. With an understanding of how TCP determines when to retransmit a segment, coverage of this protocol concludes with how TCP gracefully terminates a session.

Keep-Alives

As previously noted in this chapter, TCP represents a connection-oriented protocol. Every connection-oriented protocol requires a method to maintain the logical connection it establishes with a distant device when there is no data to transmit for a period of time. To maintain the logical connection, TCP will transmit a datagram referred to as a keep-alive. A keep-alive datagram does not contain any upper layer data. Thus, the keep-alive datagram has a Length field value of 0. Due to this, subsequent Acknowledgment Number field values do not advance.

Session Termination

If one remembers the components of the Code Bit field, one remembers that this field has a FIN bit. The purpose of this bit is to enable TCP to gracefully terminate a session. Before TCP can terminate a full-duplex communication, each party to the session must close the session. This means that both the originator and recipient must exchange segments with the FIN bit set in each segment.

Exhibit 12 illustrates the exchange of segments to gracefully terminate a TCP connection. In this example, assume station X has completed its transmission and indicates this fact by sending a segment to station Y with the FIN bit set. Station Y will acknowledge the segment with an ACK. At this point in time, station Y will no longer accept data from station X. Station Y can continue to accept data from its application to transmit to station X. If station Y does not have any more data to transmit, it will then completely close the connection by transmitting a segment to station X with the FIN bit set in the segment. Station X will then ACK that segment and terminate the connection. If an ACK should be lost in transit, segments with FIN are

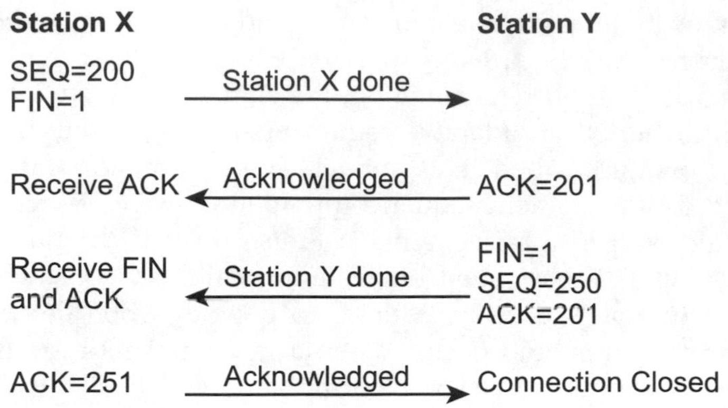

Exhibit 12. Terminating a TCP Connection

transmitted and a timer is set. Then either an ACK is received or a timeout occurs, which serves to close the connection.

TCP Timers

In concluding this discussion of TCP, we turn our attention to several types of timers used by this transport layer protocol. Those timers include a delayed ACK timer, keep-alive timer, persist timer, and fin-wait 2 timer. Each of these timers can be viewed as memory settings that are decremented as the protocol stack operates on a device.

Delayed ACK Timer

A delayed ACK timer provides TCP with the ability to more efficiently respond to the data it receives. When a device receives data that must be acknowledged but not immediately, TCP can wait up to 200 ms prior to sending an ACK. This enables TCP to transmit more data with an ACK, conserving bandwidth and making the response more efficient.

Keep-Alive Timer

We previously noted that a keep-alive is used to maintain a logical connection when there is no data to transmit. The keep-alive timer functions as a mechanism to detect if a connection is up and its expiration generates a keep-alive. That is, if a connection is idle for a fixed period of time, the keep-alive timer will expire, resulting in a probe in the form of a TCP keep-alive segment being transmitted to the other side of the connection to illicit a response. If no response is received, further keep-alives are optional and the local station is free to close the connection.

Persist Timer

The persist timer is set when the other end of a connection advertises a window size of zero as a mechanism to stop TCP from transmitting additional data. Because it is possible that a window advertisement could be lost, TCP will send one byte of data after its persist timer expires to determine if the window has opened up.

FIN-WAIT-2 Timer

As previously noted, when a station needs to close a TCP connection, it transmits a FIN command to the remote device. The destination station will then enter a FIN-WAIT-1 state.

When the acknowledgment of the termination request is received from the remote device, the local device enters the FIN-WAIT-2 state. A FIN-WAIT-2 timer is set at this point and upon expiration is reset to 75 seconds, after which the connection is dropped. This timer avoids leaving a connection in the FIN-WAIT-2 state forever while waiting for a final FIN from the remote station.

UDP

The User Datagram Protocol (UDP) is the second transport layer protocol supported by the TCP/IP protocol suite. UDP is a connectionless protocol. This means that an application using UDP can have its data transported in the form of IP datagrams without first having to establish a connection to the destination. This also means that when transmission occurs via UDP, there is no need to release a connection, thus simplifying the communications process. Other features of UDP include the fact that this protocol has no ordering capability, nor does it provide an error detection and correction capability. This in turn results in a header that is greatly simplified and is much smaller than that of TCP.

The UDP Header

Exhibit 13 illustrates the composition of the UDP header. This header consists of 64 bytes, followed by actual user data. In comparing the TCP and UDP headers, it is easy to note the relative simplicity of the latter because it lacks many of the features of the former. For example, because it does not require the acknowledgment of datagrams nor sequence of datagrams, there is no need for Sequence and Acknowledgment fields. Similarly, because UDP does not provide a flow control mechanism, the TCP Window field is removed. The result of UDP performing a best-effort delivery mechanism is a relatively small transport layer protocol header, with the protocol relatively simple in comparison to TCP. The best way to understand the operation of UDP is via

Source Port	Destination Port
Message Length	Checksum

Exhibit 13. The User Datagram Protocol Header

an examination of its header. Note that similar to TCP, an IP header will prefix the UDP header, with the resulting message consisting of the IP header, UDP header, and user data referred to as a UDP datagram.

Source and Destination Port Fields

The Source and Destination Port fields are each 16 bits (or two bytes) in length and function in a manner similar to their counterparts in the TCP header. That is, the Source Port field is optionally used, with a value either randomly selected or filled in with zeroes when not in use, while the Destination Port field contains a numeric that identifies the destination application or process.

Exhibit 6 provided many examples of well-known TCP and UDP services based upon port numbers assigned in the Destination Port field of the transport layer protocol. While both TCP and UDP actually support every port number, certain services are only implemented using a particular transport layer protocol. For example, because one would not want to initiate a file transfer on a best-effort basis, FTP is implemented under TCP. In comparison, the Simple Network Management Protocol (SNMP) operates on a best-effort basis and is transported using UDP.

Length Field

The Length field indicates the length of the UDP datagram, to include header and user data that follows the header. This two-byte field has a minimum value of 8, which represents a UDP header without data.

Checksum Field

The Checksum field is two bytes in length. The use of this field is optional and its value is set to 0 if the application does not require a checksum. If a checksum is required, it is calculated on what is referred to as a pseudo-header. The pseudo-header is a logically formed header that consists of the Source and Destination addresses and the Protocol field from the IP header.

Exhibit 14 illustrates the composition of the UDP pseudo-header. Similar to the TCP pseudo-header, the UDP pseudo-header represents the fields upon which the checksum is computed and not an actual header.

IP Source Address		
IP Destination Address		
Zero	IP Protocol	UDP Length

Exhibit 14. The UDP Pseudo-Header

By verifying the contents of the two address fields through its checksum computation, the pseudo-header ensures that the UDP datagram is delivered to the correct destination network and host on the network. This does not verify the contents of the datagram.

Operation

Because the UDP header does not include within the protocol an acknowledgment capability or a sequence numbering capability, it is up to the application layer to provide this capability. This enables some applications to add this capability, whereas other applications that run on top of UDP may elect not to include one or both. As previously described, a UDP header and its data are prefixed with an IP header to form a data frame. Upon receipt of the datagram, the IP layer strips off that header and submits the remainder to UDP software at the transport layer. The UDP layer reads the destination port number as a mechanism to demultiplex the data and send it to its appropriate application.

Applications

UDP is primarily used by applications that transmit relatively short segments and for which the use of TCP would result in a high level of overhead in comparison to UDP. Common examples of applications that use UDP as a transport protocol include the Simple Network Management Protocol (SNMP), Domain Name Service (DNS), and the newly emerging series of applications from numerous vendors that transport digitized voice over the Internet and are collectively referred to as Internet telephony. Concerning Internet telephony, most implementations applications use both TCP and UDP. TCP is used for call setup, whereas UDP is used to transport digitized voice once the setup operation is completed. Because real-time voice cannot tolerate more than a fraction of a second of delay, Internet applications do not implement error detection and correction, as retransmissions would add delays that would make reconstructed voice sound awkward. Instead, because voice does not rapidly change, applications may either "smooth" an error or drop the datagram and generate a small period of noise that cannot affect the human ear. This is because most Internet telephony applications transmit

10-ms or 20-ms slices of digitized voice, making the error or even the loss of one of a few datagrams transmitting such slices of a conversation most difficult to notice.

Chapter 6

Applications and Built-in Diagnostic Tools

The TCP/IP protocol suite includes a number of built-in diagnostic tools that developers provide as associated applications running under the operating system that supports the suite. Thus, the primary focus of this chapter is on a core set of applications that can be used to obtain insight into the flow of data across a TCP/IP network. Through the use of the application programs discussed in this chapter, one can determine if the protocol stack is operating correctly on a host, whether or not a host is reachable via a network, and the delay or latency between different networks with respect to the flow of data from one network to another. Because knowledge of the Domain Name System (DNS) is important to obtain an understanding of the operation and constraints associated with different applications that provide a diagnostic testing capability, an overview of DNS is given in the first section of this chapter. Once this is accomplished, the remainder of the chapter focuses on the operation and utilization of applications that provide a diagnostic testing capability.

The DNS

This section examines the Domain Name System (DNS), as well as the database contained on a series of servers that make up the DNS. In doing so, it examines the purpose of the DNS, its structure, and the type of records stored on a DNS server.

The series of Domain Name Servers form the Domain Name System (DNS), perhaps an unfortunate naming choice as it results in a bit of confusion when referring to the system or the servers. Recognizing this potential problem, this author uses the term "DNS" to reference the system of servers.

The DNS represents both a distributed database used by TCP/IP applications to map between host names and IP addresses as well as a protocol conveyed via UDP to distribute information between clients and servers. As discussed in another section in this chapter (The Domain Name Structure), the DNS employs a hierarchical naming scheme similar to a file system tree which facilitates the mapping of host names to IP addresses and, if required, an opposite mapping from IP addresses to host names.

Purpose

The purpose of the DNS is to provide the TCP/IP community with a mechanism to translate host addresses into IP addresses because all routing is based on an examination of IP addresses. To accomplish this translation process, a series of Domain Name Servers are used to create a distributed database that contains the names and addresses of all reachable hosts on a TCP/IP network. That network can be a corporate intranet, the portion of the Internet operated by an Internet service provider (ISP), or the entire Internet.

The Domain Name Structure

Internet host names employ a hierarchical address structure. This address structure consists of a top-level domain, a sub-domain, and a host name.

Initially, top-level domain names such as .com, .gov, and .edu, as well as IP addresses, were assigned and maintained by the Internet Assigned Numbers Authority (IANA), which was responsible for the overall coordination and management of the DNS. Controversy about the IANA having sole control of top-level domains occurred during the past few years, with the result that the Internet Corporation for Assigned Names and Numbers (ICANN) was formed as a nonprofit organization to take over responsibility for the allocation of IP address space as well as for DNS and root server management. The prior controversy resulted because DNS management and IP address allocation occurs on a global basis, while most of those functions were previously performed under U.S. Government contract by the IANA and were not globally representative. Today, ICANN is responsible for the top-level domains and the management of root servers that operate at the top of each defined domain. In comparison, domain administrators where a domain can be assigned to a government agency, university, or commercial enterprise are responsible for host names and IP address assignments within their domains.

The hierarchical naming structure used by the DNS can be viewed as being very similar to a modern computer file system. That is, the structure of the DNS forms an inverted tree, with a special node at the top referred to as the root, which is not named and can be considered to house a null label. A series of domain name servers operate under the root, with the domain name of any node in the tree representing a list of labels, commencing at that node and working up to the root, using a period ("dot") to separate the labels. The name of each node, with the exception of the root, can be up to 63 characters in length.

In a computer file system one commences reference to a file by noting its path from the drive on which it is located. In the DNS, one goes in the opposite direction, adding the labels at each node, separated by a period as we progress toward the root.

The Domain Name Tree

Exhibit 1 illustrates a portion of the initial domain name tree, with the top-level domains consisting of either three-letter top-level domains or two-letter top-level domains. The two-letter top-level domains represent country domains, such as Australia (.au), France (.fr), Israel (.il), etc. There are currently seven top-level three-letter domains as indicated in Exhibit 1. In comparison, there are over 100 two-letter country identifier domains.

In examining Exhibit 1, note that .arpa represents a special domain name that is used for IP address to host name mappings. The seven three-character domain names represent different generic types of organizations. Exhibit 2 describes the meanings associated with the seven three-character domain names shown in the prior illustration. Three of the top-level domains (.com, .net, and .org) are operated on commercial principles, while the other four (.edu, .int, .mil, and .gov) have various restrictions concerning who can register names in the associated domains.

At its meeting in November 2000, the ICANN selected seven new top-level domains for negotiation of agreements that will allow them to be used in the Internet's domain name system. Exhibit 3 lists the seven new top-level domains ICANN selected and their meanings. When this book was prepared, agreements had been reached for all domains except .pro. Readers can use the URL http://www.icann.org/tlds/ to check on the status of the agreement for the .pro top-level domain as well as to determine if any additional domains are being considered.

When an organization applies for an IP address and domain name, both entries are added to the appropriate server at the domain root. For example,

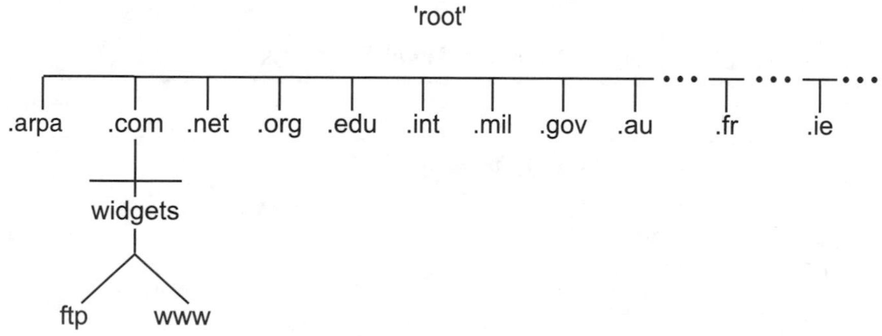

Exhibit 1. The Initial Domain Name Tree

Exhibit 2. The Seven Initial Domains

Domain Name	*Meaning*
.com	Commercial organization
.edu	Educational institution
.gov	Government institution
.mil	Military organization
.net	Network support center
.org	Organization other than above
.int	International organization

if an organization is assigned the domain *widgets.com* as a commercial organization, an entry indicating the network address for *widgets.com* and the domain widgets would be placed in the root .com domain name server.

In examining the entry under the .com domain in Exhibit 1, one notes the sub-domain labeled "widgets." Under the widgets entry, there are two entries: ftp and www. Here, ftp and www represent two host names within the widget sub-domain. The fully qualified names of each host then become ftp.widgets.com and www.widgets.com. Thus, if someone does not know the IP address of the ftp and the Web server operated by widgets.com, they can enter the fully qualified domain name for each server, and DNS will automatically perform the translation, assuming applicable DNS entries exist in a server.

Zones and Zone Transfers

In the example shown in the lower portion of Exhibit 1, "widgets" represents a sub-tree of the DNS referred to as a zone. A zone can be viewed as a DNS sub-tree that is administered separately. Whenever a new host is installed within a zone, the DNS administrator for the zone is responsible for allocating a host name and IP address for the host. The administrator would enter the host name and IP address into their name server's database. While a small organization would more than likely have only one name server, a large organization would probably have multiple domain name servers, one of

Exhibit 3. ICANN Selected New Top-Level Domains

Domain	*Meaning*
.arro	Air-transport industry
.biz	Business
.coop	Cooperatives
.info	Unrestricted use
.museum	Museums
.name	For registration by individuals
.pro	Accountants, lawyers, physicians, and other professionals

which represents a primary name server for the zone while the other servers represent secondary name servers. The primary name server will load all the information for the zone from disk files. In comparison, the secondary servers receive updates from the primary in response to their periodic queries. When a secondary domain name server receives information from its primary, the resulting transfer of information is referred to as a zone transfer.

If a domain name server does not contain the answer to a query, it must contact another name server. While each name server can be configured with the address of another name server at a higher level in the naming tree, all name servers must have a pointer to the root name server. Because the root servers know the name and IP address of each primary name server for each zone, at a minimum one zone's primary server can obtain the location for another zone's primary domain server via the services of a root server. There are currently 13 root servers located around the globe. The host names of the root servers range from A.ROOT-SERVERS.NET located in Herndon, Virginia, to M.ROOT-SERVERS.NET located in Keio, Japan. Given a general appreciation for the manner by which one domain name server can obtain information from another, one can look at how host names are converted into IP addresses, a process referred to as name resolution.

The Name Resolution Process

An IP network must have either a local DNS or employ the facilities of another organization's domain name server. For either situation, when you enter a fully qualified host name in a TCP/IP application, an application will first check its cache memory to determine if the IP address associated with the host name was previously learned. If so, it will use that IP address in memory. If not, the application will then look up the IP address of the DNS previously configured for the protocol stack to use. The local computer then transmits an address resolution request using UDP on port 53 to the IP address of the DNS. That IP address could be a DNS on the local network or the DNS operated by the organization's ISP.

The software in the TCP/IP protocol stack that examines the host name and returns the IP address (or receives an IP address and looks up the host name) is referred to as a name resolver. Exhibit 4 illustrates the relationship of the name resolver to an HTTP (HyperText Transport Protocol) Web browsing operation in which one entered a host name for the address in the browser. Note that the name resolver is invoked by the Web browser and returns the IP address prior to TCP opening a connection. If an application used UDP as the transport protocol, the result would be similar, with the name resolver returning the IP address prior to requesting UDP to open a connection.

Upon receipt of the address resolution request, the DNS first checks its cache memory in an attempt to determine if the IP address was previously resolved. If so, it responds to the computer's request with the host's associated IP address, allowing the computer to use the destination host IP address to create an IP datagram that a router can route. If the DNS did not previously

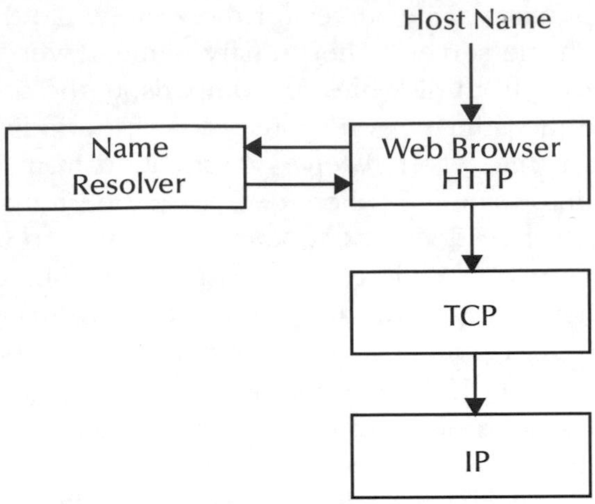

Exhibit 4. The Name Resolver Represents a Software Module in the TCP/IP Protocol Stack that Receives a Host Name and Returns an IP Address, or Receives an IP Address and Returns a Host Name

learn the IP address and is not responsible for the domain where the fully qualified domain name host resides, it will forward the request to a higher level in the DNS hierarchy. To do so requires the DNS to have a pointer record that literally points to the address of the next-level DNS. For example, a DNS on a local network would have a pointer record to the DNS operated by the Internet service provider (ISP) that provides the organization with access to the Internet. If the ISP's DNS does not have an entry for the requested host, another pointer record will be used to route the address resolution request to a "higher authority." That higher authority could be a network service provider (NSP) and eventually the top-level DNS for the domain of the fully qualified host name.

Data Flow

To illustrate the potential flow of data during the address resolution process, consider Exhibit 5. In Exhibit 5, the user at host gil.smart.edu just entered the host name www.cash.gov into his or her browser and pressed the Enter key, which in effect commences the resolution process. When the address resolution process commences, a UDP datagram flows to the local DNS on the domain smart.edu as indicated by ①. Assuming that the DNS does not have an entry for the network address of the requested host (www.cash.gov), the resolution request flows upward to the next DNS via the use of a pointer record in the local DNS. This is indicated by numbers ②, ③, and ④ in Exhibit 5. Assuming the next DNS, which is shown as serving the domain isp.com, does not have an entry for www.cash.gov, the resolution request continues its flow up the DNS hierarchy until it will either reach a server that can resolve the request

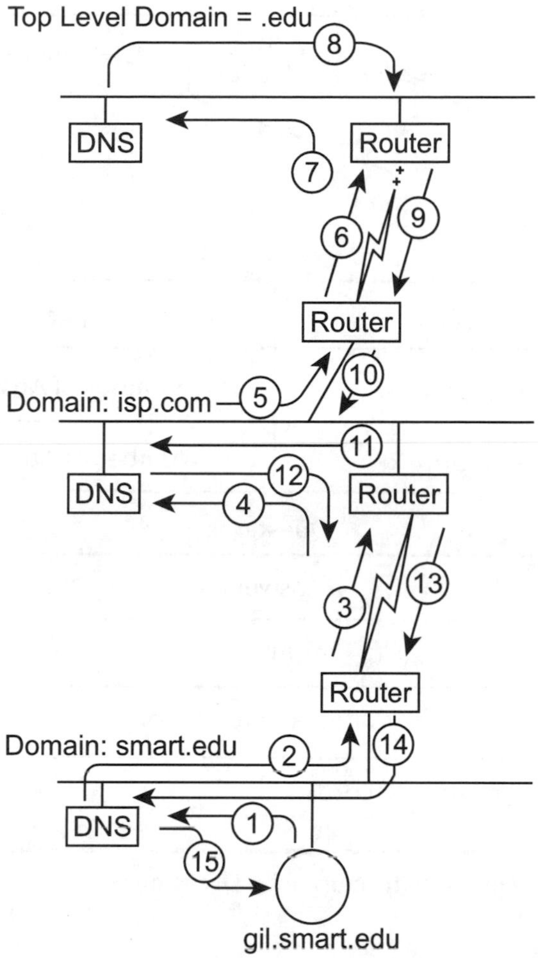

Exhibit 5. Potential Dataflow during the Address Resolution Process

or arrives at the top-level DNS for the domain for which the host name is to be resolved. This is indicated by ⑤, ⑥, and ⑦ in Exhibit 5.

Once the address is resolved, the resolution does not flow directly back to the original DNS. Instead, the resolution flows back to each DNS in the hierarchy, providing each server with the ability to update its resolution table. This is indicated by ⑨, ⑩, ⑪, ⑫, ⑬, and ⑭, in Exhibit 5. Finally, the local DNS returns the resolved IP address, as indicated in ⑮. At this point in time, the station can now form an IP datagram using a destination IP address obtained from the address resolution process. One key exception to the previously mentioned address resolution process is when a name server does not have a pointer record to a higher level name server. Because each name server must have a pointer to the top of the domain, the name would then send its query directly to the server at the top of Exhibit 5.

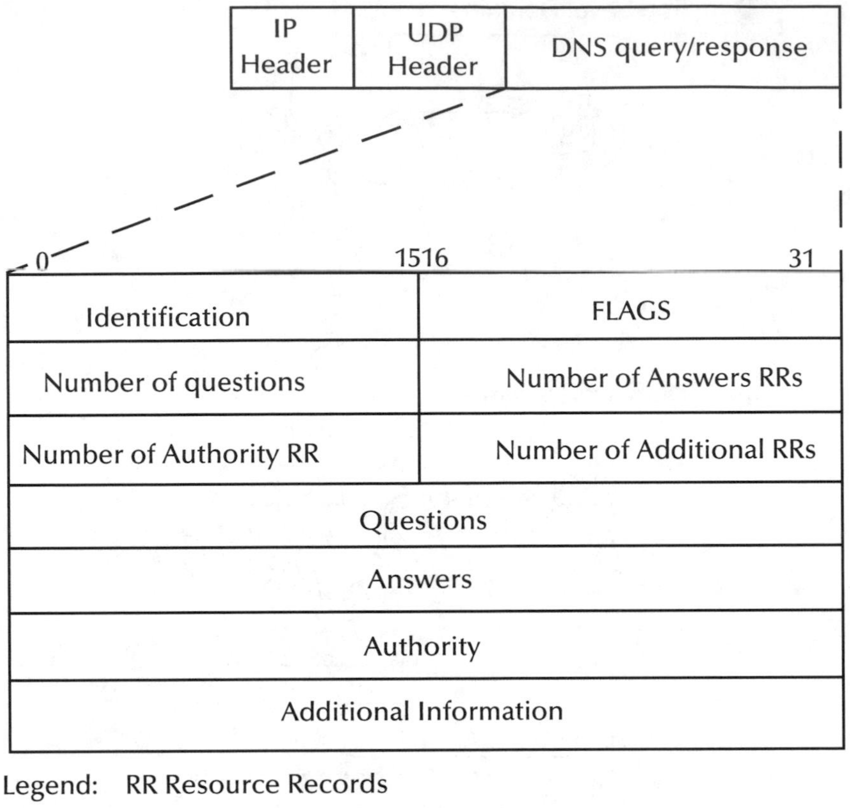

Exhibit 6. Transmission and Structure of a DNS Query and Response

Message Format

If the name resolver on the local host does not have a copy of the IP address associated with a host name (or host name associated with an IP address), it must form and transmit a DNS query to the local domain name server. The DNS query follows a predefined message format and is transported via UDP.

The top portion of Exhibit 6 illustrates the transmission of a DNS query/response within an IP datagram. The lower portion of Exhibit 6 illustrates the format of the DNS query and response. Both DNS message queries and responses use the format illustrated in the lower portion of Exhibit 6, with certain fields only applicable to each type of message. To obtain an appreciation for how the DNS message conveys information, one can examine the fields in the query and their use in both DNS queries and responses.

Identification Field

The 16-bit Identification field is set by the client and returned by the domain name server. Because clients can have multiple requests outstanding (just think of a multiprocessing system with several windows open supporting Telnet and Web browsing), the Identification field associates the response to a particular query.

Flags Field

The Flags field contains eight distinct sub-fields that vary in length from one to four bits. The Flags field is subdivided into sub-fields as indicated below:

bit 0	1-4	5	6	7	8	9-11	12 15
Q/R	OPCODE	AA	T	RD	RA	Set to 0	Return Code

- *Q/R bit sub-field.* Bit position 0 in the Flags field is set to 0 if the message is a DNS query. If the message is a response, the bit position is set to 1.
- *OPCODE sub-field.* Bits 1 through 4 define the operation to be performed. A value of 0 represents a standard host name to IP address query. In comparison, an OPCODE setting of 1 represents an inverse query. To check on the status of a DNS server, the OPCODE is set to a value of 2.
- *AA sub-field.* The fifth bit position in the Flags field denotes whether or not the domain name server is authoritative for the domain in the Question field. When set, this indicates an Authoritative Answer (AA).
- *Message Truncated bit sub-field.* The sixth bit in the Flags field is set if the message was truncated (T). When set, this indicates that the total length of the reply exceeded 512 bytes and only the first 512 bytes of the reply were returned.
- *Recursion Desired (RD) sub-field.* The seventh bit in the Flags field is the Recursion Desired (RD) sub-field. This bit can be set in a query and is then returned in the response.
- *Recursion Available (RA) sub-field.* The eighth bit in the Flags field is the Recursion Available (RA) sub-field. When set, this indicates that recursion is permitted.
- *Return Code sub-field.* The last sub-field in the Flags field is four bits in length. This sub-field represents the Return Code, which indicates if an error occurred. Current values for this sub-field include 0 for no error and 3 for a name error. Given an appreciation for the use of the sub-fields in the Flags field, one can focus on the other fields in the DNS query and response.

Number of Questions Field

The Number of Questions field contains a count of the entries in the "Questions" section in the message.

Number of Answers Field

The Number of Answers field contains the number of answers received from a remote name resolver. This number provides a count of the entries in the Answers section of the response.

Answers, Authority, and Additional Information Fields

The Answers, Authority, and Additional Information fields consist of a set of resource records (RR) that provide a description of domain names and mappings. The resource record is transmitted in response to a query contained in the Question section of a domain name server message. Thus, to obtain an appreciation of the resource record, one needs to first focus attention on the composition of the sub-fields within the Question section of a query message.

Question Field Composition

Exhibit 7 illustrates the sub-fields within the Question section of a domain name server query message. The Query Domain name sub-field is variable in length. The client is responsible for completing the entries in the sub-fields within the Question field, which are then returned by the queried domain name server with the applicable response contained in the Answers field.

Answers Field Composition

The response to a query results in the inclusion of one or more resource records in the Answers field, which is returned to the client. The format of the resource records used in messages returned by domain name servers is shown in Exhibit 8. Note that there are six sub-fields that make up a resource record. The first sub-field, Resource Domain Name, contains the destination name and is variable in length. The Type sub-field defines the type of data record conveyed, that the Class sub-field specifies the record class. The Time to Live sub-field contains an integer that indicates the time in seconds that the information in the resource record can be cached. The Resource Data Length sub-field specifies the number of bytes contained in the Resource Data sub-field, permitting the latter to be variable in length.

0	31
Query Domain Name	
Query Type	Query Class

Exhibit 7. The Subfields within the Question Field Are Completed by the Name Resolver Operating on the Client

0	31
Resource Domain Name	
Type	Class
Time to Live	Resource Data Length
Resource Data	

Exhibit 8. The Format of Domain Name Server Resource Records

Time Consideration

If a fully qualified domain name cannot have its IP address resolved by the local DNS, one or more additional servers must be queried. This means that datagrams conveying address resolution information will flow over relatively low-speed WAN connections for which the time delay then depends on the operating rate of those connections and other activity flowing on each connection, as well as the processing being performed by routers that form the WAN. Because the DNS resolution process on a host results in the setting of a timer, if too much time occurs during the resolution process, the timer will timeout or expire. When this situation occurs, an error will be generated by the protocol stack that will be used by the application to generate an error message. One popular error message generated by a browser informs the user to "check the destination name spelling and try again!" The reason this message does not mention anything about the address resolution process is probably due to the fact that most people using browsers have no knowledge of the process and a more descriptive error message might be counterproductive.

DNS Records

Each DNS can contain a series of different types of records as well as multiple records for one or more record types. Exhibit 9 lists some of the more popular types of DNS records.

In examining the record types listed in Exhibit 9, note that a domain can have multiple name servers or multiple mail exchange servers. Also note that while the A record provides information necessary for an address resolution process, the PTR record type supports reverse lookups. Exhibit 10 illustrates an example of a UNIX Zone file named "smart.edu.zone" for the domain smart.edu. Assume that the Class C address 198.78.46.0 was assigned to the domain smart.edu. Further assume that the server name, dns.smart.edu, is the name server, and that mail.smart.edu is the name of the mail server.

In examining the entries in Exhibit 10, note that the string "IN" is used to indicate an Internet address and dates from a period where different types of addresses could be placed in a DNS database. Also note that names and host addresses end with a trailing dot (.) or period to indicate that they are an absolute name or address rather than a relative address.

Exhibit 9. Examples of DNS Record Types

Record Type	*Description*
A	Contains an IP address to be associated with a host name
MX	Contains the address of a mail exchange system(s) for the domain
NS	Contains the address of the name server(s) for the domain
CNAME	Canonical Name records contain an alias host name to associate with the host names contained in the record
PTR	Contains a host name to be associated with an IP address in the record
SOA	The Start of Authority records indicate the administrative name server for a domain as well as administrative information about the server

Exhibit 10. The smart.edu.zone File

```
;Start of Authority (SOA) record
 smart.edu. IN SOA dns.smart.edu.owner.smart.edu(
                   19960105 ;serial#(date format)
                      10800 ;refresh(3 hours)
                        3600 ;retry(1 hour)
                      604800 ;expire(1 week)
                      86400) ;TTL(1 day)
;Name Server (NS) record
 smart.edu. IN NS  dns.smart.edu.

;Mail Exchange (MX) record
 smart.edu. IN MX  20 mail.smart.edu
;Address (A) records.
 router.smart.edu. IN A    198.78.46.1
 dns.smart.edu.    IN A    198.78.46.2
 mail.smart.edu.   IN A    198.78.46.3
 gil.smart.edu.    IN A    198.78.46.30
;Aliases in canonical Name (CNAME) record
 www.smart.edu IN CNAME gil.smart.edu.
```

The SOA Record

The first record normally placed in a Zone file for a domain server is the Start of Authority (SOA) record. Not only does this record govern the manner by which a domain name server and secondary servers, if any, operate, but in addition, the ability to read the contents of this record can provide information about the manner by which another domain operates. As noted later in this chapter, one can examine the contents of a domain name server database through the use of the NSLOOKUP application program.

The serial number in the SOA record identifies the version of the DNS database. This value can be used by secondary servers as a metric concerning updating as the number increments whenever the database changes. The refresh value informs the server how often to check for updated information. If the secondary server cannot connect to the primary, it will use the retry value as the time period to wait before retrying. The expire time tells the secondary server when to stop answering queries about the primary when it cannot contact the primary. This value assumes that no answer is better than a bad answer and is shown set to a week (604,800 seconds) in Exhibit 10.

Checking Records

Upon further examination of the entries in Exhibit 10, one notes that the router in the 198.78.46.0 network has the host address .1, while the DNS has the host address .2, and the mail server has the address .3. Also note that the host gil.smart.edu has the alias www.smart.edu, and that the entry of either host name will return the IP address 198.78.46.30. Thus, by checking the records in a name server, it becomes possible to not only obtain the IP address for a particularly qualified domain name, but, in addition, to discover the alias or aliases assigned to one or more hosts in a domain. Given an appreciation for the role and operation of the domain name system and the servers used in the DNS, one can now focus on use of a series of built-in diagnostic tools provided as application programs in most versions of TCP/IP.

Diagnostic Tools

Most operating systems with a TCP/IP protocol stack include several application programs that can be used to obtain information about the state of the network or a particular host. Examples of such applications include Ping, traceroute, pathping, nslookup, and finger. Each of these applications will be covered in this section.

Ping

Based on contradictory tales, the name "Ping" was given to an application because it either resembled the use of radar or functioned as an acronym for the full name, Packet Internetwork Groper. Regardless of whether the function of electronic equipment or the development of an acronym accounted for its name, Ping is one of the most widely used tools — if not *the* most widely used tool — bundled as an application in TCP/IP software.

Operation

Through the use of the Ping application program, a series of Internet Control Message Protocol (ICMP) Echo type messages are transmitted to a distant host. If the host is both reachable and active, it will respond to each ICMP Echo message with an ICMP Echo Response message. Not only does the use of Ping then tell you that the distant host is both reachable and active, but the application also notes the time the Echo left the computer and the reply was received to compute the round-trip delay time. Because timing can be very critical for such applications as Voice-over-IP and interactive query/response, the use of Ping may inform one ahead of time whether or not an application is suitable for use on the Internet or a corporate intranet.

Implementation

There is no standard that governs the manner by which Ping is implemented and different vendor versions, such as UNIX and Windows NT, may differ slightly from one another. One common form of the Ping command to invoke this application is shown below:

```
ping [-q -v] [-r] [-c Count] [-I Wait] [-s size] host
```

where:

- `-q` selects quiet mode that only results in the display of summary information at start-up and completion
- `-v` selects verbose output mode that results in display of ICMP packets received in addition to Echo Requests
- `-r` selects a route option that displays the route of returned datagrams
- `-c` specifies the number of Echo Requests to be sent prior to concluding the test
- `-i` specifies the number of seconds to wait between transmitted datagrams containing an Echo Request
- `-s` specifies the number of data bytes to be transmitted
- `host` specifies the IP address or host name of the destination to be queried

In examining the above options, note that some older implementations of Ping would run until interrupted with a CTRL-C unless a count value was specified through the use of the `-c` option. Also note that many versions of Ping differ with respect to the default wait time between transmitted Echo Requests. Some implementations may transmit echo requests 250 ms apart as a default, while other implementations may use a default of 500 ms, one second, or some other time value. A third item concerning the options listed above concerns the packet size specification variable, `-s`. This variable is used to specify the number of data bytes transmitted and results in a total packet size becoming the specified packet size plus 8, because there are eight bytes in the ICMP header. This means that the default on some implementations is

56 bytes, which results in a 64-byte packet. Given an appreciation for the options supported by Ping, one can now focus on its use within a TCP/IP environment by examining the use of the Microsoft Windows version of Ping, which one can access from the Command Prompt in Windows.

Using Windows NT Ping

Exhibit 11 illustrates the Windows NT Ping help menu that is displayed when one enters the name of the application without options. In examining the help screen shown in Exhibit 11, note that the `-t` option will result in the Ping application continuously transmitting Echo Request packets until interrupted. Unfortunately, this is a favorite attack method used by unsophisticated hackers. Its use is discusssed later in this chapter and in more detail in Chapter 8 and 9 when discussing security in more detail. Also note that Microsoft supports several route options as well as a time to live (TTL) option. Typically, most applications set a TTL default value of 250 to prevent a datagram from infinitely wandering the Internet or a private intranet. As the datagram is received by a router, it decrements the TTL value by 1 and compares the result to zero. If the value is greater than zero, it forwards the datagram; otherwise, it places the datagram into the great bit bucket in the sky. By setting the TTL value higher than the default, one can then obtain the capability to reach a host that requires routing through a large number of routers that might otherwise be unreachable from a particular location.

To illustrate the use of Ping, one can ping two locations on the Internet. The first location is the real Whitehouse Web site located at www.whitehouse.gov. The top portion of Exhibit 12 illustrates this operation. Note the response "Request timed out" displayed four times. Microsoft's implementation of Ping results in four Echo Request ICMP packets being transmitted as IP

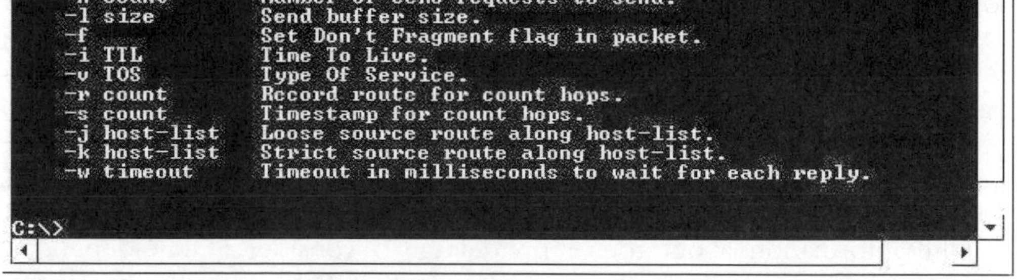


```
C:\>ping

Usage: ping [-t] [-a] [-n count] [-l size] [-f] [-i TTL] [-v TOS]
            [-r count] [-s count] [[-j host-list] | [-k host-list]]
            [-w timeout] destination-list

Options:
    -t             Ping the specifed host until interrupted.
    -a             Resolve addresses to hostnames.
    -n count       Number of echo requests to send.
    -l size        Send buffer size.
    -f             Set Don't Fragment flag in packet.
    -i TTL         Time To Live.
    -v TOS         Type Of Service.
    -r count       Record route for count hops.
    -s count       Timestamp for count hops.
    -j host-list   Loose source route along host-list.
    -k host-list   Strict source route along host-list.
    -w timeout     Timeout in milliseconds to wait for each reply.

C:\>
```

Exhibit 11. Microsoft Windows Ping Options

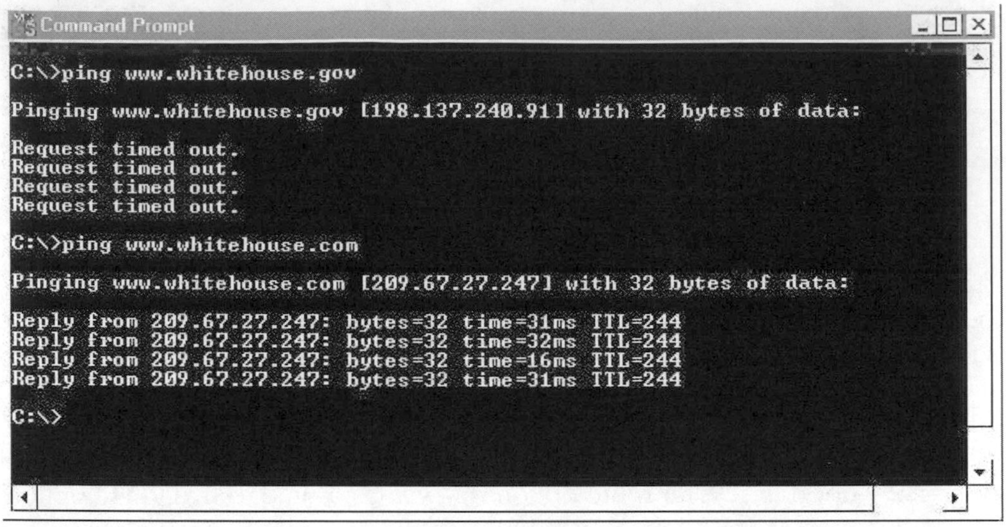

Exhibit 12. Using Ping

datagrams to the destination specified in the Ping command line. The reason the request timed out has nothing to do with the TTL value. Instead, the White House uses a firewall to block pings because it is one of a number of weapons unsophisticated hackers like to use. Chapter 8 and 9 provide greater detail concerning how one can block pings.

The lower portion of Exhibit 12 illustrates a second ping, a commercial site Web server whose address is similar, but not the same as "the White House." This commercial site Web address is www.whitehouse.com. Note that Ping automatically resolves the entered host name into an IP address. Also note from the four replies that the round-trip delay varies from a low of 16 ms to a high of 32 ms. This variance is due to the fact that the path between source and destination is subject to random dataflows from other users. This can delay the datagrams one's host is transmitting that contain ICMP Echo Requests.

Resolution Time Considerations

One item that deserves a bit of attention is the fact that it is quite possible for the first response to be much longer than subsequent responses. The reason for this is the fact that if one enters a host name that was not previously resolved, DNS will be required to obtain the IP address associated with the name entered on the command line. Although the example shown in Exhibit 12 does not indicate a long delay and, in fact, the first response was 1 ms less than the second, this is not always the case. If a site that is not that popular and whose IP address and host name was not previously learned, one might require information about round-trip delay. To consider a time-dependent application, such as Voice-over-IP, it is a good idea to periodically transmit pings throughout the day and discard the first response if it appears high due to the address resolution process.

Applications

Although Ping is quite often used to determine round-trip delay, that is not its primary use. Whenever a station is configured and connected to a network, one of the first things one should do is ping the station. If one obtains a response, this will indicate that the TCP/IP protocol stack is active. This will also mean that the station is properly cabled to the network and that its network adapter is operational. Otherwise, the protocol stack, cable, or network adapter may represent a problem. One can check out the protocol stack by pinging the address 127.0.0.1 or any address on the 127.0.0.0 network because this invokes a loopback. If one obtains a valid result, one would then run diagnostics on the network adapter card provided by the vendor and check or swap cables with a device known to work to isolate the problem. If one attempts to ping a host on a different network, it may not be a simple process to walk over to the destination if all one receives is a timeout message. The cause of a lack of response can range in scope from an inoperative router to an inactive destination. Fortunately, one can obtain insight into the route to the destination through the use of another program called traceroute.

Traceroute

Traceroute, as its name implies, traces the route to a specified destination that will be placed in the application command line. Similar to Ping, there are several variations concerning the implementation of Traceroute. A common form of the Traceroute command on a UNIX host is:

```
traceroute [-t count] [-q count] [-w count] [-p port number]
host
```

where:

- `-t` specifies the maximum time-to-live (TTL) value, with a default of 30 used
- `-q` specifies the number of UDP packets transmitted with each TTL setting; the default is usually 3
- `-w` specifies the time in seconds to wait for an answer from a router
- `-q` represents an invalid port address at the destination; port 33434 is commonly used

Operation

A better understanding of traceroute options requires an explanation of the manner by which this application operates. Thus, prior to observing the operation of the program and discussing its options, one can focus on how the program operates.

Traceroute works by transmitting a sequence of UDP datagrams to an invalid port address on the destination host. Using common default settings,

Traceroute begins by transmitting three datagrams, each with its TTL field value set to 1. As soon as the first router in the path to the destination receives the datagram, it subtracts 1 from the value of its TTL field and compares the result to 0. Because the value equals 0, the datagram will be considered to have expired, and the router will return an ICMP Time Exceeded Message (TEM) to the originator, indicating that the datagram expired. Because the originator noted the time the datagram was transmitted and the time a response was received, it is able to compute the round-trip delay to the first router. It will also note that the IP address of that router is contained in the datagram transmitting the ICMP TEM message.

To locate the second router in the path to the destination, Traceroute will increment the TTL field value by 1. Thus, the next sequence of datagrams will flow through the first router, but will be discarded by the second router, resulting in another sequence of TEM messages being returned to the originator. This process will continue until the datagrams either reach the destination or the default TTL value is reached, and the application operating on the source terminates. If the datagrams reach the destination, because they are attempting to access an invalid port on the destination host, the destination will return a sequence of ICMP destination unreachable messages, indicating to the Traceroute program that its job is finished. With an understanding of how the program operates, one can examine its use with a version included in Microsoft's Windows operating system.

Using Microsoft Windows Tracert

The Microsoft Windows version of Traceroute is named Tracert. This application program is similar to Ping in that it is operated from the command prompt within Windows.

Exhibit 13 illustrates the use of the Tracert program without any parameters to display a help screen for the program. In examining Exhibit 13, note that the Microsoft implementation of Traceroute supports four options. Probably the most commonly used option is the `-h` option, the use of which allows one to change the TTL default of a maximum of 30 hops normally used by the program. The other options available for use include the -d option, which precludes the resolution of IP addresses to host names; the -j option, which results in the use of a loose source route; and the -j option, which permits one to specify a timeout value that the program will use when waiting for a reply.

Tracing a Route

To illustrate how Tracert can supplement the use of Ping, one can utilize the former to trace the route from the author's network to the real White House, the one operated by the federal government. In the previous attempt at pinging the White House, efforts were not successful because each ping returned a timeout message.

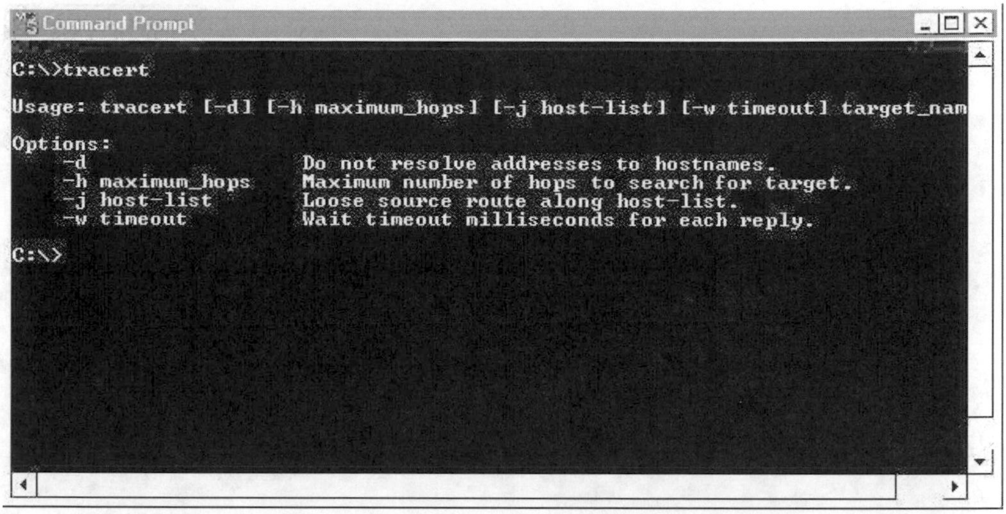

Exhibit 13. Microsoft's Implementation of Traceroute (Called Tracert) Provides Users with Four Options

Exhibit 14 illustrates the use of Microsoft's version of Traceroute to trace the route to the White House Web server. Note that when the program is first executed, it performs an address resolution and displays the IP address of the destination. Also note that the program displays the fact that it is tracing the route to the destination using a maximum of 30 hops, which represents the default value of the application.

Note from Exhibit 14 that there were eight routers in the path to the White House, after which one could not access the White House network. The eighth router was located in Herndon, Virginia, and according to information returned by the router is operated by PSI.net, an Internet service provider. It was not possible to trace the full route into the White House network because the router at the White House Web site was programmed to block both pings and traceroutes. Thus, this resulted in the generation of a "destination net unreachable" message.

In examining the entries in Exhibit 14, one also sees that the Microsoft implementation tries three times or more to accurately transmit a sequence of three datagrams with the same TTL field values. Focus now on the round-trip delay and router for each route. The first path, which is from the author's workstation to the router located at IP address 205.131.175.2, required under 10 ms for each of three datagrams to reach, and for the computer issuing the tracert to receive a response. The second path was to the router operated by bbn.planet in Atlanta and resulted in a round-trip delay of 31 ms from the author's computer to that router. Looking at the router information returned, one sees that some routers provide a description of their location and operator and other identifiers, while other routers simply provide their IP address. While all routers in this example returned some information, upon occasion some routers may not respond to a TTL field value of zero condition and will simply throw the datagram away. When this situation occurs, the Traceroute

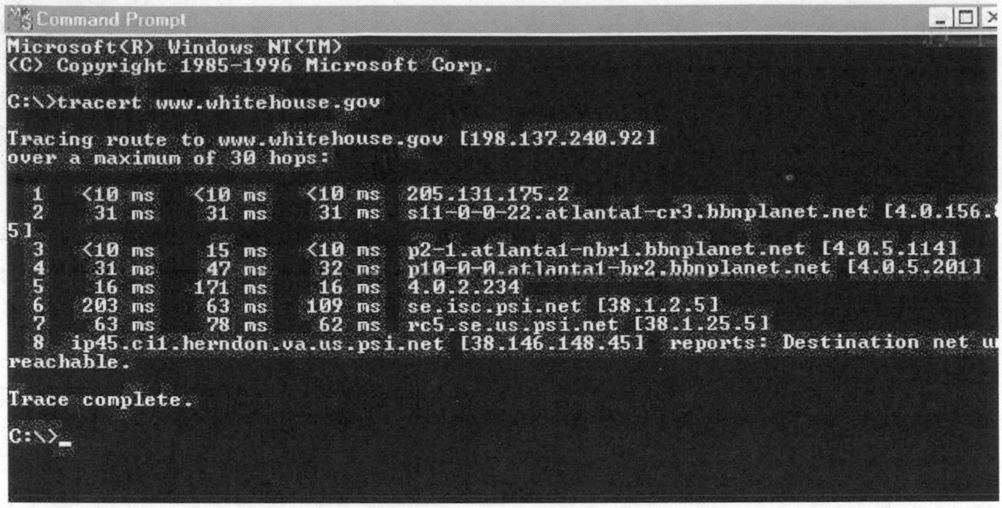

```
Command Prompt
Microsoft(R) Windows NT(TM)
(C) Copyright 1985-1996 Microsoft Corp.

C:\>tracert www.whitehouse.gov

Tracing route to www.whitehouse.gov [198.137.240.92]
over a maximum of 30 hops:

  1   <10 ms   <10 ms   <10 ms  205.131.175.2
  2    31 ms    31 ms    31 ms  s11-0-0-22.atlanta1-cr3.bbnplanet.net [4.0.156.
5]
  3   <10 ms    15 ms   <10 ms  p2-1.atlanta1-nbr1.bbnplanet.net [4.0.5.114]
  4    31 ms    47 ms    32 ms  p10-0-0.atlanta1-br2.bbnplanet.net [4.0.5.201]
  5    16 ms   171 ms    16 ms  4.0.2.234
  6   203 ms    63 ms   109 ms  se.isc.psi.net [38.1.2.5]
  7    63 ms    78 ms    62 ms  rc5.se.us.psi.net [38.1.25.5]
  8  ip45.ci1.herndon.va.us.psi.net [38.146.148.45]  reports: Destination net u
reachable.

Trace complete.

C:\>_
```

Exhibit 14. Using Microsoft's Tracert to Trace the Route to the White House Web Server

program's attempt will time out and information for that router hop will be denoted through the use of an asterisk (*) as being unavailable.

Applications

As indicated by this particular use of Traceroute, this utility program traces the route to a destination. In doing so, it displays the round-trip delay to each router hop, enabling one to determine if one or more routers are causing an excessive amount of delay on the path to a destination. Many times, Traceroute can be a valuable tool in determining where network bottlenecks reside. In addition, one can use this tool as a mechanism to identify, to a degree, where along a path a failure of a communications circuit or hardware occurred if a destination should become unreachable. The reason for "to a degree" is due to the fact that if either a circuit becomes inoperative or a router fails, Traceroute would not be able to distinguish between the two situations. Before Traceroute can be used to isolate the general location of a problem, it is a valuable tool one should consider using either by itself or as a supplement to Ping.

PathPing

Based upon our prior coverage of Ping and Traceroute, it is apparent why many people refer to them as the "dynamic duo" of testing applications. Perhaps recognizing the utility of both applications, Microsoft combined their functionality into one that was given the name PathPing. PathPing is only available under Windows 2000 and does not represent a common TCP/IP application incorporated, like Ping and Traceroute, into every protocol stack. Despite its limited availability, it is a useful tool.

PathPing can be considered to represent a route tracing tool that combines the features of Ping and Traceroute commands with additional capability. Similar to Ping and Traceroute, PathPing operates under the Command Prompt. When invoked, PathPing transmits packets to each router along the path to the specified host. Where PathPing differs from its dynamic duo cousins is in the fact that it includes options that permit testing for quality-of-service (QoS) as well as adds a statistical computation capability when the results are summarized.

Exhibit 15 illustrates the general format of the PathPing command that is obtained by entering the commands without options. While the first three and the sixth options (`-n`, `-h`, `-q`, and `-w`) are similar to those supported by Traceroute, the other four options represent significant additions that extend the capability of this utility program. Focus now on the use of these four new options.

The -p Option

The `-p` option provides the ability to define a wait period in milliseconds between pings. If one wants to gather statistics over a long period of time but issue queries on a periodic basis, one would use the -p option followed by a wait period value in milliseconds.

The -q Option

The `-q` option provides the ability to control the number of queries per hop. By using the `-q` option in conjunctions with the `-p` option, one can control

```
Command Prompt
Microsoft Windows 2000 [Version 5.00.2195]
(C) Copyright 1985-1999 Microsoft Corp.

E:\>pathping

Usage: pathping [-n] [-h maximum_hops] [-g host-list] [-p period]
                [-q num_queries] [-w timeout] [-t] [-R] [-r] target_name

Options:
    -n                  Do not resolve addresses to hostnames.
    -h maximum_hops     Maximum number of hops to search for target.
    -g host-list        Loose source route along host-list.
    -p period           Wait period milliseconds between pings.
    -q num_queries      Number of queries per hop.
    -w timeout          Wait timeout milliseconds for each reply.
    -T                  Test connectivity to each hop with Layer-2 priority tags.

    -R                  Test if each hop is RSVP aware.

E:\>_
```

Exhibit 15. Microsoft Combined the Features of Ping and Traceroute in Windows 2000 and Added Additional Functionality, Calling the New Program PathPing

the periodic testing of a route from source to destination whose results can be much more meaningful than obtained from the use of Ping or Traceroute by themselves.

The `-T` Option

The `-T` option represents one of two QoS tests added to PathPing. The `-T` option tests the connectivity with each hop in the path to the destination to determine their support of the IEEE 802.1Q and 802.1p specifications. The 802.1Q specification results in the addition of several fields to a layer 2 frame that permit virtual LANs (vLANs) to be associated with a frame. One of the fields added under the 802.1Q specification is a three-bit priority field. The use of that field is specified by the IEEE 802.1p specification.

The `-R` Option

The second option that deals with QoS is the `-R` option. This option will test each hop to determine if the router is Resource Reservation (RSVP) Protocol aware. By using PathPing with the `-R` option, one can determine if it is possible for the routers on the path to the destination to support the reservation of bandwidth for a time-critical application.

NSLOOKUP

A fourth built-in application program that can be used to provide valuable information is NSLOOKUP. Unlike Ping and Traceroute, which are implemented in essentially all versions of TCP/IP software, NSLOOKUP is available in most, but not all, operating systems that support TCP/IP.

Operation

NSLOOKUP is a name server lookup program. This program can be employed to examine entries in the DNS database of a particular host or domain. There are several ways NSLOOKUP can be implemented, with the most common being an interactive query mode. In the interactive query mode, one would simply type the command "nslookup." The other method NSLOOKUP supports is a single query mode. The general format of the latter is:

```
nslookup [IP-address\host-name]
```

If one enters the program name by itself, one will be placed in its interactive mode. In the interactive mode, the program uses the greater than sign (>) as a prompt for input. Exhibit 16 illustrates an example of the use of NSLOOKUP. In this example, after entering the command "nslookup," the program responds with the name and address of the default name server. This is the name server whose address is configured in the TCP/IP protocol stack operating on the workstation one is using to run the program. That name server, which is serv1.opm.gov. in this example, will be used to resolve each request.

In the example shown in Exhibit 16, the next step is to enter the Web server host address for Yale University. Note that NSLOOKUP not only resolved the IP address of www.yale.edu, but, in addition, provided the true name of the Web server because the response indicated that www.yale.edu is an alias.

In the lower portion of Exhibit 16, note the prompt in the form of a greater than sign (>). Because the interactive query mode of NSLOOKUP was used, this prompt indicates that it is waiting for an NSLOOKUP command. Because NSLOOKUP queries a name server, one can use the program to retrieve information about different types of name server records. To do so, one must use the "set type=" command, followed by the record type, and then inform one's local DNS server of the distant DNS to be queried.

Exhibit 17 provides a list of NSLOOKUP set of query record types one can enter to display a particular type of domain name server record. For example, entering "set q=VID" would be used to specify a query based on user ID.

Finding Information about Mail Servers at Yale

Exhibit 18 represents a continuation of the querying of the Yale University DNS. In this example, the record type was set to MX and the domain yale.edu entered. This resulted in the local DNS springing into action and returning a sequence of information about the mail server used at Yale. In examining the entries in Exhibit 18, one sees that the response to the query resulted in a listing of both mail exchanger and name server host addresses and IP addresses for that university, providing significant information about its network resources.

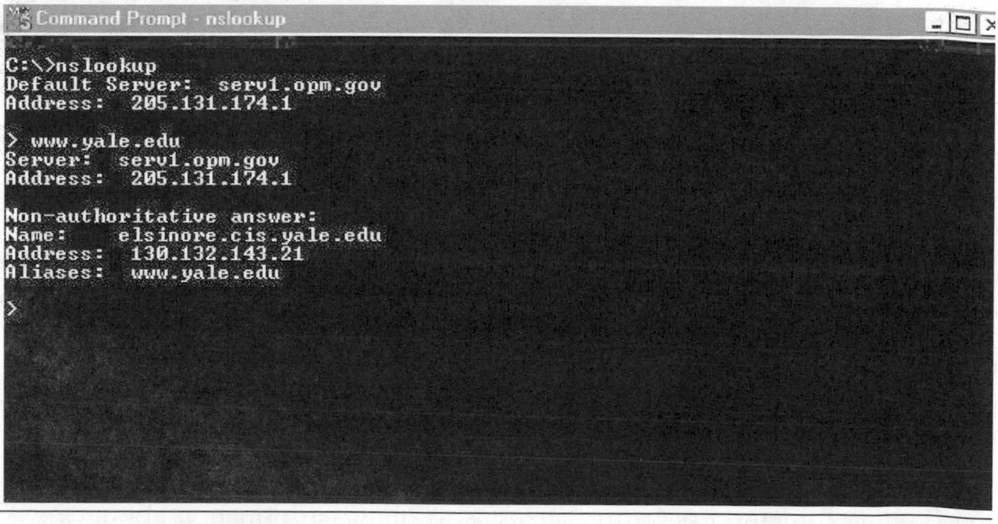

Exhibit 16. Using Microsoft's NSLOOKUP to Query the Yale University Server

Exhibit 17. NSLOOKUP Set Querytype Values

Nslookup: set q[uerytype]

Changes the type of information query. More information about types can be found in Request for Comment (RFC) 1035. (The set type command is a synonym for set querytype.)
set q[uerytype]=value
Default = A.

Parameters

Value	
A.	Computer's IP address
ANY	All types of data
CNAME	Canonical name for an alias
GID	Group identifier of a group name
HINFO	Computer's CPU and operating system type
MB	Mailbox domain name
MG	Mail group member
MINFO	Mailbox or mail list information
MR	Mail rename domain name
MX	Mail exchanger
NS	DNS name server for the named zone
PTR	Computer name if the query is an IP address, otherwise the pointer to other information
SOA	DNS domain's start-of-authority record
TXT	Text information
UID	User ID
UINFO	User information
WKS	Well-known service description

Viewing the SOA Record

One can continue the quest for knowledge about Yale University by changing the record type to SOA and again entering "yale.com" as the domain name. Exhibit 19 illustrates the resulting display from the previously described operations. In examining the entries in Exhibit 19, note that Yale University operates four name servers. Also note that the IP address for each server has also been obtained.

Protecting Server Information

One common method of hacker attack is to obtain information about one or more users by listing A records. Due to this, many organizations will block the ability of those records to be retrieved. Thus, if one sets the record type to "A" and again enters the domain yale.com, one would not obtain a listing of A records because Yale blocks their retrieval by foreign name servers.

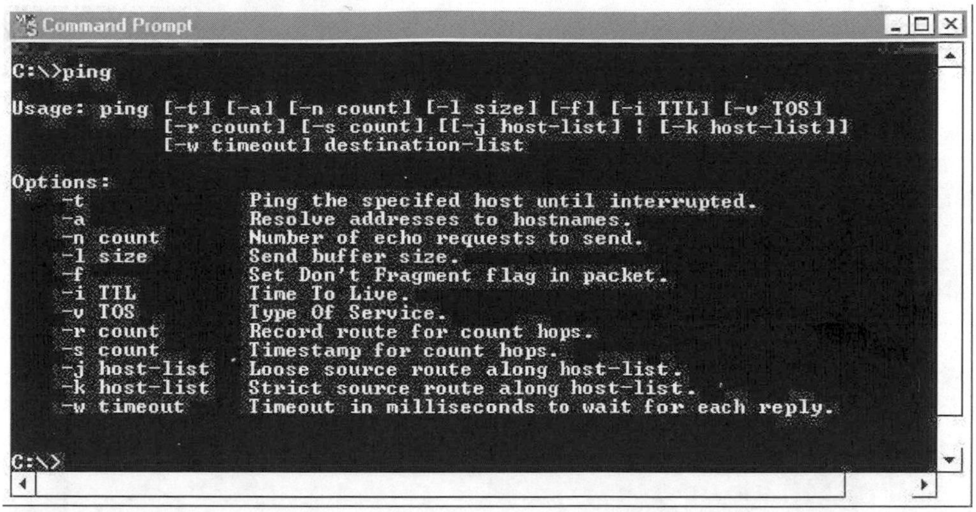

Exhibit 18. Using NSLOOKUP to Retrieve MX Records from the Yale University Name Server

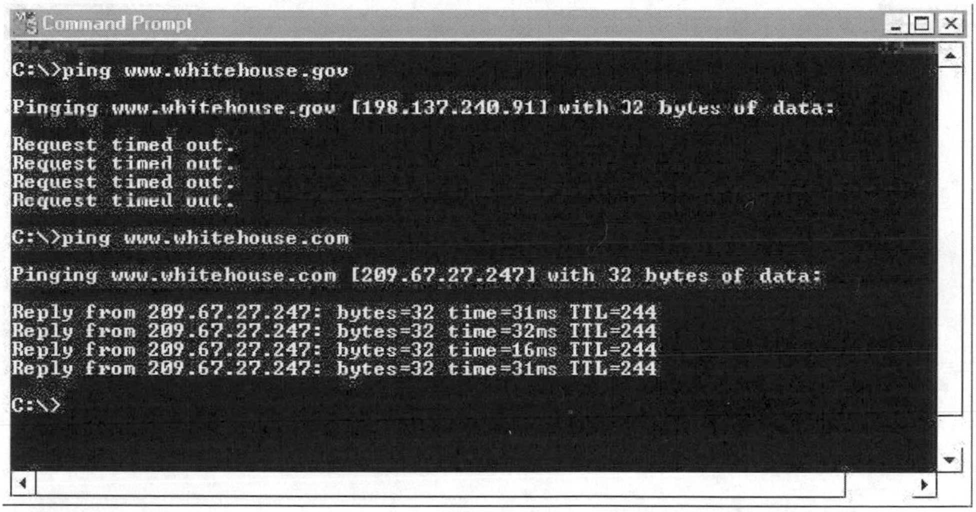

Exhibit 19. Reading the Start of Authority (SOA) Records at Yale University through the Use of NSLOOKUP

NSLOOKUP Alternative

Although NSLOOKUP represents a powerful tool for determining information about an organization, this program is not implemented in every TCP/IP protocol stack. Fortunately, one can use one of several public "nslookup" facilities on the Internet that enable one, at a minimum, to obtain the IP address associated with a host name. One example of a public nslookup site is at www.infobear.com, which is illustrated in Exhibit 20.

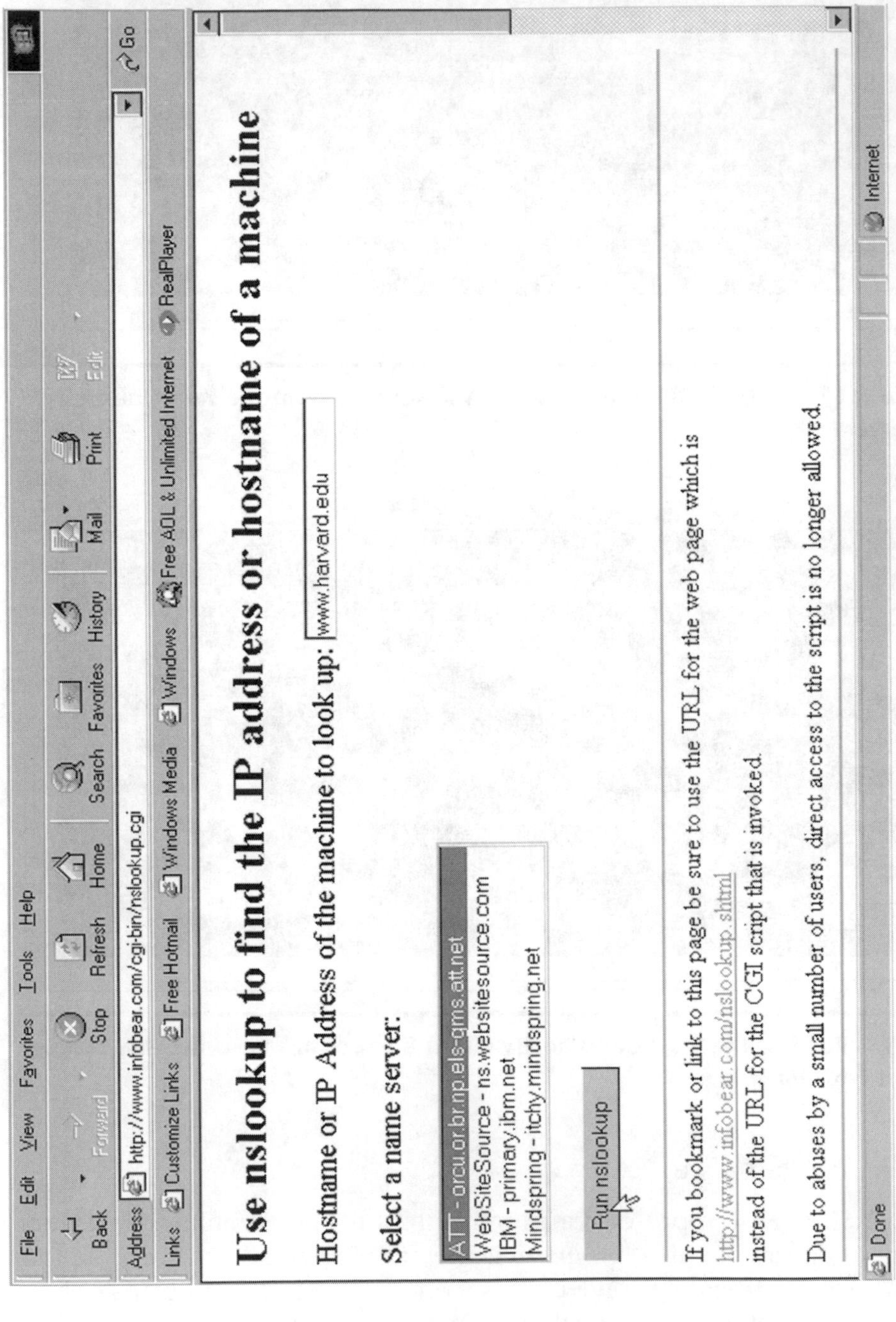

Exhibit 20. Using the Public NSLOOKUP Facility at www.infobear.com

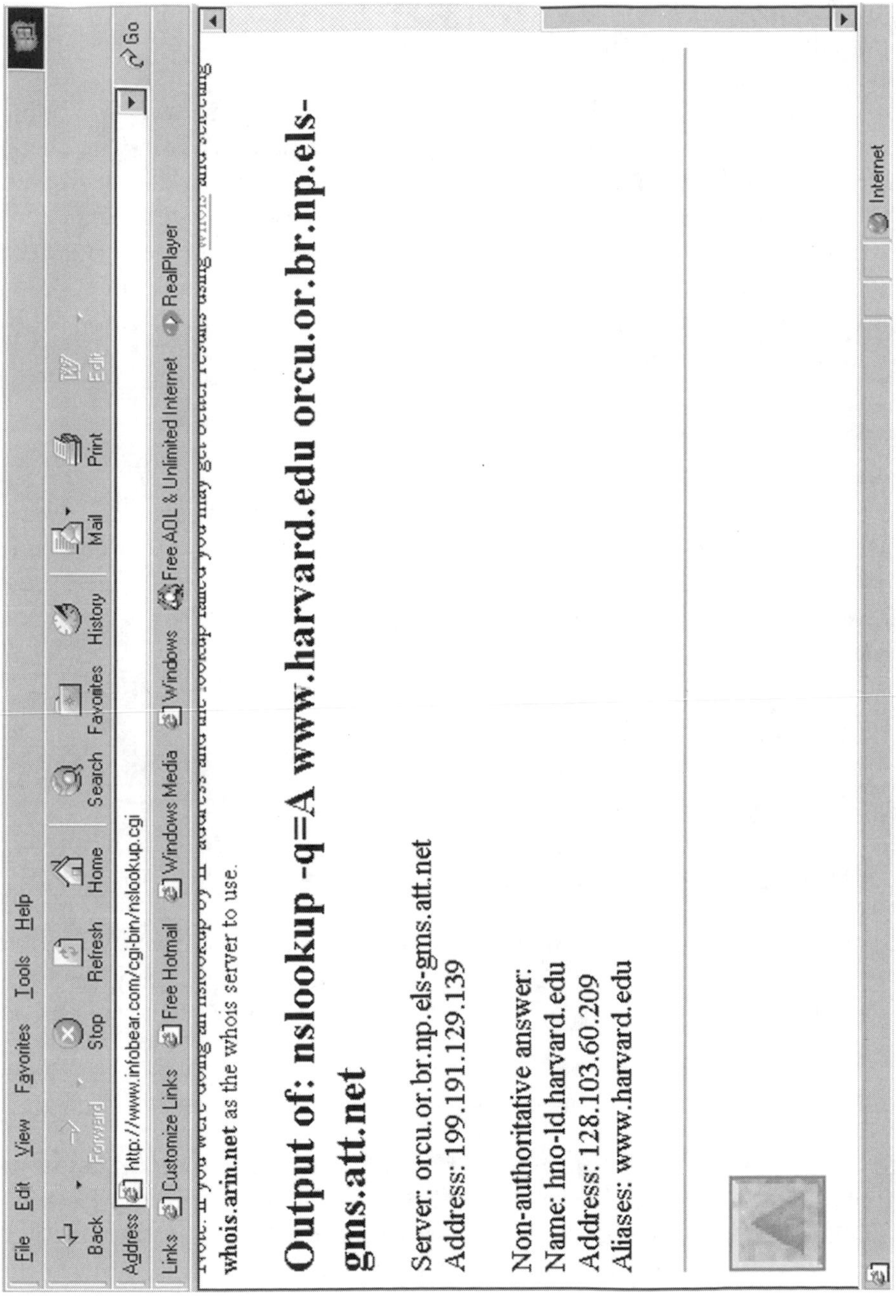

Exhibit 21. Examining the Response to the Use of a Public NSLOOKUP Site

In examining Exhibit 20, note that this public nslookup location provides the ability to specify either a host name or IP address for resolution. Also note that this site provides the ability to select one of four name servers for responding to a query.

Because we previously used Yale University for illustrative purposes in examining NSLOOKUP, it is only fair that we use Harvard when using a public nslookup facility. Thus, in Exhibit 20, we entered the Web address of Harvard University.

Once one clicks on the button labeled "Run nslookup," the Web site being accessed submits a request to the previously selected name server. The name server responds to the Web site one is viewing within the browser; however, to see the results, one needs to scroll to the bottom of the page. So, let us do so. Exhibit 21 shows the output of the nslookup operation performed by the name server operated by AT&T. Note that Harvard's Web server host name (www.harvard.edu) is an alias, with the real host name being hno-ld.harvard.edu, whose IP address is 128.103.60.209.

Finger

Finger, a fifth built-in utility, is a program that enables a user to obtain information about who is logged onto a distant computer or to determine information about a specific user. The use of this command results in a new verb referred to as "fingering," which is not a rude gesture, but a query on the Internet.

Format

The general format of the Finger command on a UNIX system is:

```
finger [username] @ {host.name\IP.address}
```

Exhibit 22 illustrates the Finger command options under Microsoft Windows operation system. Note that the `-l` option results in a long display that can provide detailed information about a user or host computer.

Security Considerations

Similar to other network utility programs under the Microsoft operating system, Finger runs in the command prompt dialog box as a DOS application. Because the use of Finger can provide detailed information about a user or host, it is normally blocked by programming a router to bar datagrams that contain the destination port that identifies a Finger application. An example of Finger blocking is shown in Exhibit 23. In this illustration, the author attempted to finger several domains. First, this author fingered ford.com without success. Next, a U.S. government agency; followed by an attempt to finger Yale University; and, finally, the Federal Bureau of Investigation. Each of these

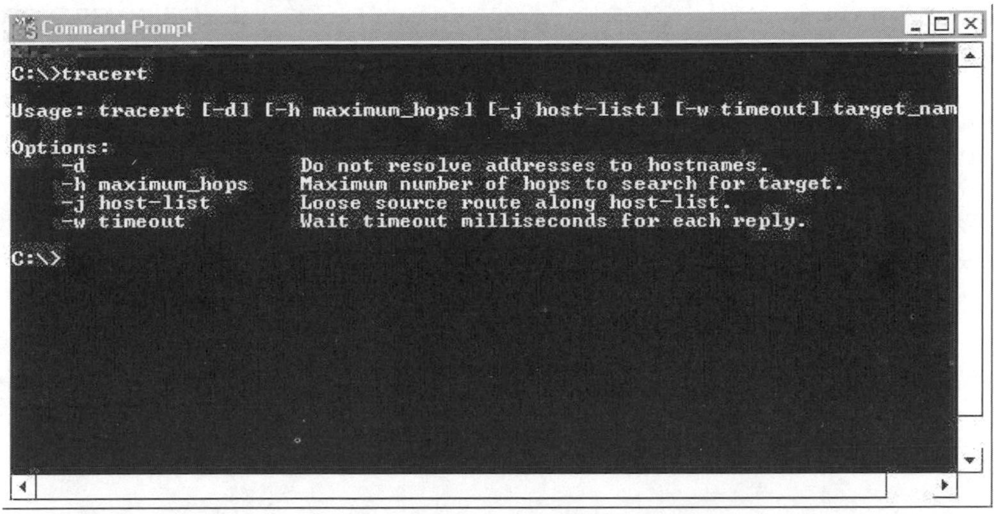

Exhibit 22. The Finger Help Screen under Microsoft Windows

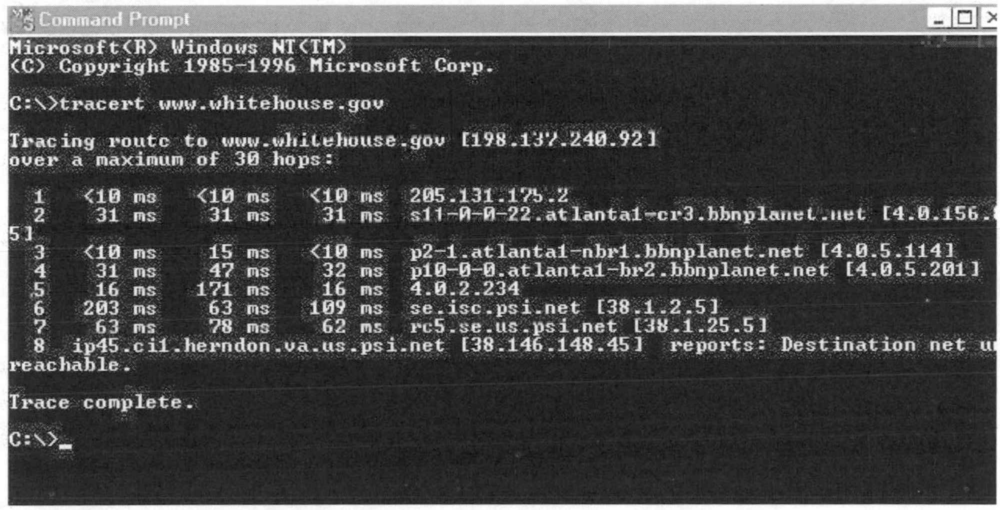

Exhibit 23. Many Organizations Will Block Fingering as a Security Measure

finger attempts was unsuccessful as those organizations block fingering as a security measure.

Applications

As indicated in Exhibit 23, many organizations block fingering as a security measure. Thus, a logical question is, "Why discuss its use?" The reason is that many organizations will operate fingering internally, but block its flow into the network. Then, people within an organization obtain the ability to query a host or user to determine who is working on the host, their telephone number, the application they are using, and other information that may be of assistance when attempting to solve a problem.

As indicated in this chapter, the TCP/IP protocol suite contains several built-in application programs that can be used to determine information about hosts, the paths between networks, and users on a host. By carefully considering the use of different application programs, one can obtain valuable tools that will assist in ensuring that if problems occur, one can focus attention on the potential location and perhaps even the cause of the problem.

Chapter 7

Routing and Routing Protocols

Having read the preceding chapters in this book, one is now aware that routing on a TCP/IP network occurs based on the IP address contained in a datagram. One is also aware of the fact that when entering a host address into an application program, that address must be translated into an IP address because routing occurs based on the destination IP address and not on the host name. Chapter 6 discussed how the address translation process occurs and the role of the domain name system (DNS) and the entries in the domain name servers that form the DNS. What has not been discussed heretofore is the manner by which a router learns where to forward a datagram based on its destination IP address. Thus, the focus of this chapter is on routing and routing protocols that enable datagrams to flow over a TCP/IP network or between separate networks so that they can reach their destination.

Both routing and routing protocols represent complex topics for which many books have been written. Because the focus of this book is on obtaining a firm understanding of how the TCP/IP protocol suite operates, the focus here is on routing concepts and methods instead of the minute details associated with numerous routing protocols. Doing so will provide the reader with an appreciation for the manner by which datagrams are routed instead of obtaining information required by some people to specifically tailor equipment for operating with a certain routing protocol.

Recognizing the importance of the Internet, this chapter first examines how this "mother of all networks" is subdivided into separate entities and how the entities are interconnected to one another. In doing so, one obtains an overview of the basic utilization of several types of routing protocols that are responsible for developing paths between networks. Because routers construct routing tables and periodically advertise the contents of such tables to other routers, this topic is also examined. For those of us from Missouri, the "show me" state, this chapter includes an examination of how two popular routing protocols operate in order to obtain an appreciation of the manner by which both routers in the Internet and on private TCP/IP networks understand where to route datagrams. Because it is important to have practical knowledge of the use of routing protocols, when applicable this chapter examines how Cisco routers are configured to support different routing protocols.

Network Routing

For a large network such as the Internet or a private network operated by a multinational corporation, it would more than likely be impractical for each router to have entries for each network address. Even if memory was free, whenever a table update was broadcast to adjacent routers, the time required to transmit routing table entries could become so long that it would preclude the ability to transport production data for significant periods of time. Recognizing this potential problem, the various committees responsible for the development of the TCP/IP protocol suite also developed a series of routing protocols. Some protocols are used to convey information within a network consisting of two or more subnetworks managed by a common entity, with the collection of networks referred to as an autonomous system. Other protocols are designed to convey information between autonomous systems. Thus, rather than one routing protocol, the TCP/IP protocol suite supports a family of routing protocols. Because routing methods within an autonomous system differ from routing protocols used to interconnect autonomous systems, one can view the Internet or a corporate enterprise network as a global network and examine the manner by which routing occurs within a global system.

Routing in a Global System

Exhibit 1 illustrates an example of a global system consisting of several interconnected autonomous systems. To facilitate reference to protocols, addressing is indicated in terms of two decimal numbers separated by a decimal point instead of true dotted decimal notation.

Autonomous Systems

In examining Exhibit 1, one can first more narrowly define an autonomous system. As previously mentioned, it represents a collection of networks managed by a common entity. In actuality, it is the routing protocol that is managed, with the result that only a single routing protocol is used within an autonomous system. Thus, one can also view an autonomous system as a group of networks that use routers to exchange routing information between subnetworks in the system via the use of a common routing protocol.

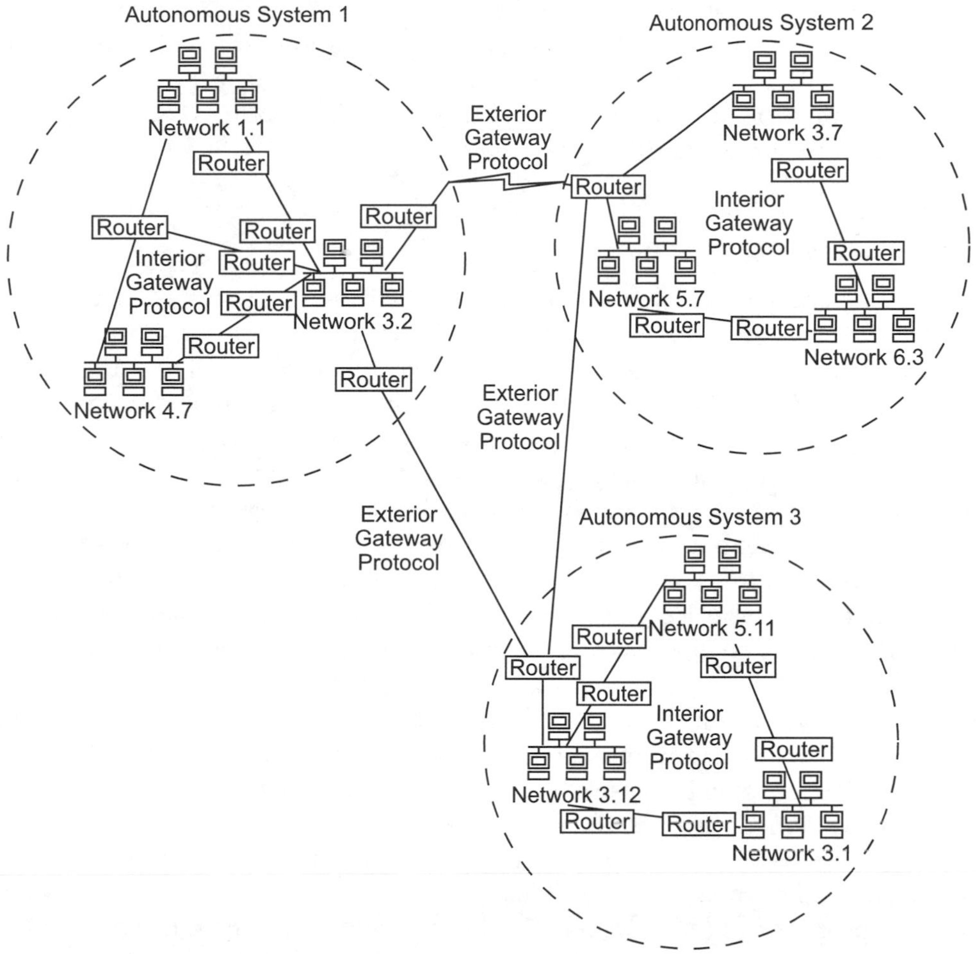

Exhibit 1. A Global System Using Different Types of Protocols to Advertise Reachable Information

Each network shown in Exhibit 1 can represent a corporate network, educational network, or governmental network. When connected to the Internet through the services of an Internet service provider (ISP), the ISP represents an autonomous system. If Exhibit 1 represents a private enterprise network, perhaps autonomous system 1 represents North America, system 2 represents South America, etc. Thus, each subnetwork in an autonomous network could represent a series of LANs and routers that connect offices in California and the Pacific Northwest, Texas, the southwestern United States, etc. Because organizations acquire IP addresses at different points in time, there is no structure associated with an address relationship between networks in an autonomous system. This explains why the individual networks in autonomous system 1 are numbered 1.1, 3.2, and 4.7 in the example, while the networks located in autonomous system 2 are numbered 3.7, 5.7, and 6.3. For example, in real life, an ISP in Chicago might be responsible for providing routing and connectivity information for a mixture of Class A, B, and C networks whose IP addresses span the gamut of the valid range of addresses available for each class. The only restriction concerning addressing is the fact that each address must be within the allowable range; no single network address can be repeated anywhere else in the global system.

Types of Routing Protocols

There are two general types or categories of routing protocols that provide routing information within and between autonomous systems. Those routing protocols are referred to as Interior Gateway Protocols (IGPs) and Exterior Gateway Protocols (EGPs). They derive their middle identifier due to the fact that when the Internet was developed, the device that provided routing between networks was referred to as a gateway. In some trade literature, the terms "Interior Router Protocol" (IRP) and "Exterior Router Protocol" (ERP) are now used. Although these latter terms are more representative of the devices used in networks to transmit routing information, this author likes both aged wine and long-used terms. Thus, the use of the term "gateway" when describing routing protocols continues to be used herein.

- *Interior Gateway Protocol.* The function of an Interior Gateway Protocol (IGP) is to transmit routing information between routers within an autonomous system. Because all routers in the autonomous system that provide interconnectivity between networks are controlled by the governing authority of the system, it becomes possible to enhance both efficiency and compatibility by specifying the use of a common routing protocol. This routing protocol is used for interconnecting separate networks within the autonomous system. Thus, routing protocols used within each network may or may not be the same as the routing protocol used to interconnect networks within the autonomous system. In fact, it is entirely possible that one or more networks in the autonomous system use "bridging" rather than routing to govern the flow of data within the network.
- *Exterior Gateway Protocol.* Because the routing method used within one autonomous system can differ from that used by another system, it is important to have a mechanism that transfers a minimum level of information between systems. Thus, the purpose of an Exterior Gateway Protocol (EGP) is to transport routing information between routers that connect one such system to another.
- *IGP versus EGP.* Because there are numerous paths between networks in an autonomous system and while one or a few connections link such systems together, there are considerable differences between an IGP and an EGP. For example, an IGP needs to construct a detailed model of the interconnection of routers within an autonomous system. This model must have a sufficient database to compute both an optimum path to a destination as well as obtain knowledge of an alternate path or paths if the least costly path should become inoperative. In

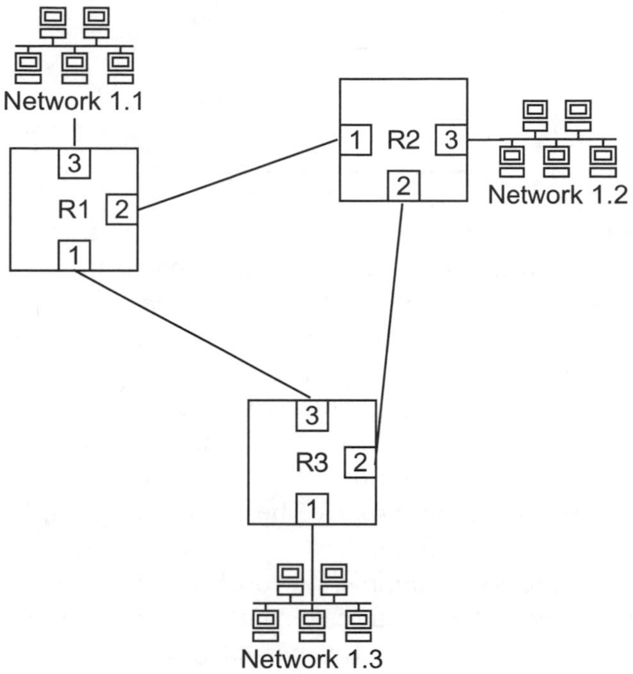

Exhibit 2. A Three-Network Autonomous System

comparison, an EGP only requires the exchange of summary information between networks. For example, within autonomous system 1, each router that connects one network to another must know the possible paths from one network to another as well as the other networks in the system. In comparison, to interconnect autonomous systems, an EGP mainly has to convey information between routers linking each system concerning the networks reachable on each system.

Recognizing the differences between an IGP and an EGP, one can now focus on the general type of information included in routing tables and the rationale for routers having to advertise the contents of their routing tables to neighbors.

Need for Routing Tables

In a small system, it is both possible and relatively easy to configure a router so that all paths to other networks are known. To illustrate this, consider Exhibit 2, which shows three interconnected networks labeled 1.1, 1.2, and 1.3. The three networks are interconnected through the use of three routers labeled R1, R2, and R3, with each router having three ports labeled 1, 2, and 3.

To facilitate the routing of datagrams, a router must know how to transmit data to another network. In actuality, a router only needs to know what port to output a datagram to reach a given network. Thus, it is entirely possible to configure a static routing table for router R1 shown in Exhibit 2 as follows:

Port	*Network*
1	1.3
2	1.2
3	1.1

In the preceding example, the term "static" is used to signify that the entries are permanent and do not vary. While there may be the need for dynamic routing tables, in many situations static routing remains a practical solution for configuring routers. For example, if an organization uses one router to connect a LAN to the Internet via an ISP, it makes sense and enhances router performance to use static routing. This is because the organization's router only needs to know the address of the ISP's router. By using static routing in this situation, the organization's router avoids transmitting router table updates, enabling less bandwidth required for overhead and more bandwidth becoming available for actual data transfer.

Returning to the previous example, a problem with the above configuration is the fact that it does not indicate alternate paths between networks, For example, if the circuit between router R1 and router R2 failed, the above configuration does not indicate that datagrams could flow to network 1.2 via router R3.

If one wanted to reconfigure router R1 with knowledge of all possible paths to the three networks, one possible port/network table would be as follows:

Port	*Network*
1	1.3
1	1.2
2	1.2
2	1.3
3	1.1

In examining the preceding port/network table, note that there is no mechanism to distinguish the fact that routing a datagram via a particular port number to a network results in either direct or indirect routing. For example, from router R1 the transfer of a datagram via port 1 provides a direct route to network 1.3. If the datagram is transmitted via port 2, the datagram will have to be relayed via router R2 to reach network 1.3. Thus, another metric is required to distinguish direct paths from indirect paths. That metric is a hop count, which indicates the number of routers a datagram must flow through to reach a particular network. Thus, the routing table for router R1 might be revised as in the following port/network/hop count table.

In cxamining the port/network/hop count table, note that a direct connection to a network results in a router hop count of zero. Also note that the preceding table provides the ability to distinguish the best route from one that requires more hops.

Port	*Network*	*Hop Count*
1	1.3	1
1	1.2	2
2	1.2	1
2	1.3	2
3	1.1	0

To continue this routing example, one can create an extended routing table for the router R2. This routing table is shown below.

Port	*Network*	*Hop Count*
1	1.1	1
1	1.3	2
2	1.3	1
2	1.1	2
3	1.2	0

Once again, one can distinguish between direct and indirect routes by the hop count value. For example, from the above table, port 1 provides a direct route to network 1.1 and an indirect route to network 1.3. Similarly, port 2 on R2 provides a direct route to network 1.3 and an indirect route to network 1.1.

Need for Information Interchange

What happens if a path between routers becomes inoperative? For example, consider the path between routers R1 and R2. If the circuit for this path becomes inoperative, how does router R1 obtain information to update its routing table? This update should allow the router to note whether or not a path is available or not available for use. Thus, to dynamically change routing, a router needs to know the state of paths between networks. To obtain this information, a router periodically transmits information to other routers. This information not only tells one router that the network is reachable via another network, but in addition, the lack of an update within a predefined period of time could be used to inform the other router that the path between routers is not available for use. Then the other router will search its routing table and, if another route to a destination is available, make that the available route. Because timing is critical, routers also timestamp information stored in their routing tables. Depending on the manner by which a particular routing protocol is implemented, the timestamp may simply be used to purge entries from a routing table, provide a mechanism for selecting one entry over another, or perform another function.

Routing Table Update Methods

There are two methods routers use to provide other routers with information concerning the contents of their routing tables. One method is for the router to periodically broadcast the contents of its routing table to other routers. This table update method is used by vector distance routing protocols. Here, the term "vector distance" relates to the type of information transmitted by the router and conveyed by the protocol. The vector identifies a network destination, while the distance represents the distance in hops from the router to a particular network destination.

As networks grew in size, the number of routers also increased. As this situation occurred, the number of entries in each router's routing table considerably expanded. At a certain point, the number of routing table entries can result in the periodic transmission of table entries between routers consuming too much network bandwidth. Thus, this potential development led to the creation of a second type of routing table update. This type of routing table update occurs by transmitting routing information only when there is a change in one of its links. The protocol that transmits such changes is referred to as a link state protocol. In addition to providing more efficient utilization of bandwidth, a link state protocol provides the ability to use multiple paths to a common destination. Unlike a vector state protocol that only supports one route at a time, a link state protocol can support load balancing on multiple paths. This is not without a price, as a link state protocol is typically more complex than a vector state protocol. One popular example of a vector distance protocol is the Routing Information Protocol (RIP). An example of a link state protocol is the Open Shortest Path First (OSPF) Protocol.

The Routing Information Protocol

As previously mentioned, the Routing Information Protocol (RIP) represents one of the most popular vector distance routing protocols. Under RIP, participants can be classified as being either active or passive. Active participants can be considered to represent routers that transmit the contents of their routing tables. In comparison, passive devices listen and update their routing tables based on information provided by active routers. Normally, host computers operate as passive participants in a network, while routers operate as active participants.

Illustrative Network

To illustrate the operation of RIP requires the presence of a network. Because an RIP database maintains information about the link between networks, each link in the network is numbered. In addition, because each router represents a node in a network, for simplicity of illustration, the contents of routing tables are shown in terms of their connected links and number of hops required to reach other nodes in a network. Thus, Exhibit 3, which will form

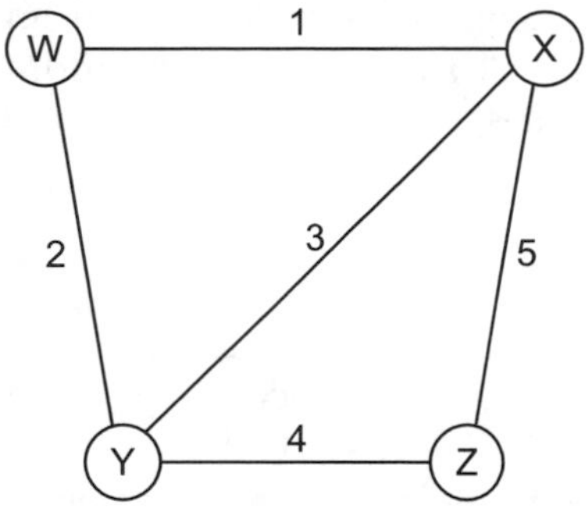

Exhibit 3. A Network of Four Nodes Using Five Links

the basis for examining how RIP operates, shows a four-node network with five numbered links.

Dynamic Table Updates

Under RIP when a router is "powered on," it only has knowledge of its local condition. The entry "local" under the link column shown below represents the network to which the router is connected. As noted later in this chapter, a router is configured during its setup process with the network addresses that are connected to different ports on the device. For simplicity of illustration of dynamic table updates, we will only consider each router to have a single local connected network, although in reality this is often not true. Thus, upon initialization, each router will construct a routing table that contains a single entry. For example, the table for router n, where n can represent any router in a network upon power-up, would have the following table entry:

From n to	*Link*	*Hop Count*
N	Local	0

Thus, for the router represented by node W in Exhibit 3, its routing table would be as follows upon initialization:

From W to	*Link*	*Hop Count*
W	Local	0

Under RIP, an active router will broadcast the contents of its routing table every 30 seconds. Thus, at t = 30 seconds after initialization, node W will broadcast its distance vector (W = 0) to all of its neighbors. Using Exhibit 3 to illustrate the operation of RIP, this means that because nodes X and Z are neighbors of node W, they will each receive the distance vector transmitted by node W.

Node X receives the distance vector W = 0 on link 1. Upon receipt of this message, node X updates its routing table by adding 1 to the distant vector supplied by node W. Thus, the distance vector table for node X would appear as follows:

From X to	*Link*	*Hop Count*
X	Local	0
W	1	1

At this point in time, node X had a change in its distance vector table. Thus, when 30 seconds expire since its last table update transmission, it transmits a new distance vector set of information. This information would inform adjacent nodes on links 1, 3, and 5 that X = 0 and W = 1.

As node X's routing table update information flows to node Y, it now becomes possible for that node to be aware of node W although there is no direct path information currently known between nodes W and Y. Because the distance vectors from node X inform node Y of the hop count from X to itself and to W, node Y adds 1 to each hop count and stores the information in its routing table. If one logically assumes that node Y was powered on, it already had an initial entry to itself in its routing table. Thus, upon receipt of the two distance vector items of information from node X, node Y's routing table will have three entries. Those entries would be:

From Y to	*Link*	*Hop Count*
Y	Local	0
X	3	1
W	3	2

Note that in the preceding routing table, node Y now knows it can reach node W via link 3 and that it requires two hops to reach that node.

While nodes X and Y exchange routing information, so do nodes W and Y. Thus, node Y would determine that node W is only one hop away via Link 2. Thus, node Y would have its routing table updated as follows:

From Y to	*Link*	*Hop Count*
Y	Local	0
X	3	1
W	2	1
W	3	2

Note that Y now knows it can reach W via two different links, with Link 2 providing the most direct method because it is only one hop away.

While node Y updates its routing table, it is safe to assume that because at least 30 seconds have transpired, node W's distance vector information reached node Z. Thus, node Z would have updated its routing table as follows:

From Z to	*Link*	*Hop Count*
Z	Local	0
W	5	2

Because the discussion of the update of node Y followed the update of node X, at least 60 seconds transpired, which enables each node to transmit two routing table updates. Thus, node Y would also receive node Z's next routing table update that would be transmitted to adjacent nodes on links 2, 3, and 4. The routing table for node X would then be updated to the following state:

From X to	*Link*	*Hop Count*
X	Local	0
W	1	1
Z	5	1
W	3	2

Note that at this point in time, node X knows two ways to reach node W: via link 1 with a hop count of 1, which represents a direct connection; or via link 3 with a hop count of 2, which represents an indirect connection. Thus, it is possible for RIP to provide a mechanism for routers to develop a routing table that contains alternate paths.

Because node Z transmits its distance vector information on links 4 and 5, that information also flows to both nodes W and Y in addition to X, whose routing table was just updated. Thus, one can also update the previously updated node Y routing table to ascertain the effect of a routing table update received from node Z. See the following Node Y routing table.

Because alternate routing entry information would grow exponentially as a mesh network grows in size, RIP does not normally store information about duplicate paths to the same node. Instead, when it computes its routing table update and adds 1 to a received hop count for a node, it compares the new value to the existing value if an entry for the node already exists in memory. If the computed value equals or exceeds the existing hop count, the information about the node received via a router table update is discarded. The

From Y to	*Link*	*Hop Count*
Y	Local	0
X	3	1
Z	4	1
W	2	1
W	3	2
W	4	3

exception to this situation is if a router is configured to maintain alternate routing entries to use in the event of a link failure.

Basic Limitations

The preceding example provides a general overview of the manner by which RIP enables nodes to learn the topology of a network. Although RIP does not normally provide alternate path information, the periodic transmission of table entries allows new paths to be learned, because existing information in router tables are time-stamped and an aging process will result in the old path being purged from memory. This process takes time, as table updates occur every 30 seconds. For example, it might take five minutes for one node that is ten hops away from a non-adjacent node to learn that a path changed. A second limitation of RIP is the fact that it is limited to the maximum hop distance it supports. This distance is 16 hops, which means that an alternative protocol must be used for very large networks.

In actuality, the maximum RIP hop count is 15. Any route that is advertised with a distance of 16 hops is considered to be unreachable through the advertised path. Because it is possible for a link to fail, RIP uses an expiration timer of 180 seconds. Thus, if a route becomes silent for a period of six updates (three minutes), the other routers that previously learned about the route will set their hop count value associated with the link to 16. In effect, this hop count value notes that the route is invalid. The other routers will then advertise the route to the previously reachable router with a new distance value for a period of 120 seconds. This new advertisement is employed to inform downstream routers of the link failure, resulting in a total period of 300 seconds (five minutes) passing until some downstream devices are aware of a link failure.

Another problem associated with the use of RIP is the fact that it is possible to generate a false connection to a network. To understand how this can happen, consider Exhibit 4 that illustrates two routers connected to one another, with router X connected to the network segment 205.131.175.0. Now suppose a failure caused router X to remove network segment 205.131.175.0 from its routing table. Because under RIP, router Y received a broadcast of router X's routing table, it previously learned that network 205.131.175.0 was one hop away via router X. Thus, router X would also view network 205.131.175.0 as two hops away via router Y. Thus, if router X loses its connection to network 205.131.175.0, it would then note from its routing table that it could send data for that network to router Y, which would then transmit it back to router X, which could not deliver the traffic because it lost its connection — sort of a "Catch-22" view of networking.

To prevent the previously mentioned problems, RIP uses a technique referred to as split horizon. Under split horizon, a router cannot advertise routes through the same interface from which the route was learned. Returning to Exhibit 4, split horizon would prevent router Y from advertising router X's local connections, and vice versa. However, some split horizon is not implemented by default on some routers and one may need to configure it to avoid the previously mentioned problem. Other routers might perform a technique referred to as poison reversal instead of split horizon. Under poison reversal, a hop count of 16 is used to corrupt the reverse path. Returning to Exhibit 4, router Y would then advertise network 205.131.175.0 with a hop count of 16 when transmitting router table updates, ensuring that the route via router Y to network 205.131.175.0 was not used by router X.

RIP Versions

The original version of RIP developed for use in TCP/IP dates to 1988 when it was adapted by the Internet Activities Board and published as RFC 1058. RIP gained widespread acceptance due to its inclusion as a routing protocol in the Berkeley 4BSD UNIX operating system. In fact, today, both UNIX and Windows NT workstations support RIP in passive mode, allowing such devices to receive and process table updates — although as a passive device, they cannot respond to RIP requests nor broadcast the contents of their tables. Workstations that support RIP do so to avoid having to request information from other routers on a network. Although good in theory, most computers today are configured with a default gateway address for simplicity.

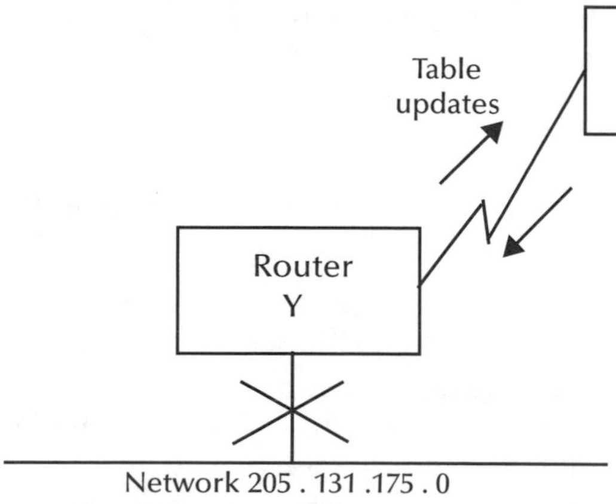

Exhibit 4. If a Connection to Network 1.1 Fails, Router X May Assume that the Network is Reachable via Router Y

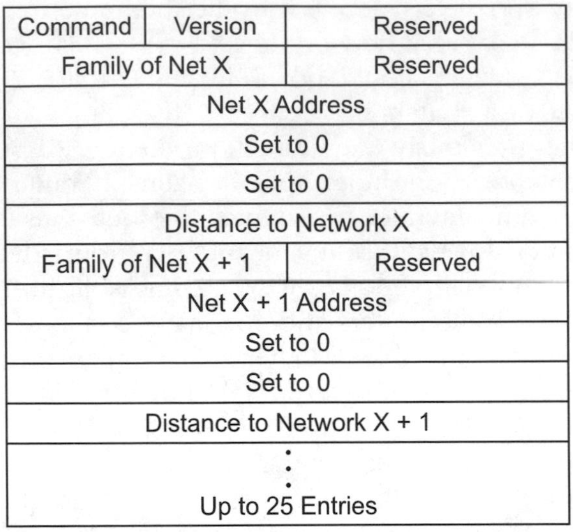

Exhibit 5. Routing Information Protocol Version 1 Packet Fields

To obtain an appreciation of the difference between the original version of RIP (now referred to as RIPv1) and its successor (RIPv2), turn attention to the fields with the original RIP packet. Once an appreciation for the use of the fields in that packet has been obtained, one will have the foundation to examine the additional features and capabilities provided by RIPv2.

The Basic RIPv1 Packet

As previously mentioned, to obtain a better appreciation of RIPv1 and Version 2 of the protocol that was standardized in 1994, one should focus on the fields in the RIP packet. Exhibit 5 illustrates the fields in the RIP packet. Before discussing those fields, one should note that RIP is transported as a UDP datagram. Thus, the fields shown in Exhibit 5 would be prefixed with a UDP header and that header, in turn, would be prefixed with an IP header.

Command Field

The Command field identifies the function of the RIP packet. There are five commands, as described below:

Command	*Description*
1	Request for partial or full routing table information
2	Response containing a routing table
3/4	Turn on (3) or turn off (4) trace mode. This is now obsolete.
5	Sun Microsystems' internal use

Version Field

The Version field identifies the version of RIP. Initially, the value of this field was 1 to indicate RIP version 1.

Family of Net X Field

This field indicates the protocol that controls the routing protocol and is set to 2 for IP. Because Xerox Network Services (XNS) also operated over networks when TCP/IP was evolving, this field was included to allow the same RIP frame to be used to support multiple protocol suites. Thus, while a value of 2 is used for IP, the routing protocol also supports RIP for AppleTalk, Novell's NetWare Internetwork Packet Exchange (IPX), and XNS.

Net X Address Field

When the Family of Net X field is set to a value of 2, the Net X Address field contains the IP address of the destination network. Under RIP version 1, only the first four bytes of a total of 12 available bytes are used, with the remaining 8 bytes set to zero.

If the command field has a value of 1, there is only one entry and the net 1 address (first IP address) is set to a value of zero, which means that the packet is a request for an entire routing table.

Distance to Network X Field

Because RIP is limited to supporting a maximum of 16 hops, this field only supports the integers 1 to 16. An entry of 16 in this field indicates that a network is unreachable. The term "count to infinity" is sometimes used to indicate too many hops for RIP to reach a target.

As indicated in Exhibit 5, up to 25 entries containing the IP address of a network and the distance of that network can be included in a RIP packet, with a maximum RIP packet limited to 512 bytes in length.

RIPv1 Limitations

In addition to supporting a maximum hop count of 16 — with only a distance of 15 supported because a count of 16 indicates a destination is unreachable — RIP has several additional disadvantages. Those disadvantages include an inability to differentiate between the bandwidth differences on different links and the fact that broadcasts can become significantly large and consume bandwidth that cannot then be used for data transmission. Another limitation of RIPv1 is the fact that this routing protocol requires a subnet mask to be uniform across an entire network. This is because RIPv1 does not support the ability to contain a subnet mask entry in its routing table. Thus, RIPv1 assumes that the subnet mask is the same for all of its configured ports as the subnet whose value it learns for the network identifier.

Command	Version	Reserved
Address Family Identifier		Route Tag
Net X Address		
Subnet Mask		
Next-Hop IP Address		
Metrix		
Address Family Identifier		Route Tag
Net X + 1 Address		
Subnet Mask		
Next-Hop IP Address		
Metrix		
⋮ Up to 25 Entries		

Exhibit 6. RIPv2 Packet Fields

RIPv2

Recognizing some of the limitations associated with RIPv1, this routing protocol was modified in 1994, resulting in the development of RIPv2. RIPv2 is backward-compatible with RIPv1. It adds several important features that enhance its capability. The additional features include a text password authentication capability, the inclusion of subnet masks in its routing tables, and a route tag that provides a mechanism for separating RIP routes from externally learned routes. Exhibit 6 illustrates the RIPv2 packet format.

In comparing the fields in RIPv1 to RIPv2 packets, one notes the use of several new fields in RIPv2, as discussed below.

Route Tag Field

The purpose of the Route Tag field is to provide RIPv2 with the ability to advertise routes that were learned externally. For example, assume a router is used to provide an interconnection between autonomous systems. It would then learn routers through the use of an EGP and would use the route tag for denoting or identifying the autonomous system from which those routers were learned.

Next Hop Field

The purpose of the Next Hop field is to provide a router with the ability to learn where the next hop is located for the specified route entry. A value of 0.0.0.0 in this field is used to indicate that the source address of the update should be used for the route. This field is primarily used when there are multiple routers on a single LAN segment that use different IGPs for routing updates to different LANs. If a point-to-point link is used, the next hop can be obtained from the source IP address of the IP header of a datagram. Thus, this field is not very useful for point-to-point links.

In examining the fields in the RIPv2 packet shown in Exhibit 6, one might be a bit puzzled as to how this newer version of RIP can support authentication. The trick used to obtain this additional feature is for the RIPv2 header to set the value of a field within the packet to a special value that tells a receiver to interpret the data differently. One can appreciate this technique by examining how RIPv2 supports authentication.

Authentication Support

When the Address Family Identifier field in a RIPv2 packet is set to a value of hex FFFF, the header of the resulting RIP datagram changes into an authentication header. Exhibit 7 illustrates the fields in a RIPv2 authentication packet.

In examining Exhibit 7, one sees that an Authentication Type field value of 2 is for using a simple password. A field of 16 bytes that allows one to convey up to a 16-character password follows this. If RIPv2 is communicating with a router supporting RIPv1, RIPv1 will ignore this entry because the value of hex FFFF in the fourth field of the header is not recognized as an IP address family.

A RIPv2-compliant router can be configured with or without authentication. If it is configured with authentication disabled, the router will accept and process both RIPv1 and RIPv2 unauthenticated messages. If the router receives a RIPv2-authenticated message, it will discard the message. If the router is configured to support authentication, then unauthenticated messages will be discarded.

Command	Version	Unused
FFFF		Authentication Type
Password		
Password		
Password		
Password		
Address Family Identifier		Route Tag
Net n + 1 Address		
Subnet Mask		
Next Hop		
Metric		

Exhibit 7. RIPv2 Authentication Packet

Scalability and Hop Count Limitations

Although RIPv2 added additional features, it maintained the maximum distance allowable between two stations at 15 hops. This means that for many medium-sized networks and just about all large-sized networks, RIP is not scalable to satisfy many organizational networking requirements. In addition, both RIPv1 and RIPv2 do not consider the fact that there could be other metrics besides a hop count that should be considered when determining a path. These shortcomings were considered in the development of a routing protocol referred to as Open Shortest Path First (OSPF), which is discusssed next.

OSPF

The use of Open Shortest Path First (OSPF) as a routing protocol in place of RIP results in both advantages and disadvantages. Although OSPF is more efficient in its overall use of bandwidth, it consumes more bandwidth during its initial discovery process and represents a more complex process that consumes more router memory cycles. This chapter section focuses on obtaining an understanding of the manner by which OSPF operates and its key features.

Overview

The Open Shortest Path First (OSPF) dates to 1988 when the Internet community realized its growth required a more scalable, nonproprietary Interior Gateway Protocol (IGP) for the TCP/IP protocol suite. An OSPF Working Group was formalized in 1991, at which time its efforts resulted in the OSPF routing protocol advancing to a Draft Internet Standard. RFC 1131 defines the initial version of OSPF (OSPF 1) and is now obsolete. RFC 1583 defines the most widespread version of OSPF (OSPF 2) in use, while RFC 2328 defines the most current version of OSPF 2. OSPF represents a link state protocol that transmits routing table updates either when a change occurs or every 30 minutes via the use of a multicast address. When configured for OSPF, each router maintains an independent database that includes information about all available networks within an administrative routing area. In doing so, OSPF uses a link state algorithm to compute the shortest path to each known destination. Although the actual algorithm can be quite complicated, one can summarize its salient operations as a four step process as follows:

1. Upon initialization or upon a change in routing information, a router generates a link state advertisement. This advertisement denotes the table of all link states maintained by the router.
2. All routers exchange link states via a flooding process. That is, each router in an administrative routing area that receives a link state update

stores a copy of the update in its database and propagates the update to other routers.

3. After the database is completed, the router computes a shortest path to each destination, placing the destinations, their associated cost, and the next hop to reach those destinations into its IP routing table.
4. If no changes in the OSPF network occur, such as the addition or deletion of a network, mainly keep-alives flow between routers when there is no data to transmit and OSPF is very quiet. However, when changes to the network occur, such changes are communicated between routers via link state packets and the shortest path is then recomputed.

The shortest path is computed using what is referred to as the Dijkstra algorithm. Under the Dijkstra algorithm, each router is placed at the root of a tree and the shortest path to each destination is computed based upon the cumulative cost required to reach the destination. This action results in each router developing its own view of the network topology although all routers construct a shortest path tree using the same link state database. That database can be considered to represent a distributed map. Later in this section we will describe the metrics that can be associated with the construction of a shortest path tree as well as the computations involved in building a shortest path tree.

Path Metrics

A key feature of OSPF is the fact that paths are based on a true metric and not just a hop count. For example, OSPF routers pass messages to each other in the form of Link State Advertisements (LSAs). One type of LSA includes the IP address of a router's interface and the cost of that interface. Here, the cost is configured by the router administrator. While it is possible for a router administrator to associate any value to a router interface, RFC 1253 defines a series of recommendations concerning the assignment of costs to router interfaces for use of OSPF. Exhibit 8 illustrates that such costs are relative to a 100-Mbps operating rate. That is, the formula used to compute the cost is:

$$\text{Cost} = 100{,}000{,}000/\text{bandwidth in bps}$$

To illustrate an example of the use of the above formula, assume a path will cross a 10BASE-T 10-Mbps Ethernet interface. Then, the cost becomes:

$$\text{Cost} = 100{,}000{,}000/10{,}000{,}000 = 10$$

which is the second entry in Exhibit 8.

Exhibit 8. Potential OSPF LSA Costs

Data Rate of Interface	*Cost*
≥100 Mbps	1
10 Mbps	10
E1 (2.048 Mbps)	48
T1 (1.544 Mbps)	65
64 kbps	1562
56 kbps	1785
19.2 kbps	5208
9.6 kbps	10416

The Link State Database

The key to the efficiency of OSPF is its link state database. Each node (router) within an OSPF area maintains a copy of the network in the form of a database, with updates flooded to other routers in the network. Using the database, each node computes the best route to all other nodes in the network. To obtain an appreciation for the manner by which a link state database is created and updated as network conditions change, consider the top portion of Exhibit 9, which illustrates a five-router network connected through the use of six links. The network map that forms the database maintained by each router would appear as indicated in the lower portion of Exhibit 9, with each link representing a single record in the database.

The records that form the link state database shown in the lower portion of Exhibit 9 are actually more comprehensive than an actual database. That is, each record would contain an interface identifier instead of a link number. In addition, each record would also contain information about the state of the link; however, for now one can ignore this additional information.

If a datagram needs to be transmitted from A to E, A will search its database and note that the shortest path to E is through B. Thus, it would transmit the datagram on link 1, with router B forwarding the datagram on link Z to E.

Database Update

As previously mentioned, database updates occur via flooding. To illustrate how this process changes the database, assume that the link between A and B failed. Both routers A and B would note that link 1 failed. Each router would then update the applicable record in its database and transmit the update to all other nodes in the network. Thus, A would send the following update message on link 2 to C:

From A to B link 1, distance = infinite

Router-based network

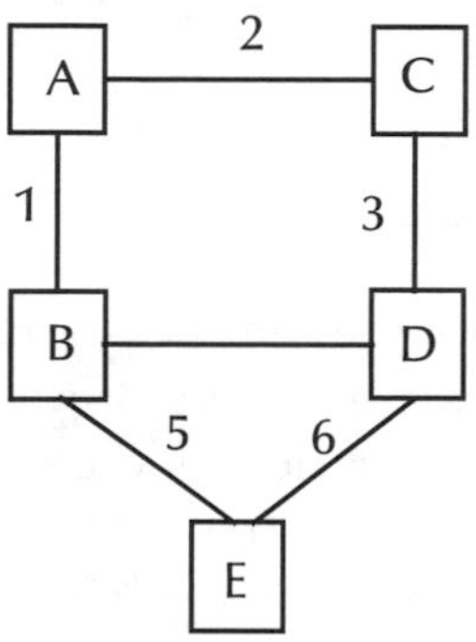

Link state database

From	*To*	*Link*	*Distance*
A	B	1	1
A	C	2	1
B	A	1	1
B	D	4	1
B	E	5	1
C	A	2	1
C	D	3	1
D	B	4	1
D	C	3	1
D	E	6	1
E	B	5	1
E	D	6	1

Exhibit 9. Creating a Link State Database

Node C would relay this message to D on link 3, which in turn would relay the message to E on link 6 and B on link 4.

Similarly, node B would transmit an update message on links 4 and 5 to nodes D and E as follows:

From B to A link 1, distance = infinite

Node D will relay the message to node C on link 3 and C would relay the message to node A on link 2.

The previous database update examples do not consider the fact that it is possible for a message to propagate through a network and inadvertently update a node that was updated with more recent information. Thus, a delayed update could adversely affect the information contained in the database. To preclude this problem from occurring, each link state table update will contain either a timestamp or a message number, permitting the recipient to distinguish old from new information.

Constructing the Shortest Path

The Dijkstra algorithm is used to compute the shortest path between nodes. Dijkstra called his algorithm shortest path first because it computes the path from each node to all other nodes in a network and returns the shortest path. Because the shortest path represents an optimum path, it should be opened first, resulting in the term "open shortest path first." To illustrate how the shortest path is computed, we need a reference network, so let us construct one.

The top portion of Exhibit 10 illustrates the use of four routers to interconnect four different networks. Each interface is shown with a cost metric that corresponds to its interface as previously noted in Exhibit 8. The lower portion of Exhibit 10 shows the network view with respect to router A. In examining the lower portion of Exhibit 10 in comparison to the costs contained in the upper portion of that illustration, it is important to consider the direction of the arrows because some interface costs are not relevant. For example, the cost of router B's interface to network 205.131.175.0 is not relevant when computing the cost to the 198.78.46.0 network.

Thus, router A can reach the 198.78.46.0 network via router B with a cost of 11 (1 + 10). Router A can also reach the 212.131.176.0 network via router C with a cost of 2 (1 + 1), or via routers B and D with a cost of 12 (1 + 10 + 1). Because the route via router C has a lesser cost, that route would become part of the shortest path tree and the link from router B to router D in Exhibit 10 would be pruned from the tree. If equal cost paths are computed to the same destination, multiple paths will be maintained. However, the maximum number of paths maintained by a router will depend on the manner by which OSPF is implemented. For example, Cisco's implementation of OSPF will keep track of up to six hops to the same destination.

Once a router constructs its shortest path tree, it will use the information to construct its routing table. This means that directly connected networks will have a cost metric of 0, while other networks will become reachable based on the costs computed when constructing the tree.

Initialization Activity

Although the original OSPF routing protocol dates to the days of ARPAnet, it was not until RFC 2178 that the protocol became available for modern TCP/IP networks. Similar to RIP, OSPF is an IGP and is designed to run within a single autonomous system. Upon initialization, each router within an autonomous system records information about each of its interfaces. Each router in the autonomous system then constructs a Link State Advertisement (LSA) packet that contains a list of all recently viewed routers and the costs previously

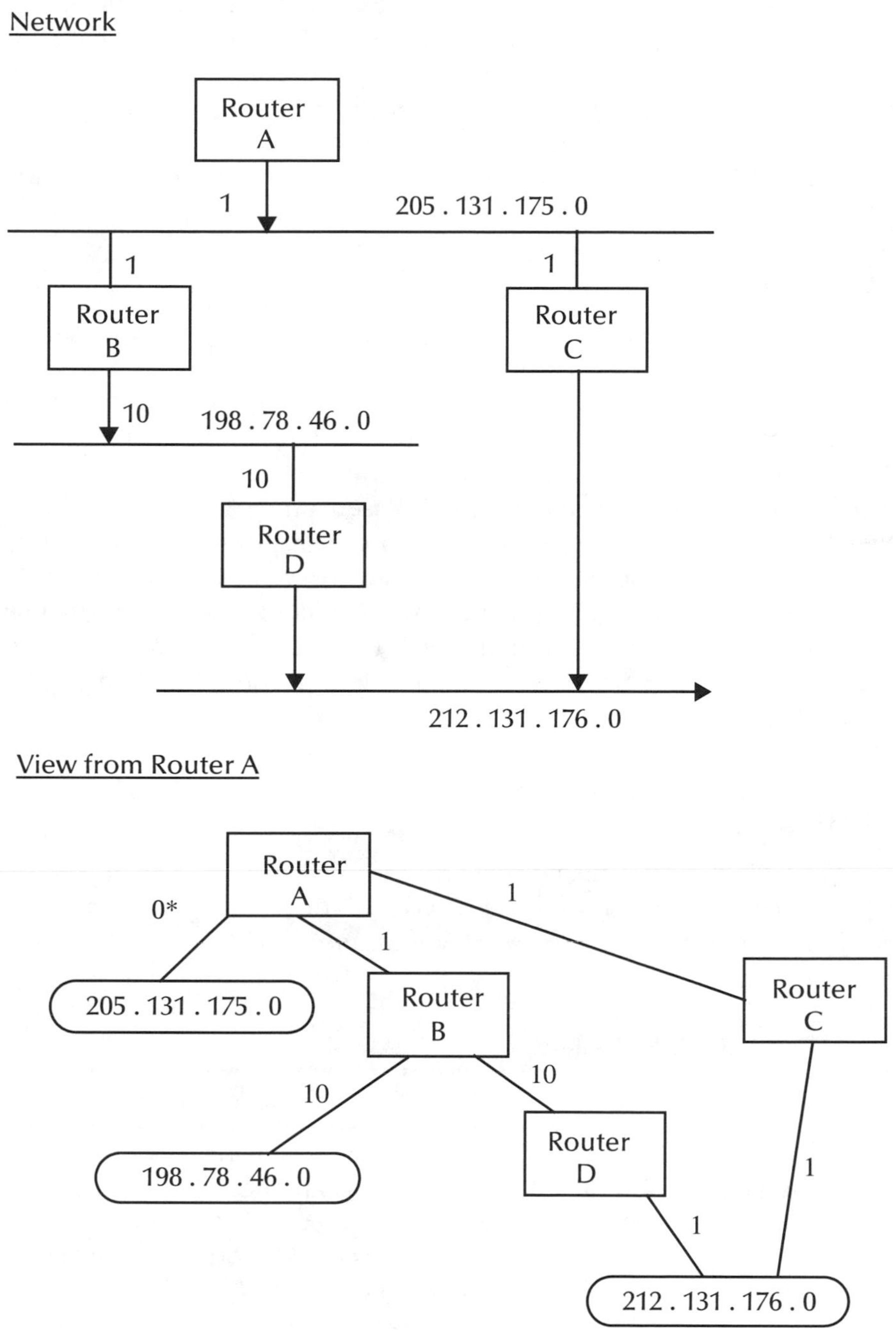

* Assigned cost = 0 a network is directly connected to router A.

Exhibit 10. Constructing the Shortest Path

associated with their interfaces. Rather than broadcasting the LSAs to all adjacent nodes as supported by RIP, OSPF subdivides a network into geographic entities (known as areas) and forwards LSA packets to routers within its area. A received LSA is then flooded to all other routers in an area, with each router updating its tables with a copy of the most recently received LSA. Thus, each router obtains complete knowledge of the topology of the area to which it was assigned.

Router Types

Under OSPF, a network or a group of networks can represent an area. Through the use of areas, routing table updates can be better controlled, with packet flooding occurring within an area while different areas communicate with one another to obtain information about networks within different areas. This subdivision of labor is based on the use of different types of routers, with the function of routers with respect to OSPF based on their type.

If there is only one area, each router maintains a database of the topology of the area and only one router has to deal with external routes beyond the area. When there are multiple areas, a number of other types of routers may be required to perform specialized operations. In fact, under OSPF, there are six types of routers that can be used. Exhibit 11 describes the function of each type of OSPF router.

Message Types

As discussed, OSPF routers transmit messages in the form of LSAs. There are currently six types of LSAs used by the protocol. This chapter section briefly discusses the function of each type of SLA message.

Exhibit 11. Types of OSPF Routers

Router Type	*Mnemonic*	*Description*
Backbone router	BR	A router that has a connect to a backbone
Area border router	ABR	A router that has an interface to multiple areas
Autonomous system boundary router	ASBR	A router that exchanges routing information with routers connected to other autonomous systems
Internal router	IR	A router that connects networks within a common area
Designated router	DR	A specified router that transfers information on behalf of adjacent routers on a subnet
Backup designated router	BDR	A router that backs up the designated router and takes over should the primary DR fail

Version Number Type Packet Length	
Router Identification	
Checksum	Autype
Authentication	

Exhibit 12. The Common LSA Message Header

Common Message Header

Each type of LSA message has a common header. That header, which is illustrated in Exhibit 12, contains eight fields. OSPF runs above IP, resulting in an IP datagram with a Protocol Type field value of 89 transporting OSPF.

The first field is an 8-bit Version Number, which is set to 2 to indicate the most current version of OSPF. The Type field indicates the OSPF message type and corresponds to the entries in Exhibit 13. The Packet Length field indicates the number of bytes in the packet to be transported as an IP datagram, while the Router Identification field represents the IP address that identifies the router. The 32-bit Area Identification field identifies the area, with 0 reserved for the backbone area. The backbone area is applicable when multiple areas are used. When this situation occurs, one of these areas has to be configured as area 0, which then becomes the backbone. The 16-bit Checksum is computed on the entire packet with the exception of the following 8-bit Autype field. Concerning that field, only two values are defined: 0 for no authentication and 1 for simple authentication. When simple authentication is employed, the Authentication field includes an eight-character password.

Type 1 Message

A Type 1 LSA message is used to transmit information about a router's interface and the cost associated with the interface. Because an interface is defined

Exhibit 13. OSPF Message Types

Type 1	Router Links Advertisement
Type 2	Network Links Advertisement
Type 3	Summary Links Advertisement
Type 4	Autonomous System Boundary Router Summary Link Advertisement
Type 5	Autonomous System External Link Advertisement
Type 6	Multicast Group Membership Link State Advertisement

with the use of an IP address, the information in a router's Link State Advertisement consists of an IP address–cost metric pair. Exhibit 13 lists the six types of SLA messages that OSPF routers use.

Type 2 Message

The purpose of a Type 2 LSA message is to inform all routers within an area of the presence of a designated router (DR). Thus, a DR floods a Type 2 LSA upon its election. This message contains information about all routers in the area, as well as the fact that one is now the DR for the area.

Type 3 Message

Because an area border router (BR) connects adjacent areas, a mechanism is needed to describe networks reachable via the adjacent border router (ABR). Thus, an ABR router floods a Type 3 message into an area to inform routers in the area about other networks that are reachable from outside the area.

Type 4 Message

A Type 4 message describes the cost from the router issuing the message to an autonomous system boundary router. Thus, this message allows a boundary router that functions as a gateway to another autonomous system to note the cost associated with accessing different networks via different paths within its system.

Type 5 Message

A boundary router that connects autonomous systems generates a Type 5 message. This message describes an external network on another system reachable by the router. Thus, this message flows to routers in one autonomous system to describe a network reachable via a different system.

Type 6 Message

The last type of LSA is a Type 6 message. A Type 6 message enables a multicast-enabled OSPF router to distribute multicast group information instead of having to transmit multiple copies of packets.

Operation

The actual initialization of OSPF in an autonomous area requires a series of datagrams to be exchanged that enables the Designated Router and Backup to be selected and router adjacencies to be noted prior to routing information being exchanged. The most basic exchange between OSPF routers occurs via the transmission of Hello messages. Such messages flow between routers that enable routers within an area to discover one another, as well as to note the relationship between routers. Once the DR and BDR are selected, additional messages are exchanged that eventually enable one area to become aware of other areas, as well as networks reachable outside of the current autonomous system.

Although the initial learning process is complex, once routing table information is constructed, updates only occur when there is a change in the network structure or every 30 minutes. Thus, although OSPF initially requires more bandwidth than RIP, it rapidly reduces its bandwidth requirements.

Configuring Cisco Routers

In concluding this chapter, we will literally put theory into practice. That is, we will turn our attention to configuring routing protocols. In doing so, we will configure Cisco routers, as that vendor has approximately 70 percent of the market for this type of communications device.

Configuring RIP

The first routing protocol to configure is the Routing Information Protocol (RIP). RIP probably represents one of the most popular routing protocols as it is used by numerous small to medium-sized networks. Although RIP is limited to supporting a maximum of 15 hops, it is relatively easy to configure. To configure RIP under Cisco's Internetwork Operating System, one would perform the steps listed in Exhibit 14.

Exhibit 15 illustrates the RIP configuration process. In this example, it is assumed that the location router being configuring is connected to two Class C networks — 198.78.46.0 and 205.131.175.0. A question one might have is:

Exhibit 14. The Steps to Configuring RIP under Cisco's Internetwork Operating System

1. At the privileged prompt (#), type `config t` and press Enter, assuming one will configure the router from the terminal.
2. At the configuration prompt (`config`), type the keywords `router rip` and press Enter to select RIP as the routing protocol.
3. After entering `router rip` in 2, the configuration prompt will change to (`config-router`). At this prompt, enter the keyword `network` followed by what is referred to as the major network number. That number is the network address for the class A, B, or C network directly connected to the router. Continue entering the keyword `network` followed by the major network number for each IP network connected to the router.
4. After entering all directly connected networks, either type `End` or press CTRL-Z to terminate the configuration session.

Exhibit 15. Configuring RIP on a Cisco Router that Has Two Major Network Numbers

```
Router>enable
Router#config t
Enter configuration commands, one per line. End with CNTL/Z.
Router(config)#router rip
Router(config-router)#network 198.78.46.0
Router(config-router)#network 205.131.175.0
Router(config-router)#^Z
```

how does the router know which interface is connected to each network? The answer to this question is based on the fact that one would configure the protocol and network address for each router interface either during its setup or later using an applicable interface configuration command. Thus, the router setup process or the subsequent use of an applicable interface configuration command allowed the router to associate IP network addresses with its interfaces.

Examining RIP Routing Tables

If one has worked with IOS for awhile, then one is probably well aware that one handy command is the `show` command. With applicable parameters, the `show` command provides the ability to display numerous types of information. Because one is working with RIP, one might be interested in displaying the RIP routing table. To do so, one would enter the `show ip route` command at either the user or privileged prompt level. To view the RIP routing table, one would type `show ip route` at either the user or privileged prompt. As a refresher, one must to be in the router's privileged mode to perform configuration operations. In comparison, to display most types of information, one can be either in the router's user or the privileged mode.

Configuring IGRP

The inability of RIP to scale beyond 15 hops makes it ill-suited for use in intermediate and large internetworks. Thus, network managers and LAN administrators who have large networks need to consider a more scalable routing protocol. One such protocol is the Interior Gateway Routing Protocol (IGRP).

IGRP represents a distance vector routing protocol. However, unlike RIP, which only uses a hop count metric, IGRP permits the use of several metrics, such as delays, bandwidth, and reliability. In comparison to RIP, which is limited to 15 hops, IGRP can support routing information for a path that transverses up to 255 hops, which makes this routing protocol well-suited for large internetworks.

The configuration process for IGRP in a Cisco router environment is similar to the steps previously described for configuring RIP. The key difference between configuring RIP and IGRP is the fact that the latter must operate on a router that belongs to an autonomous system. Here, the term "autonomous system" (AS) represents a collection of networks operating under a common administration that share a common routing strategy. To uniquely define an AS, it is assigned a 16-bit decimal number. As one might expect, all routers that belong to the same autonomous system must be configured with the same AS number.

Exhibit 16 illustrates the configuration process for enabling IGRP on a router. Similar to enabling RIP, one would enter the router's privileged mode and type `config t` to configure the router from a terminal or via a Telnet session. Next, at the configuration prompt, one would type `router igrp` followed by the AS number. In the example illustrated in Exhibit 16, this author purposely used the router's built-in help facility by entering a question mark (`?`) to display available information about the `router igrp` command. Note that the next line informs us of the need to enter an autonomous system number in the range of 1 to 65535. Continuing with the configuration process and assuming that the router is part of AS `007`, one would enter the AS number. This is followed by entering a major network number. For this example it is assumed that the router only has one network directly connected. However, if there is more than one network, one would enter the keyword `network` followed by the major network number for each network directly connected to the router. Once finished, one would then either enter CTRL-Z or type `end` to terminate the configuration process.

One can use the `show` command to display the routing table built by IGRP. To do so, one would enter the command `show ip route`. One can also view IGRP routing information using the `show ip route` command.

Under IGRP, updates are transmitted every 90 seconds or at one third the rate of RIP's 30-second interval. A route will be declared inaccessible if it does not receive an update from the first router in the route within three update periods (270 seconds). After seven update periods (630 seconds), the router will remove the route from its routing table.

Although the configuration of IGRP is very similar to RIP, internally each router using IGRP uses several types of metric information. For each path

Exhibit 16. The Cisco Router IGRP Configuration Process

```
Router#config t
Enter configuration commands, one per line. End with CNTL/Z.
Router(config)#router igrp ?
 <1-65535> Autonomous system number
Router(config)#router igrp 007
Router(config-router)#network 198.78.44.0
Router(config-router)#end
```

through an AS, IGRP records the segment with the lowest bandwidth, the delay, smallest MTU (maximum transmission unit), reliability, and traffic load. For a given route, IGRP computes a 32-bit metric that represents the sum of the segment delays and the lowest segment bandwidth. For a network of mixed media, the route with the lowest metric indicates the most desirable path to a destination. If the network is homogenous, such as all Fast Ethernet media, then the metric becomes a hop count and the lowest hop count reflects the most desirable path. The computation of the path metric occurs transparently; however, to view this information, one should use the `debug ip transaction` command.

Configuring OSPF

Configuring OSPF in a Cisco router environment represents a two-step process. First, enable OSPF using the router OSPF command whose format is shown below:

```
router ospf <process id>
```

where the `process id` represents a numeric value local to the router. Seondly, assign areas to router interfaces using the network command whose format is shown below:

```
network <network|IP address><wildcard mask><area-id>
```

Here, the wildcard mask uses a 0 bit to represent a match and a 1 bit to represent a don't care. The `area-id` represents the area number to which the router interface will belong.

To illustrate the configuration of OSPF, assume one has a three-port router as indicated in Exhibit 17. Note that two ports (E0 and E1) are connected to Ethernet segments, while the third port represents a serial port (S0). The two Ethernet ports are assumed to reside in the same area, while the serial port is in a different area.

To configure OSPF on the router illustrated in Exhibit 17 one would use the following commands:

```
interface Ethernet0
ip address 205.131.176.2 255.255.255.0
interface Ethernet1
ip address 205.131.175.1 255.255.255.0
router ospf 30
network 205.131.0.0 0.0.25.255 area 0.0.0.0
network 198.78.46.1 0.0.0.0 area 23
```

If one wanted to add simple password authentication, one would use the authentication key command show whose format is:

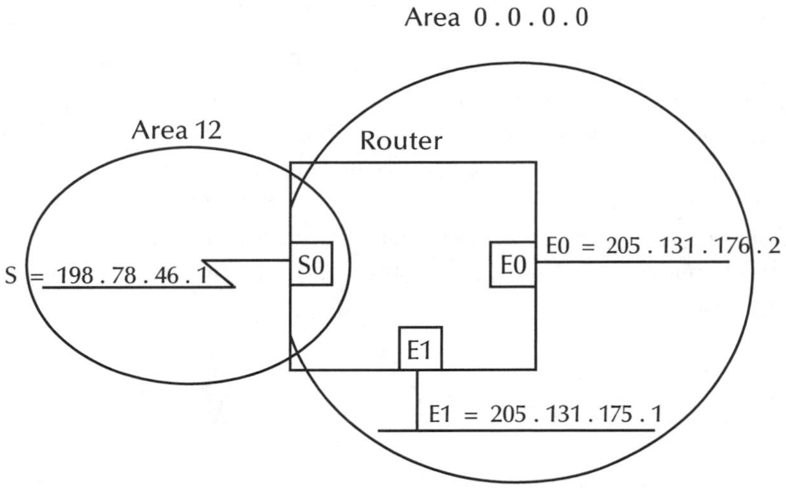

Exhibit 17. An OSPF Router that Participates in Multiple Areas

```
ip ospf authentication-key key
```

This command would be placed under a specific interface. One would also need to add the following area command under the router ospf <process-id> area:

```
area area-id authentication
```

The following example illustrates the assignment of the password hard2get to the prior OSPF configuration example for area 0 and the password treblig5 for area 23.

```
interface Ethernet0
ip address 205.131.176.2 255.255.255.0
ip ospf authentication-key hard2get
interface Ethernet1
ip address 205.131.176.1 255.255.255.0
ip ospf authentication-key hard2get
interface seriol0
ip address 198.78.46.1 255.255.255.0
ip ospf authentication-key treblig5
router ospf 30
network 205.131.0.0 0.0.255.255 area 0.0.0.0
area 0 authentication
network 198.78.46.1 0.0.0.0 area 23
area 23 authentication
```

Summary

As indicated in this section, the configuration of an applicable routing protocol represents a relatively simple process in a Cisco router environment. However, prior to configuring a router to use an applicable routing protocol, one must consider the size of the network and how one may wish to have a specific route between networks selected when there are multiple routes. By careful consideration of the routing protocol, one can make its configuration process both relatively easy as well as avoid the necessity for reconfiguring routers with a different protocol.

Chapter 8

Security Threats

The ability to counter security threats requires an understanding of those threats, which is the objective of this chapter. This chapter focuses attention on a variety of threats to both computers and the networks to which they are connected. Security threats to be examined include password cracking, network scanning, viruses, worms, and techniques that are used to deny service to legitimate users, the latter categorized as denial-of-service attacks. Information presented in this chapter can be considered to form a foundation for additional security-related material presented in Chapter 9, which focuses on techniques that can be employed to enhance security. While Chapter 9 focuses on techniques that can be used to enhance security, those techniques are primarily oriented toward the protection of the router connected to a public network, as well as the use of router access lists and firewalls to filter different types of network traffic. To ensure that readers will understand how to counter each threat discussed in this chapter, this chapter will either directly note an applicable countermeasure or reference material presented in Chapter 9.

Password Cracking

In examining the devices that form a network, one notes that one thing they all have in common is a password for controlling access. That is, regardless of whether a network device is a router, server, or access controller, the ability to access the device to issue commands, retrieve data, or obtain network access normally depends upon the use of a user identifier (user ID) and associated password. Although tokens and even biometrics are used to enhance access security, the vast majority of device access continues to be based on the use of a user ID and password. Perhaps due to this, it is a relatively easy process to locate numerous password cracking tools on the Internet.

Internet Availability

If one enters such search terms as "hacker tools," "password cracking," or even "passwords" in a Web search engine, one will be amazed at the wealth of available tools. If you can access such tools, so can hackers. For example, consider Exhibit 1 that illustrates the home page for Internet/Network Security located at http://netsecurity.about.com. Looking carefully at the lower portion of the Web page, note the section titled "Hacker Tools." Under that section, one can view a brief description of a Windows NT password cracker named Lopht Crack, followed by a barely visible second program. If one surfed to this Web page and scrolled through its listing, one would discover a series of programs one could use to gain access to different types of computers as well as other types of hacker tools. This site is just one of many Web sites that provide access to different types of password cracking programs that facilitate obtaining access to different types of devices.

Cracking Methods

There are several methods commonly employed by password cracking programs. Perhaps the oldest technique is to use the entries in an electronic dictionary as a mechanism to determine the password. However, for this and other techniques to succeed, the password cracker must also have knowledge of the user ID.

A second common password cracking technique is referred to as a brute-force technique. In this technique, a program commences operation by first trying every character for a single character position, then expanding the position by one character and trying every character combination for two character positions, etc. As noted later in this chapter, the selection of an appropriate password can defeat a dictionary attack as well as delay a brute-force attack to the point where its probability of success is negligible.

User-ID Vulnerabilities

Because many organizations create user IDs by appending first and middle initials to the last name of employees, it is relatively easy to use a telephone directory to determine employee user IDs. If an employee does not have a middle name, many organizations use the letter "X" as the middle initial when creating a user ID, making the user ID guessing process rather easy.

Once a hacker determines a user ID, he or she will typically use one or more password cracking programs in an attempt to gain illegal entry into a computer system. Because most modern operation systems permit a limit to be placed upon the number of invalid password sign-on attempts that can occur during a predefined interval, it is possible to counter a hacker through a lockout facility. However, lockouts can represent a double-edged sword.

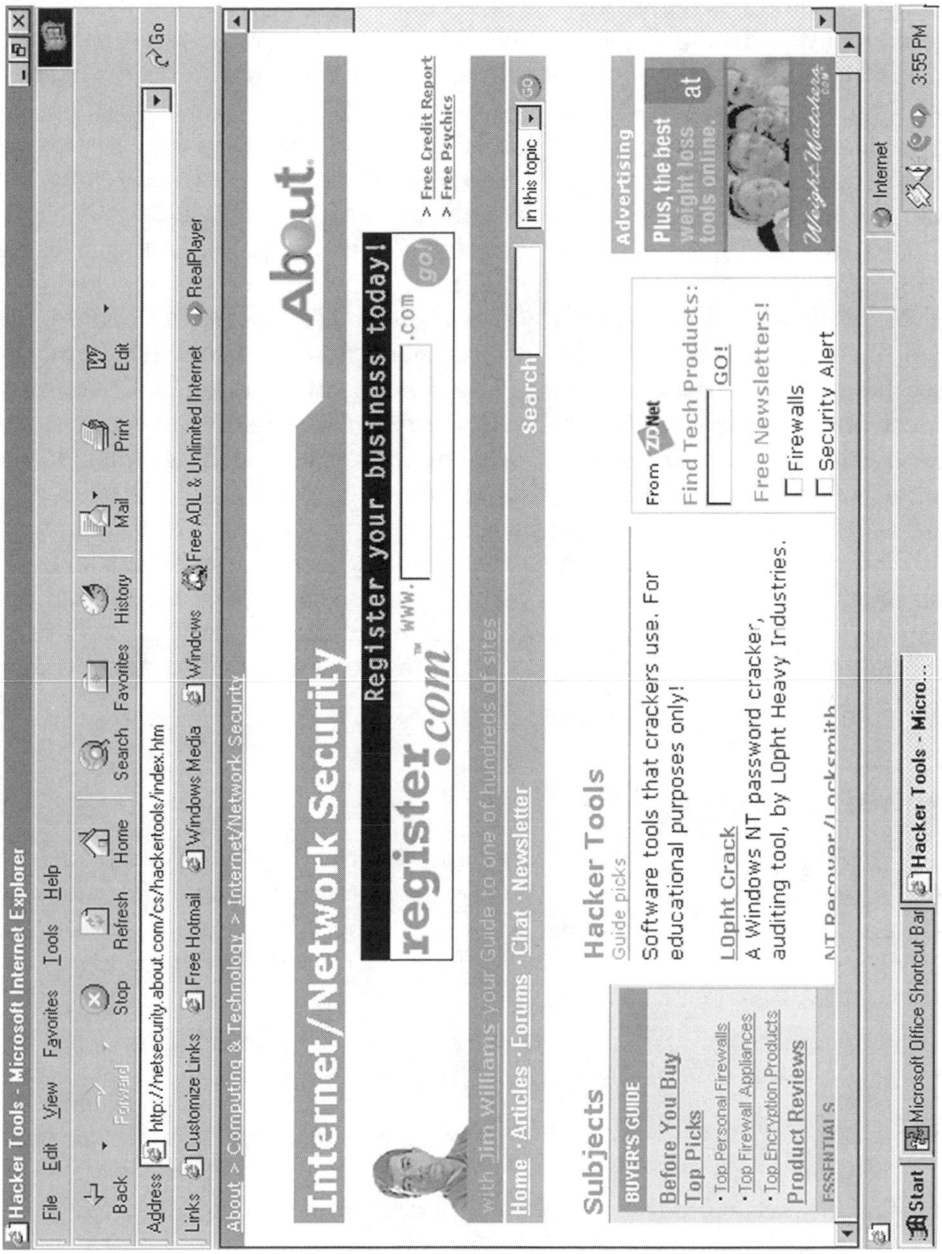

Exhibit 1. The Internet/Network Security Home Page

Lockouts

While successful password cracking can be extremely harmful, it is entirely possible for unsuccessful attempts to be dangerous to the activities of an organization. At first glance, the prior statement sounds a bit bizarre, and thus an explanation is warranted.

Many operating systems include a lockout facility. When enabled, the lockout facility tracks the number of invalid log-on attempts during a particular period of time. If the number of invalid log-on attempts reaches a predefined threshold, the account status is changed to "lockout," which precludes a hacker from additional password guesses but, in addition, blocks a legitimate user from accessing his or her account. A lockout duration, which is set by the administrator, governs the length of time the account stays in its lockout status.

If a hacker obtains a telephone directory of an organization that uses an easy-to-guess user ID creation scheme, it becomes rather easy to lock out most, if not all, employees of their accounts. To do so, the hacker could write a script that cycles through a table of intelligently guessed user IDs, typically trying three to five passwords to gain access to an account, because most lockouts are set to initiate when three to five unsuccessful log-on attempts occur. If this action occurred at 7:45 a.m. on a Monday morning, it is entirely possible that at a little after 8:00 a.m. the network administrator's telephone would be constantly ringing, with calls from employees who did not understand why they could not log on to the network server or another device.

Although it is difficult to stop lockouts from occurring because they have a relatively low threshold, the network administrator can set the duration of a lockout condition to 15 or 30 minutes. Doing so will minimize the effect of a hacker lockout attack.

Password Creation Policy

Concerning the use of dictionary attacks and other types of password cracking software, one may be able to thwart most or all password cracking attempts through a careful password creation policy. The following five password creation steps can minimize risk and should be considered when creating new accounts as well as when account users need to change their passwords.

1. Avoid using names, places, or items that are easily guessed.
2. Avoid the use of words that are in English and foreign dictionaries.
3. Include one or more numbers in a password to preclude a successful dictionary attack.
4. Ensure passwords are at least six or more characters in length.
5. Consider adding non-alphanumeric characters to the password.

In examining the above steps, the last two require a degree of elaboration. Because a brute-force password cracking program commences operation by cycling through all the letters and numbers for one position and then doing

Exhibit 2. Potenential Password Combinations Based upon 46 Distinct Values Permitted per Position

Password Length	*Combinations*
1	46 × 1 = 46
2	46 ×46 = 2116
3	46 ×46 ×46 = 97,336
4	46 ×46 ×46 × 46 = 4,477,456
5	46 × 46 ×46 ×46 ×46 = 205,962,976
6	46 ×46 ×46 ×46 ×46 ×46 = 9.4742969e + 09
7	46 ×46 ×46 ×46 ×46 ×46 ×46 = 4.35817657e +11
8	46 ×46 ×46 ×46 ×46 ×46 ×46 ×46 = 2.0473122e + 13
9	46 ×46 ×46 ×46 ×46 ×46 ×46 ×46 × 46 = 9.22190468e + 14

it for two positions, continuously expanding the attempts, a short password is more susceptible to breaking than a longer password. Thus, expanding the length of a password as well as using non-alphanumeric characters, such as the asterisk or the exclamation point, considerably expands the number of combinations a password cracking program needs to try. For example, assume the use of a two-character alphanumeric password. Then, the maximum number of combinations a password cracking program needs to try becomes:

$$36 \times 36 = 1296$$

Now assume each character position can include both alphanumerics as well as such special characters as the pound sign (#), asterisk (*), exclamation point (!), greater than (>), less than (<), left bracket ([), right bracket (]), at sign (@), carrot (^), and plus (+), for a total of ten additional characters. The maximum number of combinations associated with a two-position password then becomes:

$$46 \times 46 = 2116$$

Note that the addition of ten characters that can be used in the password resulted in a 2116/1296 × 100, or a 163 percent increase in the number of combinations a password cracking program needs to try. Now expand the number of positions in the password. For example, a three-position password that supports alphanumerics as well as the ten special characters just mentioned results in 46 × 46 × 46, or 97336 potential combinations. Exhibit 2 indicates the potential combinations for a password of n positions, with n varying from 1 to 9 when each position can have one of 46 distinct values.

In examining the entries in Exhibit 2, assume a computer can attempt 1000 log-on attempts per minute, which is rather high for remote access where datagrams are delayed as they flow through a network. Then, for a six-position password, the time required to cycle through all combinations would be:

$$\frac{9{,}474{,}296{,}900}{1000} = 9{,}474{,}290 \text{ seconds}$$

or 6579 days. Hopefully, someone would realize during a 6579-day period that you were under attack! Given an appreciation for password cracking, one can now focus on several other attack areas that warrant attention.

File and Print Sharing

Under Microsoft Windows, the use of its built-in File and Print Sharing feature in effect turns a computer into a file server. While the intent of file and print sharing is to allow one computer to use resources on another, it can also be dangerous. By examining how it is put into effect one can learn how to control its potential vulnerability.

Enabling

One can enable File and Print Sharing through the Control Panel, selecting the network icon. From the dialog box labeled Network, one will note a button labeled "File and Print Sharing" which, when selected, generates a pop-up box that enables one to enable file sharing and/or print sharing. Exhibit 3 illustrates the File and Print Sharing dialog box.

In examining Exhibit 3, note that by itself the File and Print Sharing dialog box is only concerned with enabling or disabling one or both sharing methods. Thus, it is relatively easy to enable sharing and not realize that one, in effect, just turned the computer into a server without any access controls.

Establishing Access Controls

If one knows where to look and what to do, it is possible to establish access controls on one's shares. For example, under Windows 98, one would click on the tab labeled Access Control as illustrated in Exhibit 4. As noted in the referenced illustration, one can enable share-level access control and provide a password for each shared resource, or one can select user-level access control and specify users and groups who have access to each shared resource.

Once sharing has been set, one can control files and printers to share by right-clicking on a resource. Under Windows 2000 and other more modern versions of the Windows operating system, it is possible to obtain some additional controls beyond that offered by earlier versions of Windows. The left portion of Exhibit 5 illustrates the Properties dialog box after this author right-clicked on the folder labeled Temp and selected sharing from the resulting pop-up window. Note that the radio button associated with the label "Share this folder" was selected to share the folder. Also note that one can add comments concerning a share as well as limit the maximum number of users that can access a share.

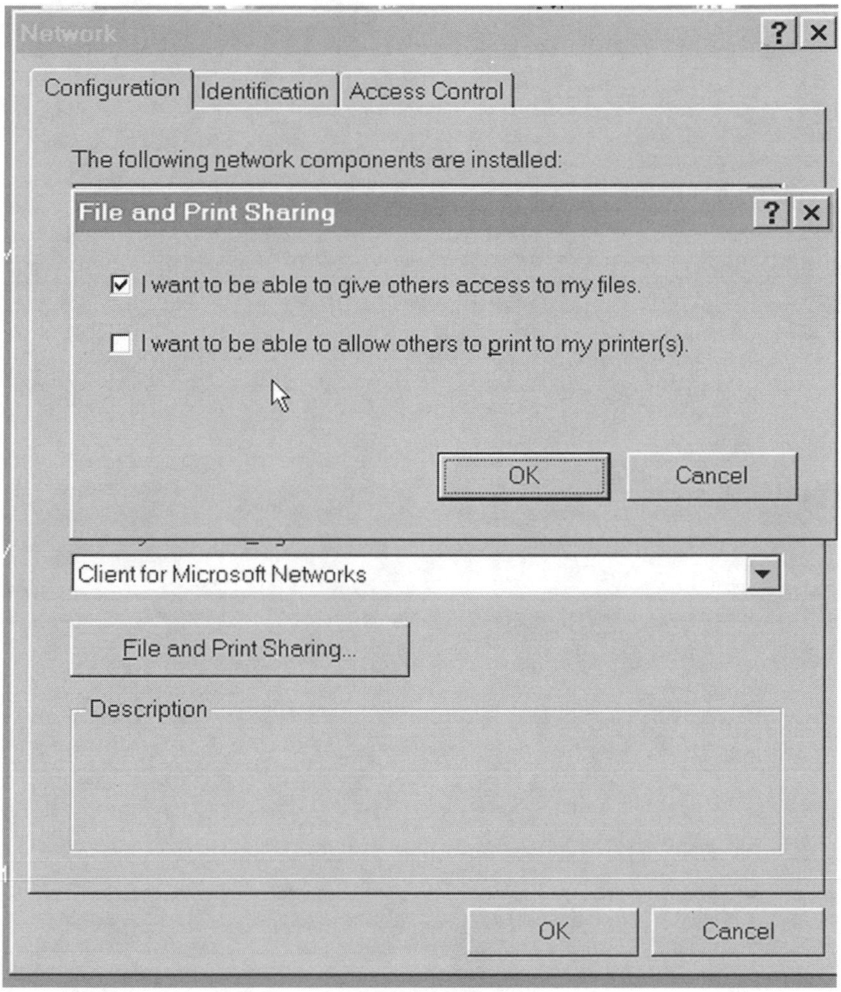

Exhibit 3. The File and Print Sharing Dialog Box

The selection of the Permissions button results in the display of the dialog box shown in the right portion of Exhibit 5. Similar to Windows NT, under Windows 2000 one can simply click on the buttons labeled Add and Remove to change users and user groups that can access a share. Thus, if one takes the time to select an appropriate password or control those users that should access a share, one can obtain a reasonable level of security for shares.

Viruses and Worms

One of the modern plagues of computing is the creation of programs that include code designed to harm data or replicate itself, with the latter either taking up all available storage or propagating itself to other computers on a network. A virus can be considered to represent code that causes some type

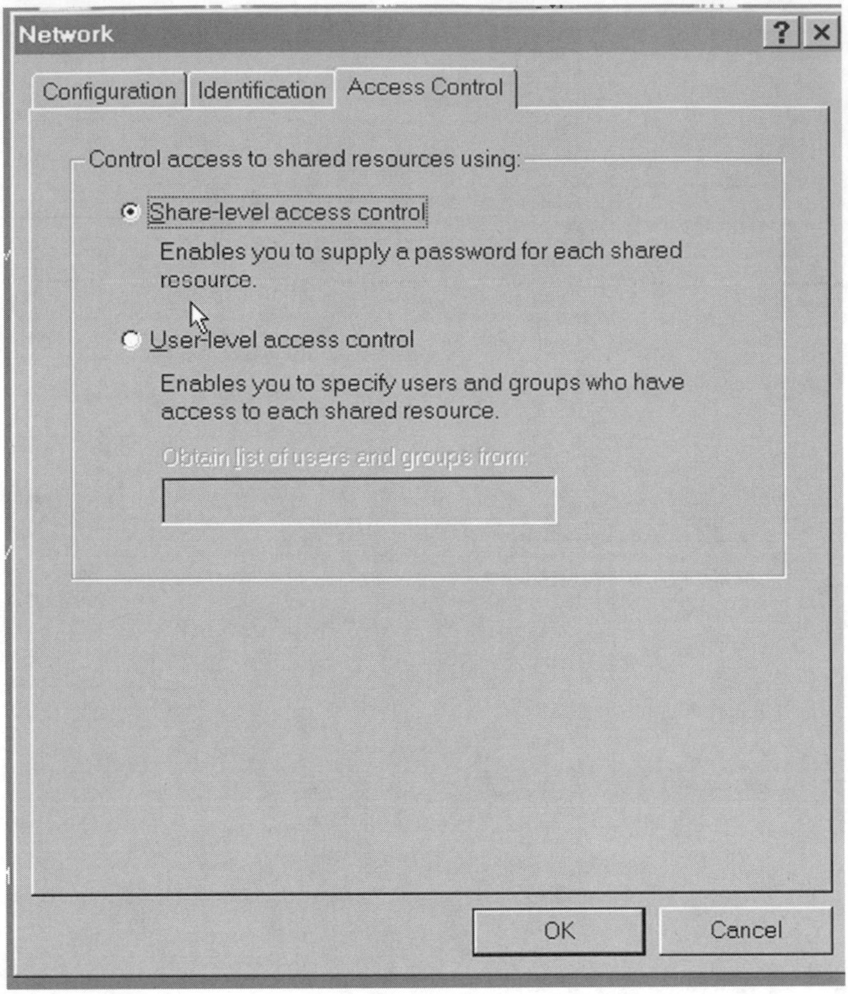

Exhibit 4. The Access Control Tab in the Network Dialog Box

of harmful effect and which must be executed to operate. In comparison, a worm represents a self-contained program that spreads copies of itself, usually automatically, to other computers. Because viruses are normally more harmful than worms, we will focus our attention upon the former as well as methods that can be used to control their effect.

Types of Viruses

The majority of viruses can be classified into four main categories. Those categories include boot sector, file infector, multi-partite, and macro viruses. A boot sector virus infects the boot sector of a drive, loading itself into memory prior to system files being loaded. This enables the boot sector virus to take control of a computer as well as spread itself.

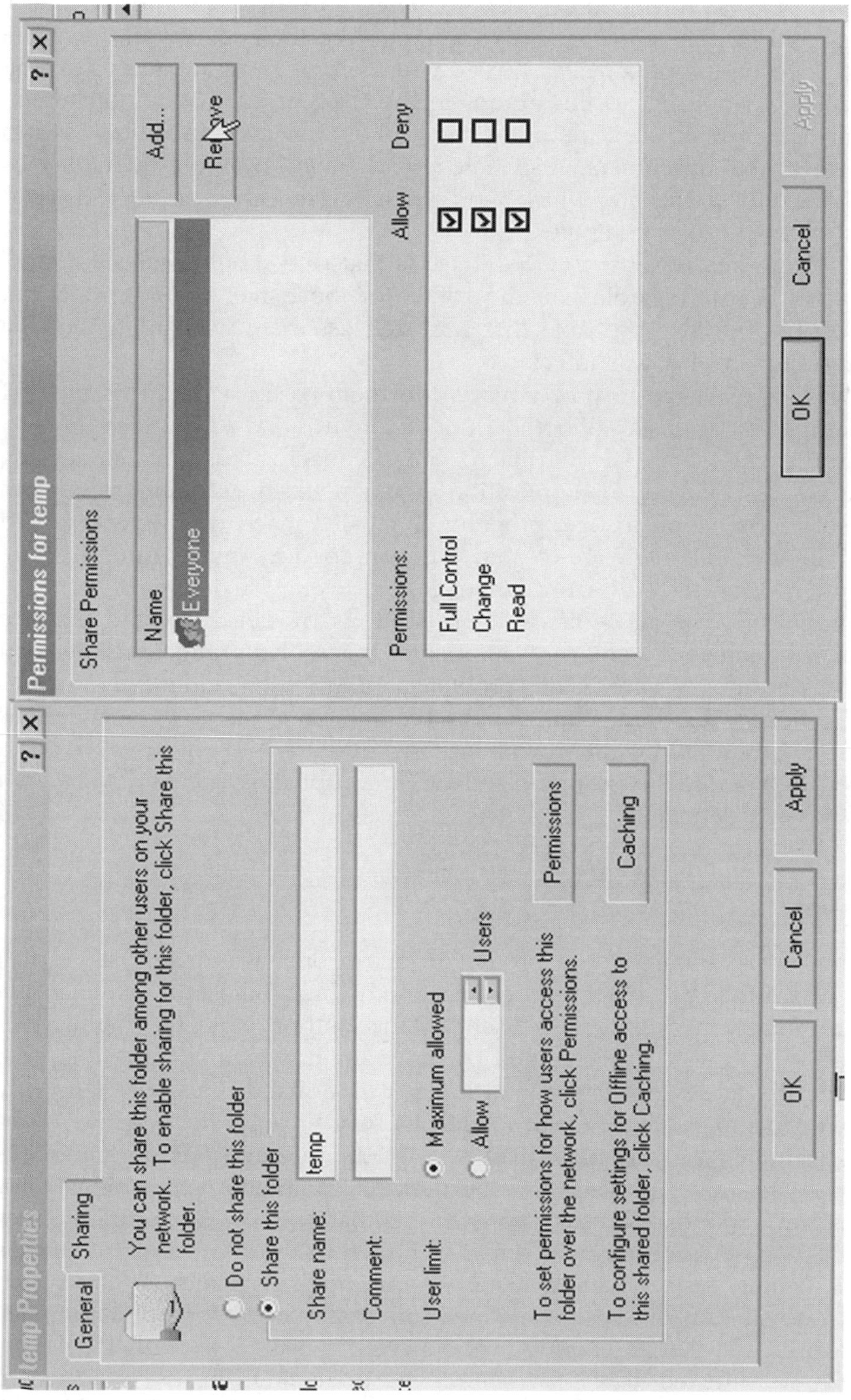

Exhibit 5. Configuring Access to a Shared Folder under Windows 2000

A second type or category of virus is a file infector. File infector viruses are created as executable files and typically have the extension .com, .exe, .bin, .ovl, or .sys. Such viruses become active whenever an infected file is activated and can remain in memory long after the file is executed. Over the past two decades, approximately 10,000 viruses have been identified. Exhibit 6 illustrates a virus sent to this author in the form of an e-mail attachment. Note that this author used the anti-virus facility provided by Yahoo Mail to check the e-mail attachment. Also note that the virus was masquerading as an audio/x-midi sound file, which indicates how far some people will go to harm another person's computer.

One of the key lessons from Exhibit 6 is that one should scan all attachments. This is true regardless of the source of the e-mail, because it is not only possible but also probable that a trusted associate will unintentionally relay a document that was infected.

A third type or category of virus is the multi-partite virus. This type of virus has the characteristics of both a boot sector virus and a file infecting virus.

A fourth type of virus is the macro virus. A macro virus is created using the macro capability of an application program, such as Microsoft's word processor or Excel spreadsheet program. Typically, macro viruses are spread via e-mail. Although many are created using an application program, they are also written using the Perl script language and even Visual Basic.

Until a few years ago, Microsoft applications by default would execute macros, resulting in a significant number of macro virus infections. As end users became more aware of the problem and Microsoft added warnings to its applications prior to executing macros, the number of macro virus infections decreased. Despite of this improvement, organizations and end users need to consider the use of virus scanning software and updating such software with the latest virus definitions.

Scanning

To obtain a maximum level of protection on an organizational basis, e-mail should be scanned as it enters an organization. Exhibit 7 illustrates an example of e-mail scanning of a message sent to this author. Note the highlighted information automatically generated by the scanner, which tells the recipient that while the message was scanned it is possible that a virus with currently unknown operation characteristics made its way through the scanning software. In addition to scanning e-mail as it enters an organization, employees should use scanning software on their desktop computers. The rationale for this apparent redundancy results from the fact that it is possible for employees to easily bypass an enterprise e-mail scanner using a browser to access Hotmail, Yahoo Mail, or another service. Although it is nice to think that employees will scan all e-mail attachments, in reality many forget. In addition, it is also possible that an employee could bring a disk to work that contains one or more infected files. Based upon the preceding, the use of desktop virus scanners provides protection against viruses transported via floppy disk

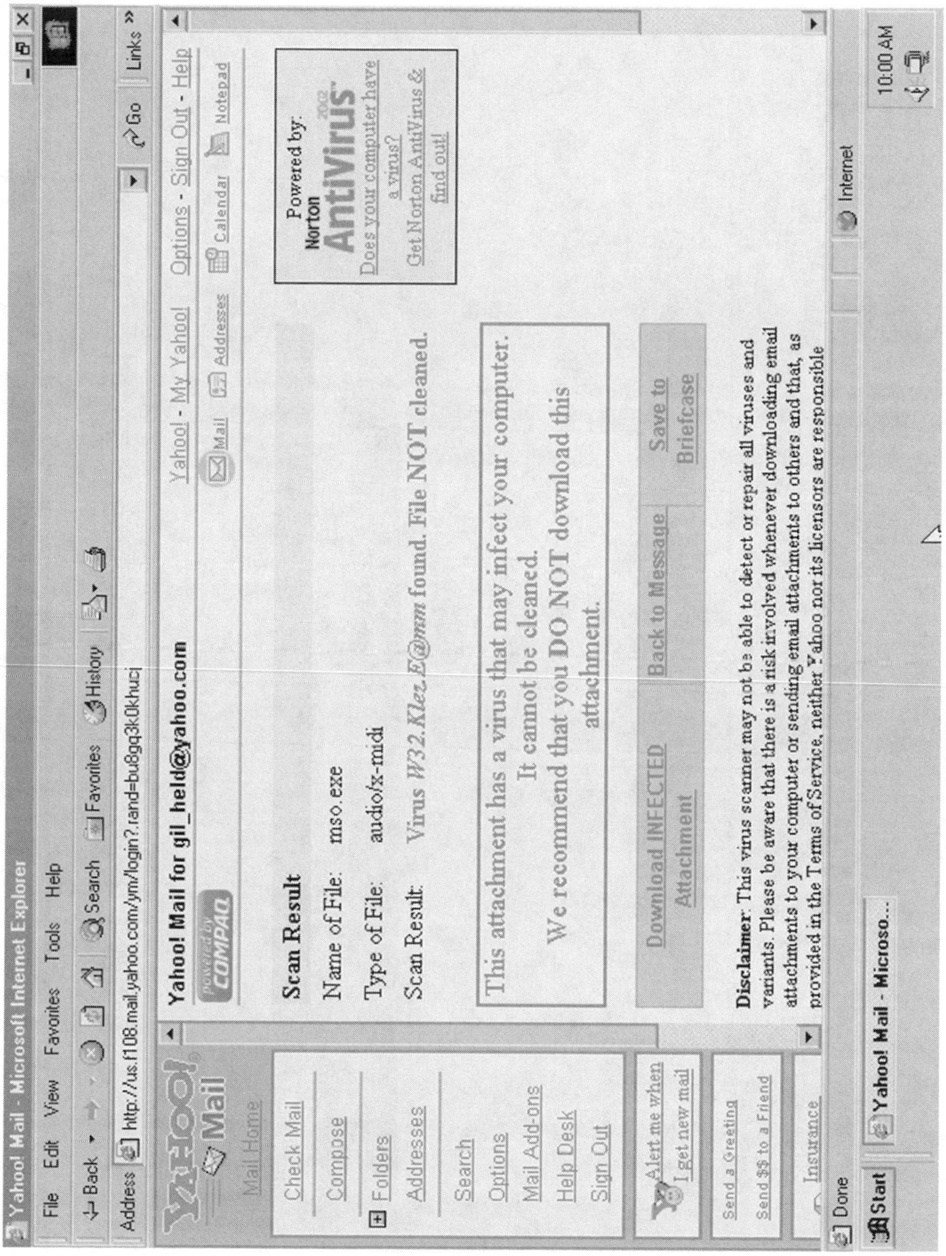

Exhibit 6. Scanning an E-mail Attachment

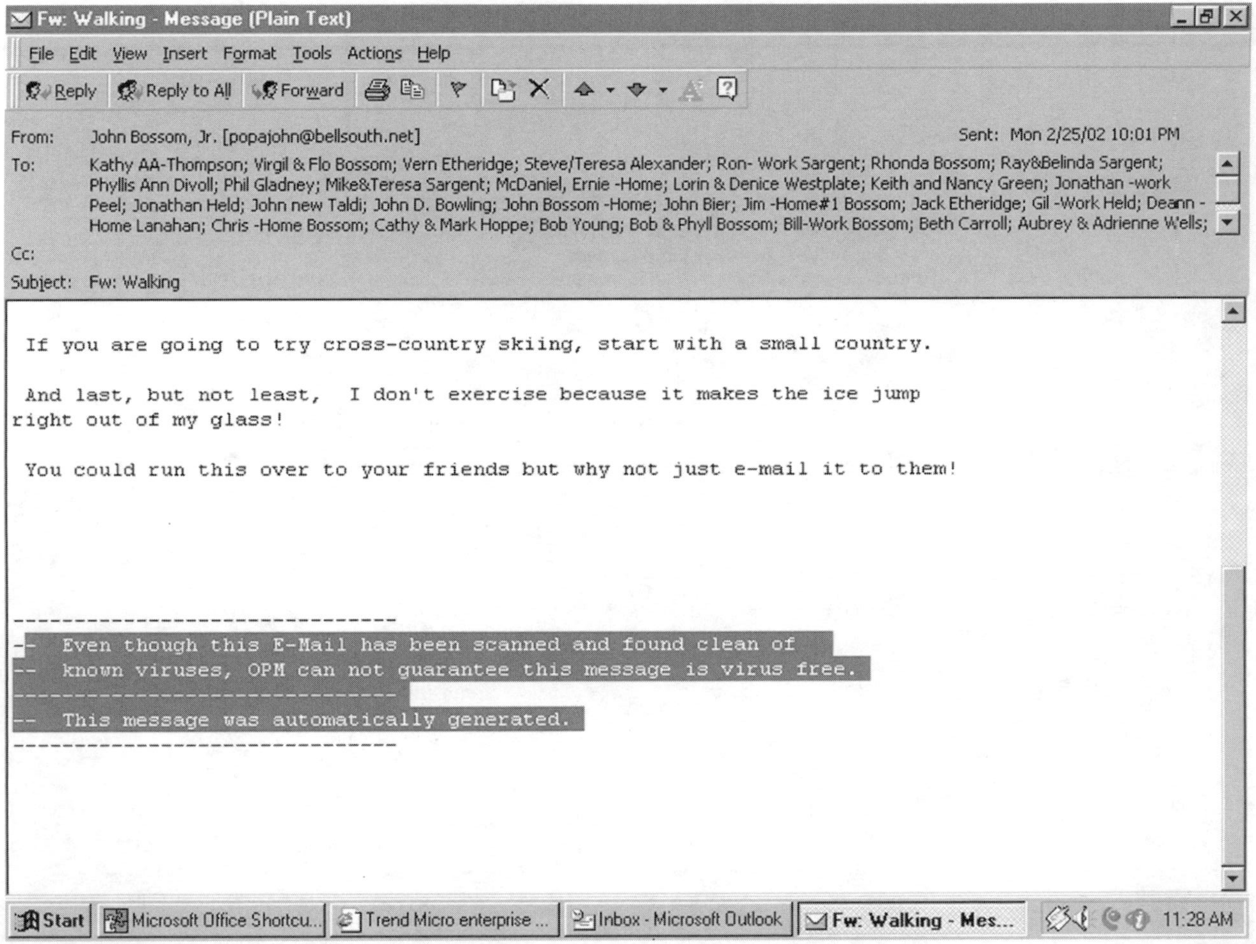

Exhibit 7. An Enterprise Virus Scanner

as well as those that could be inadvertently obtained through a Web-based e-mail service or even an FTP data transfer.

Network Attacks

While viruses and worms are designed to self-propagate, they are rarely developed to attack specific networks. Instead, they attempt to either create random IP addresses or use the address book contained in an e-mail application to perform a continuation of their dirty deed. Through the use of virus scanners, regularly updating virus definitions, and obtaining and applying software patches, one can minimize the potential damage resulting from self-propagating code. Another threat that is a bit more difficult to counter is intrusion via the Internet, in which one's network and computer resources are the direct target. Thus, this section focuses on a series of attacks that target computers or hardware devices.

Using Whois

While some hackers scan blocks of IP addresses for vulnerabilities, other hackers use specific tools to locate targets of interest. One such tool is operated by the Internet Network Information Center (InterNIC) as a mechanism to provide public information concerning Internet domain name registrations. This tool, known as Whois, represents a double-edged sword because it can also be used by persons to determine information about targets of interest.

Exhibit 8 illustrates the home page of the InterNIC Web site, located at www.internic.net. Note the cursor pointing to the term "Whois," which when clicked takes the user to the Whois search facility.

Exhibit 9 illustrates the InterNIC Whois search page. Note that a Whois search is applicable for eight top-level domains; however, .gov is not supported. For this example, this author entered harvard.edu for the domain name in an attempt to determine applicable information stored by the registry service. Then, simply clicking on the Submit button resulted in the display of a significant amount of information concerning Harvard University.

Exhibit 10 illustrates a portion of the information returned from the Whois search. Note that the search returns the name of the administrative contact as well as his telephone number and e-mail address. In addition, the name servers used by Harvard, to include their host names and IP addresses, are also returned. From this information it is relatively easy to develop several types of attacks. For example, by noting the IP address of the two name servers, a hacker could initiate a scan to determine all active hosts on each network. That scan could include testing different ports to determine what services are supported by each address. In fact, there are a large number of port scanning tools available on the Internet that can both simplify the life of a hacker as well as be put to good use by network operators. Concerning the latter, by using a port scanner from outside a network, one can determine possible

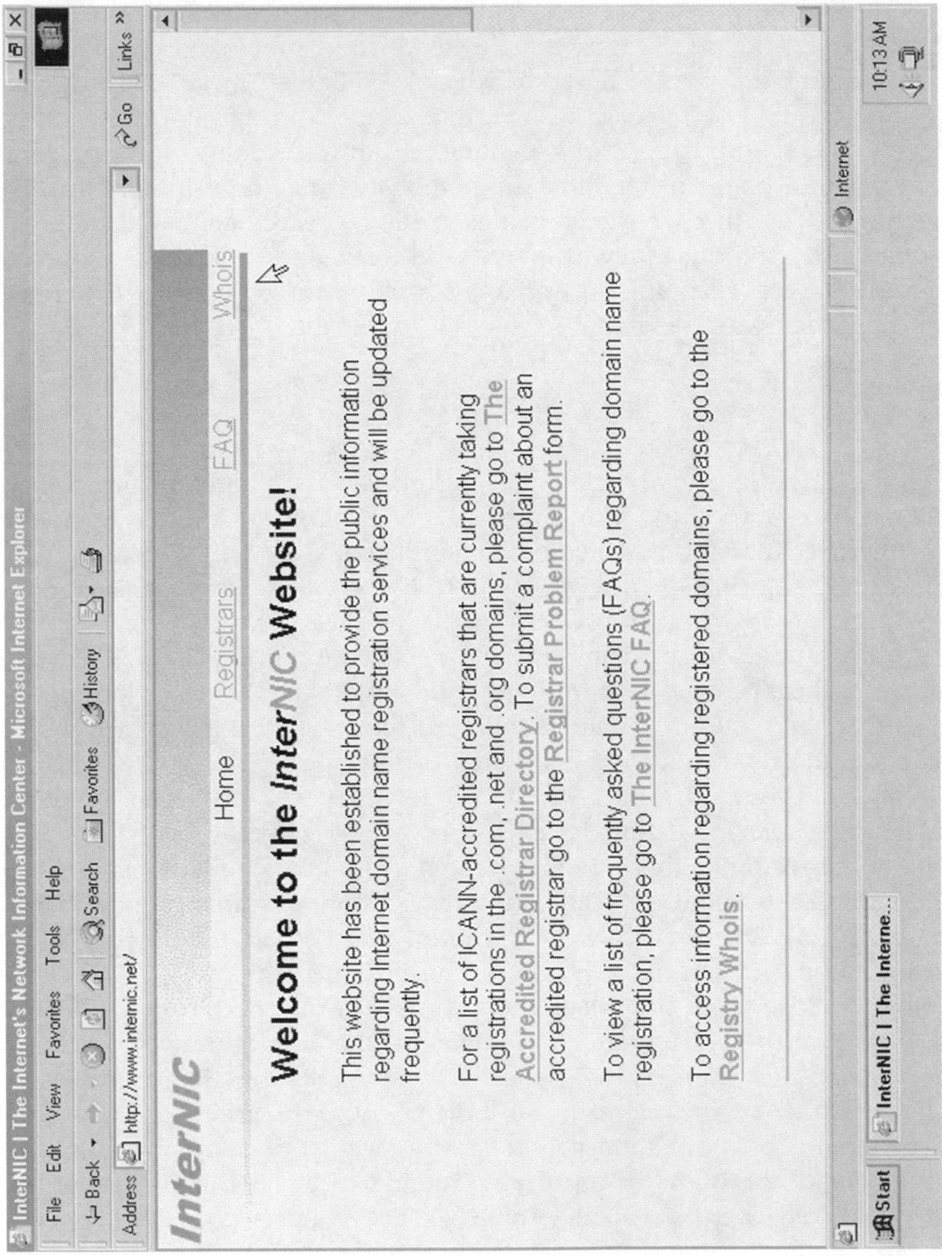

Exhibit 8. The Internet Network Information Center (InterNIC) Home Page

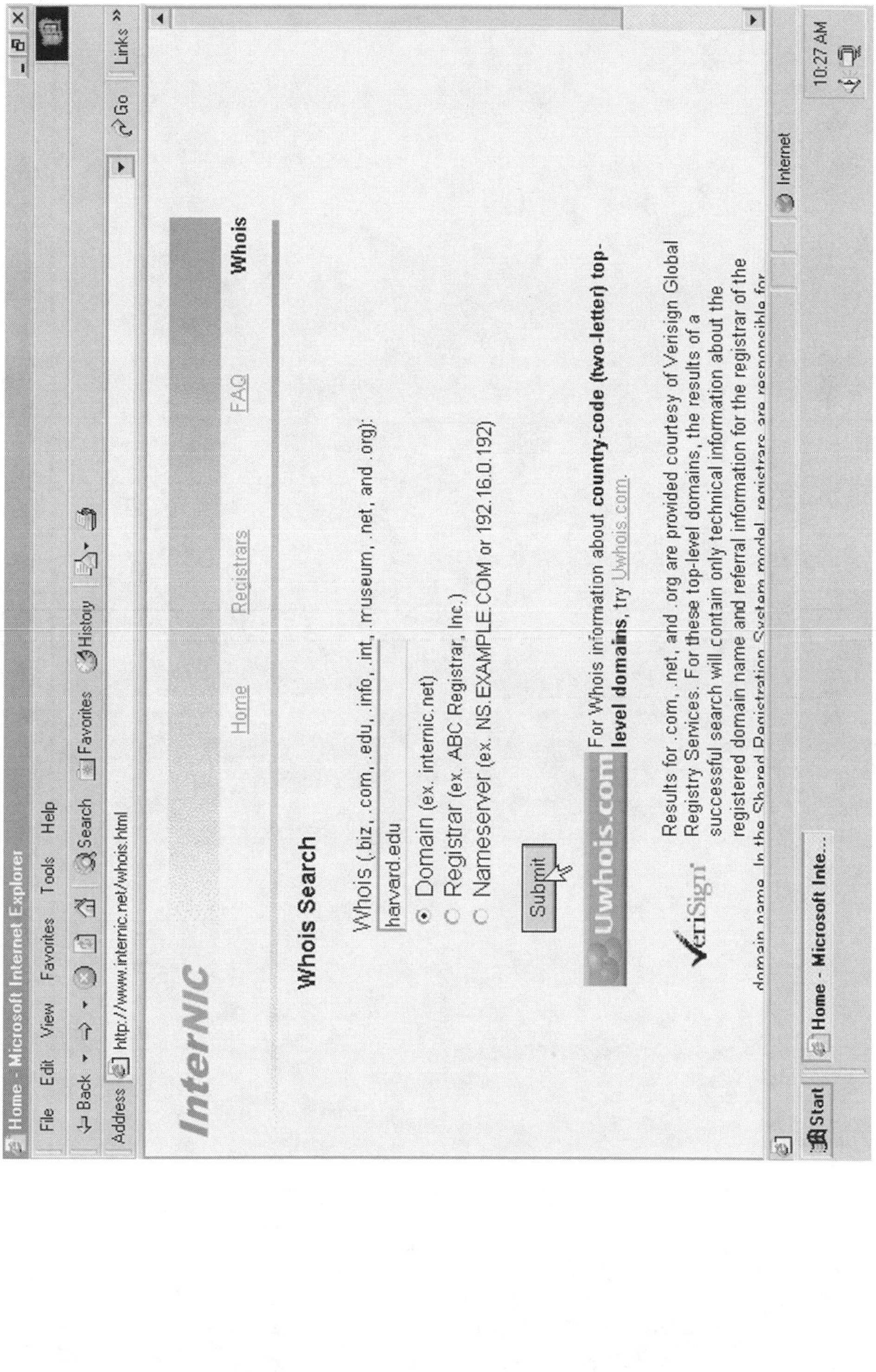

Exhibit 9. Using the Whois Search Facility Operated by the InterNIC

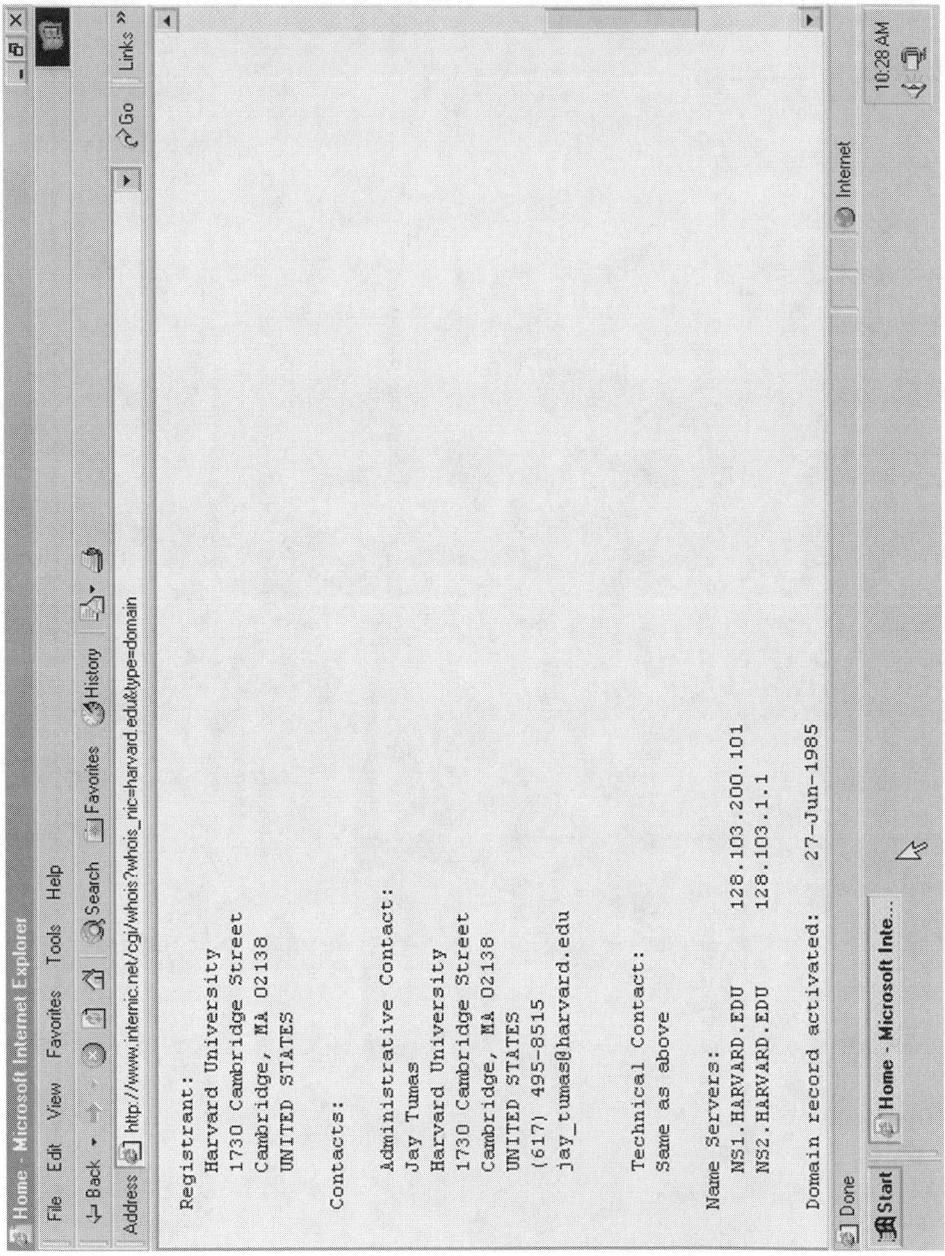

Exhibit 10. Examining the Results of a Whois Search of the Harvard University Domain

network vulnerabilities and initiate action to close any security holes found. In fact, the Internet/Network Security Web page previously shown in Exhibit 1 included links to several scanning programs, to include one that specifically looks for Windows shares within an IP range.

Hacker Search Techniques

Once hackers select a target, there are a variety of techniques they can consider using to cause harm to both computers and networks. First, they can search for well-known ports that are supported by different addresses as a mechanism to note different processes and services that can be attacked. Once ports are located, hackers can consider a literal "bag of tricks" in an attempt to cause harm. For example, one common trick is to transmit datagrams with peculiar features, such as being too long or too short, hoping to cause overflow or underflow conditions. Because it takes time for a hacker to scan a network and attempt to gain access to a process or service or initiate a buffer overflow or similar attack, it is important to detect the occurrence of such in-progress attacks. In fact, a large number of intrusion detection software (IDS) products are available from vendors designed to detect port scanning, ping sweeps and in some instances the uploading of executables, the attempted exploitation of an operating system, and similar attacks. To make readers aware of the many types of network and host attacks, this section examines some of the more prominent ones.

Ping Sweeps

A ping sweep occurs when a person writes a script to ping a series of IP addresses. Through the use of a ping sweep it becomes possible to determine the active hosts on a network. This is typically followed by many hackers with a ping attack or a directed broadcast attack, or both. Thus, let us focus on these two attack methods.

Ping Attack

A ping attack represents an unsophisticated attack method that can, under certain conditions, cause havoc to a network. To understand how this is possible, assume the target one wishes to attack has a 64-kbps connection to the Internet.

One of the options of the Microsoft version of Ping is `-t`, which provides for continuous pinging of the target host until a CTRL-C is entered to terminate the program. Another valuable option is `-w`, which permits one to define a timeout in milliseconds to wait for a reply. A third option worth considering is the `-l` option, which provides the ability to set the number of bytes (default is 32) transmitted when a ping occurs. By incorporating all three options, one can saturate the connection of a target. For example, consider Exhibit 11, which illustrates the use of a ping attack against the host www.opm.gov. Note that the `-l` option is followed by 128, which results in the reply containing 128 bytes. Because the Microsoft version of Ping will transmit one echo request per second, using a size of 128 bytes results in the target transmitting 128 bytes × 8 bits/byte, or 1024 bps in the form of ping replies. If the hacker goes into a university computer laboratory and sets ping on 30 computers, he or she will force the target to use half its Internet bandwidth replying to the continuous string of pings. If the hacker uses the `-l` option with a value of 256, each reply will contain 256 bytes. In this situation, the hacker could consume all available bandwidth by setting ping on 30 workstations to attack a common target. Similarly, increasing the `-l` option value to 512 would result in the target replying with 512 bytes to each ping, a situation that would require 15 workstations to, in effect, saturate a 64-kbps Internet connection. In Chapter 9, when examining how one can use router access lists, there is

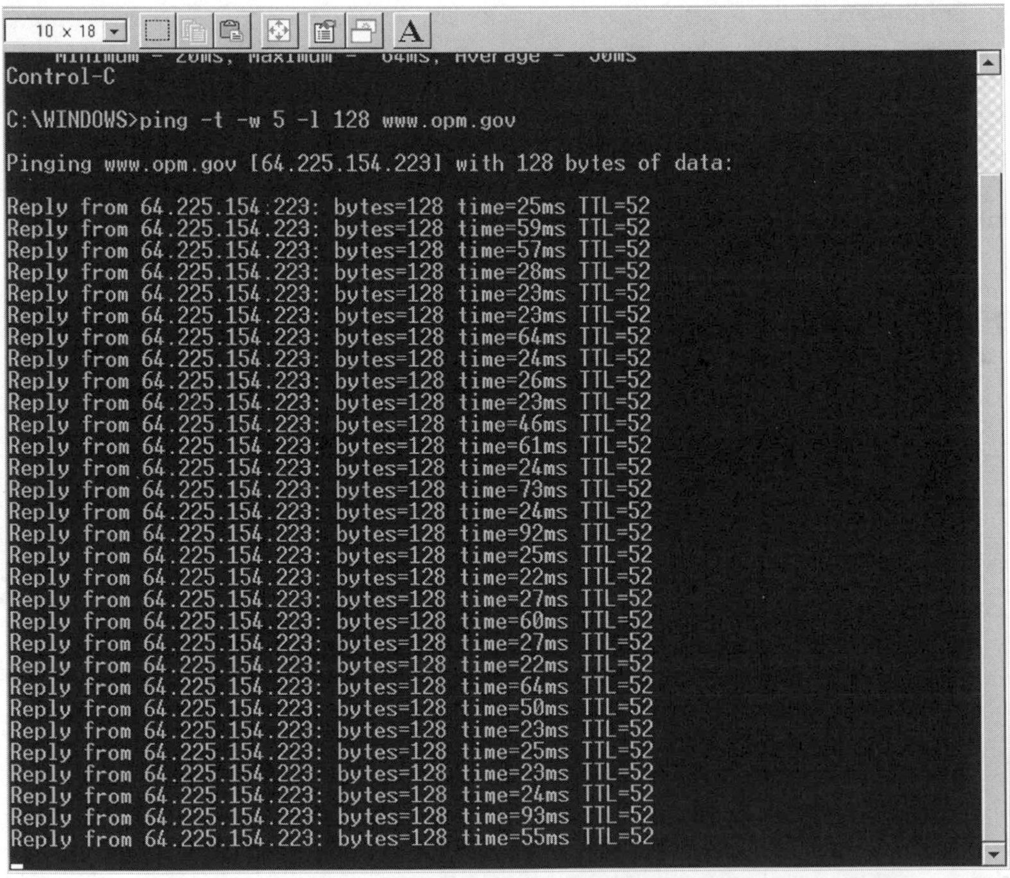

Exhibit 11. Continuously Pinging the Host www.opm.gov to Consume Network Bandwidth

a technique that can be used to block pings from the Internet but which will enable users on a corporate network to ping hosts on the Internet.

Directed Broadcast

A second attack method commonly employed by hackers as a mechanism to consume bandwidth and deny service to legitimate users is a directed broadcast attack. To understand how a directed broadcast attack works, focus first on the term "directed broadcast."

Each class A, B, and C network has a broadcast address. For example, the network 205.131.175.0 has the broadcast address 205.131.175.255. By directing one ping to the broadcast address, the router serving that network converts the layer 3 broadcast into a layer 2 broadcast. This means that each active station on the network will respond to the ping. For example, if there are 200 active stations on the network, a single ping will result in 200 replies!

Although the generation of a large amount of ping replies is bad enough, if the attacker spoofs his IP address, the effect is to disrupt two networks at the same time. For example, suppose an attacker configured his TCP/IP protocol stack with the IP address of the FBI's Web server and attacked the OPM network. Each host on the OPM network would transmit an echo reply to the FBI Web server, in effect causing two networks to be attacked. This type of attack is commonly referred to as a "smurf" attack. To prevent this attack, turn off the directed broadcast capability on each interface of any routers and switches connected to a public network. To do so in a Cisco environment, one would enter the IOS command:

```
no ip directed-broadcast
```

It should be noted that until recently, by default, directed broadcasts were enabled on Cisco routers. However, due to the growth in smurf attacks, recent revisions of the Cisco Internetwork Operating System now disable directed broadcasts by default.

UDP Echo

A related attack to directed broadcast concerns the UDP echo facility enabled on some routers. By transmitting a sequence of characters to a router's echo (UDP port 7) facility, the router echoes the characters back to the originator. If a hacker spoofs an IP address, the responding echoes are targeted to a third party, in effect disrupting another device.

In a Cisco router environment, there are three diagnostic ports which at one point were by default enabled for echo, chargen (character generator), and discard for both TCP and UDP tests. When a host transmits to one of those three router services, a small amount of router CPU activity occurs. If a hacker transmits a stream of requests to one or more of those services with spoofed IP addresses, it becomes possible to consume a large portion of a router's CPU capacity, preventing it from processing its other router functions. Prior to IOS release 12.0, one had to disable this rarely used router capability that Cisco refers to under the term "small-servers." To do so, one needs to enter the following IOS commands:

```
no service udp-small-servers
no service tcp-small-servers
```

Due to the abuse of small-servers, Cisco changed its IOS with the release of 12.0, which was introduced during 2000. Under IOS version 12.0, by default small-servers is now disabled. However, if one is using an earlier release of the Cisco operating system, it is a good idea to enter the two previously listed IOS commands.

Buffer Overflows

In concluding this discussion of network attack methods, we turn our attention to a series of attacks that have a common characteristic. That characteristic is the exploitation of an error in operating system software that enables a program to be executed when it should not. While it may be difficult to believe, there are a large number of very intelligent programmers who spend a considerable amount of time performing what may appear to be illogical operations, such as transmitting an illegally sized TCP segment to a server. The reason people perform such operations is to locate "holes" in an operating system that permit the transmission of executable code following the generation of the hole to be executed. The generation of a hole in an operating system commonly results from the overflow of an internal buffer, resulting in the attack method being referred to as a buffer overflow attack. Because the developers of the operating system may not have included code to prevent an illegal length segment or datagram from being processed, the operating system code may allow data following the illegal activity to be executed. In fact, several major attacks during 2002 occurred due to weaknesses in operating systems that hackers exploited.

While there is basically no way for an end user to stop a buffer overflow attack that is just discovered, one can eliminate one's vulnerability once the attack method is known. This is because vendors will quite often publish a software patch very soon after a buffer overflow exploit becomes known. Once the patch is published, one should apply it to the affected computers to eliminate the security hole that was discovered.

Chapter 9

Enhancing Security

Chapter 8 focused attention on security threats, examining viruses, directed broadcasts, and other techniques that can cause harm to both computers and networks. This chapter changes direction concerning the field of security and examines proactive techniques one can implement to protect networks and computers connected to networks.

The need to enhance security results from the structure of the TCP/IP protocol suite.

One of the key advantages of the TCP/IP protocol suite is also a disadvantage. The advantage is its openness, with RFCs used to identify the manner by which the protocol suite operates. Unfortunately, this openness has a price: it allows just about any person to determine how the various components that make up the protocol suite operate. This capability enables people who wish to do harm to IP networks and computers operating on those networks to develop techniques to do so. In comparison, other protocol suites that were developed by commercial organizations may not be as extensively documented. Thus, people who wish to exploit the weaknesses of a protocol suite developed by a commercial organization may face a far more daunting task.

Because the use of the Internet has expanded at an almost exponential rate, another problem associated with the TCP/IP protocol suite involves the connection of private networks to the Internet. With almost 100 million users now connected to the Internet on a global basis, this means that if only a very small fraction of Internet users attempt to break into different hosts, the total number would become considerable. Recognizing the openness of the TCP/IP protocol suite and the ability of people from Bangladesh to Belize to hack computers, security has become a major consideration of network managers and LAN administrators and is the focus of this chapter.

This chapter focuses on a series of TCP/IP security enhancement topics. Because the router represents both the entryway into a network as well as the first line of defense, this device is considered first. One can consider using this examining measure to prevent unauthorized entry into a router's configuration subsystem. Also discussed are other methods one can use to create access lists that perform packet filtering. Although the use of router access lists can considerably enhance the security of a network, there are certain functions and features that they do not perform. Thus, many network managers and LAN administrators rightly supplement the security capability of a router with a firewall, the operation of which is also covered in this chapter. In concluding this chapter we turn our attention to a set of protocols developed by the Internet Engineering Task Force (IETF) to support the secure exchange of packets at the IP layer. This set of protocols is collectively referred to as IPSec, a mnemonic for IP Security.

Router Access Considerations

Any network connected to the Internet gains connectivity through the use of a router. This means that if a remote user can gain access into an organization's router, it becomes possible for that user to reprogram the router. This reprogramming could result in the creation of a hole in a previously created access list that enables the person to overcome any barrier the access list created to the flow of packets. If the person is not a simple hacker, but a paid agent, he or she might then reprogram an organization's router to initially transport packets to a location where they are recorded and then forwarded onto their destination. Thus, the ability to control access to a router's configuration capability cannot be overlooked. This represents one of the first facts that one should consider if and when connecting an organization's private network to the Internet.

Router Control

Most routers provide several methods that can be used to control their operation. Although routers produced by different vendors may not support all of the methods discussed herein, they will usually support one or more of the methods to be discussed in this section. Those methods include direct cabling via a control port into the router, Telnet access, and Web access.

Direct Cabling

All routers include a control port that enables a terminal device to be directly cabled to a router. The terminal device can be a PC or a dumb asynchronous terminal. Once connected to the router, a user normally must enter a password to access the configuration system of the router. The exception to this occurs the first time a person accesses the router via a direct connection, because most routers are shipped without a password being enabled. Thus, if someone has unpacked a router, connected a terminal to its direct connect configuration port, and configured an access password, the next person to use the terminal would have to know the password to be able to configure the router.

Benefits and Limitations

The key benefit of a direct cabling configuration method is that only people who can physically access the terminal can configure the router. Thus, this configuration method precludes the ability of a remote user (to include potential hackers) from gaining access to an organization's router configuration substation and changing one or more parameters. Unfortunately, this advantage is also a disadvantage: it precludes the ability to remotely configure a router. Thus, if one's organization has trained personnel at each router location, or if one's budget permits the accumulation of frequent flyer mileage as one sends employees on the road to reconfigure routers, one can consider the use of direct cabling. If the organization needs to be responsive to changing requirements and cannot afford to have trained employees at each router location, one would then prefer a technique that provides remote router management capability. This capability can be obtained through the use of Telnet or Web access to the router.

Telnet and Web Access

Some routers include the ability for remote configuration via Telnet. Other routers extend remote router configuration capability to Web browsers via the use of the HyperText Transport Protocol (HTTP). For either situation, all that is required for a remote user to gain access to the configuration subsystem of a router is its IP address and password, assuming a password was previously configured to block casual access into the router's configuration subsystem. An IP address is required because both Telnet and Web access, while possible via a host name resolved into an IP address as well as via a directly entered IP address, are usually not obtainable via the former. This is because many organizations do not assign a host name to a router.

Although it may appear that obtaining the IP address of a router to target might require some effort, in actuality it can represent a simple process. This is because common practice is to configure a router with the dot1 (.1) address on a network, which makes it easy to discover. Even if the network manager or LAN administrator uses an IP address other than dot1, it is still a relatively easy process to locate a router. This is because most routers respond to an attempted Telnet access in a predefined manner. Thus, it is also relatively easy for a hacker to write a script that results in his computer cycling through a block of IP addresses. Because certain types of routers generate a particular type of prompt, such as "User Access Verification" in a Cisco environment, the script simply looks for a predefined prompt and logs the IP address where the prompt was observed.

To illustrate how easy it is to locate a router, one can examine the use of Telnet. Exhibit 1 shows the use of the Microsoft Windows Telnet client program in an attempt to gain access to a Cisco Systems router.

In the example shown in Exhibit 1, access to a Cisco router can require the use of two passwords. The first password is used to gain access to the router's virtual terminal (vt) port that allows a person to display router information, but precludes the ability to configure the router. If one types the command "enable" to gain access to the router's privileged mode of operation, one will be prompted to enter a second password. When this password is successfully entered, one obtains the ability to both display information as well as to configure the router.

In a Cisco router environment, once one types the command "enable" and enters an applicable password, the system prompt changes from a greater than sign (>) to a pound sign (#). In the example shown in Exhibit 1, the name "Macon" was previously assigned to the router being accessed, resulting in the router name prefixing the prompt that denotes the mode being occupied. Once in the privileged mode, one can change the router's configuration.

Protection Limitation

One of the problems associated with remote access to routers is that the basic method of protection via a password can be overcome if care is not taken during the password creation process. This is because most routers will simply disconnect the Telnet or Web connection after three failed password entry attempts, enabling a user to try three more passwords. Because of this limitation, several hackers in the past are known to have written scripts that would try three entries at a time from an electronic dictionary. If the network manager or LAN administrator used a name, object, or expression that could be extracted from an electronic dictionary, it was not long before the hacker gained entry into a router's virtual terminal capability and essentially took control of the device. Thus, it is extremely important to use an alphanumeric password combination that is not in a dictionary for password creation. In addition, through the use of an access list, it becomes possible to restrict access to a router's virtual terminal (vt) port from a known IP address. Therefore, it is possible — with some effort — to make it extremely difficult for a remote user other than a designated employee or group of employees to remotely access an organization's routers. There is one limitation associated with the use of a router's access list that warrants discussion. Because an access list would be developed to allow packets from a known IP address to access a router's virtual terminal (vt) port, this means the address cannot be dynamically assigned. In addition to requiring a fixed IP address, the use of an access list to protect access to a vt port also restricts the ability of traveling employees to gain access to a router's vt port. This is because ISPs commonly assign IP addresses dynamically. For example, an employee communication from San Francisco at 3:00 p.m. would have a different temporary IP address than that assigned when

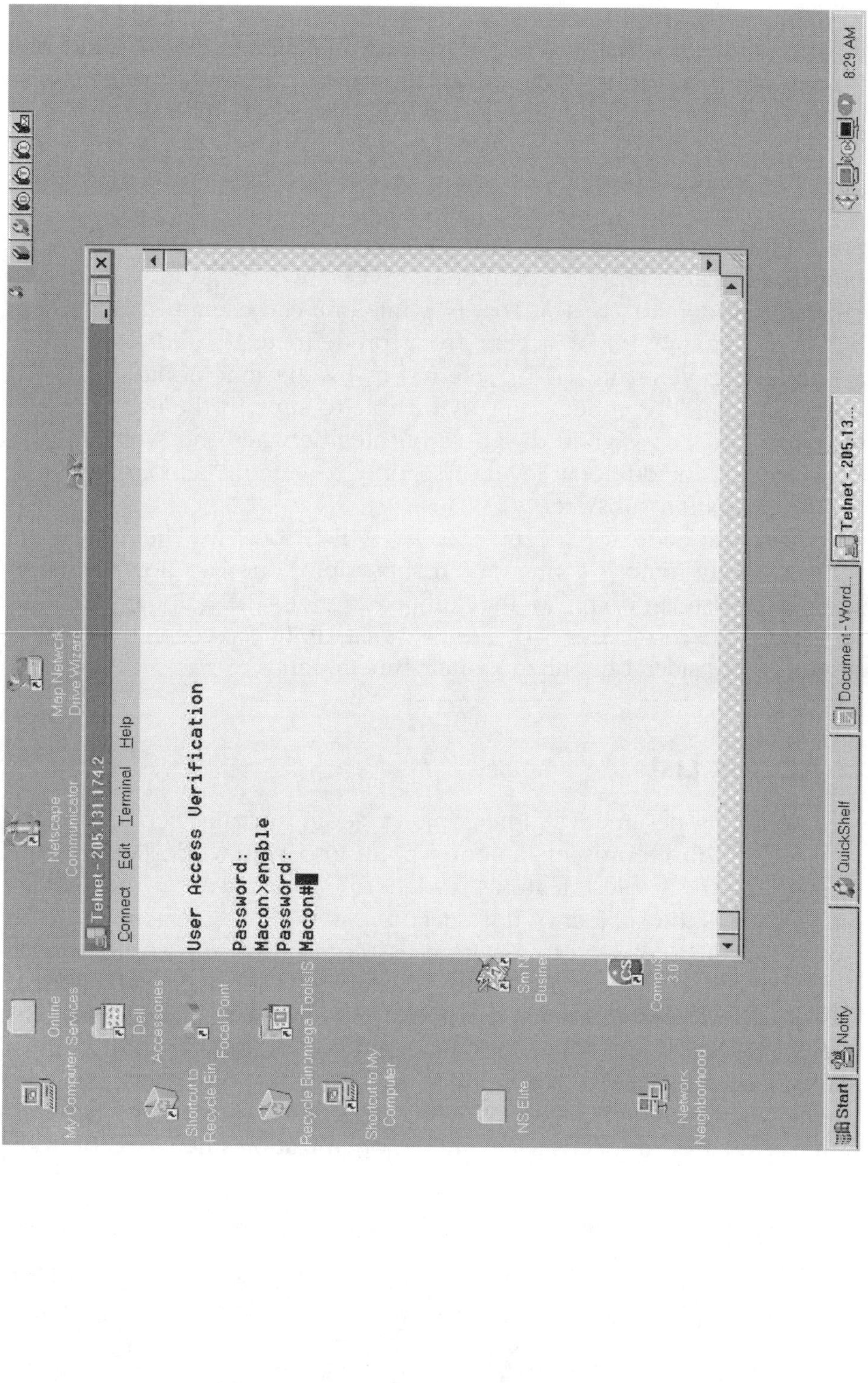

Exhibit 1. Using Telnet to Access the Configuration Subsystem on a Router

he or she accessed the Internet at 2:00 p.m. Similarly, if the employee took a trip to San Jose at 6:00 p.m. and accessed the Internet, another IP address would be temporarily assigned to the employee's notebook computer.

One method to overcome the previously described problem is for traveling employees to dial an access server that is directly connected to the organization's network. If one configures the server to accept a static IP address assigned to an employee's notebook, then a router's access list could be used to allow remote access for authorized employees who travel around the country or around the globe. This action, of course, results in the necessity for employees to use long distance instead of potentially more economical Internet access. Because many organizations only periodically require traveling employees to reconfigure organizational routers, the cost of potential long-distance support may not represent a detriment to its use.

Although the previous discussion focused on Telnet access to a router's vt port, some routers also support configuration via a Web browser that results in similar, but not identical, issues. That is, while one can use a router's access list capability to allow HTTP access from predefined IP addresses, Web browsers also support secure HTTP, referred to by the mnemonic HTTPS. If the router supports HTTPS, then one may be able to support the use of public key encryption and preassigned digital certificates between the Web browser and router, adding an additional level of security to gaining remote access to a router's configuration subsystem.

Given an appreciation for the manner by which local and remote users can gain access to a router's configuration subsystem, one can now focus on the use of access lists. In doing so, the author examines the rationale for their use, the basic types of access lists, and new capabilities recently added to access lists that considerably enhance their functionality.

Router Access Lists

Because a router is designed to interconnect geographically separated networks, this device also represents an entry point into a network. Recognizing this fact, one of the earliest features added to routers was an access list capability, which is the subject of this section.

An access list, also referred to as an access control list, represents one or more statements that, when executed by a router, perform packet filtering. Access lists can be configured for a variety of network protocols, such as Apple Talk, IP, IPX, DECnet, and Vines. Once an access list is created, it must be applied to an interface to take effect. In doing so, one must consider whether one wants to filter packets flowing into the organization's network from an untrusted area, or packets leaving the organization's network, or both.

Rationale for Use

While the primary use of access lists is to bar traffic to enhance network security, there are other reasons to use this router feature. One reason that is gaining acceptance is the ability to filter packets based upon the IP Type of Service (ToS) field. This allows traffic to be prioritized when entering or leaving a queue. Another reason for using access lists is to implement corporate policy concerning the use of different services on an intranet or accessible via the Internet. For example, corporate policy may be to bar all or certain employees from Web surfing.

Two additional reasons for configuring access lists include restricting the contents of routing updates and providing a mechanism for traffic flow. While each of these reasons can be sufficient in and of themselves to use access lists, the primary reason for their use is to obtain a basic level of security.

This chapter section primarily focuses on the use of access lists to enhance network security. Because Cisco Systems has a dominant market share of the installed base of routers, examples in this section focus on Cisco access lists. However, other router vendors follow a similar methodology by which access lists are created and applied to an interface, either inbound or outbound. While one may have to tailor examples in this section to the access list format supported by other router manufacturers, the basic concepts are applicable to most routers. Thus, the information presented in this section should serve as a guide to the use of a router's access list as the first line of defense of a network, regardless of the manufacturer of the device.

Although access lists were developed to support different protocols, the primary focus here is on the IP. This is because IP is the only protocol supported for use on the Internet, and most organizations that use access lists for security do so with respect to data flowing to and from the Internet with respect to an organization's private network.

Exhibit 2 illustrates the use of a router to connect two LANs — both to each other as well as to the Internet. In this example, the router provides a gateway from the LANs to the Internet. Because many, if not most, organizations do not want to allow any user that accesses the Internet to gain access to their private network, it is quite common for the network manager or LAN administrator to program the router to restrict the flow of packets. This packet flow restriction is accomplished through the use of a router's access list capability, and the technique used by the router in examining packets specified by an access list is referred to as packet filtering.

Ports Govern Data Flow

In examining Exhibit 2, note the three router ports labeled S0, E0, and E1. Port S0 represents a serial port that provides connectivity from the router to and from Internet data flows. Ports labeled E0 and E1 represent Ethernet ports that provide connectivity to individual Ethernet LANs that represent an organization's private network.

To use a router to obtain a packet filtering capability requires one to perform two functions. First, one or more access lists must be created. Next, each access list that is created must be applied to a specific port in a specific data flow direction. Data flow direction is defined as follows: data flowing

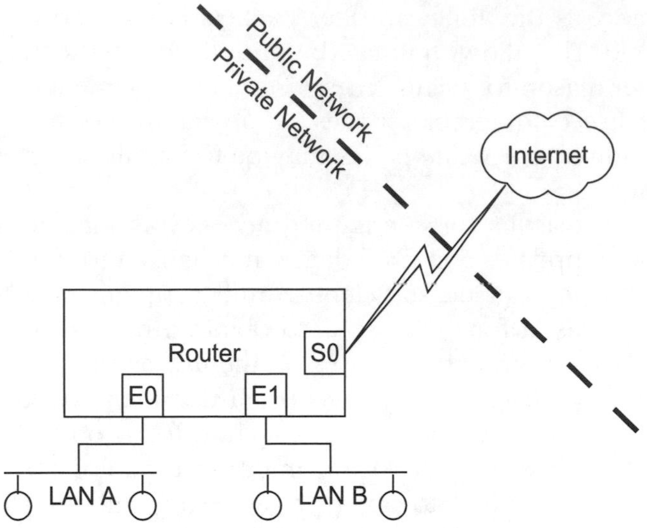

Exhibit 2. Connecting a Private Network Consisting of Two LANs to the Internet

toward a router is considered to flow in, while the direction of data leaving a router is considered to flow out. Thus, in a Cisco router environment, the key words "in" and "out" are used when an access list is applied to an interface to indicate which data flow direction packet filtering specified by the access list should occur.

Data Flow Direction

Because one can apply up to two access lists per router port (one inbound, one outbound), it becomes possible to filter packets at different locations with respect to a router's interfaces. In general, it is a good rule to apply an access list as close as possible to the data source to be filtered. For example, if one wants to filter packets entering the organization's private network from the Internet, one should apply an access list to port S0 in the inbound direction. Although one could create access lists for ports E0 and E1, if one applies the access list to port S0, it would protect the entire network with one access list and avoid some duplication of effort. This duplication would be necessary if one needed to permit or deny similar data flows to or from each network. For example, if one wanted to block Web surfing from stations on both LANs, one could either code an applicable access list and apply it to interface S0, or code two access lists and apply one to interface E0 and the other to interface E1. Similarly, if one wanted to restrict the ability of network users on LAN A to surf the Web, it would be easier to apply an access list to port E0 in the inbound direction to filter all HTTP data flows than to apply the access list to port S0. If one applied the list to port S0 and simply filtered on HTTP, one could adversely affect the ability of users on LAN B to surf the Internet. This would then require one to program a more complex access list to apply to port S0 to block LAN A users while allowing LAN B users to surf the Web. Thus, for most situations, one should attempt to place an access list as close as possible to the source of data to be filtered.

Given an appreciation for the general use of access list, one can now probe deeper into the specific types of access lists that can be used.

Types of Access Lists

There are two basic types of access lists supported by Cisco routers: standard and extended. A standard access list is limited to performing filtering on source addresses. In comparison, an extended access list permits filtering based upon source address, destination address, source port, destination port, and even the setting of bits within certain fields of a packet.

Standard Access Lists

The basic format of a standard IP access list is shown below.

```
access-list list # {permit | deny } source [wildcard-
mask] [log]
```

Although one access list can be assigned to one direction on an interface, a router can support multiple access lists. Thus, the `list #` represents a decimal from 1 to 99 that identifies a particular access list. In addition, because Cisco assigns numeric ranges to different types of access lists with respect to the protocols they operate upon, the `list #` also serves to identify the protocol that will be filtered. This means that a `list #` from 1 to 99 identifies a standard IP access list.

In examining the above format, note that one would specify either the keyword `permit` or `deny` in an access list statement. The use of `permit` enables a packet to flow through an interface when conditions specified in the access list are matched. Similarly, the use of `deny` sends a packet to the great bit bucket in the sky when conditions specified in the access list are matched.

The `source` entry in the standard access list format represents the IP address of a host or network from which the packet was transmitted. One can specify the source either via the use of a 32-bit IP address denoted in dotted decimal notation, or using the keyword `any` to represent any IP address. The `wildcard-mask` functions as a reverse-network address subnet mask; that is, one would place 1's in the bit positions to be ignored. For example, assume an organization has the IP class C network address of 198.78.46.0. When configuring the TCP/IP protocol stack, one would use the subnet mask 255.255.255.0 to specify the absence of subnets. Here, the trailing byte of 0s indicates a don't care condition, and results in hosts 1 through 254 being considered as residing on the network. If configuring Cisco access lists, the wildcard mask uses an inverse of the subnet mask, with 1 bits in positions one wants to ignore. Thus, if one wants to allow all hosts on network 198.78.46.0, the wildcard mask would be 0.0.0.255. An example of a standard IP access list statement permitting IP packets from all hosts on the 198.78.46.0 network would be:

```
access-list 1 permit 198.78.46.0 0.0.0.255
```

Note that list number 1 is in the range 1 to 99. Thus, the list number identifies the access list as a standard IP access list. Also note that the keyword `access-list` is entered with a dash (-) between "access" and "list."

For a second example of a standard IP access list, assume one wants to permit packets from hosts 198.78.46.12 and 198.78.46.14. Because the hosts do not represent a contiguous block of IP addresses, it is not feasible to develop a single statement. Thus, the access list would include the following two statements:

```
access-list 1 permit 198.78.46.12 0.0.0.0
access-list 1 permit 198.78.46.14 0.0.0.0
```

As we will shortly note, under Cisco's Internetwork Operating System (IOS), one can use the keyword `host` as a prefix to an IP address to replace a trailing wildcard mask of 0.0.0.0.

Returning to the format of the standard IP access list, note the optional term `log`. When used, this option results in an informational logging message about packets that match an access list statement being sent to the console. Logging can be an effective tool for both developing complex access lists as well as for generating information about the number of packets permitted or denied by an access list.

Because it can be tedious to enter wildcard masks for specific network addresses when constructing an access list with a large number of statements, one can use the keyword `host` to reference a specific address. That is, instead of having to enter `198.78.46.8 0.0.0.0` to reference the specific IP address of 198.78.46.8, one could enter `host 198.78.46.8` as a shortcut reference.

Access lists are processed sequentially, with instructions or statements executed as they occur in the list. This means one must carefully consider the placement of statements in an access list because once a match occurs, the packet is processed against the match conditions. Another access list feature worth noting is the fact that although syntax errors will be flagged, the router operating system will not inform you if you code an improper IP address, use an incorrect wildcard mask, or create another mistake when creating access list statements. Thus, similar to any programming effort, one must carefully consider the variables used in each access list statement.

To illustrate the use of a standard access list, assume one simply wants to block the ability of users on LAN A in Exhibit 2 from accessing the Internet. Further assume that the IP address of the LAN A network is 198.78.46.0.

Because the access list one creates will be applied to port E0, one must specify that port in an interface command. In addition, one would use the `ip access-group` command to apply an access list to a particular direction. The format of that command is shown below:

```
ip access-group [list number] {in/out}
```

Thus, the access list would be as follows:

```
interface S0
ip access-group 1 out
access-list 1 deny 198.78.46.0 0.0.0.255
```

Note that the preceding access list blocks all packets from LAN A from flowing into the Internet. The reason one does not use the E0 interface is because if one did, it would block LAN A users from accessing LAN B. Also note that when one uses a standard access list, there is no way to specify a particular TCP or UDP application. Thus, one could not use a standard access list to allow FTP, but block HTTP. Similarly, another limitation associated with standard access lists is the fact that they can only filter based upon the source address in a packet. This means one cannot use a standard access list if one wants to control the flow of packets based upon their destination address. To obtain an additional packet-filtering capability requires the use of an extended access list.

Extended Access Lists

An extended access list considerably extends the capability of router packet filtering. As previously mentioned, through the use of an extended access list one can filter on source and destination addresses, layer 4 ports, protocol, and even the bit settings within certain packet fields. The general format of an extended IP access list is as follows:

```
access-list list # {permit|deny} [protocol] source address
source- wildcard [port] destination address destination -
wildcard [port] [established] [log] [other options]
```

Similar to a standard access list, the list number defines the type of list. To define an extended IP access list, one would use a list number between 100 and 199. Because IP includes ICMP, TCP, and UDP, one can create a more explicit access list statement by specifying a specific IP protocol. In fact, one can even specify a routing protocol in an access list. Note that unlike a standard access list, which is restricted to filtering based on a source address for all IP traffic, one can filter based upon a particular IP protocol, source and destination address, source and destination ports, as well as use such keywords as `established`, `log`, and other options.

Both source and destination ports are optional and are used when filtering on layer 4 information. One can specify a port number, the mnemonic of a port number such as SNMP, or use the keyword `RANGE` to create specific ranges of port numbers. One can also use mnemonics to represent numeric operations, such as GT for "greater than," LT for "less than," and EQ for "equal to." For example, one could specify filtering based on SMTP for source or destination ports or both by substitution, either "EQ 25" or "EQ SMTP" for source port and/or destination port because port number 25 represents SMTP.

The keyword `established` is only applicable for the TCP protocol. When used in an access list statement, a match occurs if a TCP datagram has either its ACK or RST bits sets. This situation occurs when a packet flowing in one direction represents a response to a session initiated in the opposite direction. One common use of an extended IP access list with the keyword `established` is to only permit packets to enter a network from the Internet that represent a response to a session initiated via the trusted private network side of a router. For example, consider the following extended IP access list statement.

```
access-list 101 permit tcp any any established
```

The list number of 101 identifies the access list as an extended IP access list. The protocol specified is TCP and one permits packets to flow from any source to any destination address if their ACK or RST bit is set, which indicates the packet is part of an established conversation. Thus, one would normally want to apply the preceding statement to a serial interface connecting a router to the Internet. However, one would also want to apply the access list containing the preceding statement in the inbound direction if one wants to consider restricting TCP traffic from the Internet to sessions established by hosts on one's internal network or networks connected via the router to the Internet.

To provide the reader with a bit (no pun intended) more information about extended IP access lists, consider the following access list consisting of three statements.

```
access-list 101 permit tcp any any established
access-list 101 permit ip any host 198.78.46.8
access-list 101 permit icmp any any echo-reply
```

The first statement permits TCP datagrams that are part of an established conversation. The second statement permits IP from any host to the specific host whose IP address is 198.78.46.8. Here, the keyword `host` followed by an IP address is equivalent to an IP address followed by a wildcard mask of 0.0.0.0. The third statement in the access list permits ICMP from any host to any host if the packet is a response to a ping request (`echo-reply`). Note that if one applies this access list in the inbound direction on a serial interface connecting a router to the Internet, the result will be to allow responses to pings originating from the trusted side of the router.

Because an access list is based on the premise that all is denied unless explicitly allowed, if one applies the preceding access list in the inbound direction, pings originating on the Internet destined to all hosts on the 198.78.46.0 network other than host 198.78.46.8 will be blocked. The reason pings can flow to host 198.78.46.8 is due to the fact that the second statement permits IP traffic to include ICMP to that host. If one wanted to preclude pings to that host, one could insert a deny ICMP statement prior to the permit IP statement. This fact illustrates an important concept concerning access list processing. The contents of packets are matched against statements in an access list in their sequence. If access list statement n permits or denies a packet, then statement n + 1 will not be matched against the packet. Thus, it is important to review the order in which statements are entered into an access list.

When working with protocols in an extended IP access list, it is important to consider specificity. That is, because an IP header prefixes ICMP, TCP, and UDP, once one permits or denies IP to or from a specific address, one also permits or denies ICMP, TCP, and UDP to or from those addresses. For example, consider the following sequence of access list statements:

```
access-list 101 permit ip any host 198.78.48.6
access-list 101 deny tcp any host 198.78.48.6
```

Because the first statement permits IP from any location to the host whose IP address is 198.78.46.6, whenever a packet meeting the criteria is encountered, it is permitted through the router. Thus, the second statement would never be executed. To correctly block TCP while allowing other IP protocols, one would need to reverse the order of the statements as follows:

```
access-list 101 deny tcp any host 198.78.46.6
access-list 101 permit ip any host 198.78.46.6
```

To illustrate the additional capability afforded by the use of extended access lists, reconsider the previous problem where all users on LAN A were blocked from accessing the Internet. Now assume one wants to allow employees to Telnet to any location on the Internet, but block Web surfing from users on both LANs. To accomplish this, one would create the following router commands:

```
interface S0
ip access-group 101 out
access-list 101 permit telnet any any
```

Note that it was not necessary to encode a specific access-list deny statement. This is because the end of each access-list has an implicit deny all statement that blocks anything that is not explicitly permitted. Although all types of Cisco access lists include a "deny all" statement at the end of each list, many programmers prefer to code their own. Thus, it is common to see the following statement at the end of many extended access lists:

```
access-list list # deny any any
```

where `list #` represents the numeric value of the access list. As indicated by this small series of examples and the prior examples in this section, an extended access list significantly extends the capability to perform complex packet filtering operations beyond that supported by standard access lists.

New Capabilities in Access Lists

In tandem with several relatively recent updates to the Cisco Internetwork Operating System (IOS) were improvements to the functionality and capability of access lists. Four additions to access lists include named access lists, reflexive access lists, time-based access lists, and TCP intercept. In actuality, these additions represent additional capabilities added to access lists and not new types of access lists.

Named Access Lists

Because each type of access list has a limited range of acceptable numbers, it is theoretically possible — although highly unlikely — that one could run out of numbers when configuring an enterprise router. Perhaps a more important reason for named access lists is the fact that a name can be more meaningful than a number. In any event, named access lists were introduced in IOS Version 11.2.

As its name implies, a named access list is referenced by a name instead of a number. Named access lists are applicable for both standard and extended access list operations. The structure of a named access list requires adding a name to the `ip access-group` statement as well as for a single `ip access-list` statement that defines the type of access list, standard or extended. Because the name replaces the access list number, each `permit` or `deny` statement in the access list is then coded without requiring an access list number. When coding a named access list, the format of the `ip access-group` command becomes:

```
ip access-group name [in|out]
```

where the variable `name` represents the name assigned to the access list.

The format of the required `access-list` statement then becomes:

```
ip access-list [standard|extended] name
```

where one would use the keyword `standard` when defining a standard named access list while the keyword `extended` would be used when defining an extended named access list. The variable `name` would be replaced by the name of the access list. Revising a previously presented access list into a named extended IP access list called "inbound," one would obtain the following statements:

```
ip access-group inbound in
ip access-list extended inbound
     permit tcp any any established
     permit ip any host 198.78.46.8
     permit icmp any any echo-reply
```

An important aspect of named access lists that deserves mention is the fact that they enable one to delete specific entries in the list. This is accomplished by entering a "no" version of a specific statement contained in a named access list. This action is not possible with a numbered access list. Instead, to revise a numbered access list, one would create a new list, delete the old list, and apply the new list to the appropriate interface.

Reflexive Access Lists

One of the limitations associated with the use of the keyword `established` in an extended IP access list is that it is only applicable to TCP. To control other upper layer protocols, such as UDP and ICMP, one would either permit all incoming traffic or define a large number of permissible source/destination host/port addresses. Along with being a very tedious and time-consuming task, the resulting access list could conceivably require more memory than available on the router. Perhaps recognizing this problem, Cisco introduced reflexive access lists in IOS Version 11.3.

A reflexive access list creates a dynamic, temporary opening in an access list. That opening results in the creation of a mirror image or "reflected" entry in an existing access list, hence the name of this list. The opening is triggered when a new IP traffic session is initiated from inside the network to an external network. The temporary opening is always a permit entry and specifies the same protocol as the original outbound packet. The opening also swaps source and destination IP addresses and upper-layer port numbers and will exist until either the session initiated on the trusted network is closed or an idle timeout value is reached.

To illustrate the operation of a reflexive access list, assume a user behind the router initiates a Web session from IP address 198.78.46.12 to IP address 205.131.175.11. Further assume that the source TCP port number, which was selected at random, is 1099, while the well-known destination port number (as one might expect) is 80 for Web browsing. Thus, the originating outbound packet would have the following key characteristics:

Source IP address: 198.78.46.12

Source TCP port: 1099

Destination IP address: 205.131.175.11

Destination TCP port: 80 (http)

When a reflexive access list is enabled, the characteristics of the outbound packet are used to automatically create an opening in an inbound access list. The resulting entry would be:

```
permit tcp host 205.131.175.11 eq 80 host 198.78.46.12
eq 1099
```

In examining the preceding entry, note that it is a mirror image of the outbound packet. That is, the source and destination IP addresses and the source and destination port numbers were exchanged. Given an appreciation for how a reflexive access list operates upon packets, one can now examine the tasks required to place this type of access list into effect.

There are four general tasks associated with the creation of a reflexive access list. First, one would create an extended named access list. In an IP environment, the following command format would be used:

ip access-list extended name

where name represents the name of the access list.

Next, one would create one or more permit entries to establish reflected openings. Because a reflexive access list is applied to outbound traffic, it will result in temporary openings appearing in an inbound access list. When defining permit statements for the outbound access list, one would use the following statement format:

permit protocol **any any reflect** name [**timeout** seconds]

One can use the keyword timeout to assign a timeout period to each specific reflexive entry created in the inbound direction. If one elects not to use this option, a default timeout of 300 seconds will be used for the opening. One can also elect to place a global timeout on all reflexive statements. To do so, use the following global command:

ip reflexive-list timeout value

where value is the global timeout value in seconds.

The third task is to create an access list for inbound filtering into which dynamic reflexive entries are added. Conclude the operation with the following command:

evaluate name

where name represents the name of the access list and causes packets to be evaluated by reflexive entries.

The following example illustrates the creation of a reflexive access list where the reflected openings are limited to 180 seconds of idle time. In examining the following statements, note that the three deny statements in the extended access list named "inbound" are conventional statements that are not reflected. Also note that those statements are commonly referred to as anti-spoofing entries. That is, many times, hackers use RFC 1918 private network IP addresses in an attempt to preclude network operators from identifying the source address of an attack.

```
!
ip reflexive-list timeout 180
!
ip access-list extended outbound
     permit tcp any any reflect my_session
     permit udp any any reflect my_session
     permit icmp any any reflect my_session
!
ip access-list extended inbound
     deny ip 10.0.0.0 0.255.255.255 any
     deny ip 172.16.0.0 0.31.255.255 any
     deny ip 192.168.0.0 0.0.255.255 any
evaluate my_session
```

Before moving on, it should be noted that while reflexive access lists considerably extend the capability of packet filtering, they are limited to single-channel connections. This means applications such as FTP that use multiple port numbers or channels cannot be supported by reflexive access lists. However, a special release of IOS, initially referred to as the Firewall Feature Set (FFS), introduced support for dynamic openings in access lists for multi-channel applications. Now referred to as Context Based Access Control (CBAC) in IOS Release 12.0, CBAC also adds Java blocking, denial-of-service prevention and detection, real-time alerts, and audit trails. Unfortunately, CBAC is only applicable for certain platforms.

Time-Based Access Lists

Until IOS Version 12.0, there was no easy method for an administrator to establish different security policies based on the time of day or date. Although an administrator could create multiple access lists and apply them at different times, doing so could be a complex process. In addition, does anyone really want to stay in the office until 6 p.m. on a Friday to implement a new security policy? With the introduction of IOS Version 12.0, time-based access lists provided the flexibility to implement different policies based on time.

In the wonderful world of IP, the use of time-based access lists is a relatively easy, two-step process. First, one would define a time range, and then reference that time range in an access list entry. One can specify a time range using a time-range statement whose format is shown below.

```
time-range time-range-name
```

where `time-range-name` is the name assigned to the time range.

Once the preceding is accomplished, one can specify a time range in one of two ways: use an `absolute` statement or a `periodic` statement, with the format of each shown below:

```
absolute [start time date] [end time date]
periodic days-of-the-week hh:mm to [days-of-the-week]
hh:mm
```

The `time` parameter is entered in the format hh:mm, where hours (hh) are expressed in a 24-hour format. If one does not include a start time, the access list will immediately go into effect. If one does not include an end time, the access list will remain in effect until the list is removed or replaced. If one does not include an `absolute` statement in the time-based access list, the list will go into effect when applied to an interface and remain in effect until removed or replaced. Continuing this examination of the format of the two statements, one can list the days of the week separated by spaces or use the keywords `daily` or `weekend`. Once the time range is created, it can be referenced through the optional keyword `time-range` in a traditional access list entry. The following example illustrates the creation of a time-based access list that restricts Web access to Monday through Friday from 8 a.m. to 5 p.m.

```
time-range allow-http
     Periodic weekdays 8:00 to 17:00
!
access-list 101 permit tcp any any eq 80 time-range
        allow-http
```

Note that the above example did not include an `absolute` statement. Thus, that time-based access list would go into effect when it is applied to an interface and remain in effect until the access list is removed or replaced.

To illustrate the use of `absolute` and `periodic` statements in a time-based access list, assume one wants to restrict Web access to Saturday and Sunday between 8:00 a.m. and 5:00 p.m. as well as on weekdays from noon to 1:00 p.m. Also assume that this time-based access list will go into effect immediately and terminate on 31 December 2003 at midnight. One would code the following statement for the time-based access list:

```
time-range allow-http
     absolute end 24:00 31 December 2003
     periodic weekdays 12:00 to 13:00
     periodic weekends 8:00 to 17:00
!
access-list 101 permit tcp any any eq 80 time-range
        allow-http
```

In examining the preceding time-based access list, note that there are two `periodic` statements. While there can only be one `absolute` statement, there can be multiple `periodic` statements in a time-based access list.

TCP Intercept

This examination of enhancements to access lists concludes with TCP intercept. This feature was added in IOS Version 11.3 as a mechanism to alleviate a special type of denial-of-service attack referred to as SYN flooding.

Under TCP's three-way handshake, the first packet in a session has the SYN bit sent. The recipient of this initial packet requesting a service, such as HTTP, responds with a packet in which the SYN and ACK bits are set and waits for an ACK from the originator of the session. If the originator of the request fails to respond, the host times-out the connection. However, while the host is waiting for the conclusion of the three-way handshake, the half-open connection consumes resources.

Suppose an unscrupulous person modifies software to transmit tens of thousands of packets with their SYN bit set, using forged IP source addresses. This will result in the attacked host never receiving a response to its request to complete each three-way handshake. Thus, its resources will be consumed as it times-out each session, only to be faced with a new flood of additional bogus packets with their SYN bit set. As host resources are consumed, its ability to be usable decreases to a point where little or no useful work occurs. Because of the popularity of this method of attack, TCP intercept was added as a mechanism to limit half-open connections flowing through a router.

The TCP intercept feature works by intercepting and validating TCP connection requests. The feature operates in one of two modes: intercept or watch. When in intercept mode, the router intercepts inbound TCP synchronization requests and establishes a connection with the client on behalf of the server and with the server on the behalf of the client, in effect functioning as a proxy agent. If both connections are successful, the router will merge them. To prevent router resources from being fully consumed by a SYN attack, the router has aggressive thresholds and will automatically delete connections until the number of half-open connections falls below a particular threshold.

The second mode of operation of TCP intercept is watch mode. Under watch mode, the router passively monitors half-open connections and actively closes connections on the server after a configurable length of time.

Enabling TCP intercept is a two-step process. First, configure either a standard or extended IP access list permitting the destination address one wants to protect. Once this is accomplished, enable TCP intercept using the following statement:

```
ip tcp intercept list list#
```

Because the default mode of operation of TCP intercept is intercept mode, a third step may be required to set the mode. To do so, use the following command:

```
ip tcp intercept mode {intercept | watch}
```

As previously mentioned, TCP intercept includes aggressive thresholds to prevent router resources from being adversely consumed by a SYN attack. There are four thresholds maintained by routers that one can adjust. Those thresholds are set using the following TCP intercept commands, with the default value indicated for each setting:

```
ip tcp intercept max-incomplete low number 90
ip tcp intercept max-incomplete high number 1100
ip tcp intercept one-minute low number 900
ip tcp intercept one-minute high number 1100
```

To illustrate the use of TCP intercept, assume one wants to protect the host 198.78.46.8. To do so while selecting default thresholds would require the following `access-list` statements.

```
ip tcp intercept list 107
access-list 107 permit tcp any host 198.78.46.8
```

Applying a Named Access List

Until now, it has only briefly been mentioned that access lists are applied to an interface. Because some of us are from Missouri, the "show me" state, the following paragraphs review how they are applied by supporting a named access list instead of a numbered one.

As previously mentioned, one applies an access list through the use of the `access-group` command. The general format of that command is:

```
ip access-group {list# | name } {in | out}
```

Note that one would use a name in the `access-group` command to reference a named access list. Also note that one would use either `in` or `out` to reference the direction with respect to the router interface where filtering occurs. Because the `access-group` command only associates the direction of filtering to an access list number or name, one would use an `interface` command before the `access-group` command to tie everything to an interface. For example, assume one wants to apply the extended IP access list named "inbound" previously created to a router's serial port in the inbound direction. The statements would be as follows:

```
interface serial 0
    ip access-group inbound in
!
ip access-list extended inbound
    permit tcp any any established
    permit ip any host 198.78.46.9
    permit icmp any any echo-reply
```

Configuration Principles

Although access lists can be used as the first line of defense to protect a network, there are several configuration principles to note to prevent good intentions from creating protection holes. First, Cisco access lists are evaluated sequentially, top-down. This means that as soon as a match occurs, access list processing against a packet terminates. Thus, it is important to place more specific entries toward the top of an access list. Second, if adding new entries to an access list, they are added to the bottom of the list. This can result in undesirable results and one may wish to consider creating a new list, deleting the old one, and applying the new list instead of attempting to patch an existing list.

Limitations

While router access lists represent an important tool for providing a barrier against unwanted intrusion, they are limited in their capability. For example, if one needs to provide access to a Web server, filtering via a router access list to allow any user on the Internet to only access the server does not block such users from attempting to break into the server. This limitation results from the fact that a router access list does not actually examine the contents of data within a packet. Instead, a router access list examines packet headers for port numbers and IP addresses and enables or disables the flow of information by comparing those metrics against the parameters coded in one or more `access-list` statements. Thus, for many networks, a more powerful security tool in the form of a firewall is both required and added as a network component.

Firewalls

A firewall in some respects is similar to a router in that it is designed to enforce a network access control policy by monitoring all traffic flowing to or from a network. There are many firewall products being marketed, with some devices consisting of software that users load onto a usual LAN port PC, while other products represent a combined hardware and software solution in one package. Regardless of the method by which a firewall is constructed, it is important to note the manner by which it should be installed.

Installation Location

Because a firewall is designed to inspect the contents of packets, it is important to locate the device where it will do the most good. That location is commonly between a public and private network boundary. The term used to denote the location is referred to as a DMZ (for demilitarized) LAN.

Exhibit 3 illustrates the installation of a firewall on a DMZ LAN to protect a private network. Note that the term "DMZ" references a LAN with no attached workstations or servers. Because the only connections to the DMZ are from a router and a firewall, all traffic that flows from the Internet to the private network, and vice versa, must flow through the firewall. Thus, the use of a DMZ in the manner illustrated in Exhibit 3 results in all packets flowing from or to the Internet being examined by the firewall.

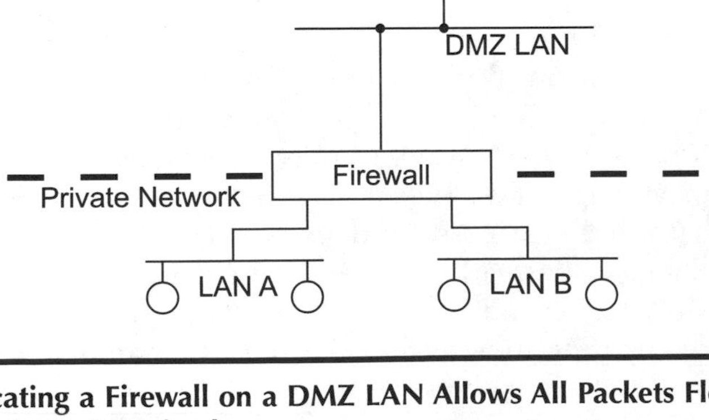

Exhibit 3. Locating a Firewall on a DMZ LAN Allows All Packets Flowing from and to the Internet to Be Examined

Basic Functions

There are several functions firewalls can perform. On a basic level, most firewalls, as a minimum, perform packet filtering similar to the filtering performed by router access lists.

Through the ability to "look" into the contents of packets, firewalls become capable of being programmed to examine the contents of information being transferred. This functionality is referred to as "stateful" inspection by one vendor and enables a firewall to look for suspicious activity, such as repeated log-on attempts. Upon determining that a repeated sequence is occurring, such as an attempted log-on, the firewall would either alert the network operator or bar further attempts, with the specific action based on the manner in which the firewall was configured.

When comparing the capability of a firewall to a router, one notes several functions performed by firewalls that are not commonly associated with routers. Those functions include proxy services, authentication, encryption, and network address translation, as discussed next.

Proxy Services

A proxy can be considered an intermediary that acts on behalf of another. When discussing firewall proxy services, a firewall answers requests on behalf of another computer, first examining the request to ensure it is acceptable. If found to be so, the firewall will then pass the request to the indicated computer. Rather than responding directly to the original requester, the destination host responds to the proxy service on the firewall. Exhibit 4 illustrates the data flow for a proxy service function operated on a firewall.

There are two types of proxy services firewalls can provide. The first is an application-level proxy under which packets are inspected at the application layer to determine if their behavior is acceptable. The second type of proxy service is a circuit-level proxy. A circuit-level proxy service occurs at the session layer. This type of proxy service can be viewed as falling between an application-level proxy and a filtering firewall. In effect, a circuit-level proxy uses predefined security files whose contents are compared against datagrams to determine if they are safe and should be allowed through a firewall. At one time when processor speed was relatively low, a circuit-level proxy provided a lesser performance delay that could be meaningful. With 1 GHz and above microprocessors readily available, the delays associated with the use of an application-layer proxy firewall have become minimal and they now by far represent the most common type of proxy service. Thus, the remainder of this section focuses on application-level proxy services.

There are several applications for which proxy services were developed, such as FTP and HTTP. To understand how proxy services operate and why they are an important security tool, assume an FTP proxy is operational on the firewall shown in Exhibit 4. After describing how the proxy operates, one can focus on the flow of data in the example.

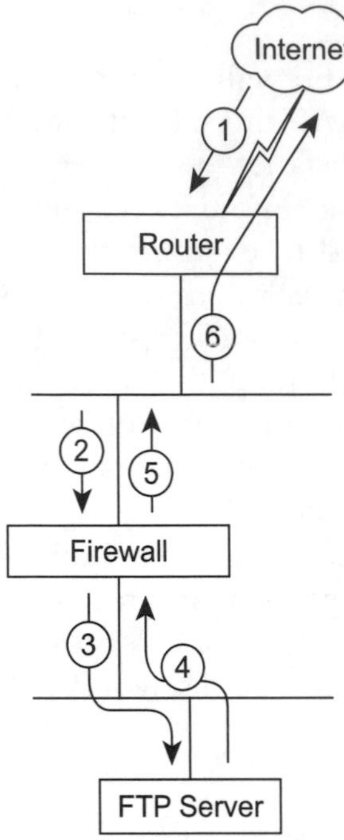

Exhibit 4. Dataflow When a Firewall Supports Proxy Services

FTP includes several commands whose use can be harmful if invoked under certain circumstances. Two of those commands are `MGET` and `MPUT`, with the `M` prefix in the `GET` and `PUT` commands used to denote that multiple files will be retrieved from or transferred to an FTP server. To illustrate how these commands might represent a problem, assume an organization has a 56-kbps connection to the Internet. Further assume that the organization operates a combined FTP/Web server, and FTP provides access to a directory with 10 GB of data.

If a remote user on the Internet accesses the organization's FTP server and enters the command `MGET *.*`, this action would cause every file in the directory of the server currently accessed to be downloaded. If there were 10 GB of data in the directory, this one command would result in 396 hours of transmission. This action, in effect, would significantly impact the ability of users to access the organization's Web server and to receive a timely response. Because an FTP application supports all FTP commands, one cannot block MGET and MPUT via an FTP initialization screen. Instead, one must employ a proxy service on a firewall, as illustrated in Exhibit 4. In this example, an FTP request from the Internet (1) flows first to the router whose access list would be programmed to permit inbound FTP to the FTP server. Next, the FTP request would be intercepted and examined by the proxy service on the firewall (2). If the FTP operation was allowed, the firewall would pass the request to the server (3). If not, the firewall would reject the request (5), and the rejection would flow back to the originator via the router (6). Assuming the FTP request was allowed, the firewall forms a new packet to indicate that the request came from that device and records the originator's address plus the source port number in a table in memory prior to forwarding the packet to the server (3). The server will respond to the firewall (4), which will then check its tables and create a new packet, so the original source address is now its destination address. Once this packet reformatting is complete, the firewall transmits the packet to the router (5), which forwards it to the Internet (6) toward its destination.

As indicated by the preceding example, an application proxy service on a firewall intercepts packets, allowing the firewall to compare actions within the packet against a predefined configuration that either allows or prohibits such actions. For an FTP proxy, one would more than likely block the use of `MGET` and `MPUT` commands as they could significantly increase network traffic. Although a person could still request one file after another or write a script to execute a series of `PUT` or `GET` commands, this action would be more difficult than simply issuing a single `MGET` or `MPUT` command. In addition, some firewall proxy services permit the user to configure a maximum amount of traffic that can flow to or from a specific IP address, further limiting the use of FTP as a denial-of-service weapon.

Authentication

Although a user-ID/password sequence is commonly considered to represent an authentication method, it provides a limited level of security in comparison to other methods. One common firewall authentication method is obtained through token support. A token represents an algorithm that is used to produce a pseudo-random value that changes every minute. A remote user is then provided with a credit-card sized token generator that displays a five- or six-digit number that changes every minute based on an algorithm embedded in the circuitry on the card. A remote user who needs to be authenticated is blocked from gaining access to services on the network by the firewall. The firewall prompts the user for his or her PIN (personal identification number) and the five- or six-digit authentication number. The firewall uses the PIN with an algorithm in its software to generate an authentication number that is compared to the transmitted number. If the two match, the user is then authenticated.

The key safety feature of the token lies in the fact that the loss of the card by a remote user does not allow a finder to access the network. A PIN is required for authentication and, once authenticated, a user must still have the applicable passwords to gain access to hosts on the network. Because of this, a token-based authentication scheme is probably the most popular method to authenticate remote users.

Encryption

Another feature added to some firewalls is encryption. Because data flow over the Internet is subject to viewing by numerous organizations that operate routers, encryption is a necessity when using the Internet as a virtual private network (VPN) to interconnect two or more organizational locations. To ensure that organizational information is not read, an encryption firewall will allow the firewall manager to define network addresses for packet encapsulation. Then, packets destined to a different organizational network via the Internet will flow through the Internet in encrypted form, with a newly formed header using the address of a firewall on the destination network because that firewall will now be responsible for decryption. Although the use of VPNs is in its infancy, as their usage increases, one can expect an increase in demand for encryption performing firewalls.

Network Address Translation

In concluding this examination of firewall features, this section focuses on network address translation (NAT). NAT represents both a security mechanism and an address extension mechanism.

The use of NAT results in the translation of an IP address behind a firewall into a new IP address for routing via the Internet. Thus, NAT hides organizational addresses and serves as a mechanism to prevent direct attacks to hosts on a network.

A second function performed by NAT, addressing extension, allows an organization to operate using RFC 1918 addresses behind a firewall and translate those addresses into a single "valid for public network usage" IP address. Because an organization might have hundreds or thousands of hosts behind a firewall, the reader may be curious as to how a firewall can accomplish the previously descried translation process. The answer to this is the use of high port addresses. For example, consider the network address 198.78.46.1 assigned to the public side of a firewall. Each host requiring access to the Internet would have its IP source datagram address converted into IP address 198.78.46.1 so that the firewall can differentiate datagrams flowing back to different IP addresses that were created by different hosts behind the firewall. The firewall will assign distinct source port numbers to the UDP or TCP header in each datagram and update a table of IP address/port-number assignments. Then, when a datagram is returned from the Internet to the firewall, it will search the IP address/port-number assignment table, retrieve the original source address, and form a new datagram so that it can flow to the correct destination. Thus, NAT provides both a security feature as well as address extension capability. Because IPv4 addresses are becoming quite scarce, many organizations view the ability of a firewall to perform NAT as an extremely important criterion, although its security function is not as important as the other firewall features previously described in this section.

IPSec

In concluding this discussion of tools and techniques that can be used to enhance security, we turn our attention to a set of extensions to the IP protocol family collectively referred to as IPSec. IPSec represents a set of protocols that provides cryptographic security services that support authentication, data integrity, access control, and confidentiality. Under IPSec, one can transmit data that secures each application from eavesdropping as well as from modification. Although IPSec is transparent to operations, this set of extensions to the IP protocol family must operate on both source and destination host. While IPSec can be used by pairs of hosts, it is often employed to secure the creation of a virtual private network (VPN) through the Internet, a topic that is examined in Chapter 10.

Protocols

The ability of IPSec to provide confidentiality, data integrity, authentication, and access control results from the use of two security-related protocols referred to as Authentication Header (AH) and Encapsulated Security Payload (ESP). Because AH and ESP operate based upon the use of shared secret keys, it can become a burden to manage such keys. Thus, a third protocol — referred to as the Internet Key Exchange (IKE) — provides a mechanism to negotiate the use of keys. Unlike AH and ESP, IKE is optional as it is possible to configure secret keys manually; however, it is doubtful if one would want to maintain the use of the same key for a long period of time as this could compromise security.

AH versus ESP

The use of the Authentication Header results in the creation of cryptographic hashes of the data and key parts of the IP header, such as source and destination IP addresses, that provide data integrity to the datagram. While AH provides support for authentication, data integrity, and access control, it does not support confidentiality. In comparison, ESP adds support for confidentiality by rewriting the IP payload in encrypted form.

Modes

Both AH and ESP support two modes of operation referred to as transport mode and tunnel mode.

Transport Mode

In transport mode, security headers are added before the transport layer headers (TCP, UDP) and the IP header. Thus, the use of AH results in the hashing of the TCP or UDP header and key fields within the IP header. In comparison, when ESP is used, the ESP header will cover the encryption of the TCP or UDP header and data, but not the IP header. The top portion of Exhibit 5 illustrates examples of AH and ESP transport modes (A and B). Because the use of ESP cannot authenticate the outer IP header, it is often

A. Transport mode AH packet

IP Header	AH	TCP/UDP Header	Data

B. Transport mode ESP packet

IP Header	ESP	TCP/UDP Header	Encrypted Data

C. Combined AH and ESP transport mode (transport adjacency)

IP Header	AH	ESP	TCP/UDP Header	Encrypted Data

Exhibit 5. Transport Mode Packet Formats

practical to combine both an AH and ESP header, a situation illustrated in the lower portion of Exhibit 5 (C). This is referred to as transport adjacency.

AH is identified by the IPv4 header having a value of 51 in its Protocol field. In comparison, ESP is identified by a value of 50 in the IPv4 header Protocol field. Both AH and ESP are applicable to IPv4 and IPv6. When IPv6 is used, AH and ESP are denoted by the value of 51 and 50, respectively, in the Next Header field.

The transport mode of operation is employed by a host generating packet. As indicated in Exhibit 5, security headers are added after the transport layer headers but prior to the IP header being prefixed to the packet. When AH is used, the TCP or UDP header and source and destination IP addresses in the IP header are hashed. In comparison, the use of an ESP header results in the encryption of the transport layer header and data.

Tunnel Mode

A second IPSec operational mode is referred to as the tunnel mode. The tunnel mode is employed when an IP header is already attached to the packet and one end of the secure connection is a gateway. Under the tunnel mode of operation, AH and ESP headers are used to cover the entire packet, requiring a new IP header to be prefixed to the AH or ESP header.

The use of the tunnel mode enables many clients to transmit securely to a common gateway located at the entry to a network. The gateway decrypts data when an ESP header is used or re-computes the hash when an AH is used. The gateway also removes the security header and routes the data to its intended destination. The most common use of tunnel-mode IPSec is for enabling multiple client locations to communicate with a common device at a central location, such as a corporate network being accessed by multiple branch offices.

The top two examples (A and B) in Exhibit 6 illustrate the format of a tunnel-mode AH packet and a tunnel-mode ESP packet. Similar to the transport

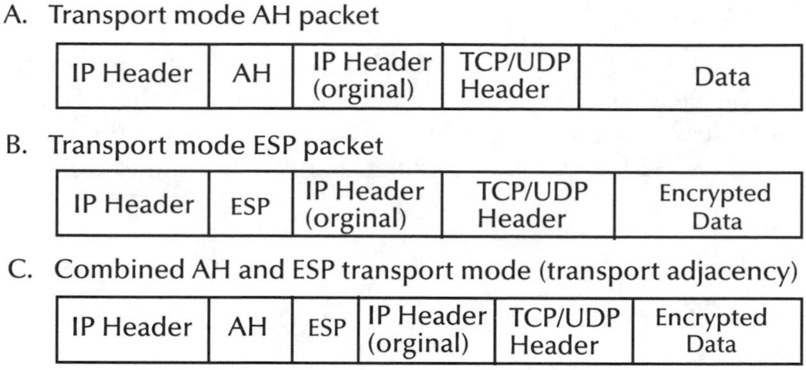

Exhibit 6. Tunnel Mode Packet Formats

mode, one can combine an AH and an ESP header to authenticate the entire packet less a few fields in the IP header and also encrypt the payload. Referred to as transport adjacency, the tunneling version is indicated in the lower portion (C) of Exhibit 6.

AH Header Format

Exhibit 7 illustrates the format of the AH. Note that there are six fields in the AH header, with one 16-bit field currently reserved.

Next Header Field

The Next Header field is an eight-bit field whose value identifies the next field after the Authentication Header. A value of 50 in this field would indicate that the AH is followed by an ESP Header.

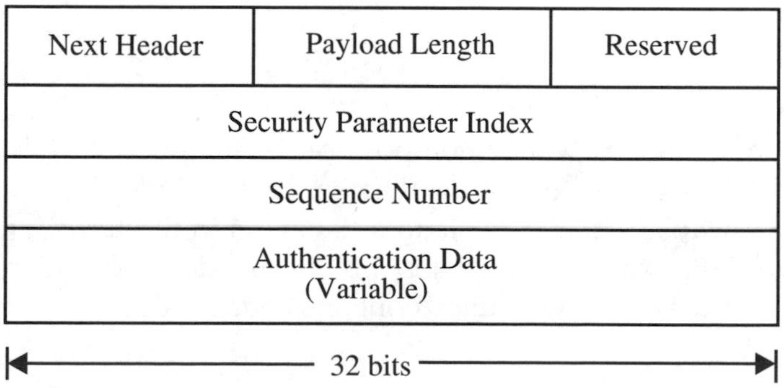

Exhibit 7. The AH Format

Payload Length Field

The function of the Payload Length field is to indicate the length of the Authentication Header. This field denotes the length of the AH in terms of 32-bit words, less 2. The default value of this field is 4 for three 32-bit fixed words plus three 32-bit words of authentication data, minus two.

Reserved Field

Currently, 16 bits are reserved for future use. The bits in this field are set to zero.

Security Parameter Index Field

This field is 32 bits in length and functions as an identifier of a security associate (SA), where an SA represents a unidirectional logical connection between two IPSec systems. The value in the Security Parameter Index field is normally selected by the destination system and permits different security sessions with the same destination address to be supported.

Sequence Number Field

This 32-bit field represents a counter whose value increases with each packet transmitted. Because sequence numbers cannot repeat, the maximum number of packets that can be transmitted during a single security association is $2^{32} - 1$.

Authentication Data Field

Authentication Data field is used to convey a hash or integrity check value computed over the payload. Several algorithms are supported for computing the integrity check, with the algorithm to be used selected when the security length of this field is a variable number of 32 bits.

ESP Header and Trailer

In comparison to the AH whose composition is relatively straightforward, the ESP header is only part of the story. That is, ESP includes both a header and trailer, which encapsulates the payload and results in the term "encapsulating" being used in ESP. Exhibit 8 illustrates the ESP header and trailer. The header contains two fields while the trailer contains four fields.

Security Parameter Index Field

This 32-bit field functions in the same manner as described for the Authentication Header.

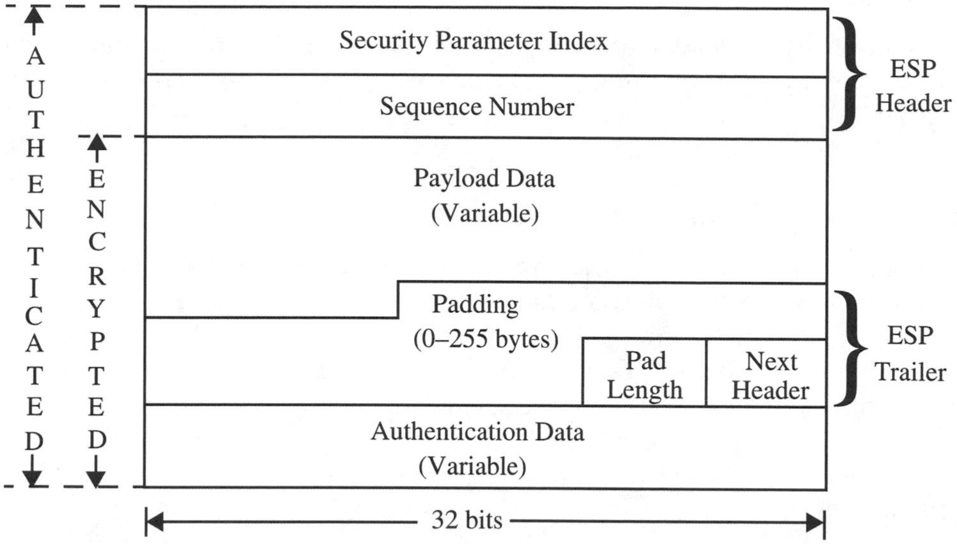

Exhibit 8. ESP Header and Trailer

Sequence Number Field

This 32-bit field also functions in the same manner as described for AH.

Payload Data Field

The Payload Data field is not actually part of the ESP header or trailer. It represents instead the encrypted payload whose encryption method was selected during the security association process.

Padding Field

Because most encryption algorithms operate on an integral number of blocks, a Padding field permits the payload to be extended to accommodate a particular encryption algorithm. Because padding may not be necessary if the algorithm operates on a byte basis or if the payload ends on a block boundary, the Padding field is optional.

Pad Length Field

This 1-bit field denotes the number of preceding padding bytes. This field is always present and has a value of 0 if no padding occurred.

Next Header Field

The eight-bit Next Header field indicates the type of data transported in the Payload Data field. The value used in the Next Header field corresponds to the set of IP protocol number values.

Authentication Data Field

The Authentication Data field is variable in length and contains an integrity check value (ICV) computed for the ESP packet. The ICV is computed from the Security Parameter Index field to the Next Header field. This field is optional and is only included when integrity check and authentication is selected during the security association initialization process.

Operations

From a logical perspective, IPSec can work in three different ways:

1. Host-to-Host
2. Host-to-Network
3. Network-to-Network

Host-to-Host

Host-to-host operations result in an IPSec connection between two hosts. Either transport mode or tunnel mode can be used under host-to-host operations. In transport mode, one can use AH, ESP, or AH can be applied after ESP (transport adjacency). The same combinations can be supported in tunnel mode.

Host-to-Network

In a host-to-network environment, a gateway provides IPSec support for multiple clients. Each client host communicates with the gateway instead of a particular host on a destination network.

Network-to-Network

In a network-to-network operational environment, hosts on one network communicate with a gateway that operates the IPSec protocol stack. That gateway communicates with a second gateway connected to the destination network that also operates the IPSec protocol stack. Clients on each network do not need to have any knowledge of IPSec because the gateways automatically perform all required security operations.

Chapter 10

Emerging Technologies

The widespread adoption of the TCP/IP protocol suite by business, government, and academia has resulted in a significant amount of development effort being devoted to this protocol suite. This development effort recognizes that Internet usage has grown exponentially, from a few hundred thousand users at the beginning of the 1990s to over 100 million users at the beginning of the new millennium. With this vast market of Internet users, the acquisition of equipment by Internet service providers (ISPs) also became an extensive market for hardware and software developers. With the vast amount of funds that ISPs are expending in providing support to their customer base, they are also favorably viewing the development of new technologies that they could use for additional billing, enhancing customer retention, and differentiating their service from other ISPs. Thus, there is a receptive market from both end users and ISPs for the use of new technologies that add functionality to the TCP/IP protocol suite.

This chapter focuses on four emerging technologies related to the TCP/IP protocol suite: virtual private networking, mobile IP, Voice-over-IP, and IPv6. Although each of these technologies has been in existence for a number of years, they can be considered emerging technologies as their potential use is now being recognized, and products are rapidly being developed that utilize these technologies.

Virtual Private Networking

In the wonderful world of the TCP/IP protocol suite, virtual private networking and the creation of virtual private networks (VPNs) are being driven by the growth of the Internet and economics. With the rapid growth of the Internet, this global network now provides connectivity to just about every city on the

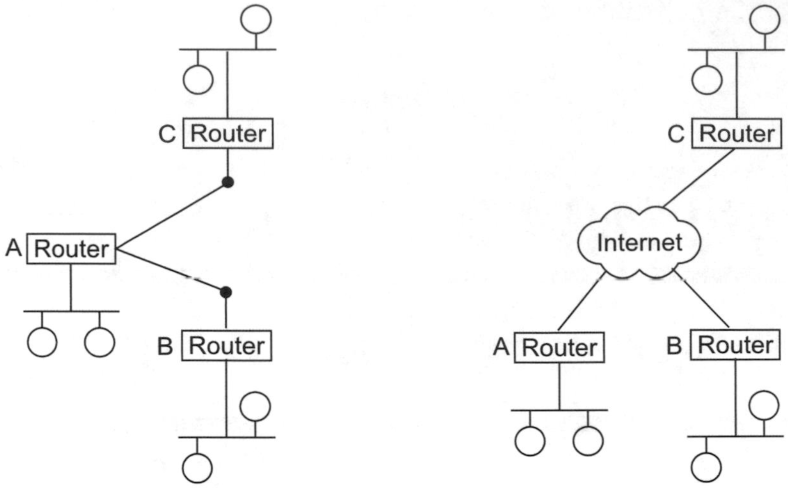

Exhibit 1. Comparing a Leased Line-Based Network versus the Use of a VPN over the Internet

globe. Thus, the use of the Internet represents a potential replacement for the expensive leased lines used by many organizations to interconnect geographically separated locations.

Benefits

To understand the benefits associated with the use of a VPN created via transmitting data over the Internet, one can compare and contrast the use of a private leased line-based network to the Internet. The left portion of Exhibit 1 illustrates a three-location, leased line-based network. The right portion of Exhibit 1 illustrates the use of a VPN created over the Internet to provide connectivity between the three locations.

Reducing Hardware Requirements

In examining Exhibit 1, note that the use of a private network requires more router ports than the creation of a VPN to interconnect three or more geographically separated locations. The use of a private network requires each location to be interconnected to other locations. To do so, the private network designer may have to interconnect some locations to multiple locations, such as connecting location A to locations B and C. In comparison, when a packet network such as the Internet is used, each location requires only one connection to the network and can use the routing capability of the packet network to access multiple locations via one serial connection. Thus, the use of the Internet can reduce hardware costs associated with obtaining connectivity, such as the number of router ports required for connecting three or more locations together.

Reliability

In addition to hardware savings, the use of a VPN via a packet network enables an organization to obtain the ability to use the mesh structure of the packet network. This means that if a router or transmission line within the Internet should fail, alternate routing within the Internet may alleviate the problem, providing additional reliability. Although a private organization can construct a mesh-structured network to obtain a similar degree of additional reliability, this is not common due to the high cost associated with establishing this type of network structure.

Economics

Although the ability to use less hardware and to obtain long-distance reliability are important advantages associated with a VPN, they are not the only advantages. Perhaps the key advantage is the ability of organizations to interconnect geographically separated locations under certain situations for a fraction of the cost of using leased lines. To illustrate the potential economic savings associated with the use of a VPN in comparison to a leased line-based network, reconsider Exhibit 1.

Assume that the private three-node network illustrated in the left portion of Exhibit 1 results in location A being 500 miles from location B and a similar distance from location C. Thus, the network would have a total of 1000 miles of leased lines. If one assumes that those leased lines are T1 circuits that operate at 1.544 Mbps and the monthly cost of each circuit is $4 per mile, then the long-distance cost of the leased line network becomes 1000 miles at $4 per mile per month, or $4000 per month.

In looking at the VPN created via the Internet shown in the right portion of Exhibit 1, one can see that the use of the Internet is distance insensitive for corporate users. The only charge is an access fee that connects each location via an Internet service provider (ISP) to the Internet. If it is further assumed that each of the three locations is within a city or surrounding suburban area, then the monthly fee charged by an ISP to support T1 access can be expected to range between $1000 and $1500 per location. This means that to provide three locations with T1 Internet access, the monthly cost would range between $3000 and $4500. Thus, while it might be possible to save some money, it is also possible that the use of the Internet can result in an additional expenditure of funds versus a private leased line-based network. By now the reader might be a bit confused because this author previously mentioned that economics is the driving force for the creation of a VPN via the Internet. And because this author does not want readers to be confused, assume now that the three locations shown in the left portion of Exhibit 1 are New York City, Miami, and San Francisco.

Based on the previously mentioned revised locations, the distance between the three locations has now expanded to approximately 5000 miles. Thus, the monthly cost of a private leased line-based network using T1 circuits would now become 5000 miles at $4 per mile per month, or $20,000 per month. Because the cost of accessing the Internet in major metropolitan areas is the same, the cost associated with connecting each location to the other via a VPN over the Internet remains the same. Thus, the cost would remain between $3000 and $4500 per month.

The preceding revision illustrates that the distance-insensitive cost associated with the use of the Internet can result in considerable savings when locations to be interconnected are relatively far apart. This also means that the further distance one location is from another, the greater the possible monthly cost savings. This also means that the global reach of the Internet could provide considerable economic savings for multinational organizations because they use international circuits that are relatively expensive in comparison to leased lines installed within a country. Given an appreciation for the benefits associated with the use of VPNs, one must also be aware of some of the limitations associated with the technology.

Limitations

Although not thought of as such each time a user transmits or receives e-mail via the Internet, that user employs a VPN that was created on a temporary basis. In fact, the use of VPNs by corporations follows a similar structure, with routing occurring on a packet-by-packet basis through the Internet. Unlike the transmission of conventional e-mail that might represent an update about family life or another personal matter, a VPN used by a company requires several features that are not normally needed on a personal messaging basis. Those features include authentication and encryption, as well as the use of a firewall because corporate information will now be flowing through the Internet. This opens the corporate network to potential attack from the Internet community of users.

In Chapter 9 we examined the use of IPSec as a mechanism to enhance security. There, it was noted that, through the use of the AH and ESP protocols, one can enhance IP security by providing support for authentication and encryption. Thus, let us turn our attention to both of these important topics and how they relate to IPSec.

Authentication

Authentication represents the process of verifying that a person is the person he or she claims to be. As discussed in Chapter 9, one of the most popular methods of authentication is based on the use of token generating cards. In an IPSec environment, the use of public key encryption can be employed to provide authentication. As a refresher for readers not familiar with public key encryption, its use involves two keys. One key is published and referred to as a public key while the second key is kept secret and referred to as a secret key. The public and private keys are mathematically related such that a message encrypted through the use of a public key can be decrypted by the use of the corresponding private key. When the private key is used for encryption, anyone with access to the corresponding public key can decrypt the message, resulting in a lack of security. However, the very fact that one can decrypt a message with a public key verifies the fact that it was encrypted with a private key. Thus, this verifies the identity of the sender and forms the basis for a popular authentication method supported by IPSec. Regardless of the type of authentication used, one must factor in its cost to determine the true cost of using a VPN versus a leased line network. Normally, authentication is not required on a leased line network as the network connects fixed locations. Thus, a leased line network commonly represents a "closed" network that outsiders cannot access. In comparison, the Internet represents an "open" network. Once a person notes the host or IP address of a device, that person can attempt to transmit information to that device.

Encryption

Because it is doubtful that an organization would allow vital corporate information to flow clear across the Internet where it could possibly be intercepted, another commonly required VPN feature is encryption. However, VPN encryption is both more difficult to perform and more expensive than conventional encryption products used to secure transmission via leased lines.

The reason VPN encryption is more complex and costly than encryption performed on point-to-point leased lines results from the fact that routing via a VPN is more complex. For example, consider Exhibit 2, which illustrates the assignment of Class C IP addresses to each of three networks to be interconnected via the Internet. Note that a fourth network on which a public server resides, such as www.whitehouse.com, is shown with the network address xxx.yyy.zzz.0 to indicate that it can be any address other than the three network addresses of the geographically separated networks to be interconnected via a VPN. Because a user on network 198.78.46.0 may periodically surf the Web while at other times access a server on network 207.121.131.0 or network 205.131.175.0, the device performing encryption must be configured to distinguish a VPN destination address. In addition, because one would not want to use the same encryption key between all sites, the equipment must support multiple keys.

In an IPsec environment, the Encapsulating Security Payload (ESP) protocol discussed in Chapter 9 provides a mechanism to encrypt packet payload data. Although one might anticipate that public key encryption is supported, in actuality ESP is limited to supporting such private symmetrical encryption techniques as the Data Encryption Standard (DES) and triple-DES. The reason for the lack of support of public key encryption results from the high processing requirements of that technique. In comparison, DES and triple-DES

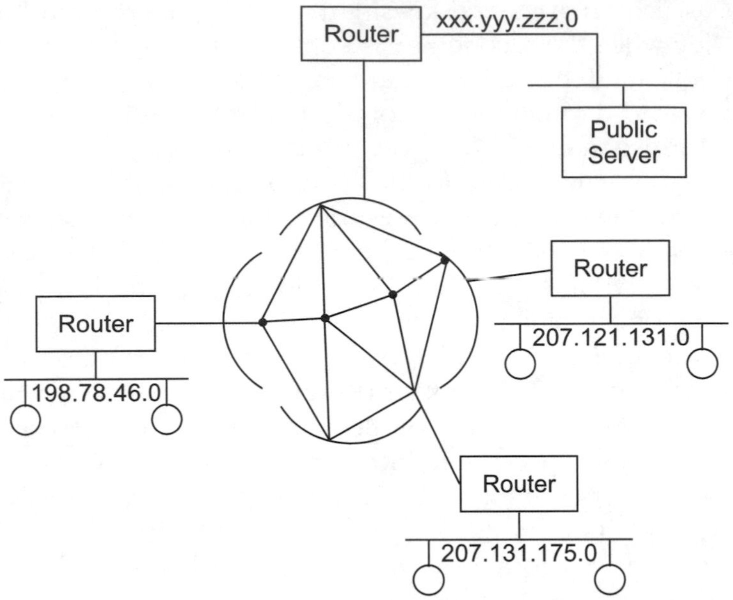

Exhibit 2. When Encryption Is Used on a VPN, the Destination of Packets Must Be Examined as a Basis for Determining Whether or Not to Encrypt the Packet

are relatively processor benign and enable a gateway to easily support multiple encryption sessions.

Other Issues to Consider

In addition to security, there are two additional issues one must consider when thinking about the use of a VPN. Those issues are management control and the latency or delay through the Internet. Concerning management control, unlike the use of leased lines that can contact a single communications carrier in an attempt to resolve a problem, if a problem occurs on the Internet, one's ability to communicate with a carrier is restricted when dealing with an ISP. Concerning latency, because other traffic carried on the Internet is not predictable, the delay packets experience will be random. This means that certain delay-sensitive applications, such as real-time command and control for numeric machinery as well as Voice-over-IP, may or may not be suitable for a VPN. Despite such problems, VPNs represent an emerging technology, with support even included in Microsoft's popular Windows NT server. Thus, this section concludes with a discussion of how one can set up an NT server to allow dial-up access that in turn permits a remote user to connect to the organization's internal network. If that network is in turn connected to the Internet, one can then provide employees with the ability to access other organizational locations via a local telephone call even if those locations are thousands of miles away or are on another continent.

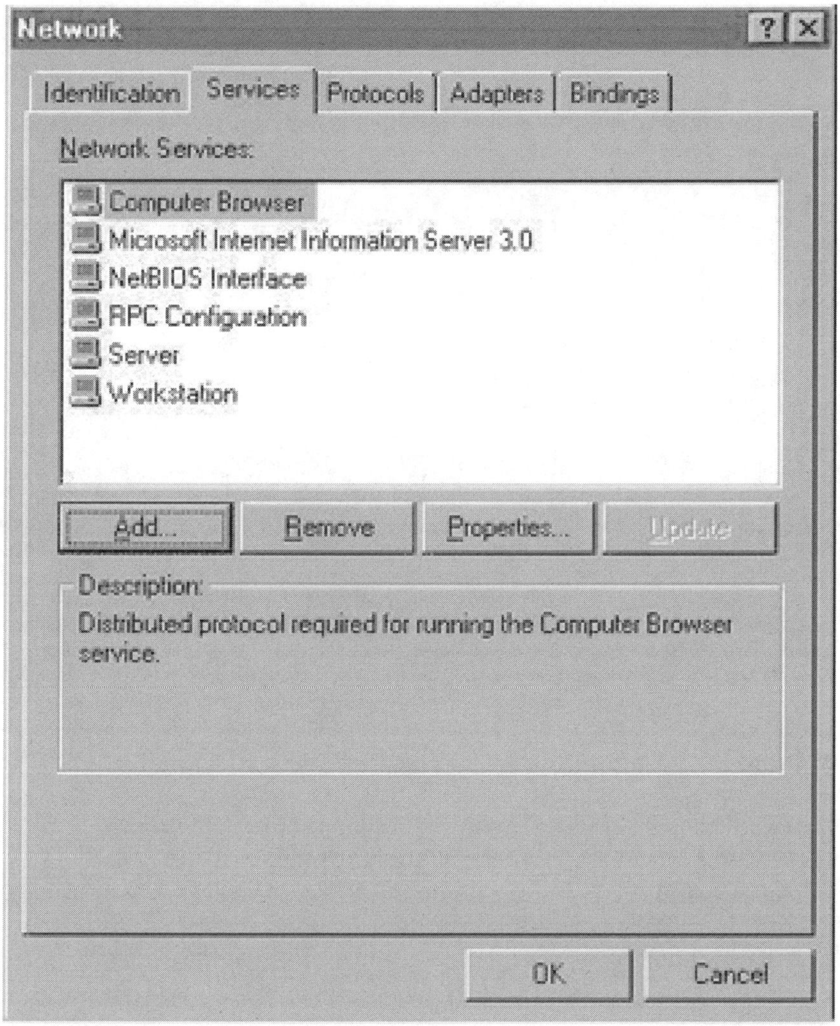

Exhibit 3. Installing Remote Access Services on an NT Server Requiring Selection of Services Tab from the Network Dialog Box

Setting Up Remote Access Service

Exhibit 3 illustrates how one would begin to install Microsoft's Remote Access Service on a Windows NT server. In this example, one would enter Start > Settings > Control Panel and then select Network. Once the Network dialog box is displayed, click on the Services tab in the box and the Add button located on that tab.

By performing the previously described operations, a dialog box labeled "Select Network Service" will be displayed. Exhibit 4 illustrates an example of that dialog box. Note that the Remote Access Service entry is shown highlighted. Click on the button labeled "OK" and Windows will prompt you for

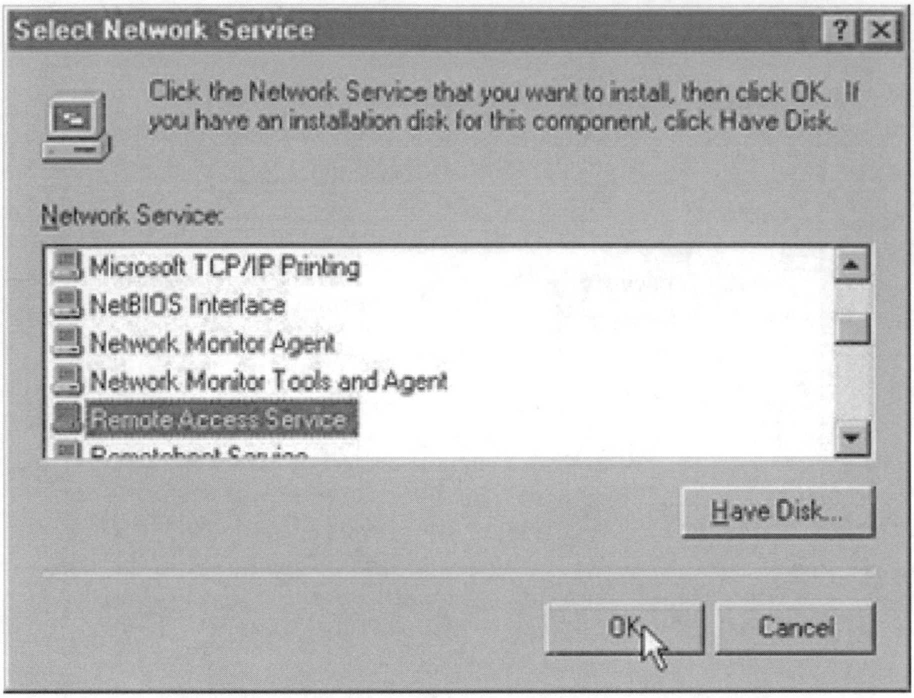

Exhibit 4. Installing RAS from the Select Network Service Dialog Box

a disk or a CD that is provided with NT. After entering Windows NT, CD RAS will be both located and a portion of the program will be installed.

After RAS is installed, different devices can be added that will allow access to services. This is shown in Exhibit 5, where the author has added a generic 28,800-bps modem to support dial-in service. Exhibit 6 shows the result of the previous action, with the modem installed on the COM1 serial communications port.

By examining the right portion of Exhibit 6, one notes a button labeled "Network." Clicking on this button provides the ability to allow a remote client to use NetBEUI, TCP/IP, and IPX protocols. This capability is shown in Exhibit 7. Note that this dialog box also provides the capability to require authentication and encryption for the remote user.

If one clicks on the Configure box next to the TCP/IP option, one obtains the ability to configure a variety of TCP/IP options. Exhibit 8 illustrates the resulting dialog box, labeled "RAS Server TCP/IP Configuration." Note from Exhibit 8 that one can enable RAS service for the entire network or the server. Also note that one can provide a dynamic or static IP address to remote clients or even allow them to request a predefined IP address. Thus, Microsoft's Remote Access Service server provides support for different addressing schemes. When combined with other Microsoft products, Windows NT servers can be used for routing, which allows an organization to spend a few thousand dollars per location to interconnect geographically separated networks via the

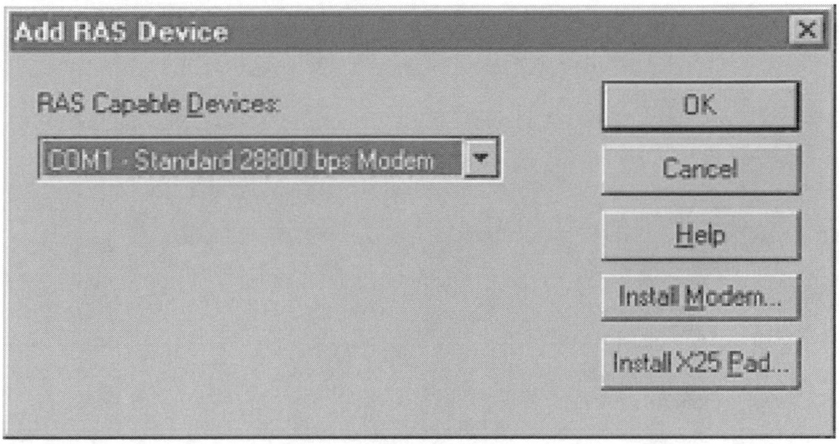

Exhibit 5. Adding a Generic 28,800-bps Modem to Support Dial-Up Access to a RAS Server

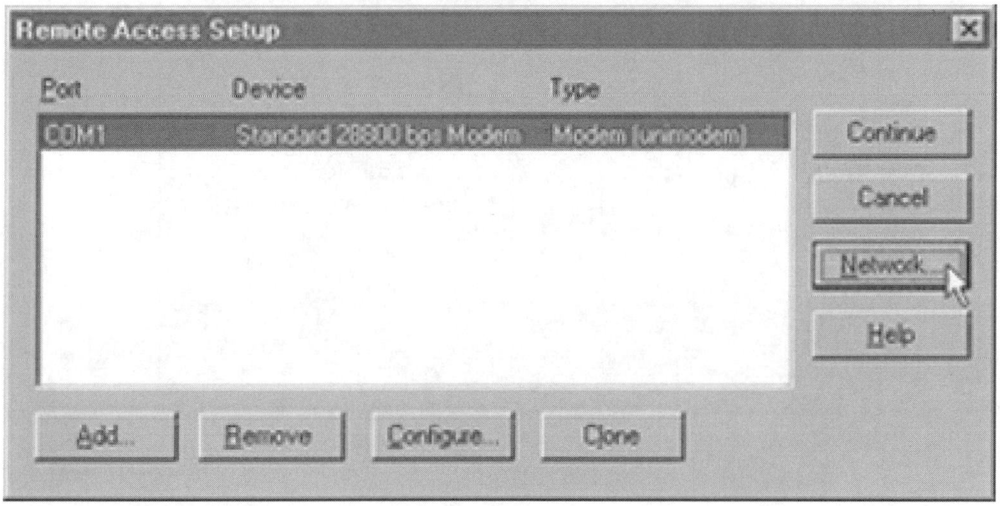

Exhibit 6. Examining the Remote Access Setup Dialog Box after Dial-In Access Is Configured

Internet. Thus, many products are appearing in the marketplace that provide a VPN capability and represent another driving force for adopting VPNs.

Mobile IP

Although a mobile person can access their home location via the dial-up services of an ISP, there is no method for host computers on an internal corporate network to easily note the mobile user's identity and imitate communications with the person's computer. Because of this, a TCP/IP network

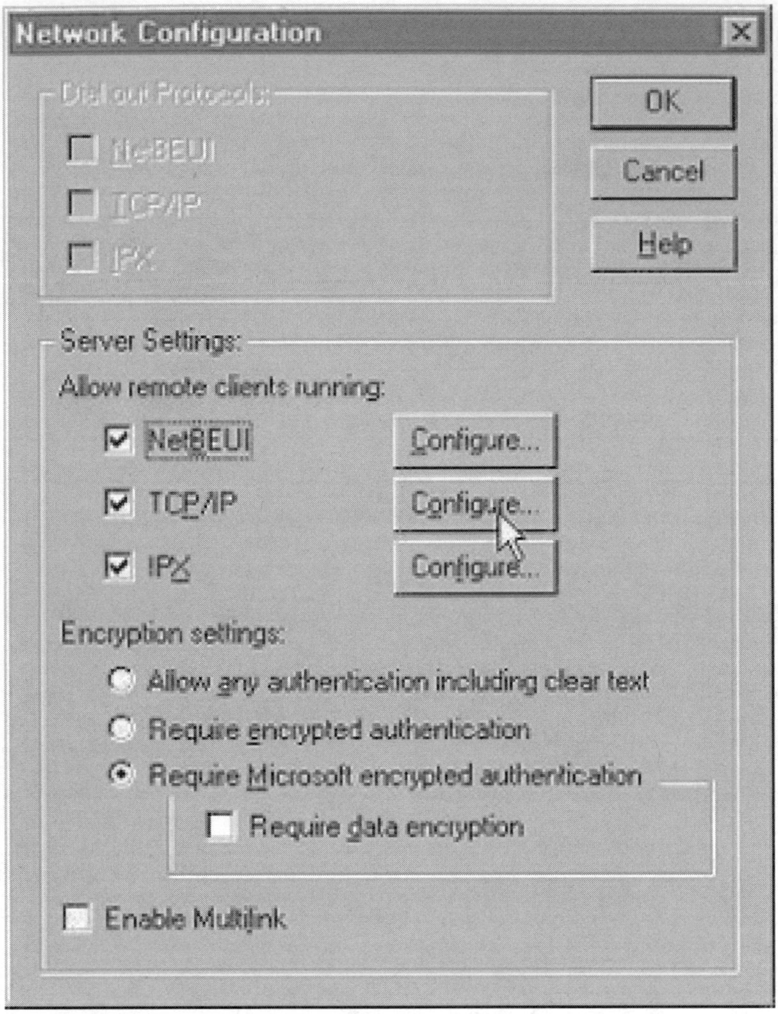

Exhibit 7. Specifying the Protocols the Server Will Support and the Use of Authentication and Encryption through the Network Configuration Dialog Box

can be considered to represent a client-driven network, with the client having to initiate communications sessions.

With the growth in the use of cell phones and the development of a limited e-mail and browsing capability by those devices, it becomes possible to employ server-side session initiation. That is, a server can be configured to interface the telephone network and transmit messages to mobile cell phone subscribers. However, a similar mechanism is not available for the traveling notebook operator who may be required to check several mail systems to determine what messages, if any, are awaiting his or her action. Recognizing this problem

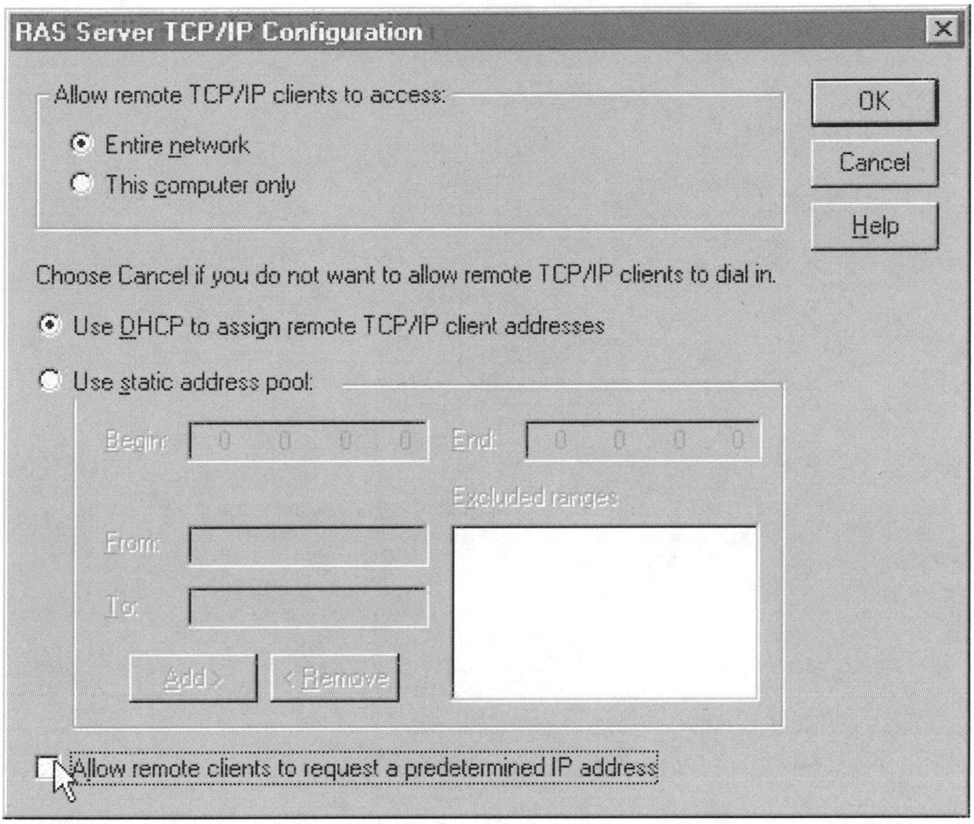

Exhibit 8. RAS Server TCP/IP Configuration Dialog Box

was probably a contributing factor to the development of mobile IP, which represents a second emerging technology to be discussed in this chapter.

Overview

Under mobile IP, a user makes a connection to his home network and registers his presence with a mobile IP server. If the remote user is using the services of an ISP and has a temporary IP address, that address is also registered with the mobile IP server. A second feature or function of that server is to serve as a focal point for applications that need to communicate with the mobile user. Thus, it becomes possible for e-mail and other server-side applications to note the presence of a mobile IP user and communicate with the user through the services of the mobile IP server.

Operation

Exhibit 9 provides an example of how a mobile IP server might be used. In this example, assume that the mobile user was previously registered with the

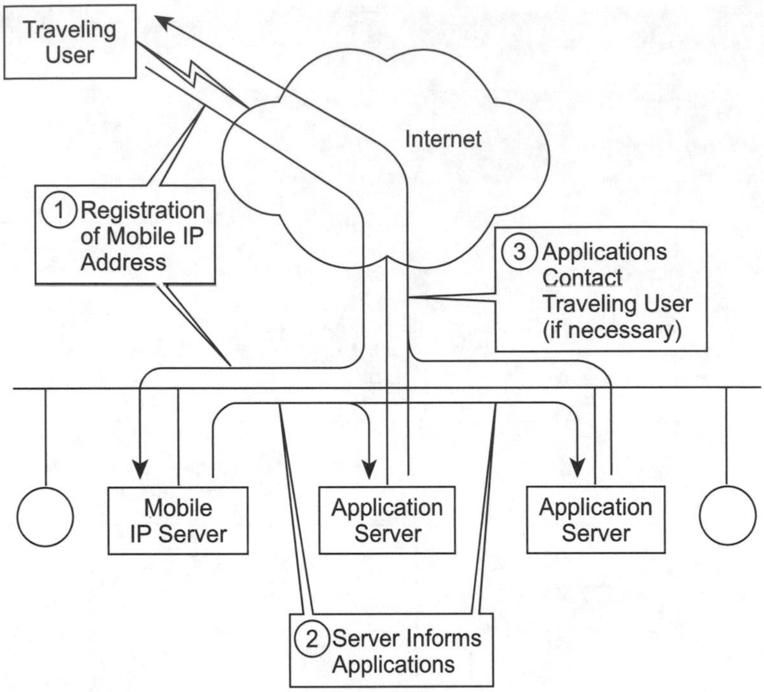

Exhibit 9. Mobile IP in Operation

server, and applications that need to reach the user to know his or her presence will be established via notification from the server.

On a trip to Japan, the traveling executive dials the Internet via the hotel where he or she is staying. While online, the ISP serving Japan assigns a temporary IP address to the user. This address is noted by the mobile IP server (1), which informs predefined applications that the distant user is online. This is illustrated by (2). Next, each application, such as e-mail (3) and digitized voice mail (3), uses the temporary IP address to establish communications with the traveling executive.

While the concept behind mobile IP has been around for a few years, until recently it was easier for a person to simply communicate with his or her e-mail system than support server-side initiation. Because there are emerging applications beyond e-mail that people may wish to access, it may be easier to allow the applications to contact the user when they access the home network than to require persons to check numerous servers.

Voice-over-IP

The transmission of voice over an IP network, which is referred to as Voice-over-IP, represents an evolving technology that offers both individuals and organizations the potential to realize substantial economic savings. In fact, if one can obtain a Voice-over-IP transmission capability by upgrading existing equipment through the installation of voice modules on a router or the use of a getaway on an existing network infrastructure, it becomes possible to transmit a digitized voice call over an intranet or the Internet for as little as 0.1 cent per minute. This cost is low enough to make the Sprint dime lady blush and explains the key interest of organizations in applying this technology.

Constraints

There are several key constraints governing the ability of digitized voice to be transmitted over an IP network and successfully reconstructed at the destination. Those constraints include end-to-end latency, the random nature of packet networks, the voice digitization method used, and the need to subdivide packets containing data into minimum-length entities. Each of these constraints is interrelated.

Latency

Latency or end-to-end delay governs the ability of reconstructed voice to sound normal or awkward. The total one-way delay that a packet experiences as it flows from source to destination via an IP network depends on several factors. Those factors include the speed of the ingress and egress lines from locations connected to the Internet or a private intranet, the voice coding algorithm used to digitize voice, the number of router hops through the Internet or a private intranet from source to destination, and the activity occurring at and between each hop. When all of these factors are considered as an entity, the one-way delay of a packet should not exceed 250 ms and should probably be under 200 ms to obtain a good quality of reconstructed voice.

Because delays on the Internet can easily exceed 200 ms without considering the voice coding algorithm delay, this explains why it is not possible to consider the Internet as fully ready to support digitized voice at this time. Because it is relatively easy but costly to add bandwidth to a private intranet, one can do so to reduce delays. However, the additional cost associated with reducing latency can increase the cost of transporting Voice-over-IP. In the near future, the hundreds of thousands of miles of fiber-optic cable being installed throughout the United States, western Europe, and other locations around the globe should result in an increase in transmission capacity by several orders of magnitude over existing transmission facilities. As ISPs upgrade their backbones, it may be possible within a few years for the problem of latency to be considerably reduced in comparison to the role it plays today in hampering Internet telephony from achieving widespread acceptance.

Packet Network Operation

The operation of a packet network can be considered to represent a random process, with data arriving at routers occurring on a random basis. This means that the delay experienced by a series of packets transporting digitized voice will not only result in a random transit delay through the network, but will also result in random delays between packets. This also means that the ability to transport digitized voice and reconstruct it so that it sounds natural requires the use of a "jitter buffer."

A jitter buffer represents a small portion of memory at the recipient equipment that temporarily stores received packets transporting voice. To ensure that packets are extracted in their appropriate time sequence, each packet must be timestamped. In a Voice-over-IP environment, most applications currently use a protocol referred to as the Real Time Protocol (RTP). RTP provides the capability to both timestamp and sequence number packets. RTP is commonly implemented over UDP. UDP is used to transmit digitized voice because no error checking is necessary, as erroneous packets cannot be retransmitted. Although RTP is important for the appropriate use of a jitter buffer, this new header adds a bit of delay to the flow of packets. In addition, the use of a jitter buffer for temporary data storage also adds to end-to-end delay. Although many jitter buffers are capable of being configured to store from 0 (not operational) to 255 ms of speech, the wider the buffer, the greater the potential delays to voice transporting packets. Thus, the configuration of a jitter buffer must be considered with respect to other potential delays as well as the voice digitization coding method to be used.

Voice Digitization Method

There are currently over half a dozen voice digitization methods supported by most Voice-over-IP hardware products. These methods vary with respect to the coding rate they operate at, the coding delay, and the legibility of reconstructed voice. The latter is normally specified by a subjective measurement referred to as Mean Optimum Score (MOS). In general, the lower the data rate, the higher the coding delay and the lower the MOS. For example, pulse code modulation (PCM), which is used extensively on the public switched telephone network (PSTN), operates at 64 kbps, has a coding delay of approximately 1 ms, and has the highest MOS of all coding methods. In comparison, a popular voice coder used on packet networks referred to as G.723 operates at 5.3 kbps or 6.2 kbps, but has a coding delay of 30 ms and a much lower MOS than PCMs.

Exhibit 10 lists four popular voice coding methods. The first two, pulse code modulation (PCM) and adaptive differential pulse code modulation (ADPCM), represent waveform coding techniques primarily used on the PSTN (PCM) and on international circuits (ADPCM) over which public network calls are routed between countries. Both coding methods are referred to as "toll quality" and represent the sound of reconstructed voice for which other methods are commonly compared. The algorithm delay for coding a voice sample via PCM or ADPCM is very fast, typically 1 ms. However, the resulting bit rate is relatively high in comparison to recently developed voice coding

Exhibit 10 Common Speech Coding Algorithms

Standard	*Coding Method*	*Bit Rate*	*Delay*	*MOS*
G.711	PCM	64 kbps	1 ms	4.4
G.726	ADPCM	32 kbps	1 ms	4.4
G.728	LD-CELP	16 kbps	10 ms	4.2
G.723.1	MP-MLQ	5.3/6.3 kbps	30 ms	3.9

methods that use both waveform sampling and speech synthesis — a technique that is referred to as hybrid coding.

Two popular hybrid voice coding techniques standardized by the ITU are G.728 and G.723.1, the latter a multi-rate coder. G.728 is a low-delay coder, with the algorithm requiring 10 ms. This delay is still a thousand times greater than the delay associated with PCM and ADCPM. Also note that the G.723.1 standard is 30 ms, which can represent a considerable period of time when overall end-to-end delay to include the coding algorithm is limited.

Because end-to-end delay must be less than 250 ms and preferably below 200 ms, many times the use of a very low bit rate voice digitization technique will result in an excessive amount of delay. If one's equipment supports multiple coders, one technique to consider to enhance the quality of reconstructed voice is the use of a different coder.

A second problem concerning the use of voice coders is the fact that at the present time there are not any standards that enable equipment produced by different vendors to negotiate the use of a voice coder. Although the Frame Relay Forum developed a standard for Voice-over-Frame Relay during 1997, a similar standard is still missing for use on TCP/IP networks. Thus, equipment interoperability can be considered in its infancy, and organizations may have to experiment using different coders to select an optimum one based upon a series of factors to include routing delays through the packet network.

Packet Subdivision

As indicated earlier in this book, a datagram can be up to 65,535 bytes in length. Unfortunately, if a long datagram should flow between two datagrams transporting digitized voice, the lengthy datagram can introduce a significant delay that makes the reconstruction of quality-sounding voice difficult, if not impossible. Due to this, it is necessary to use equipment to limit the length of packets transporting data. Unfortunately, there are two constraints associated with packet subdivision. First, one can only use equipment at the entrance to a packet network to subdivide lengthy packets. This means that one cannot control lengthy packets transmitted by other organizations through the packet network. Second, by taking one lengthy packet transporting data and subdividing it into two or more packets, one increases network traffic and reduces transmission efficiency. This results from the fact that one now has more overhead in the form of multiple headers rather than one header. This additional traffic can overtax routers and result in routers doing what they are programmed to do under an overload condition — drop packets. Thus, it is entirely possible that the medicine in the form of packet subdivision could kill the patient. Despite the previously mentioned problems, Voice-over-IP is a viable emerging technology. To understand why organizations are excited about the use of this technology, one can explore two networking configurations suitable for consideration on the Internet or an intranet, assuming end-to-end latency can be obtained at an acceptable level.

Networking Configurations

Two of the most popular methods for transporting voice over an IP network are through the use of voice modules installed in a router and the use of a stand-alone voice gateway. This section examines the use of each method.

Router Voice Module Utilization

Recognizing the fact that many organizations can benefit from the convergence of voice and data and that they already operate private IP networks, several router manufacturers have introduced voice modules that are designed for installation within different router products. While voice modules can vary in capability and functionality between vendors, they perform a set of common features. These features include providing an interface to different signaling methods associated with the direct connection of PBX ports or individual telephone instruments, supporting several voice coding algorithms, and prioritizing the flow of datagrams transporting voice into router queues for faster placement onto a serial communications line. Exhibit 11 illustrates the potential

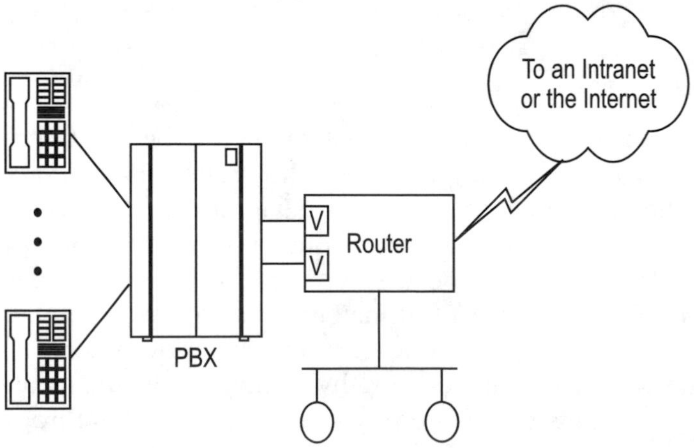

Exhibit 11. Using Router Voice Modules to Obtain an Integrated Voice/Data Networking Capability

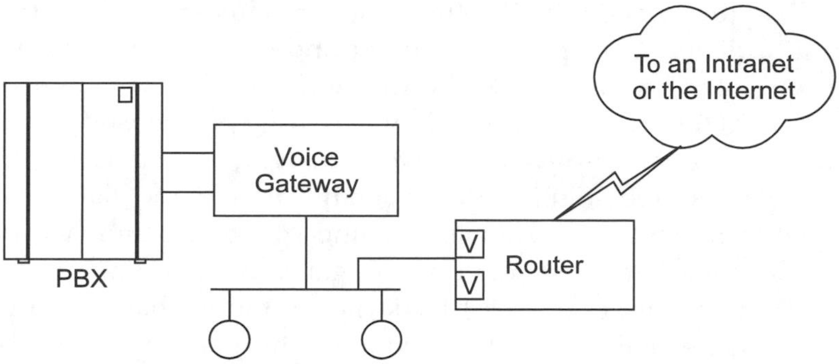

Exhibit 12. Using a Voice Gateway

use of voice digitization modules installed in a router to provide the ability to transmit both voice and data over a common network infrastructure.

In examining Exhibit 11, note that an organization would program the PBX to establish a new prefix for voice users to access the router's voice modules. For example, dialing a "6" might route calls to the router, while dialing a prefix of "9" would be used to connect to an outside line for calling via the PSTN. One would also configure the voice modules via the router's operating system, such as selecting a specific voice coding algorithm and setting a specific priority for voice in comparison to data so that datagrams transporting voice will receive preference for extraction from the queue in the router for transmission onto the serial port connecting the router to a private intranet or the public Internet.

Voice Gateway

A second common method to consider for integrating the transmission of voice and data over an IP network is obtained through the use of a voice gateway. Exhibit 12 illustrates the potential use of this communications device.

In examining Exhibit 12, one would interface a voice gateway to a PBX similar to the manner by which one would connect a PBX to voice modules installed in a router. Unlike the use of a router where packets transporting digitized voice do not flow on a LAN, when a gateway is used, the packets flow on the local network. Thus, take care to ensure that the utilization level of the network is not over 50 percent. Otherwise, an excessive amount of collisions could occur that add to the latency of packets transporting voice.

A key advantage to the use of stand-alone voice gateways over the use of voice modules installed in routers is the fact that the former scale better than the latter. For example, current voice gateways are obtainable that typically support 4, 8, 16, 32, 64, and 128 voice ports, with expansion possible on some getaways that allow up to 1024 ports to be supported. In comparison, many routers only support the addition of two to four voice modules, with each module capable of supporting a limited number of ports.

Although a few routers now offer voice modules that can be directly interfaced to a digital ISDN port on a router and can directly accept 24 voice calls, such modules are only supported on high-end routers whose basic cost can exceed $50,000. In comparison, low-end routers that support a limited number of voice connections may have pricing that begins at $1500 and represent a more viable solution for integrating voice and data at a branch office. Low-end routers have a limited scaling capability, and one may wish to carefully consider the use of a voice gateway that has an expansion capability. If an organization uses LAN switches rather than a shared media network, it then becomes possible to connect the gateway to a switch port and avoid potential latency problems associated with the use of shared media networks.

IPv6

This section on emerging technologies concludes with a discussion of the new version of the Internet Protocol, IPv6. As noted earlier in this book, the near-exponential growth in the use of the Internet has rapidly depleted the quantity of available IP network addresses and has resulted in such addresses becoming a precious commodity. In examining IPv6, note that its addressing capability ensures that every man, woman, and child on the planet — as well as every electronic device — can obtain an IPv6 address. This capability provides a mechanism to enable the development of intelligent network-based home appliances and other devices that could be managed by a service organization or the homeowner from their office. Thus, IPv6 can be considered to provide a foundation for extending the capabilities of the Internet to new applications that can be expected to arise during the new millennium.

Overview

IPv6 was developed as a mechanism to simplify the operation of the Internet Protocol, provide a mechanism for adding new operations as they are developed through a header daisy-chain capability, add built-in security and authentication, and extend source and destination addresses to an address space that could conceivably meet every possible addressing requirement for generations. The latter is accomplished through an expansion of source and destination addresses to 128 bits and is the focus of this section.

Address Architecture

IPv6 is based on the same architecture used in IPv4, resulting in each network interface requiring a distinct IP address. The key differences between IPv6 and IPv4 with respect to addresses are the manner by which an interface can be identified, and the size and composition of the address. Under IPv6, an interface can be identified by several addresses to facilitate routing and management. In comparison, under IPv4, an interface can only be assigned one address. Concerning address size, IPv6 uses 128 bits, or 96 more bits than an IPv4 address.

Address Types

IPv6 addresses include unicast and multicast, which were included in IPv4. In addition, IPv6 adds a new address category known as anycast. Although an anycast address identifies a group of stations similar to a multicast address, a packet with an anycast address is delivered to only one station, the nearest member of the group. The use of anycast addressing can be expected to facilitate network restructuring while minimizing the amount of configuration changes required to support a new network structure. This is because one can use an anycast address to reference a group of routers, and the alteration of a network when stations use anycast addressing would enable them to continue to access the nearest router without a user having to change the address configuration of their workstation.

Address Notation

Because IPv6 addresses consist of 128 bits, a mechanism is required to facilitate their entry as configuration data. The mechanism used is to replace those bits with eight 16-bit integers separated by colons, with each integer represented by four hexadecimal digits. For example:

6ACD:00001:00FC:B10C:0001:0000:0000:001A

To facilitate the entry of IPv6 addresses, one can skip leading zeros in each hexadecimal component. That is, one can write 1 instead of 0001 and 0 instead of 0000. Thus, this ability to suppress zeroes in each hexadecimal component would reduce the previous network address to:

6ACD:1:FC:B10C:1:0:0:1A

Under IPv6, a second method of address simplification was introduced, the double-colon (::) convention. Inside an address, a set of consecutive null 16-bit numbers can be replaced by two colons (::). Thus, the previously reduced IP address could be further reduced to:

6ACD:1:FC:B10C:1::1A

It is important to note that the double-colon convention can only be used once inside an address. This is because the reconstruction of the address requires the number of integer fields in the address to be subtracted from eight to determine the number of consecutive fields of zero value the double-colon represents. Otherwise, the use of two or more double-colons would create ambiguity that would not allow the address to be correctly reconstructed.

Address Allocation

The use of a 128-bit address space provides a high degree of address assignment flexibility beyond that available under IPv4. IPv6 addressing enables Internet service providers to be identified as well as includes the ability to identify local and global multicast addresses, private site addresses for use within an organization, hierarchical geographical global unicast addresses, and other types of addresses. Exhibit 13 lists the initial allocation of address space under IPv6.

The Internet Assigned Numbers Authority (IANA) was assigned the task of distributing portions of IPv6 address space to regional registries around the world, such as the InterNIC in North America, RIPE in Europe, and APNIC in Asia. To illustrate the planned use of IPv6 addresses, the discussion continues with what will probably be the most common type of IPv6 address — the provider-based address.

Exhibit 9.13. IPv6 Address Space Allocation

Allocation	*Prefix (binary)*	*Fraction of Address Space*
Reserved	0000 0000	1/256
Unassigned	0000 0001	1/256
Reserved for NSAP allocation	0000 001	1/128
Reserved for IPX allocation	0000 010	1/128
Unassigned	0000 011	1/128
Unassigned	0000 1	1/32
Unassigned	0001	1/16
Unassigned	001	1/8
Provider-Based Unicast Address	010	1/8
Unassigned	011	1/8
Reserved for Geographic-Based Unicast Address	100	1/8
Unassigned	101	1/8
Unassigned	110	1/8
Unassigned	1110	1/16
Unassigned	1111 0	1/32
Unassigned	1111 10	1/64
Unassigned	1111 110	1/128
Unassigned	1111 1110 0	1/512
Link-Local Use Addresses	1111 1110 10	1/1024
Site-Local Use Addresses	1111 1110 11	1/1024
Multicast Addresses	1111 1111	1/256

Prefix	Registry ID	Provider ID	Subscriber ID	Subnet ID	Station ID

Legend:

Prefix	three bits set to 010
Registry	5 bits identify organization that allocated the address
Provider	24 bits with 16 used to identify ISP and 8 used for future extensions
Subscriber	32 bits with 24 used to identify the subscriber and 8 for extension
Subnet	16 bits to identify the subnetwork
Station	48 bits to identify the station

Exhibit 14. Provider-Based Address Structure

Provider-Based Addresses

The first official distribution of IPv6 addresses will be accomplished through the use of provider-based addresses. Based on the initial allocation of IPv6 addresses as shown in Exhibit 13, each provider-based address will have the three-bit prefix 010. That prefix will be followed by fields that identify the registry that allocated the address, the service provider, and the subscriber. The latter field actually consists of three sub-fields: a subscriber ID that can represent an organization, and variable network and interface identification fields used in a similar manner to IPv4 network and host fields. Exhibit 14 illustrates the initial structure for a provider-based address.

Special Addresses

Under IPv6, five special types of unicast addresses were defined, of which one deserves special attention. That address is the Version 4 address, which was developed to provide a migration capability from IPv4 to IPv6.

In a mixed IPv4/IPv6 environment, devices that do not support IPv6 will be mapped to version 6 addresses using the following form:

0:0:0:0:0:FFFF:w.x.y.z

Here, w.x.y.z represents the original IPv4 address. Thus, IPv4 addresses will be transported as IPv6 addresses through the use of the IPv6 version 4 address format. This means that an organization with a large number of workstations and servers connected to the Internet only has to upgrade its router to support IPv6 addressing when IPv6 is deployed. Then, the network can be gradually upgraded on a device-by-device basis to obtain an orderly migration to IPv6.

Although IPv6 is being used on an experimental portion of the Internet, its anticipated movement into a production environment was delayed due to the more efficient use of existing IPv4 addresses. This occurred via network address translation, which was described in Chapter 9. While the use of IPv6 is less pressing than thought just a few years ago, no matter how efficient the allocation of the remaining IPv4 addresses becomes, it is a known fact that within the next few years, all available addresses will be used. Prior to that time, one can expect a migration to IPv6 to occur.

APPENDICES: TCP/IP PROTOCOL REFERENCE NUMBERS

The appendices provide a comprehensive reference to several key TCP/IP protocol numbers. As indicated earlier in this book, TCP/IP is not a single protocol. Instead, it represents a layered protocol that has several components.

One of the major components of TCP/IP includes the Internet Control Message Protocol (ICMP) used to convey different types of control messages within an IP datagram. Because of the flexible design of the ICMP format, different types of messages can be conveyed by altering the value of its Type field. In addition, many ICMP Type field values have a Code field whose value further clarifies the type of message being conveyed. Thus, Appendix A is included in this book to provide a reference to ICMP Type and Code values.

A second major component of the TCP/IP protocol suite is the Internet Protocol (IP). Because an IP datagram can transport an ICMP message, a TCP segment, or a UDP datagram, as well as other higher layer protocols, a mechanism is required to define the upper layer protocol being conveyed. That mechanism is provided by the Protocol Type field, which identifies the header following the IP datagram. Appendix B contains a listing of the values of the Protocol Type field.

A third major characteristic of the TCP/IP protocol suite is the use of port numbers to identify applications, enabling the multiplexing of different types of application-based traffic from and to common addresses. The use of port numbers explains how, for example, a Web server could also support FTP and Telnet operations. The first 1024 port numbers, referred to as Well-Known Ports, are summarized in Appendix C.

Appendix A

ICMP Type and Code Values

This appendix provides a listing of ICMP Type and Code values. One can use the information in this appendix when configuring router access lists or a firewall that performs a packet filtering operation. For examplc, if one creates a router access list that only allows ICMP Type 0 (Echo Reply) messages in the inbound direction from an Internet connection, in effect one permits responses to echo messages originated by users behind the router but blocks all other ICMP messages. Thus, this would allow one's employees to ping distant hosts while blocking users on the Internet from pinging hosts on one's organizational network.

ICMP Type Numbers

The Internet Control Message Protocol (ICMP) has many messages that are identified by a "Type" field as listed below.

Type	*Name*
0	Echo Reply
1	Unassigned
2	Unassigned
3	Destination Unreachable
4	Source Quench
5	Redirect
6	Alternate Host Address
7	Unassigned
8	Echo
9	Router Advertisement
10	Router Selection

(continues)

Type	*Name (continued)*
11	Time Exceeded
12	Parameter Problem
13	Timestamp
14	Timestamp Reply
15	Information Request
16	Information Reply
17	Address Mask Request
18	Address Mask Reply
19	Reserved (for Security)
20–29	Reserved (for Robustness Experiment)
30	Traceroute
31	Datagram Conversion Error
32	Mobile Host Redirect
33	IPv6 Where-Are-You
34	IPv6 I-Am-Here
35	Mobile Registration Request
36	Mobile Registration Reply
37	Domain Name Request
38	Domain Name Reply
39	SKIP
40	Photuris
41–255	Reserved

ICMP Code Values

Many of these ICMP types have a Code field. One can view the Code field as providing a specific clarifier for the value in the Type field. For example, a router generating a Type field value of 3 indicates that the IP destination address was unreachable, but does not specifically indicate why it was unreachable. Here, the Code field value would clarify the reason why the destination address was unreachable. The following table lists the Type field values and their applicable Code field values, if any:

Message Type	*Code Field Value*
0	Echo Reply **Codes** 0 No Code
1	Unassigned
2	Unassigned
3	Destination Unreachable

Codes

0 Net Unreachable
1 Host Unreachable
2 Protocol Unreachable
3 Port Unreachable
4 Fragmentation Needed and Don't Fragment Was Set
5 Source Route Failed
6 Destination Network Unknown
7 Destination Host Unknown
8 Source Host Isolated
9 Communication with Destination Network Is Administratively Prohibited
10 Communication with Destination Host Is Administratively Prohibited
11 Destination Network Unreachable for Type of Service
12 Destination Host Unreachable for Type of Service
13 Communication Administratively Prohibited
14 Host Precedence Violation
15 Precedence Cutoff in Effect

4 Source Quench

Codes

0 No Code

5 Redirect

Codes

0 Redirect Datagram for the Network (or subnet)
1 Redirect Datagram for the Host
2 Redirect Datagram for the Type of Service and Network
3 Redirect Datagram for the Type of Service and Host

6 Alternate Host Address

Codes

0 Alternate Address for Host

7 Unassigned

8 Echo

Codes

0 No Code

9 Router Advertisement

Codes

0 No Code

10 Router Selection

Codes

0 No Code

(continues)

Message Type	*Code Field Value (continued)*
11	Time Exceeded **Codes** 0 Time to Live Exceeded in Transit 1 Fragment Reassembly Time Exceeded
12	Parameter Problem **Codes** 0 Bad IP Header 1 Missing a Required Option 2 Bad Length
13	Timestamp **Codes** 0 No Code
14	Timestamp Reply **Codes** 0 No Code
15	Information Request **Codes** 0 No Code
16	Information Reply **Codes** 0 No Code
17	Address Mask Request **Codes** 0 No Code
18	Address Mask Reply **Codes** 0 No Code
19	Reserved (for Security)
20–29	Reserved (for Robustness Experiment)
30	Traceroute
31	Datagram Conversion Error
32	Mobile Host Redirect
33	IPv6 Where-Are-You
34	IPv6 I-Am-Here
35	Mobile Registration Request
36	Mobile Registration Reply

39	SKIP
40	Photuris **Codes** 0 Reserved 1 Unknown Security Parameters Index 2 Valid Security Parameters, but Authentication Failed 3 Valid Security Parameters, but Decryption Failed

Appendix B

Internet Protocol (IP) Protocol Type Field Values

In the Internet Protocol Version 4 (IPv4), an 8-bit Protocol field is used to identify the next level protocol. The purpose of this appendix is to provide a comprehensive reference to IP Protocol Type field values. If one is monitoring the flow of datagrams, one can use the information contained in this appendix to facilitate obtaining an understanding of the flow of information. For example, if a monitor program does not provide a full decode capability it might simply indicate the value of the IP Protocol Type field, such as "protocol type = 50." From this appendix, one would note that a Protocol Type field value of 50 indicates that an Encapsulation Security Payload (ESP) follows the IP header. The values of the Assigned Internet Protocol Numbers and associated protocols are listed in the following table.

Decimal	*Keyword*	*Protocol*
0	HOPOPT	IPv6 Hop-by-Hop Option
1	ICMP	Internet Control Message
2	IGMP	Internet Group Management
3	GGP	Gateway-to-Gateway
4	IP	IP in IP (encapsulation)
5	ST	Stream
6	TCP	Transmission Control
7	CBT	CBT
8	EGP	Exterior Gateway Protocol
9	IGP	Any private interior gateway (used by Cisco for their IGRP)
10	BBN-RCC-MON	BBN RCC Monitoring
11	NVP-II	Network Voice Protocol

(continues)

Decimal	*Keyword*	*Protocol (continued)*
12	PUP	PUP
13	ARGUS	ARGUS
14	EMCON	EMCON
15	XNET	Cross Net Debugger
16	CHAOS	Chaos
17	UDP	User Datagram
18	MUX	Multiplexing
19	DCN-MEAS	DCN Measurement Subsystems
20	HMP	Host Monitoring
21	PRM	Packet Radio Measurement
22	XNS-IDP	XEROX NS IDP
23	TRUNK-1	Trunk-1
24	TRUNK-2	Trunk-2
25	LEAF-1	Leaf-1
26	LEAF-2	Leaf-2
27	RDP	Reliable Data Protocol
28	IRTP	Internet Reliable Transaction
29	ISO-TP4	ISO Transport Protocol Class 4
30	NETBLT	Bulk Data Transfer Protocol
31	MFE-NSP	MFE Network Services Protocol
32	MERIT-INP	MERIT Internodal Protocol
33	SEP	Sequential Exchange Protocol
34	3PC	Third Party Connect Protocol
35	IDPR	Inter-Domain Policy Routing Protocol
36	XTP	XTP
37	DDP	Datagram Delivery Protocol
38	IDPR-CMTP	IDPR Control Message Transport Proto
39	TP++	TP++ Transport Protocol
40	IL	IL Transport Protocol
41	IPv6	IPv6
42	SDRP	Source Demand Routing Protocol
43	IPv6-Route	Routing Header for IPv6
44	IPv6-Frag	Fragment Header for IPv6
45	IDRP	Inter-Domain Routing Protocol
46	RSVP	Reservation Protocol
47	GRE	General Routing Encapsulation
48	MHRP	Mobile Host Routing Protocol
49	BNA	BNA
50	ESP	Encapsulation Security Payload for IPv6 and IPv4
51	AH	Authentication Header for IPv6 and IPv4
52	I-NLSP	Integrated Net Layer Security TUBA
53	SWIPE	IP with Encryption
54	NARP	NBMA Address Resolution Protocol
55	MOBILE	IP Mobility
56	TLSP	Transport Layer Security Protocol using Kryptonet key management

57	SKIP	SKIP
58	IPv6-ICMP	ICMP for IPv6
59	IPv6-NoNxt	No Next Header for IPv6
60	IPv6-Opts	Destination Options for IPv6
61		Any host internal protocol
62	CFTP	CFTP
63		Any local network
64	SAT-EXPAK	SATNET and Backroom EXPAK
65	KRYPTOLAN	Kryptolan
66	RVD	MIT Remote Virtual Disk Protocol
67	IPPC	Internet Pluribus Packet Core
68		Any distributed file system
69	SAT-MON	SATNET Monitoring
70	VISA	VISA Protocol
71	IPCV	Internet Packet Core Utility
72	CPNX	Computer Protocol Network Executive
73	CPHB	Computer Protocol Heart Beat
74	WSN	Wang Span Network
75	PVP	Packet Video Protocol
76	BR-SAT-MON	Backroom SATNET Monitoring
77	SUN-ND	SUN ND PROTOCOL-Temporary
78	WB-MON	WIDEBAND Monitoring
79	WB-EXPAK	WIDEBAND EXPAK
80	ISO-IP	ISO Internet Protocol
81	VMTP	VMTP
82	SECURE-VMTP	SECURE-VMTP
83	VINES	VINES
84	TTP	TTP
85	NSFNET-IGP	NSFNET-IGP
86	DGP	Dissimilar Gateway Protocol
87	TCF	TCF
88	EIGRP	EIGRP
89	OSPFIGP	OSPFIGP
90	Sprite-RPC	Sprite RPC Protocol
91	LARP	Locus Address Resolution Protocol
92	MTP	Multicast Transport Protocol
93	AX.25	AX.25 Frames
94	IPIP	IP-within-IP Encapsulation Protocol
95	MICP	Mobile Internetworking Control Pro.
96	SCC-SP	Semaphore Communications Sec. Pro.
97	ETHERIP	Ethernet-within-IP Encapsulation
98	ENCAP	Encapsulation Header
99		Any private encryption scheme
100	GMTP	GMTP
101	IFMP	Ipsilon Flow Management Protocol
102	PNNI	PNNI over IP
103	PIM	Protocol Independent Multicast

(continues)

Decimal	*Keyword*	*Protocol (continued)*
104	ARIS	ARIS
105	SCPS	SCPS
106	QNX	QNX
107	A/N	Active Networks
108	IPComp	IP Payload Compression Protocol
109	SNP	Sitara Networks Protocol
110	Compaq-Peer	Compaq Peer Protocol
111	IPX-in-IP	IPX in IP
112	VRRP	Virtual Router Redundancy Protocol
113	PGM	PGM Reliable Transport Protocol
114		Any 0-hop protocol
115	L2TP	Layer Two Tunneling Protocol
116	DDX	D-II Data Exchange (DDX)
117	IATP	Interactive Agent Transfer Protocol
118	STP	Schedule Transfer Protocol
119	SRP	SpectraLink Radio Protocol
120	UTI	UTI
121	SMP	Simple Message Protocol
122	SM	SM
123	PTP	Performance Transparency Protocol
124		ISIS over IPv4
125	FIRE	
126	CRTP	Combat Radio Transport Protocol
127	CRUDP	Combat Radio User Datagram
128	SSCOPMCE	
129	IPLT	
130	SPS	Secure Packet Shield
131	PIPE	Private IP Encapsulation within IP
132	SCTP	Stream Control Transmission Protocol
133	FC	Fibre Channel
134–254		Unassigned
255		Reserved

Appendix C

Port Numbers

Port numbers are commonly used to identify an application or destination process and are divided into three ranges: Well-Known Ports, Registered Ports, and Dynamic or PrivatePorts. Well-Known Ports are those from 0 through 1023. Registered Ports are those from 1024 through 49151. The Dynamic or Private Ports are those from 49152 through 65535. This appendix contains the listing of all registered Well-Known Port numbers (0 through 1023). These port numbers were originally assigned by the Internet Assigned Numbers Authority (IANA) and are now managed by The Internet Corporation for Assigned Names and Numbers (ICANN). Similar to the potential use of ICMP Type and Code values discussed in Appendix A, one can use this appendix of port numbers to assist in developing router and firewall filtering operations. For example, if one needs to permit Telnet one would configure the device one is operating to allow packets with a destination port address of 23. Similarly, if one wants to support SMTP, one would configure the device to permit packets with a destination port address of 25. The following table provides a summary of Well-Known Port numbers.

Port Assignments:

Keyword	*Decimal*	*Description*
	0/tcp	Reserved
	0/udp	Reserved
tcpmux	1/tcp	TCP Port Service Multiplexer
tcpmux	1/udp	TCP Port Service Multiplexer
compressnet	2/tcp	Management Utility
compressnet	2/udp	Management Utility
compressnet	3/tcp	Compression Process
compressnet	3/udp	Compression Process

(continues)

Keyword	Decimal	Description (continued)
	4/tcp	Unassigned
	4/udp	Unassigned
rje	5/tcp	Remote Job Entry
rje	5/udp	Remote Job Entry
	6/tcp	Unassigned
	6/udp	Unassigned
echo	7/tcp	Echo
echo	7/udp	Echo
	8/tcp	Unassigned
	8/udp	Unassigned
discard	9/tcp	Discard
discard	9/udp	Discard
	10/tcp	Unassigned
	10/udp	Unassigned
systat	11/tcp	Active Users
systat	11/udp	Active Users
	12/tcp	Unassigned
	12/udp	Unassigned
daytime	13/tcp	Daytime
daytime	13/udp	Daytime
	14/tcp	Unassigned
	14/udp	Unassigned
	15/tcp	Unassigned [was netstat]
	15/udp	Unassigned
	16/tcp	Unassigned
	16/udp	Unassigned
qotd	17/tcp	Quote of the Day
qotd	17/udp	Quote of the Day
msp	18/tcp	Message Send Protocol
msp	18/udp	Message Send Protocol
chargen	19/tcp	Character Generator
chargen	19/udp	Character Generator
ftp-data	20/tcp	File Transfer [Default Data]
ftp-data	20/udp	File Transfer [Default Data]
ftp	21/tcp	File Transfer [Control]
ftp	21/udp	File Transfer [Control]
ssh	22/tcp	SSH Remote Login Protocol
ssh	22/udp	SSH Remote Login Protocol
telnet	23/tcp	Telnet
telnet	23/udp	Telnet
	24/tcp	Any private mail system
	24/udp	Any private mail system
smtp	25/tcp	Simple Mail Transfer
smtp	25/udp	Simple Mail Transfer

	26/tcp	Unassigned
	26/udp	Unassigned
nsw-fe	27/tcp	NSW User System FE
nsw-fe	27/udp	NSW User System FE
	28/tcp	Unassigned
	28/udp	Unassigned
msg-icp	29/tcp	MSG ICP
msg-icp	29/udp	MSG ICP
	30/tcp	Unassigned
	30/udp	Unassigned
msg-auth	31/tcp	MSG Authentication
msg-auth	31/udp	MSG Authentication
	32/tcp	Unassigned
	32/udp	Unassigned
dsp	33/tcp	Display Support Protocol
dsp	33/udp	Display Support Protocol
	34/tcp	Unassigned
	34/udp	Unassigned
	35/tcp	Any private printer server
	35/udp	Any private printer server
	36/tcp	Unassigned
	36/udp	Unassigned
time	37/tcp	Time
time	37/udp	Time
rap	38/tcp	Route Access Protocol
rap	38/udp	Route Access Protocol
rlp	39/tcp	Resource Location Protocol
rlp	39/udp	Resource Location Protocol
	40/tcp	Unassigned
	40/udp	Unassigned
graphics	41/tcp	Graphics
graphics	41/udp	Graphics
name	42/tcp	Host Name Server
name	42/udp	Host Name Server
nameserver	42/tcp	Host Name Server
nameserver	42/udp	Host Name Server
nicname	43/tcp	Who Is
nicname	43/udp	Who Is
mpm-flags	44/tcp	MPM FLAGS Protocol
mpm-flags	44/udp	MPM FLAGS Protocol
mpm	45/tcp	Message Processing Module [recv]
mpm	45/udp	Message Processing Module [recv]
mpm-snd	46/tcp	MPM [default send]

(continues)

Keyword	*Decimal*	*Description (continued)*
mpm-snd	46/udp	MPM [default send]
ni-ftp	47/tcp	NI FTP
ni-ftp	47/udp	NI FTP
auditd	48/tcp	Digital Audit Daemon
auditd	48/udp	Digital Audit Daemon
tacacs	49/tcp	Login Host Protocol (TACACS)
tacacs	49/udp	Login Host Protocol (TACACS)
re-mail-ck	50/tcp	Remote Mail Checking Protocol
re-mail-ck	50/udp	Remote Mail Checking Protocol
la-maint	51/tcp	IMP Logical Address Maintenance
la-maint	51/udp	IMP Logical Address Maintenance
xns-time	52/tcp	XNS Time Protocol
xns-time	52/udp	XNS Time Protocol
domain	53/tcp	Domain Name Server
domain	53/udp	Domain Name Server
xns-ch	54/tcp	XNS Clearinghouse
xns-ch	54/udp	XNS Clearinghouse
isi-gl	55/tcp	ISI Graphics Language
isi-gl	55/udp	ISI Graphics Language
xns-auth	56/tcp	XNS Authentication
xns-auth	56/udp	XNS Authentication
	57/tcp	Any private terminal access
	57/udp	Any private terminal access
xns-mail	58/tcp	XNS Mail
xns-mail	58/udp	XNS Mail
	59/tcp	Any private file service
	59/udp	Any private file service
	60/tcp	Unassigned
	60/udp	Unassigned
ni-mail	61/tcp	NI MAIL
ni-mail	61/udp	NI MAIL
acas	62/tcp	ACA Services
acas	62/udp	ACA Services
whois++	63/tcp	whois++
whois++	63/udp	whois++
covia	64/tcp	Communications Integrator (CI)
covia	64/udp	Communications Integrator (CI)
tacacs-ds	65/tcp	TACACS-Database Service
tacacs-ds	65/udp	TACACS-Database Service
sql*net	66/tcp	Oracle SQL*NET
sql*net	66/udp	Oracle SQL*NET
bootps	67/tcp	Bootstrap Protocol Server
bootps	67/udp	Bootstrap Protocol Server

bootpc	68/tcp	Bootstrap Protocol Client
bootpc	68/udp	Bootstrap Protocol Client
tftp	69/tcp	Trivial File Transfer
tftp	69/udp	Trivial File Transfer
gopher	70/tcp	Gopher
gopher	70/udp	Gopher
netrjs-1	71/tcp	Remote Job Service
netrjs-1	71/udp	Remote Job Service
netrjs-2	72/tcp	Remote Job Service
netrjs-2	72/udp	Remote Job Service
netrjs-3	73/tcp	Remote Job Service
netrjs-3	73/udp	Remote Job Service
netrjs-4	74/tcp	Remote Job Service
netrjs-4	74/udp	Remote Job Service
	75/tcp	Any private dial out service
	75/udp	Any private dial out service
deos	76/tcp	Distributed External Object Store
deos	76/udp	Distributed External Object Store
	77/tcp	Any private RJE service
	77/udp	Any private RJE service
vettcp	78/tcp	vettcp
vettcp	78/udp	vettcp
finger	79/tcp	Finger
finger	79/udp	Finger
http	80/tcp	World Wide Web HTTP
http	80/udp	World Wide Web HTTP
www-http	80/tcp	World Wide Web HTTP
www-http	80/udp	World Wide Web HTTP
hosts2-ns	81/tcp	HOSTS2 Name Server
hosts2-ns	81/udp	HOSTS2 Name Server
xfer	82/tcp	XFER Utility
xfer	82/udp	XFER Utility
mit-ml-dev	83/tcp	MIT ML Device
mit-ml-dev	83/udp	MIT ML Device
ctf	84/tcp	Common Trace Facility
ctf	84/udp	Common Trace Facility
mit-ml-dev	85/tcp	MIT ML Device
mit-ml-dev	85/udp	MIT ML Device
mfcobol	86/tcp	Micro Focus Cobol
mfcobol	86/udp	Micro Focus Cobol
	87/tcp	Any private terminal link
	87/udp	Any private terminal link
kerberos	88/tcp	Kerberos
kerberos	88/udp	Kerberos

(continues)

Keyword	*Decimal*	*Description (continued)*
su-mit-tg	89/tcp	SU/MIT Telnet Gateway
su-mit-tg	89/udp	SU/MIT Telnet Gateway
dnsix	90/tcp	DNSIX Securit Attribute Token Map
dnsix	90/udp	DNSIX Securit Attribute Token Map
mit-dov	91/tcp	MIT Dover Spooler
mit-dov	91/udp	MIT Dover Spooler
npp	92/tcp	Network Printing Protocol
npp	92/udp	Network Printing Protocol
dcp	93/tcp	Device Control Protocol
dcp	93/udp	Device Control Protocol
objcall	94/tcp	Tivoli Object Dispatcher
objcall	94/udp	Tivoli Object Dispatcher
supdup	95/tcp	SUPDUP
supdup	95/udp	SUPDUP
dixie	96/tcp	DIXIE Protocol Specification
dixie	96/udp	DIXIE Protocol Specification
swift-rvf	97/tcp	Swift Remote Virtural File Protocol
swift-rvf	97/udp	Swift Remote Virtural File Protocol
tacnews	98/tcp	TAC News
tacnews	98/udp	TAC News
metagram	99/tcp	Metagram Relay
metagram	99/udp	Metagram Relay
newacct	100/tcp	[Unauthorized use]
hostname	101/tcp	NIC Host Name Server
hostname	101/udp	NIC Host Name Server
iso-tsap	102/tcp	ISO-TSAP Class 0
iso-tsap	102/udp	ISO-TSAP Class 0
gppitnp	103/tcp	Genesis Point-to-Point Trans Net
gppitnp	103/udp	Genesis Point-to-Point Trans Net
acr-nema	104/tcp	ACR-NEMA Digital Imag. & Comm. 300
acr-nema	104/udp	ACR-NEMA Digital Imag. & Comm. 300
cso	105/tcp	CCSO name server protocol
cso	105/udp	CCSO name server protocol
csnet-ns	105/tcp	Mailbox Name Nameserver
csnet-ns	105/udp	Mailbox Name Nameserver
3com-tsmux	106/tcp	3COM-TSMUX
3com-tsmux	106/udp	3COM-TSMUX
rtelnet	107/tcp	Remote Telnet Service
rtelnet	107/udp	Remote Telnet Service
snagas	108/tcp	SNA Gateway Access Server
snagas	108/udp	SNA Gateway Access Server
pop2	109/tcp	Post Office Protocol - Version 2
pop2	109/udp	Post Office Protocol - Version 2

pop3	110/tcp	Post Office Protocol - Version 3
pop3	110/udp	Post Office Protocol - Version 3
sunrpc	111/tcp	SUN Remote Procedure Call
sunrpc	111/udp	SUN Remote Procedure Call
mcidas	112/tcp	McIDAS Data Transmission Protocol
mcidas	112/udp	McIDAS Data Transmission Protocol
ident	113/tcp	
auth	113/tcp	Authentication Service
auth	113/udp	Authentication Service
audionews	114/tcp	Audio News Multicast
audionews	114/udp	Audio News Multicast
sftp	115/tcp	Simple File Transfer Protocol
sftp	115/udp	Simple File Transfer Protocol
ansanotify	116/tcp	ANSA REX Notify
ansanotify	116/udp	ANSA REX Notify
uucp-path	117/tcp	UUCP Path Service
uucp-path	117/udp	UUCP Path Service
sqlserv	118/tcp	SQL Services
sqlserv	118/udp	SQL Services
nntp	119/tcp	Network News Transfer Protocol
nntp	119/udp	Network News Transfer Protocol
cfdptkt	120/tcp	CFDPTKT
cfdptkt	120/udp	CFDPTKT
erpc	121/tcp	Encore Expedited Remote Pro. Call
erpc	121/udp	Encore Expedited Remote Pro. Call
smakynet	122/tcp	SMAKYNET
smakynet	122/udp	SMAKYNET
ntp	123/tcp	Network Time Protocol
ntp	123/udp	Network Time Protocol
ansatrader	124/tcp	ANSA REX Trader
ansatrader	124/udp	ANSA REX Trader
locus-map	125/tcp	Locus PC-Interface Net Map Ser
locus-map	125/udp	Locus PC-Interface Net Map Ser
nxedit	126/tcp	NXEdit
nxedit	126/udp	NXEdit
unitary	126/tcp	Unisys Unitary Login (prior assignment)
unitary	126/udp	Unisys Unitary Login (prior assignment)
locus-con	127/tcp	Locus PC-Interface Conn Server
locus-con	127/udp	Locus PC-Interface Conn Server
gss-xlicen	128/tcp	GSS X License Verification
gss-xlicen	128/udp	GSS X License Verification
pwdgen	129/tcp	Password Generator Protocol
pwdgen	129/udp	Password Generator Protocol
cisco-fna	130/tcp	cisco FNATIVE

(continues)

Keyword	Decimal	Description (continued)
cisco-fna	130/udp	cisco FNATIVE
cisco-tna	131/tcp	cisco TNATIVE
cisco-tna	131/udp	cisco TNATIVE
cisco-sys	132/tcp	cisco SYSMAINT
cisco-sys	132/udp	cisco SYSMAINT
statsrv	133/tcp	Statistics Service
statsrv	133/udp	Statistics Service
ingres-net	134/tcp	INGRES-NET Service
ingres-net	134/udp	INGRES-NET Service
epmap	135/tcp	DCE endpoint resolution
epmap	135/udp	DCE endpoint resolution
profile	136/tcp	PROFILE Naming System
profile	136/udp	PROFILE Naming System
netbios-ns	137/tcp	NETBIOS Name Service
netbios-ns	137/udp	NETBIOS Name Service
netbios-dgm	138/tcp	NETBIOS Datagram Service
netbios-dgm	138/udp	NETBIOS Datagram Service
netbios-ssn	139/tcp	NETBIOS Session Service
netbios-ssn	139/udp	NETBIOS Session Service
emfis-data	140/tcp	EMFIS Data Service
emfis-data	140/udp	EMFIS Data Service
emfis-cntl	141/tcp	EMFIS Control Service
emfis-cntl	141/udp	EMFIS Control Service
bl-idm	142/tcp	Britton-Lee IDM
bl-idm	142/udp	Britton-Lee IDM
imap	143/tcp	Internet Message Access Protocol
imap	143/udp	Internet Message Access Protocol
uma	144/tcp	Universal Management Architecture/News
uma	144/udp	Universal Management Architecture/News
uaac	145/tcp	UAAC Protocol
uaac	145/udp	UAAC Protocol
iso-tp0	146/tcp	ISO-IP0
iso-tp0	146/udp	ISO-IP0
iso-ip	147/tcp	ISO-IP
iso-ip	147/udp	ISO-IP
jargon	148/tcp	Jargon
jargon	148/udp	Jargon
aed-512	149/tcp	AED 512 Emulation Service
aed-512	149/udp	AED 512 Emulation Service
sql-net	150/tcp	SQL-NET
sql-net	150/udp	SQL-NET
hems	151/tcp	HEMS
hems	151/udp	HEMS

bftp	152/tcp	Background File Transfer Program
bftp	152/udp	Background File Transfer Program
sgmp	153/tcp	SGMP
sgmp	153/udp	SGMP
netsc-prod	154/tcp	NETSC
netsc-prod	154/udp	NETSC
netsc-dev	155/tcp	NETSC
netsc-dev	155/udp	NETSC
sqlsrv	156/tcp	SQL Service
sqlsrv	156/udp	SQL Service
knet-cmp	157/tcp	KNET/VM Command/Message Protocol
knet-cmp	157/udp	KNET/VM Command/Message Protocol
pcmail-srv	158/tcp	PCMail Server
pcmail-srv	158/udp	PCMail Server
nss-routing	159/tcp	NSS-Routing
nss-routing	159/udp	NSS-Routing
sgmp-traps	160/tcp	SGMP-TRAPS
sgmp-traps	160/udp	SGMP-TRAPS
snmp	161/tcp	SNMP
snmp	161/udp	SNMP
snmptrap	162/tcp	SNMPTRAP
snmptrap	162/udp	SNMPTRAP
cmip-man	163/tcp	CMIP/TCP Manager
cmip-man	163/udp	CMIP/TCP Manager
cmip-agent	164/tcp	CMIP/TCP Agent
cmip-agent	164/udp	CMIP/TCP Agent
xns-courier	165/tcp	Xerox
xns-courier	165/udp	Xerox
s-net	166/tcp	Sirius Systems
s-net	166/udp	Sirius Systems
namp	167/tcp	NAMP
namp	167/udp	NAMP
rsvd	168/tcp	RSVD
rsvd	168/udp	RSVD
send	169/tcp	SEND
send	169/udp	SEND
print-srv	170/tcp	Network PostScript
print-srv	170/udp	Network PostScript
multiplex	171/tcp	Network Innovations Multiplex
multiplex	171/udp	Network Innovations Multiplex
cl/1	172/tcp	Network Innovations CL/1
cl/1	172/udp	Network Innovations CL/1
xyplex-mux	173/tcp	Xyplex
xyplex-mux	173/udp	Xyplex

(continues)

Keyword	Decimal	Description (continued)
mailq	174/tcp	MAILQ
mailq	174/udp	MAILQ
vmnet	175/tcp	VMNET
vmnet	175/udp	VMNET
genrad-mux	176/tcp	GENRAD-MUX
genrad-mux	176/udp	GENRAD-MUX
xdmcp	177/tcp	X Display Manager Control Protocol
xdmcp	177/udp	X Display Manager Control Protocol
nextstep	178/tcp	NextStep Window Server
nextstep	178/udp	NextStep Window Server
bgp	179/tcp	Border Gateway Protocol
bgp	179/udp	Border Gateway Protocol
ris	180/tcp	Intergraph
ris	180/udp	Intergraph
unify	181/tcp	Unify
unify	181/udp	Unify
audit	182/tcp	Unisys Audit SITP
audit	182/udp	Unisys Audit SITP
ocbinder	183/tcp	OCBinder
ocbinder	183/udp	OCBinder
ocserver	184/tcp	OCServer
ocserver	184/udp	OCServer
remote-kis	185/tcp	Remote-KIS
remote-kis	185/udp	Remote-KIS
kis	186/tcp	KIS Protocol
kis	186/udp	KIS Protocol
aci	187/tcp	Application Communication Interface
aci	187/udp	Application Communication Interface
mumps	188/tcp	Plus Five's MUMPS
mumps	188/udp	Plus Five's MUMPS
qft	189/tcp	Queued File Transport
qft	189/udp	Queued File Transport
gacp	190/tcp	Gateway Access Control Protocol
gacp	190/udp	Gateway Access Control Protocol
prospero	191/tcp	Prospero Directory Service
prospero	191/udp	Prospero Directory Service
osu-nms	192/tcp	OSU Network Monitoring System
osu-nms	192/udp	OSU Network Monitoring System
srmp	193/tcp	Spider Remote Monitoring Protocol
srmp	193/udp	Spider Remote Monitoring Protocol
irc	194/tcp	Internet Relay Chat Protocol
irc	194/udp	Internet Relay Chat Protocol
dn6-nlm-aud	195/tcp	DNSIX Network Level Module Audit

dn6-nlm-aud	195/udp	DNSIX Network Level Module Audit
dn6-smm-red	196/tcp	DNSIX Session Mgt Module Audit Redir
dn6-smm-red	196/udp	DNSIX Session Mgt Module Audit Redir
dls	197/tcp	Directory Location Service
dls	197/udp	Directory Location Service
dls-mon	198/tcp	Directory Location Service Monitor
dls-mon	198/udp	Directory Location Service Monitor
smux	199/tcp	SMUX
smux	199/udp	SMUX
src	200/tcp	IBM System Resource Controller
src	200/udp	IBM System Resource Controller
at-rtmp	201/tcp	AppleTalk Routing Maintenance
at-rtmp	201/udp	AppleTalk Routing Maintenance
at-nbp	202/tcp	AppleTalk Name Binding
at-nbp	202/udp	AppleTalk Name Binding
at-3	203/tcp	AppleTalk Unused
at-3	203/udp	AppleTalk Unused
at-echo	204/tcp	AppleTalk Echo
at-echo	204/udp	AppleTalk Echo
at-5	205/tcp	AppleTalk Unused
at-5	205/udp	AppleTalk Unused
at-zis	206/tcp	AppleTalk Zone Information
at-zis	206/udp	AppleTalk Zone Information
at-7	207/tcp	AppleTalk Unused
at-7	207/udp	AppleTalk Unused
at-8	208/tcp	AppleTalk Unused
at-8	208/udp	AppleTalk Unused
qmtp	209/tcp	The Quick Mail Transfer Protocol
qmtp	209/udp	The Quick Mail Transfer Protocol
z39.50	210/tcp	ANSI Z39.50
z39.50	210/udp	ANSI Z39.50
914c/g	211/tcp	Texas Instruments 914C/G Terminal
914c/g	211/udp	Texas Instruments 914C/G Terminal
anet	212/tcp	ATEXSSTR
anet	212/udp	ATEXSSTR
ipx	213/tcp	IPX
ipx	213/udp	IPX
vmpwscs	214/tcp	VM PWSCS
vmpwscs	214/udp	VM PWSCS
softpc	215/tcp	Insignia Solutions
softpc	215/udp	Insignia Solutions
CAIlic	216/tcp	Computer Associates Int'l License Server
CAIlic	216/udp	Computer Associates Int'l License Server
dbase	217/tcp	dBASE Unix
dbase	217/udp	dBASE Unix

(continues)

Keyword	Decimal	Description (continued)
mpp	218/tcp	Netix Message Posting Protocol
mpp	218/udp	Netix Message Posting Protocol
uarps	219/tcp	Unisys ARPs
uarps	219/udp	Unisys ARPs
imap3	220/tcp	Interactive Mail Access Protocol v3
imap3	220/udp	Interactive Mail Access Protocol v3
fln-spx	221/tcp	Berkeley rlogind with SPX auth
fln-spx	221/udp	Berkeley rlogind with SPX auth
rsh-spx	222/tcp	Berkeley rshd with SPX auth
rsh-spx	222/udp	Berkeley rshd with SPX auth
cdc	223/tcp	Certificate Distribution Center
cdc	223/udp	Certificate Distribution Center
masqdialer	224/tcp	masqdialer
masqdialer	224/udp	masqdialer
	225–241	Reserved
direct	242/tcp	Direct
direct	242/udp	Direct
sur-meas	243/tcp	Survey Measurement
sur-meas	243/udp	Survey Measurement
inbusiness	244/tcp	inbusiness
inbusiness	244/udp	inbusiness
link	245/tcp	LINK
link	245/udp	LINK
dsp3270	246/tcp	Display Systems Protocol
dsp3270	246/udp	Display Systems Protocol
subntbcst_tftp	247/tcp	SUBNTBCST_TFTP
subntbcst_tftp	247/udp	SUBNTBCST_TFTP
bhfhs	248/tcp	bhfhs
bhfhs	248/udp	bhfhs
	249–255	Reserved
rap	256/tcp	RAP
rap	256/udp	RAP
set	257/tcp	Secure Electronic Transaction
set	257/udp	Secure Electronic Transaction
yak-chat	258/tcp	Yak Winsock Personal Chat
yak-chat	258/udp	Yak Winsock Personal Chat
esro-gen	259/tcp	Efficient Short Remote Operations
esro-gen	259/udp	Efficient Short Remote Operations
openport	260/tcp	Openport
openport	260/udp	Openport
nsiiops	261/tcp	IIOP Name Service over TLS/SSL
nsiiops	261/udp	IIOP Name Service over TLS/SSL
arcisdms	262/tcp	Arcisdms

arcisdms	262/udp	Arcisdms
hdap	263/tcp	HDAP
hdap	263/udp	HDAP
bgmp	264/tcp	BGMP
bgmp	264/udp	BGMP
x-bone-ctl	265/tcp	X-Bone CTL
x-bone-ctl	265/udp	X-Bone CTL
sst	266/tcp	SCSI on ST
sst	266/udp	SCSI on ST
td-service	267/tcp	Tobit David Service Layer
td-service	267/udp	Tobit David Service Layer
td-replica	268/tcp	Tobit David Replica
td-replica	268/udp	Tobit David Replica
	269–279	Unassigned
http-mgmt	280/tcp	http-mgmt
http-mgmt	280/udp	http-mgmt
personal-link	281/tcp	Personal Link
personal-link	281/udp	Personal Link
cableport-ax	282/tcp	Cable Port A/X
cableport-ax	282/udp	Cable Port A/X
rescap	283/tcp	rescap
rescap	283/udp	rescap
corerjd	284/tcp	corerjd
corerjd	284/udp	corerjd
	285	Unassigned
fxp-1	286/tcp	FXP-1
fxp-1	286/udp	FXP-1
k-block	287/tcp	K-BLOCK
k-block	287/udp	K-BLOCK
	288–307	Unassigned
novastorbakcup	308/tcp	Novastor Backup
novastorbakcup	308/udp	Novastor Backup
entrusttime	309/tcp	EntrustTime
entrusttime	309/udp	EntrustTime
bhmds	310/tcp	bhmds
bhmds	310/udp	bhmds
asip-webadmin	311/tcp	AppleShare IP WebAdmin
asip-webadmin	311/udp	AppleShare IP WebAdmin
vslmp	312/tcp	VSLMP
vslmp	312/udp	VSLMP
magenta-logic	313/tcp	Magenta Logic
magenta-logic	313/udp	Magenta Logic
opalis-robot	314/tcp	Opalis Robot
opalis-robot	314/udp	Opalis Robot
dpsi	315/tcp	DPSI

(continues)

Keyword	Decimal	Description (continued)
dpsi	315/udp	DPSI
decauth	316/tcp	decAuth
decauth	316/udp	decAuth
zannet	317/tcp	Zannet
zannet	317/udp	Zannet
pkix-timestamp	318/tcp	PKIX TimeStamp
pkix-timestamp	318/udp	PKIX TimeStamp
ptp-event	319/tcp	PTP Event
ptp-event	319/udp	PTP Event
ptp-general	320/tcp	PTP General
ptp-general	320/udp	PTP General
pip	321/tcp	PIP
pip	321/udp	PIP
rtsps	322/tcp	RTSPS
rtsps	322/udp	RTSPS
	323–332	Unassigned
texar	333/tcp	Texar Security Port
texar	333/udp	Texar Security Port
	334–343	Unassigned
pdap	344/tcp	Prospero Data Access Protocol
pdap	344/udp	Prospero Data Access Protocol
pawserv	345/tcp	Perf Analysis Workbench
pawserv	345/udp	Perf Analysis Workbench
zserv	346/tcp	Zebra server
zserv	346/udp	Zebra server
fatserv	347/tcp	Fatmen Server
fatserv	347/udp	Fatmen Server
csi-sgwp	348/tcp	Cabletron Management Protocol
csi-sgwp	348/udp	Cabletron Management Protocol
mftp	349/tcp	mftp
mftp	349/udp	mftp
matip-type-a	350/tcp	MATIP Type A
matip-type-a	350/udp	MATIP Type A
matip-type-b	351/tcp	MATIP Type B
matip-type-b	351/udp	MATIP Type B
bhoetty	351/tcp	bhoetty
bhoetty	351/udp	bhoetty
dtag-ste-sb	352/tcp	DTAG
dtag-ste-sb	352/udp	DTAG
bhoedap4	352/tcp	bhoedap4
bhoedap4	352/udp	bhoedap4
ndsauth	353/tcp	NDSAUTH
ndsauth	353/udp	NDSAUTH

bh611	354/tcp	bh611
bh611	354/udp	bh611
datex-asn	355/tcp	DATEX-ASN
datex-asn	355/udp	DATEX-ASN
cloanto-net-1	356/tcp	Cloanto Net 1
cloanto-net-1	356/udp	Cloanto Net 1
bhevent	357/tcp	bhevent
bhevent	357/udp	bhevent
shrinkwrap	358/tcp	Shrinkwrap
shrinkwrap	358/udp	Shrinkwrap
tenebris_nts	359/tcp	Tenebris Network Trace Service
tenebris_nts	359/udp	Tenebris Network Trace Service
scoi2odialog	360/tcp	scoi2odialog
scoi2odialog	360/udp	scoi2odialog
semantix	361/tcp	Semantix
semantix	361/udp	Semantix
srssend	362/tcp	SRS Send
srssend	362/udp	SRS Send
rsvp_tunnel	363/tcp	RSVP Tunnel
rsvp_tunnel	363/udp	RSVP Tunnel
aurora-cmgr	364/tcp	Aurora CMGR
aurora-cmgr	364/udp	Aurora CMGR
dtk	365/tcp	DTK
dtk	365/udp	DTK
odmr	366/tcp	ODMR
odmr	366/udp	ODMR
mortgageware	367/tcp	MortgageWare
mortgageware	367/udp	MortgageWare
qbikgdp	368/tcp	QbikGDP
qbikgdp	368/udp	QbikGDP
rpc2portmap	369/tcp	rpc2portmap
rpc2portmap	369/udp	rpc2portmap
codaauth2	370/tcp	codaauth2
codaauth2	370/udp	codaauth2
clearcase	371/tcp	Clearcase
clearcase	371/udp	Clearcase
ulistproc	372/tcp	ListProcessor
ulistproc	372/udp	ListProcessor
legent-1	373/tcp	Legent Corporation
legent-1	373/udp	Legent Corporation
legent-2	374/tcp	Legent Corporation
legent-2	374/udp	Legent Corporation
hassle	375/tcp	Hassle
hassle	375/udp	Hassle
nip	376/tcp	Amiga Envoy Network Inquiry Proto

(continues)

Keyword	Decimal	Description (continued)
nip	376/udp	Amiga Envoy Network Inquiry Proto
tnETOS	377/tcp	NEC Corporation
tnETOS	377/udp	NEC Corporation
dsETOS	378/tcp	NEC Corporation
dsETOS	378/udp	NEC Corporation
is99c	379/tcp	TIA/EIA/IS-99 modem client
is99c	379/udp	TIA/EIA/IS-99 modem client
is99s	380/tcp	TIA/EIA/IS-99 modem server
is99s	380/udp	TIA/EIA/IS-99 modem server
hp-collector	381/tcp	hp performance data collector
hp-collector	381/udp	hp performance data collector
hp-managed-node	382/tcp	hp performance data managed node
hp-managed-node	382/udp	hp performance data managed node
hp-alarm-mgr	383/tcp	hp performance data alarm manager
hp-alarm-mgr	383/udp	hp performance data alarm manager
arns	384/tcp	A Remote Network Server System
arns	384/udp	A Remote Network Server System
ibm-app	385/tcp	IBM Application
ibm-app	385/udp	IBM Application
asa	386/tcp	ASA Message Router Object Def.
asa	386/udp	ASA Message Router Object Def.
aurp	387/tcp	Appletalk Update-Based Routing Protocol
aurp	387/udp	Appletalk Update-Based Routing Protocol
unidata-ldm	388/tcp	Unidata LDM
unidata-ldm	388/udp	Unidata LDM
	389/tcp	Lightweight Directory Access Protocol
ldap	389/udp	Lightweight Directory Access Protocol
uis	390/tcp	UIS
uis	390/udp	UIS
synotics-relay	391/tcp	SynOptics SNMP Relay Port
synotics-relay	391/udp	SynOptics SNMP Relay Port
synotics-broker	392/tcp	SynOptics Port Broker Port
synotics-broker	392/udp	SynOptics Port Broker Port
dis	393/tcp	Data Interpretation System
dis	393/udp	Data Interpretation System
embl-ndt	394/tcp	EMBL Nucleic Data Transfer
embl-ndt	394/udp	EMBL Nucleic Data Transfer
netcp	395/tcp	NETscout Control Protocol
netcp	395/udp	NETscout Control Protocol
netware-ip	396/tcp	Novell Netware over IP
netware-ip	396/udp	Novell Netware over IP
mptn	397/tcp	Multi Protocol Trans. Net.
mptn	397/udp	Multi Protocol Trans. Net.

kryptolan	398/tcp	Kryptolan
kryptolan	398/udp	Kryptolan
iso-tsap-c2	399/tcp	ISO Transport Class 2 Non-Control over TCP
iso-tsap-c2	399/udp	ISO Transport Class 2 Non-Control over TCP
work-sol	400/tcp	Workstation Solutions
work-sol	400/udp	Workstation Solutions
ups	401/tcp	Uninterruptible Power Supply
ups	401/udp	Uninterruptible Power Supply
genie	402/tcp	Genie Protocol
genie	402/udp	Genie Protocol
decap	403/tcp	decap
decap	403/udp	decap
nced	404/tcp	nced
nced	404/udp	nced
ncld	405/tcp	ncld
ncld	405/udp	ncld
imsp	406/tcp	Interactive Mail Support Protocol
imsp	406/udp	Interactive Mail Support Protocol
timbuktu	407/tcp	Timbuktu
timbuktu	407/udp	Timbuktu
prm-sm	408/tcp	Prospero Resource Manager Sys. Man.
prm-sm	408/udp	Prospero Resource Manager Sys. Man.
prm-nm	409/tcp	Prospero Resource Manager Node Man.
prm-nm	409/udp	Prospero Resource Manager Node Man.
decladebug	410/tcp	DECLadebug Remote Debug Protocol
decladebug	410/udp	DECLadebug Remote Debug Protocol
rmt	411/tcp	Remote MT Protocol
rmt	411/udp	Remote MT Protocol
synoptics-trap	412/tcp	Trap Convention Port
synoptics-trap	412/udp	Trap Convention Port
smsp	413/tcp	SMSP
smsp	413/udp	SMSP
infoseek	414/tcp	InfoSeek
infoseek	414/udp	InfoSeek
bnet	415/tcp	BNet
bnet	415/udp	BNet
silverplatter	416/tcp	Silverplatter
silverplatter	416/udp	Silverplatter
onmux	417/tcp	Onmux
onmux	417/udp	Onmux
hyper-g	418/tcp	Hyper-G
hyper-g	418/udp	Hyper-G
ariel1	419/tcp	Ariel
ariel1	419/udp	Ariel
smpte	420/tcp	SMPTE

(continues)

Keyword	Decimal	Description (continued)
smpte	420/udp	SMPTE
ariel2	421/tcp	Ariel
ariel2	421/udp	Ariel
ariel3	422/tcp	Ariel
ariel3	422/udp	Ariel
opc-job-start	423/tcp	IBM Operations Planning and Control Start
opc-job-start	423/udp	IBM Operations Planning and Control Start
opc-job-track	424/tcp	IBM Operations Planning and Control Track
opc-job-track	424/udp	IBM Operations Planning and Control Track
icad-el	425/tcp	ICAD
icad-el	425/udp	ICAD
smartsdp	426/tcp	smartsdp
smartsdp	426/udp	smartsdp
svrloc	427/tcp	Server Location
svrloc	427/udp	Server Location
ocs_cmu	428/tcp	OCS_CMU
ocs_cmu	428/udp	OCS_CMU
ocs_amu	429/tcp	OCS_AMU
ocs_amu	429/udp	OCS_AMU
utmpsd	430/tcp	UTMPSD
utmpsd	430/udp	UTMPSD
utmpcd	431/tcp	UTMPCD
utmpcd	431/udp	UTMPCD
iasd	432/tcp	IASD
iasd	432/udp	IASD
nnsp	433/tcp	NNSP
nnsp	433/udp	NNSP
mobileip-agent	434/tcp	MobileIP-Agent
mobileip-agent	434/udp	MobileIP-Agent
mobilip-mn	435/tcp	MobilIP-MN
mobilip-mn	435/udp	MobilIP-MN
dna-cml	436/tcp	DNA-CML
dna-cml	436/udp	DNA-CML
comscm	437/tcp	comscm
comscm	437/udp	comscm
dsfgw	438/tcp	dsfgw
dsfgw	438/udp	dsfgw
dasp	439/tcp	dasp
dasp	439/udp	dasp
sgcp	440/tcp	sgcp
sgcp	440/udp	sgcp
decvms-sysmgt	441/tcp	decvms-sysmgt
decvms-sysmgt	441/udp	decvms-sysmgt

cvc_hostd	442/tcp	cvc_hostd
cvc_hostd	442/udp	cvc_hostd
https	443/tcp	http protocol over TLS/SSL
https	443/udp	http protocol over TLS/SSL
snpp	444/tcp	Simple Network Paging Protocol
snpp	444/udp	Simple Network Paging Protocol
microsoft-ds	445/tcp	Microsoft-DS
microsoft-ds	445/udp	Microsoft-DS
ddm-rdb	446/tcp	DDM-RDB
ddm-rdb	446/udp	DDM-RDB
ddm-dfm	447/tcp	DDM-RFM
ddm-dfm	447/udp	DDM-RFM
ddm-ssl	448/tcp	DDM-SSL
ddm-ssl	448/udp	DDM-SSL
as-servermap	449/tcp	AS Server Mapper
as-servermap	449/udp	AS Server Mapper
tserver	450/tcp	TServer
tserver	450/udp	TServer
sfs-smp-net	451/tcp	Cray Network Semaphore server
sfs-smp-net	451/udp	Cray Network Semaphore server
sfs-config	452/tcp	Cray SFS config server
sfs-config	452/udp	Cray SFS config server
creativeserver	453/tcp	CreativeServer
creativeserver	453/udp	CreativeServer
contentserver	454/tcp	ContentServer
contentserver	454/udp	ContentServer
creativepartnr	455/tcp	CreativePartnr
creativepartnr	455/udp	CreativePartnr
macon-tcp	456/tcp	macon-tcp
macon-udp	456/udp	macon-udp
scohelp	457/tcp	scohelp
scohelp	457/udp	scohelp
appleqtc	458/tcp	apple quick time
appleqtc	458/udp	apple quick time
ampr-rcmd	459/tcp	ampr-rcmd
ampr-rcmd	459/udp	ampr-rcmd
skronk	460/tcp	skronk
skronk	460/udp	skronk
datasurfsrv	461/tcp	DataRampSrv
datasurfsrv	461/udp	DataRampSrv
datasurfsrvsec	462/tcp	DataRampSrvSec
datasurfsrvsec	462/udp	DataRampSrvSec
alpes	463/tcp	alpes
alpes	463/udp	alpes

(continues)

Keyword	*Decimal*	*Description (continued)*
kpasswd	464/tcp	kpasswd
kpasswd	464/udp	kpasswd
	465	Unassigned
digital-vrc	466/tcp	digital-vrc
digital-vrc	466/udp	digital-vrc
mylex-mapd	467/tcp	mylex-mapd
mylex-mapd	467/udp	mylex-mapd
photuris	468/tcp	photuris
photuris	468/udp	photuris
rcp	469/tcp	Radio Control Protocol
rcp	469/udp	Radio Control Protocol
scx-proxy	470/tcp	scx-proxy
scx-proxy	470/udp	scx-proxy
mondex	471/tcp	Mondex
mondex	471/udp	Mondex
ljk-login	472/tcp	ljk-login
ljk-login	472/udp	ljk-login
hybrid-pop	473/tcp	hybrid-pop
hybrid-pop	473/udp	hybrid-pop
tn-tl-w1	474/tcp	tn-tl-w1
tn-tl-w2	474/udp	tn-tl-w2
tcpnethaspsrv	475/tcp	tcpnethaspsrv
tcpnethaspsrv	475/udp	tcpnethaspsrv
tn-tl-fd1	476/tcp	tn-tl-fd1
tn-tl-fd1	476/udp	tn-tl-fd1
ss7ns	477/tcp	ss7ns
ss7ns	477/udp	ss7ns
spsc	478/tcp	spsc
spsc	478/udp	spsc
iafserver	479/tcp	iafserver
iafserver	479/udp	iafserver
iafdbase	480/tcp	iafdbase
iafdbase	480/udp	iafdbase
ph	481/tcp	Ph service
ph	481/udp	Ph service
bgs-nsi	482/tcp	bgs-nsi
bgs-nsi	482/udp	bgs-nsi
ulpnet	483/tcp	ulpnet
ulpnet	483/udp	ulpnet
integra-sme	484/tcp	Integra Software Management Environment
integra-sme	484/udp	Integra Software Management Environment
powerburst	485/tcp	Air Soft Power Burst
powerburst	485/udp	Air Soft Power Burst

avian	486/tcp	avian
avian	486/udp	avian
saft	487/tcp	saft Simple Asynchronous File Transfer
saft	487/udp	saft Simple Asynchronous File Transfer
gss-http	488/tcp	gss-http
gss-http	488/udp	gss-http
nest-protocol	489/tcp	nest-protocol
nest-protocol	489/udp	nest-protocol
micom-pfs	490/tcp	micom-pfs
micom-pfs	490/udp	micom-pfs
go-login	491/tcp	go-login
go-login	491/udp	go-login
ticf-1	492/tcp	Transport Independent Convergence for FNA
ticf-1	492/udp	Transport Independent Convergence for FNA
ticf-2	493/tcp	Transport Independent Convergence for FNA
ticf-2	493/udp	Transport Independent Convergence for FNA
pov-ray	494/tcp	POV-Ray
pov-ray	494/udp	POV-Ray
intecourier	495/tcp	intecourier
intecourier	495/udp	intecourier
pim-rp-disc	496/tcp	PIM-RP-DISC
pim-rp-disc	496/udp	PIM-RP-DISC
dantz	497/tcp	dantz
dantz	497/udp	dantz
siam	498/tcp	siam
siam	498/udp	siam
iso-ill	499/tcp	ISO ILL Protocol
iso-ill	499/udp	ISO ILL Protocol
isakmp	500/tcp	isakmp
isakmp	500/udp	isakmp
stmf	501/tcp	STMF
stmf	501/udp	STMF
asa-appl-proto	502/tcp	asa-appl-proto
asa-appl-proto	502/udp	asa-appl-proto
intrinsa	503/tcp	Intrinsa
intrinsa	503/udp	Intrinsa
citadel	504/tcp	citadel
citadel	504/udp	citadel
mailbox-lm	505/tcp	mailbox-lm
mailbox-lm	505/udp	mailbox-lm
ohimsrv	506/tcp	ohimsrv
ohimsrv	506/udp	ohimsrv
crs	507/tcp	crs
crs	507/udp	crs

(continues)

Keyword	Decimal	Description (continued)
xvttp	508/tcp	xvttp
xvttp	508/udp	xvttp
snare	509/tcp	snare
snare	509/udp	snare
fcp	510/tcp	FirstClass Protocol
fcp	510/udp	FirstClass Protocol
passgo	511/tcp	PassGo
passgo	511/udp	PassGo
exec	512/tcp	remote process execution
comsat	512/udp	
biff	512/udp	Used by mail system to notify users of new mail received
rlogin	513/tcp	Remote login via telnet
who	513/udp	Maintains databases showing who's logged in to computer
syslog	514/udp	
printer	515/tcp	spooler
printer	515/udp	spooler
videotex	516/tcp	videotex
videotex	516/udp	videotex
talk	517/tcp	similar to a tenex link
talk	517/udp	
ntalk	518/tcp	
ntalk	518/udp	
utime	519/tcp	unixtime
utime	519/udp	unixtime
efs	520/tcp	extended file name server
router	520/udp	local routing process (on site)
ripng	521/tcp	ripng
ripng	521/udp	ripng
ulp	522/tcp	ULP
ulp	522/udp	ULP
ibm-db2	523/tcp	IBM-DB2
ibm-db2	523/udp	IBM-DB2
ncp	524/tcp	NCP
ncp	524/udp	NCP
timed	525/tcp	timeserver
timed	525/udp	timeserver
tempo	526/tcp	newdate
tempo	526/udp	newdate
stx	527/tcp	Stock IXChange
stx	527/udp	Stock IXChange
custix	528/tcp	Customer IXChange

custix	528/udp	Customer IXChange
irc-serv	529/tcp	IRC-SERV
irc-serv	529/udp	IRC-SERV
courier	530/tcp	rpc
courier	530/udp	rpc
conference	531/tcp	chat
conference	531/udp	chat
netnews	532/tcp	readnews
netnews	532/udp	readnews
netwall	533/tcp	For emergency broadcasts
netwall	533/udp	For emergency broadcasts
mm-admin	534/tcp	MegaMedia Admin
mm-admin	534/udp	MegaMedia Admin
iiop	535/tcp	iiop
iiop	535/udp	iiop
opalis-rdv	536/tcp	opalis-rdv
opalis-rdv	536/udp	opalis-rdv
nmsp	537/tcp	Networked Media Streaming Protocol
nmsp	537/udp	Networked Media Streaming Protocol
gdomap	538/tcp	gdomap
gdomap	538/udp	gdomap
apertus-ldp	539/tcp	Apertus Technologies Load Determination
apertus-ldp	539/udp	Apertus Technologies Load Determination
uucp	540/tcp	uucpd
uucp	540/udp	uucpd
uucp-rlogin	541/tcp	uucp-rlogin
uucp-rlogin	541/udp	uucp-rlogin
commerce	542/tcp	commerce
commerce	542/udp	commerce
klogin	543/tcp	
klogin	543/udp	
kshell	544/tcp	krcmd
kshell	544/udp	krcmd
appleqtcsrvr	545/tcp	appleqtcsrvr
appleqtcsrvr	545/udp	appleqtcsrvr
dhcpv6-client	546/tcp	DHCPv6 Client
dhcpv6-client	546/udp	DHCPv6 Client
dhcpv6-server	547/tcp	DHCPv6 Server
dhcpv6-server	547/udp	DHCPv6 Server
afpovertcp	548/tcp	AFP over TCP
afpovertcp	548/udp	AFP over TCP
idfp	549/tcp	IDFP
idfp	549/udp	IDFP
new-rwho	550/tcp	new-who
new-rwho	550/udp	new-who

(continues)

Keyword	Decimal	Description (continued)
cybercash	551/tcp	cybercash
cybercash	551/udp	cybercash
deviceshare	552/tcp	deviceshare
deviceshare	552/udp	deviceshare
pirp	553/tcp	pirp
pirp	553/udp	pirp
rtsp	554/tcp	Real Time Stream Control Protocol
rtsp	554/udp	Real Time Stream Control Protocol
dsf	555/tcp	
dsf	555/udp	
remotefs	556/tcp	rfs server
remotefs	556/udp	rfs server
openvms-sysipc	557/tcp	openvms-sysipc
openvms-sysipc	557/udp	openvms-sysipc
sdnskmp	558/tcp	SDNSKMP
sdnskmp	558/udp	SDNSKMP
teedtap	559/tcp	TEEDTAP
teedtap	559/udp	TEEDTAP
rmonitor	560/tcp	rmonitord
rmonitor	560/udp	rmonitord
monitor	561/tcp	
monitor	561/udp	
chshell	562/tcp	chcmd
chshell	562/udp	chcmd
nntps	563/tcp	nntp protocol over TLS/SSL (was snntp)
nntps	563/udp	nntp protocol over TLS/SSL (was snntp)
9pfs	564/tcp	plan 9 file service
9pfs	564/udp	plan 9 file service
whoami	565/tcp	whoami
whoami	565/udp	whoami
streettalk	566/tcp	streettalk
streettalk	566/udp	streettalk
banyan-rpc	567/tcp	banyan-rpc
banyan-rpc	567/udp	banyan-rpc
ms-shuttle	568/tcp	microsoft shuttle
ms-shuttle	568/udp	microsoft shuttle
ms-rome	569/tcp	microsoft rome
ms-rome	569/udp	microsoft rome
meter	570/tcp	demon
meter	570/udp	demon
meter	571/tcp	udemon
meter	571/udp	udemon
sonar	572/tcp	sonar

sonar	572/udp	sonar
banyan-vip	573/tcp	banyan-vip
banyan-vip	573/udp	banyan-vip
ftp-agent	574/tcp	FTP Software Agent System
ftp-agent	574/udp	FTP Software Agent System
vemmi	575/tcp	VEMMI
vemmi	575/udp	VEMMI
ipcd	576/tcp	ipcd
ipcd	576/udp	ipcd
vnas	577/tcp	vnas
vnas	577/udp	vnas
ipdd	578/tcp	ipdd
ipdd	578/udp	ipdd
decbsrv	579/tcp	decbsrv
decbsrv	579/udp	decbsrv
sntp-heartbeat	580/tcp	SNTP HEARTBEAT
sntp-heartbeat	580/udp	SNTP HEARTBEAT
bdp	581/tcp	Bundle Discovery Protocol
bdp	581/udp	Bundle Discovery Protocol
scc-security	582/tcp	SCC Security
scc-security	582/udp	SCC Security
philips-vc	583/tcp	Philips Video-Conferencing
philips-vc	583/udp	Philips Video-Conferencing
keyserver	584/tcp	Key Server
keyserver	584/udp	Key Server
imap4-ssl	585/tcp	IMAP4+SSL (use 993 instead)
imap4-ssl	585/udp	IMAP4+SSL (use 993 instead)
password-chg	586/tcp	Password Change
password-chg	586/udp	Password Change
submission	587/tcp	Submission
submission	587/udp	Submission
cal	588/tcp	CAL
cal	588/udp	CAL
eyelink	589/tcp	EyeLink
eyelink	589/udp	EyeLink
tns-cml	590/tcp	TNS CML
tns-cml	590/udp	TNS CML
http-alt	591/tcp	FileMaker, Inc. - HTTP Alternate (see Port 80)
http-alt	591/udp	FileMaker, Inc. - HTTP Alternate (see Port 80)
eudora-set	592/tcp	Eudora Set
eudora-set	592/udp	Eudora Set
http-rpc-epmap	593/tcp	HTTP RPC Ep Map
http-rpc-epmap	593/udp	HTTP RPC Ep Map
tpip	594/tcp	TPIP
tpip	594/udp	TPIP

(continues)

Keyword	Decimal	Description (continued)
cab-protocol	595/tcp	CAB Protocol
cab-protocol	595/udp	CAB Protocol
smsd	596/tcp	SMSD
smsd	596/udp	SMSD
ptcnameservice	597/tcp	PTC Name Service
ptcnameservice	597/udp	PTC Name Service
sco-websrvrmg3	598/tcp	SCO Web Server Manager 3
sco-websrvrmg3	598/udp	SCO Web Server Manager 3
acp	599/tcp	Aeolon Core Protocol
acp	599/udp	Aeolon Core Protocol
ipcserver	600/tcp	Sun IPC server
ipcserver	600/udp	Sun IPC server
	601–605	Unassigned
urm	606/tcp	Cray Unified Resource Manager
urm	606/udp	Cray Unified Resource Manager
nqs	607/tcp	nqs
nqs	607/udp	nqs
sift-uft	608/tcp	Sender-Initiated/Unsolicited File Transfer
sift-uft	608/udp	Sender-Initiated/Unsolicited File Transfer
npmp-trap	609/tcp	npmp-trap
npmp-trap	609/udp	npmp-trap
npmp-local	610/tcp	npmp-local
npmp-local	610/udp	npmp-local
npmp-gui	611/tcp	npmp-gui
npmp-gui	611/udp	npmp-gui
hmmp-ind	612/tcp	HMMP Indication
hmmp-ind	612/udp	HMMP Indication
hmmp-op	613/tcp	HMMP Operation
hmmp-op	613/udp	HMMP Operation
sshell	614/tcp	SSLshell
sshell	614/udp	SSLshell
sco-inetmgr	615/tcp	Internet Configuration Manager
sco-inetmgr	615/udp	Internet Configuration Manager
sco-sysmgr	616/tcp	SCO System Administration Server
sco-sysmgr	616/udp	SCO System Administration Server
sco-dtmgr	617/tcp	SCO Desktop Administration Server
sco-dtmgr	617/udp	SCO Desktop Administration Server
dei-icda	618/tcp	DEI-ICDA
dei-icda	618/udp	DEI-ICDA
digital-evm	619/tcp	Digital EVM
digital-evm	619/udp	Digital EVM
sco-websrvrmgr	620/tcp	SCO WebServer Manager
sco-websrvrmgr	620/udp	SCO WebServer Manager

escp-ip	621/tcp	ESCP
escp-ip	621/udp	ESCP
collaborator	622/tcp	Collaborator
collaborator	622/udp	Collaborator
aux_bus_shunt	623/tcp	Aux Bus Shunt
aux_bus_shunt	623/udp	Aux Bus Shunt
cryptoadmin	624/tcp	Crypto Admin
cryptoadmin	624/udp	Crypto Admin
dec_dlm	625/tcp	DEC DLM
dec_dlm	625/udp	DEC DLM
asia	626/tcp	ASIA
asia	626/udp	ASIA
passgo-tivoli	627/tcp	PassGo Tivoli
passgo-tivoli	627/udp	PassGo Tivoli
qmqp	628/tcp	QMQP
qmqp	628/udp	QMQP
3com-amp3	629/tcp	3Com AMP3
3com-amp3	629/udp	3Com AMP3
rda	630/tcp	RDA
rda	630/udp	RDA
ipp	631/tcp	IPP (Internet Printing Protocol)
ipp	631/udp	IPP (Internet Printing Protocol)
bmpp	632/tcp	bmpp
bmpp	632/udp	bmpp
servstat	633/tcp	Service Status update (Sterling Software)
servstat	633/udp	Service Status update (Sterling Software)
ginad	634/tcp	ginad
ginad	634/udp	ginad
rlzdbase	635/tcp	RLZ DBase
rlzdbase	635/udp	RLZ DBase
ldaps	636/tcp	ldap protocol over TLS/SSL (was sldap)
ldaps	636/udp	ldap protocol over TLS/SSL (was sldap)
lanserver	637/tcp	lanserver
lanserver	637/udp	lanserver
mcns-sec	638/tcp	mcns-sec
mcns-sec	638/udp	mcns-sec
msdp	639/tcp	MSDP
msdp	639/udp	MSDP
entrust-sps	640/tcp	entrust-sps
entrust-sps	640/udp	entrust-sps
repcmd	641/tcp	repcmd
repcmd	641/udp	repcmd
esro-emsdp	642/tcp	ESRO-EMSDP V1.3

(continues)

Keyword	Decimal	Description (continued)
esro-emsdp	642/udp	ESRO-EMSDP V1.3
sanity	643/tcp	SANity
sanity	643/udp	SANity
dwr	644/tcp	dwr
dwr	644/udp	dwr
pssc	645/tcp	PSSC
pssc	645/udp	PSSC
ldp	646/tcp	LDP
ldp	646/udp	LDP
dhcp-failover	647/tcp	DHCP Failover
dhcp-failover	647/udp	DHCP Failover
rrp	648/tcp	Registry Registrar Protocol (RRP)
rrp	648/udp	Registry Registrar Protocol (RRP)
aminet	649/tcp	Aminet
aminet	649/udp	Aminet
obex	650/tcp	OBEX
obex	650/udp	OBEX
ieee-mms	651/tcp	IEEE MMS
ieee-mms	651/udp	IEEE MMS
udlr-dtcp	652/tcp	UDLR_DTCP
udlr-dtcp	652/udp	UDLR_DTCP
repscmd	653/tcp	RepCmd
repscmd	653/udp	RepCmd
aodv	654/tcp	AODV
aodv	654/udp	AODV
tinc	655/tcp	TINC
tinc	655/udp	TINC
spmp	656/tcp	SPMP
spmp	656/udp	SPMP
rmc	657/tcp	RMC
rmc	657/udp	RMC
tenfold	658/tcp	TenFold
tenfold	658/udp	TenFold
url-rendezvous	659/tcp	URL Rendezvous
url-rendezvous	659/udp	URL Rendezvous
mac-srvr-admin	660/tcp	MacOS Server Admin
mac-srvr-admin	660/udp	MacOS Server Admin
hap	661/tcp	HAP
hap	661/udp	HAP
pftp	662/tcp	PFTP
pftp	662/udp	PFTP
purenoise	663/tcp	PureNoise
purenoise	663/udp	PureNoise

secure-aux-bus	664/tcp	Secure Aux Bus
secure-aux-bus	664/udp	Secure Aux Bus
sun-dr	665/tcp	Sun DR
sun-dr	665/udp	Sun DR
mdqs	666/tcp	
mdqs	666/udp	
doom	666/tcp	doom Id Software
doom	666/udp	doom Id Software
disclose	667/tcp	campaign contribution disclosures - SDR Technologies
disclose	667/udp	campaign contribution disclosures - SDR Technologies
mecomm	668/tcp	MeComm
mecomm	668/udp	MeComm
meregister	669/tcp	MeRegister
meregister	669/udp	MeRegister
vacdsm-sws	670/tcp	VACDSM-SWS
vacdsm-sws	670/udp	VACDSM-SWS
vacdsm-app	671/tcp	VACDSM-APP
vacdsm-app	671/udp	VACDSM-APP
vpps-qua	672/tcp	VPPS-QUA
vpps-qua	672/udp	VPPS-QUA
cimplex	673/tcp	CIMPLEX
cimplex	673/udp	CIMPLEX
acap	674/tcp	ACAP
acap	674/udp	ACAP
dctp	675/tcp	DCTP
dctp	675/udp	DCTP
vpps-via	676/tcp	VPPS Via
vpps-via	676/udp	VPPS Via
vpp	677/tcp	Virtual Presence Protocol
vpp	677/udp	Virtual Presence Protocol
ggf-ncp	678/tcp	GNU Gereration Foundation NCP
ggf-ncp	678/udp	GNU Generation Foundation NCP
mrm	679/tcp	MRM
mrm	679/udp	MRM
entrust-aaas	680/tcp	entrust-aaas
entrust-aaas	680/udp	entrust-aaas
entrust-aams	681/tcp	entrust-aams
entrust-aams	681/udp	entrust-aams
xfr	682/tcp	XFR
xfr	682/udp	XFR
corba-iiop	683/tcp	CORBA IIOP
corba-iiop	683/udp	CORBA IIOP
corba-iiop-ssl	684/tcp	CORBA IIOP SSL

(continues)

Keyword	Decimal	Description (continued)
corba-iiop-ssl	684/udp	CORBA IIOP SSL
mdc-portmapper	685/tcp	MDC Port Mapper
mdc-portmapper	685/udp	MDC Port Mapper
hcp-wismar	686/tcp	Hardware Control Protocol Wismar
hcp-wismar	686/udp	Hardware Control Protocol Wismar
asipregistry	687/tcp	asipregistry
asipregistry	687/udp	asipregistry
realm-rusd	688/tcp	REALM-RUSD
realm-rusd	688/udp	REALM-RUSD
nmap	689/tcp	NMAP
nmap	689/udp	NMAP
vatp	690/tcp	VATP
vatp	690/udp	VATP
msexch-routing	691/tcp	MS Exchange Routing
msexch-routing	691/udp	MS Exchange Routing
hyperwave-isp	692/tcp	Hyperwave-ISP
hyperwave-isp	692/udp	Hyperwave-ISP
connendp	693/tcp	connendp
connendp	693/udp	connendp
ha-cluster	694/tcp	ha-cluster
ha-cluster	694/udp	ha-cluster
ieee-mms-ssl	695/tcp	IEEE-MMS-SSL
ieee-mms-ssl	695/udp	IEEE-MMS-SSL
rushd	696/tcp	RUSHD
rushd	696/udp	RUSHD
uuidgen	697/tcp	UUIDGEN
uuidgen	697/udp	UUIDGEN
	698–703	Unassigned
elcsd	704/tcp	errlog copy/server daemon
elcsd	704/udp	errlog copy/server daemon
agentx	705/tcp	AgentX
agentx	705/udp	AgentX
silc	706/tcp	SILC
silc	706/udp	SILC
borland-dsj	707/tcp	Borland DSJ
borland-dsj	707/udp	Borland DSJ
	708	Unassigned
entrust-kmsh	709/tcp	Entrust Key Management Service Handler
entrust-kmsh	709/udp	Entrust Key Management Service Handler
entrust-ash	710/tcp	Entrust Administration Service Handler
entrust-ash	710/udp	Entrust Administration Service Handler
cisco-tdp	711/tcp	Cisco TDP
cisco-tdp	711/udp	Cisco TDP

	712–728	Unassigned
netviewdm1	729/tcp	IBM NetView DM/6000 Server/Client
netviewdm1	729/udp	IBM NetView DM/6000 Server/Client
netviewdm2	730/tcp	IBM NetView DM/6000 send/tcp
netviewdm2	730/udp	IBM NetView DM/6000 send/tcp
netviewdm3	731/tcp	IBM NetView DM/6000 receive/tcp
netviewdm3	731/udp	IBM NetView DM/6000 receive/tcp
	732–740	Unassigned
netgw	741/tcp	netGW
netgw	741/udp	netGW
netrcs	742/tcp	Network based Rev. Cont. Sys.
netrcs	742/udp	Network based Rev. Cont. Sys.
	743	Unassigned
flexlm	744/tcp	Flexible License Manager
flexlm	744/udp	Flexible License Manager
	745–746	Unassigned
fujitsu-dev	747/tcp	Fujitsu Device Control
fujitsu-dev	747/udp	Fujitsu Device Control
ris-cm	748/tcp	Russell Info Sci Calendar Manager
ris-cm	748/udp	Russell Info Sci Calendar Manager
kerberos-adm	749/tcp	kerberos administration
kerberos-adm	749/udp	kerberos administration
rfile	750/tcp	
loadav	750/udp	
kerberos-iv	750/udp	kerberos version iv
pump	751/tcp	
pump	751/udp	
qrh	752/tcp	
qrh	752/udp	
rrh	753/tcp	
rrh	753/udp	
tell	754/tcp	send
tell	754/udp	send
	755–756	Unassigned
nlogin	758/tcp	
nlogin	758/udp	
con	759/tcp	
con	759/udp	
ns	760/tcp	
ns	760/udp	
rxe	761/tcp	
rxe	761/udp	
quotad	762/tcp	
quotad	762/udp	

(continues)

Keyword	*Decimal*	*Description (continued)*
cycleserv	763/tcp	
cycleserv	763/udp	
omserv	764/tcp	
omserv	764/udp	
webster	765/tcp	
webster	765/udp	
	766	Unassigned
phonebook	767/tcp	phone
phonebook	767/udp	phone
	768	Unassigned
vid	769/tcp	
vid	769/udp	
cadlock	770/tcp	
cadlock	770/udp	
rtip	771/tcp	
rtip	771/udp	
cycleserv2	772/tcp	
cycleserv2	772/udp	
submit	773/tcp	
notify	773/udp	
rpasswd	774/tcp	
acmaint_dbd	774/udp	
entomb	775/tcp	
acmaint_transd	775/udp	
wpages	776/tcp	
wpages	776/udp	
multiling-http	777/tcp	Multiling HTTP
multiling-http	777/udp	Multiling HTTP
	778–779	Unassigned
wpgs	780/tcp	
wpgs	780/udp	
	781–785	Unassigned
concert	786/tcp	Concert
concert	786/udp	Concert
qsc	787/tcp	QSC
qsc	787/udp	QSC
	788–799	Unassigned
mdbs_daemon	800/tcp	
mdbs_daemon	800/udp	
device	801/tcp	
device	801/udp	
	802–809	Unassigned
fcp-udp	810/tcp	FCP
fcp-udp	810/udp	FCP Datagram
	811–827	Unassigned

itm-mcell-s	828/tcp	itm-mcell-s
itm-mcell-s	828/udp	itm-mcell-s
pkix-3-ca-ra	829/tcp	PKIX-3 CA/RA
pkix-3-ca-ra	829/udp	PKIX-3 CA/RA
	830–872	Unassigned
rsync	873/tcp	rsync
rsync	873/udp	rsync
	874–885	Unassigned
iclcnet-locate	886/tcp	ICL coNETion locate server
iclcnet-locate	886/udp	ICL coNETion locate server
iclcnet_svinfo	887/tcp	ICL coNETion server info
iclcnet_svinfo	887/udp	ICL coNETion server info
accessbuilder	888/tcp	AccessBuilder
accessbuilder	888/udp	AccessBuilder
cddbp	888/tcp	CD Database Protocol (unassigned but widespread use)
	889–899	Unassigned
omginitialrefs	900/tcp	OMG Initial Refs
omginitialrefs	900/udp	OMG Initial Refs
smpnameres	901/tcp	SMPNAMERES
smpnameres	901/udp	SMPNAMERES
ideafarm-chat	902/tcp	IDEAFARM-CHAT
ideafarm-chat	902/udp	IDEAFARM-CHAT
ideafarm-catch	903/tcp	IDEAFARM-CATCH
ideafarm-catch	903/udp	IDEAFARM-CATCH
	904–910	Unassigned
xact-backup	911/tcp	xact-backup
xact-backup	911/udp	xact-backup
	912–988	Unassigned
ftps-data	989/tcp	ftp protocol, data, over TLS/SSL
ftps-data	989/udp	ftp protocol, data, over TLS/SSL
ftps	990/tcp	ftp protocol, control, over TLS/SSL
ftps	990/udp	ftp protocol, control, over TLS/SSL
nas	991/tcp	Netnews Administration System
nas	991/udp	Netnews Administration System
telnets	992/tcp	telnet protocol over TLS/SSL
telnets	992/udp	telnet protocol over TLS/SSL
imaps	993/tcp	imap4 protocol over TLS/SSL
imaps	993/udp	imap4 protocol over TLS/SSL
ircs	994/tcp	irc protocol over TLS/SSL
ircs	994/udp	irc protocol over TLS/SSL
pop3s	995/tcp	pop3 protocol over TLS/SSL (was spop3)
pop3s	995/udp	pop3 protocol over TLS/SSL (was spop3)
vsinet	996/tcp	vsinet
vsinet	996/udp	vsinet
maitrd	997/tcp	

(continues)

Keyword	*Decimal*	*Description (continued)*
maitrd	997/udp	
busboy	998/tcp	
puparp	998/udp	
garcon	999/tcp	
applix	999/udp	Applix ac
puprouter	999/tcp	
puprouter	999/udp	
cadlock2	1000/tcp	
cadlock2	1000/udp	
	1001–1009	Unassigned
surf	1010/tcp	surf
surf	1010/udp	surf
1011–1022	Reserved	
	1023/tcp	Reserved
	1023/udp	Reserved

Index

E

F

G

H

I

J

K

L

M

N

Q

R

S

U

V

W

X

Y

Z